Who's *REALLY!* Who

COMPTON MILLER

HARDEN'S BOOKS
London

First published in Great Britain by
Blond & Briggs Ltd 1983
Revised editions published by Sphere Books Ltd 1984 and 1987
This fully revised edition published by Harden's Books 1997
29 Villiers Street, London WC2N 6ND

ISBN 0-9531436-1-9

A catalogue record for this book is available from the British Library

Printed and bound in Finland by Werner Söderström Osakeyhtiö

To my wee mum

Acknowledgments

My special thanks must go to Richard Young, whose pictures comprise the illustrated sections of this book. In the 20-odd years since we first worked together he has ceased to be just a paparazzo and become a world-recognised photographer. Future social historians will consider his work to be one of their main sources covering British social life in the last three decades of the 20th century.

A reference book like *Who's REALLY! Who* borrows material from many published sources, particularly newspapers and magazines. I am therefore grateful for the researches of my fellow Fleet Street scribes. I have also constantly consulted those indispensable snobs' bibles, *Who's Who* (A&C Black), *The International Who's Who* (Europa) and *Debrett's Peerage and Baronetage* (Macmillan). Other volumes that I have found useful are: *Whitaker's Almanac* (Whitaker), *Britain's Richest 1000* (Sunday Times), the *Radio Times Film and Video Guide* (Hodder & Stoughton), *The Television Encyclopaedia* by Jeff Evans (Guinness), *Nigel Dempster's Address Book* (Pan), *Britain's Top 100 Eligible Bachelors* by Nesta Wynn Ellis (Blake), *The Best of British Men* and *The Best of British Women* (Best of British), *Who's Who on Television* (ITV), *The Book of Birthdays* by Deirdre Chapple (Hodder & Stoughton), *The Royal Handbook* by Alan Hamilton (Mitchell Beazley), *The Royal Encyclopaedia* (Macmillan), *Secret Lives* by John Sachs and Piers Morgan (Blake), *The Book of British Hit Singles* (Guinness) and *The A-Z of TV Stars* by Anthony Hayward (Boxtree).

Finally I am extremely grateful to Jane Warren for her support and kindness, particularly in setting up my Pentium computer. My special thanks are also due to my sister Sylvia Compton Miller, agent Andrew Lownie, publishers Richard and Peter Harden and distributor Charles Arnold. I am also indebted to Larry King who commissioned the first edition of *Who's REALLY! Who* and to Anthony Blond who supplied the title.

Foreword

With thousands of potential names to choose from it is difficult to pick just 400. *Who's REALLY! Who* supplies the cast-list of those who populate the pages of the people-watching glossies, the Sunday supplements and the scandal sheets. They are the figures pounced on by the paparazzi as they alight from stretch limos at West End film premieres: the Hollywood heart-throb, the thigh-revealing supermodel, the arrogant pop idol, the stroppy deejay. They are the decadent duchesses, boisterous baronets and prancing playboys who feature in the Nigel Dempster and "William Hickey" columns. They are the flamboyant tycoons in the City pages, the literary lions (and lionesses) in the best-seller lists, the superchefs plugging their latest TV series, the charismatic politicians and musical divas fawned over by Sir David Frost and Melvyn Bragg. In short they supply the spice and fun. Without them our lives would be duller.

This is the fourth edition of *Who's REALLY! Who*, compiled in response to the hundreds of readers who have urged me to update the last one. A decade has passed and I have had to be ruthless in jettisoning the names of those who have lost their allure. It has provided the challenge of creating an exciting new *dramatis personae*. The choice is entirely subjective, of course. As always, I have confined the entries to Brits or at least to people who mainly reside in this country. You may look in vain for the very latest Britpop or soccer sensation. Tempting though their inclusion would be they have yet to manifest the staying-power that is an essential qualification for those who are to be listed in this definitive directory of fame, fortune and occasionally notoriety.

Since its birth in 1983, *Who's REALLY! Who* has profiled over 1,000 celebrities, from the late Cary Grant, David Niven and Freddie Mercury to Koo Stark and Camilla Parker Bowles before they were publicly proclaimed as royal lovers. Over the years, I have had to drop some 600 people to ensure that each edition of *Who's REALLY! Who* features only the most cutting-edge selection. This has sometimes been poignant: some of the *refusés* have been close friends. Why, apart from space reasons, do I confine the book to just 400 names? In social circles this has been a magic number ever since the insufferably grand 19th century Manhattan hostess Mrs Astor built her ballroom just large enough for 400, deeming this sufficient to entertain everyone who mattered in New York society. Thereafter "the 400" became the nickname of New York's Social Register, which contained the names and addresses of the "old money" families that cut the mustard. In London the most popular post-war nightclub, where the Princess Margaret Set used to dance – in full evening dress to a live orchestra – was called.....the Four Hundred Club.

A relatively new addition to *Who's REALLY! Who* is to include the birth date of each entrant. This has proved to be a source of unexpected difficulty. Most public figures cannot hide their age because it already appears in reference tomes like *Who's Who*, newspaper libraries and company filings. But some – like actress Joan Collins and Society hostess Anouska Hempel – have on occasions sought to subtract a few years from their *Who's Who* entry. Others, like animal rights campaigner and scriptwriter Carla Lane, only include the day and month of their birthday. "It's none of anybody's business", Ms Lane says, "I refuse to be categorized or labelled by reason of my age". Even younger ladies try to bamboozle the unwary researcher. Party girl Tamara Beckwith knocked off three years from her age when I asked her. To unravel award-winning writer Lynda La Plante's "secret", recourse to the Registrar of Births was necessary!

It was the late Sam White, doyen of Paris correspondents, who wrote that a diarist's job was to treat the frivolous things in life seriously and the serious things frivolously. I therefore make no excuse for defining *Who's REALLY! Who* in its less serious, social sense.

Sadly, the greatest star of all, Diana Princess of Wales, cannot now be included. She was to have adorned our cover, but her tragic death came just four weeks before publication. As a mark of respect we have completely revised and reprinted this book.

GUIDE TO SYMBOLS

Party-loving	◁	Stylish	※
Narcissistic	❈	Dynamic	◥
Heart-breaker	♡	Waspish	🐟
Old money	▦	New money	£
Beautiful	👁	Witty	◡
Gourmet	🍴	Snobbish	👃

A

Adam, Piers, 17th March 1964, club owner, nicknamed "the Urban Cowboy". This livewire bachelor is determined to become the Peter Stringfellow/Johnny Gold of the early 21st century. Already his clubs and restaurants attract the trustafarian sets which are making London swing again. Young socialites like Tara Palmer-Tomkinson, Vanessa von Bismarck and Emily Oppenheimer not only hang out at Kartouche along Fulham Road's "Beach" but are former girlfriends. Jemima Goldsmith, a founder member of Kartouche's social committee, met Imran Khan there.

Adam grew up in North London where his father was a solicitor and his mother an art teacher. He attended Highgate School and then read estate management at Portsmouth Poly and business studies at Oxford Poly. "I was the most useless student and didn't finish either course." Instead he discovered a flair for organising "raves". In 1987 he rented a field from former royal equerry Sir John Miller at Shotover House, near Oxford, and hosted an alternative May Ball. The same year he briefly became a City commodity broker – "it was just my luck that I joined the week before Black Monday". Capitalising on his database of teenybopper trendies he began hiring London venues like the Limelight, Roberto's and Roxanne for weekly discos.

In 1991 Adam linked with Eddie Davenport, controversial organiser of the Gatecrasher balls, and founded a weekend disco, SW1, near Victoria Station. Three years later he launched his first West End club, the Hanover Grand, in a former Masonic hall. But it was the 1994 opening of Kartouche and its drinking-den beneath that made him the coolest club owner in Chelsea. His reputation took something of a knock when a new restaurant venture, Kassoulet in Notting Hill, lasted for only a few months of 1997.

The "two loves of my life" have been baronet's niece Lucy Sykes and property tycoon's daughter Caroline Hickman. Next step? Clubs in all the major university towns. Oh yes, and then he wants to buy Tottenham Hotspur.

Aherne, Caroline (aka Mrs Merton), 24th December 1963, spoof chat show hostess. It is hard to disentangle the two egos. The blue-rinsed, bespectacled Mrs Merton is forgiven her wince-making comments because they are couched in such a disarmingly innocent way.

To Tony Curtis: "In Britain there are only three great film stars – you," (preen), "Cagney", (preen, preen) "and Lacey" (deflate, deflate). She asked Debbie McGee: "Tell me, Debbie, what was it that first attracted you to the short, balding, middle-aged millionaire Paul Daniels?" No wonder a critic described her as "part Dame Edna, part Lily Savage, with a dash of Pol Pot's DNA for good measure". As Ms Aherne she is a petite, quite sexy, 34D blonde who is on the B-celebrity party list. Indeed in 1997 she temporarily eclipsed Mrs M at the Manchester opening of Bill Wyman's restaurant Sticky Fingers. A punch-up ensued between her then boyfriend Matt Bowers and her estranged husband Peter Hook, bass guitarist with the Mancunian band New Order.

The Mrs Merton Show transformed this convent-educated lass, from a working-class Irish-Catholic family, into a BAFTA award-winning star. She was working as a secretary and part-time barmaid when she began to develop her talent for "doing voices". Two of her original creations were a comic nun, Sister Mary Immaculate, and a country-and-western singer Mitzie Goldberg. She first began impersonating Mrs Merton in a stage show produced by writer comedian Chris Sievey in 1989. She developed her into an agony aunt on local radio and the Granada sketch series *The Dead Good Show*, co-starring Steve Coogan.

The quick-witted impersonator married the blokeish "Hooky" at the Elvis Presley Memorial Chapel, Las Vegas in 1994. It was over in 18 months, partly because of her growing success. She is on a roll now, with Mrs Merton even transmitting her show from Las Vegas once and starring in British Gas commercials with her "son" Malcolm. But will she, like Barry Humphries, be able to develop other believable characters?

Al-Fayed, Mohammed, 27th January 1929, multi-millionaire storekeeper. Supremely British in outlook, suave and impeccably tailored, he is a Middle Eastern Rex Harrison. Before his £615 million takeover of the House of Fraser in 1985 he was best-known as the father of Dodi Fayed, producer of *Chariots of Fire* who died with Princess Diana in a car crash in August 1997. Mohammed's bitter fight with Lonrho chairman Tiny Rowland for control of the Harrods group brought him unwanted publicity. But he proved adept at swapping insults and ultimately won the battle, if not the propaganda war. He relishes his rôle running Britain's top department store, even if his dictatorial style has often ruffled feathers. But the City still asks: does the Sultan of Brunei control his purse-strings?

Al-Fayed, a teacher's son, was born in modest circumstances in Alexandria during its cosmopolitan heyday. He left Egypt when

Colonel Nasser seized power from King Farouk in 1952, and dabbled in property, construction, banking, oil and shipping throughout the Middle East. His £25 million purchase of the Ritz Hotel, Paris shot him into the big league of Arab spenders dominated by his former brother-in-law Adnan Khashoggi. In 1986 he bought the Duchess of Windsor's former home near Paris which he has painstakingly restored at a cost of £30 million.

The luxury-loving Mohammed is based in Park Lane and owns properties in Surrey, Scotland and St Tropez. He and his Finnish-born wife Heini have three children. Dodi, from his brief first marriage to Samira Khashoggi, was said to be about to marry Diana at the time of their death.

This brilliant Knightsbridge Pharaoh, with a temperament as quixotic as the currents of the Nile, is a dangerous man to cross. He believes there is an Establishment conspiracy against him which prevents him being granted British citizenship, despite over 30 years' residence. To embarrass John Major's government he exposed two Tory MPs who took bribes from him to ask questions in the House of Commons. His formation of Liberty Publishing in 1995 and re-launch of *Punch* marks a first step to becoming a newspaper magnate. A major benefactor of Great Ormond Street Children's Hospital, he is said to have contributed £250,000 to the Tory Party.

Albarn, Damon, 23rd March 1968, post-modern pop pin-up. Blur were the original exponents of Britpop, with their *Parklife* album becoming the *Sergeant Pepper* of the Nineties. The so-called battle of the bands saw them locked in deadly Top 10 combat with Oasis. But quiet, well-mannered, sensible Albarn was never a rock lout like the Gallagher brothers. Nor is he the Cockney wide boy he pretended to be. He is too middle-class – writing lyrics that actually mean something and hiring controversial artist Damien Hirst to direct videos. "We're an art school band and always will be!"

Comprehensive-educated Albarn grew up in a converted Essex bakery that was filled with his parents' own paintings and sculpture. His father ran Colchester Institute's art and design department and his mother worked as Joan Littlewood's stage designer.

As a lonely teenager Damon would spend hours practising the piano and synthesiser and taping his songs. At drama school he befriended guitarist Graham Coxon who was studying fine art at Goldsmith's College. They began composing songs with the same strong melodies and guitar riffs as Sixties groups like the Beatles, Kinks and Small Faces. But their lyrics borrow from the contemporary literary scene. "He's reading Balzac/Knocking back Prozac" is a typical Albarn lyric.

This jubilant Chelsea-supporter lives in Kensington with Elastica's lead singer, Justine Frischmann. "I keep reading that Damon's having a nervous breakdown. Then I get home and find him listening to *The Archers* and cooking dinner." He also has a flat in Reykjavik where he enjoys the native-American ritual of "blissing out" over hot rocks in a tepee. He has the talent and temperament to develop into a Phil Collins.

Allott, Nick, 25th March 1954, Crown Prince of Shaftesbury Avenue. It needed all his diplomatic skills to endure being Mr Anneka Rice and then resume his life when in 1988 she deserted him for TV producer Tom Gutteridge. Cheerful, easy-going and gregarious he launched himself into a frenzy of socialising. His dates included journalist Annabel Heseltine, ballerina Bryony Brind and model Carol Ashby. "Nick is like the little boy everyone wants to mother", explains an admirer. His most serious romance was with TV presenter Mariella Frostrup, but she could not cope with Anneka's constant telephone calls on his mobile and the dramas.

In his trademark jeans, white open-neck shirt and Doc Martens, Allott often resembles an off-duty garagiste. But he comes from a distinguished military family. His father, lost in a helicopter crash in 1969, was a brigadier and his grandfather a lieutenant-colonel. He first became involved in the theatre at Charterhouse. He filled a succession of leading female rôles, although he was already over 6ft tall. He dropped out of Exeter University after a year to become a £11-a-week scenery-shifter. Within three years he was stage manager at the Royal Theatre, Northampton. "Nick had a happy knack of getting on with people and making the right sort of noises in the right sort of places", says a contemporary. In 1981 he joined rising West End impresario Cameron Mackintosh as theatrical manager for *Cats*. Four years later he joined the board. "They're like twin souls, sharing the same loyalty to the firm and a schoolboyish sense of humour", says an insider. Will Allott ever branch out on his own?

West End hits like *Miss Saigon*, *Les Miserables* and *Phantom of the Opera* have made Allott a millionaire, although he lives modestly in Notting Hill. His girlfriend, journalist Christa D'Souza, is expecting a baby. Does he really keep an exotic aphrodisiac in his fridge?

Amis, Martin, 25th August 1949, the baby boomers' pet novelist. Despite being close to his difficult father Sir Kingsley Amis, they were always literary rivals. The death of "Kingers" in 1995 coincided with a personal and professional mid-life crisis for his son. Martin's demand for a £500,000 advance for his novel *The Information* caused a publishing furore. He sacked his agent Pat Kavanagh in favour of Andrew "The Jackal" Wylie. This severed his long friendship with novelist Julian Barnes, Pat's husband. Old friends complain about his greed and arrogance. He condescendingly calls his book reviews and other journalism "writing with my left hand".

The pixie-like Amis was much bullied at his Battersea grammar school because of his stature and cockiness. He began writing bestsellers after leaving Oxford with a first in English. His first novel, *The Rachel Papers*, won the 1974 Somerset Maugham Award. Fuelled by his ubiquitous roll-ups he effortlessly went on to write modern masterpieces like *Dead Babies, Success, Money, London Fields* and *Time's Arrow*. Critics praised him for his "hip, fast, slick language, his street wisdom and his caricaturist's obsession with the low, the vile, the humiliating". During the Seventies he established a second reputation as a literary Mick Jagger, entwined with well-connected girlfriends like Tina Brown, Victoria Rothschild and Emma Soames. It was 20 years later he discovered he had a secret love-child called Delilah.

This husky-voiced poker player once boasted that "whereas most writers stop outside the bedroom door, not only do I like to look inside but to go into the bathroom too". The words returned to haunt him when journalists quizzed him about the breakup of his 1984 marriage to art historian Antonia Phillips, mother of their two sons, Jacob and Louis. Her replacement was American heiress Isabel Fonseca, aptly pronounced Fun-Seeker, by whom he has a baby, Fernanda. Given his constant ridiculing of America and its "infantile" people in his novels this relationship is ironic. He now behaves like the literary fat cats he once derided. After paying £20,000 to have his teeth fixed in New York his rivals jested he would soon be having a hairweave or liposuction.

Anderson, Clive, 10th December 1952, barrister turned entertainer. This small, sly, balding rapscallion has become the scourge of the chattering classes. His chat show *Clive Anderson Talks Back* was never short of A-list guests prepared to be insulted, from Lord Healey and Roy Hattersley to Kenneth Branagh and Boy George. He loves to ask cheeky, irrelevant questions. "Why is your nickname Tarzan?", he inquired of Michael Heseltine and, on discovering his hobby was growing trees, added: "oh, is that so you can swing on them?" But Anderson's dry, sardonic wit upset Richard Branson, who tipped a glass of water over his head.

This bank manager's son from suburban Stanmore has successfully beaten rivals like Terry Wogan, Jonathan Ross and Michael

Aspel. On his shows you never quite know whether he will be friendly or naughty, perhaps producing a long-forgotten home video from his victim's childhood or even a dildo from beneath his studio desk. Underestimate him at your peril.

Anderson, ex-Harrow County Grammar School, learnt his trade at university. As president of the Cambridge Footlights he acted opposite Mel Smith, Douglas Adams and TV producer John Lloyd. From writing and performing in student revues he then transferred to that other theatre: the law. Called to the Bar in 1976 he defended drunken drivers, bank robbers and minor fraudsters. But his night-time job – compiling radio sketches and performing at the Comedy Store – gradually took over. His switch from radio in 1988 to compere Ch 4's *Whose Line Is It Anyway?* made him famous.

This pinstripe-suited inquisitor's bumbling, slightly bemused persona is not entirely an act. He leads a fogeyish, unglitzy life in Highbury with his wife Jane, a consultant specialising in AIDS, and their three children, Isabella, Flora and Edmund. He now faces the classic John Mortimer dilemma: to ditch law completely or continue with both careers?

Annis, Francesca, 14th May 1945, free spirit. She may be over 50 and a mother of three but she packs a sexual punch stronger than Patsy Kensit and Elizabeth Hurley. In 1995 she seduced Hollywood heart-throb Ralph Fiennes, 17 years her junior, when she played his mother in a stage production of *Hamlet*. Both the Press and her parents portrayed her as a 'scarlet woman' because he was already married to actress Alex Kingston. "Fran" just shrugged: "I don't expect everybody's approval. You just have to bite the bullet and get on with it."

This was the third young leading man in ten years that this classical beauty with the willowy physique and brown eyes had ensnared. She captivated Old Etonian actor Ian Ogilvy when they appeared in Chekhov's *Three Sisters* in 1987. Four years later Trevor Eve fell for her while they were making BBC1's *Parnell and The Englishwoman*, a relationship complicated by his marriage to Gold Blend ads star Sharon Maughan.

Fiery, petite, uninhibited Francesca is the daughter of a Portuguese film director and a French-Brazilian heiress. She relishes her independence and non-conformity. She has three children, Charlotte, Taran and Andreas, by photographer-turned-scriptwriter Patrick Wiseman. Despite 23 years together she never felt the need to marry him. "To me, marriage has always been bureaucratic. It's the dynamics of a relationship that matters." Her saintly house-husband forgave her the dalliances with Ogilvy and Eve but, after being cuckolded so publicly, will he welcome her back post-Fiennes? Bizarrely for one so liberal, Fran once wanted to be a Carmelite nun and admits to being haunted by her lost Catholic faith.

Professionally she began as a ballet-dancer at the Corona School but switched to drama after appearing in an *Armchair Theatre* TV play. Aged 21 she had her nose resculpted ("it was heavier-looking before"). As an actress with the RSC and the National Theatre she starred as Ophelia, Lady Macbeth and Juliet. She first became a TV femme fatale in two Seventies series, *Madame Bovary*, and *Lillie*, in which she played Edward VII's mistress Lillie Langtry.

Anson, Lady Elizabeth, 7th June 1941, party queen. Who better to organise the cocktail parties, dances, weddings and business receptions of the *nouveaux riches* than the Queen's cousin? For over 30 years this red-haired, well-upholstered, slightly formidable baronet's wife has run Party Planners. Helped by a loyal team of young Sloanes she will transform a paddock into a gypsy camp with Romany caravans, fortune-tellers, dancers and musicians. A London townhouse can become a Paris bordello, a Star Wars fantasy or a Sixties disco. But not even the pushiest deb's mum can force her to supply a guest list of eligible gels and chaps.

Liz Anson also assists nobby friends and relations. She was behind Princess Margaret's lavish 50th birthday ball at the Ritz Hotel, Sonia Lady Melchett's black and gold dance, Mick Jagger's hooley at London Zoo and Sir Jocelyn Stevens' 50th birthday celebrations halfway up a Swiss mountain!

Her own 40th birthday party at Claridge's, following Prince Charles's wedding, attracted almost the entire royal family. The Queen was so pooped she discreetly kicked off her shoes! Lady Elizabeth has since organised wedding bashes for Lady Helen Windsor, Viscount Linley and Sting, as well as Ivana Trump's party for her husband Riccardo Mazzucchelli's 50th birthday.

Liz, a goddaughter of George VI and sister of the Earl of Lichfield, attended Queensgate School and then did the Season. At 18 she founded Party Planners with a deb friend and her business has survived every recession, indeed it thrived under Harold Wilson's Labour government. In 1972 she married photographer Sir Geoffrey Shakerley, from whom she is separated. They have a daughter Fenella and, yes, she too did the Season and had a sumptuous party. Failing health – Liz suffers from ME – could soon lead to a less active presence on the social scene. Sometimes her condition has been so bad that to move about was "like trying to walk with broken bones on splintered glass".

Archer, Lord, 15th April 1940, the human squash ball. This multi-millionaire novelist, politician and controversialist takes himself very seriously. He is convinced journalists are ill-disposed towards him. Guesting on *The Clive Anderson Show* his host mildly observed "there's no beginning to your talents, Jeffrey...". But Archer exploded: "that's the sort of ill-informed, stupid remark you make from time to time." He has the last laugh, with worldwide sales of over 150 million and a three-book publishing deal worth £20 million!

This brash, bombastic, egotistical Walter Mitty was the son of a n'er-do-well Army father and a journalist mother Lola whom he adored. He went to the minor Somerset public school Wellington (not the pukka one in Berkshire). He originally trained to be a policeman but in 1963 began an education diploma at Oxford. He gained blues in athletics and gymnastics and became the Bob Geldof of his generation, raising over £1 million for Oxfam with the Beatles.

Archer turned from professional fund-raising to politics in 1966, becoming the Greater London Council's youngest ever member and in 1969 Tory MP for Louth. But he had to resign from Parliament five years later after an unwise investment in a Canadian firm almost bankrupted him. He was forced to sell his South Kensington mansion, modern art collection and Rolls-Royce (registration ANY 1). His bacon was saved by his brilliant wife Mary, mother of his two sons William and Jamie. Her earnings as a Cambridge solar energy expert enabled him to try his hand at writing. Bestselling novels like *Not A Penny More, Not a Penny Less, Shall We Tell The President?* and *Kane and Abel* enabled him to repay his debts and reclaim his tycoon lifestyle. This includes a magnificent penthouse overlooking the Thames and the old vicarage at Grantchester.

For all his faults Archer also raises millions of pounds for good causes (and the Tory party), particularly through his auctioneering skills at charity balls. He retains a quirky sense of humour. "We've a couple of Kurdish refugees working with us," he once said. "We call them Lemon Kurd and Bean Kurd!" He has always been accident-prone. In 1986 a Sunday newspaper revealed he had paid a prostitute £2,000. He felt obliged to resign as Tory deputy-chairman, which he had hoped was going to lead to the Cabinet, but subsequently won over £500,000 in libel damages. He is now worth an estimated £50 million. What new controversy will this colourful character provoke?

Ashdown, Paddy, 27th February 1941, third party irrelevance. With his broad shoulders, rugged face and eyes like tank-slits he is a political James Bond – and knows it. The 1997 general election provided a huge endorsement for his leadership. The Liberal Democrats gained 27 seats, boosting his total number of MPs to 46 – the party's best performance since 1929. He has no truck with spin doctors. "My core beliefs will never be altered by someone who comes along and says 'that policy is going to lose you votes. Ditch it!'" Ironically, he finds the Commons, with all its clubbiness, gossip and procedures, "a trial", preferring life on the stump.

He was born Jeremy John Durham Ashdown in New Delhi, but "Paddy" sounds matier for a radical politician. Although he came into politics "to destroy the class system" his background is rather Establishment. His Tory father was a colonel in the Indian Army and his family were Anglo-Irish gentry. "My grandfather was the first man in Ireland to buy a car!" On leaving Bedford School Jeremy won a naval scholarship and served in the Royal Marines. Aged 20, he needed special permission from the Admiralty to marry his wife Jane. As commander of a Special Boat Section unit he once quelled a rebellion in Brunei, but denies he ever killed anyone with his bare hands. He spent five years in the Foreign Office and learnt Mandarin Chinese while seconded to Hong Kong. In 1976 he returned to Britain to break into Liberal politics – and for a time was broke and unemployed.

Lib Dem peer Lord McNally describes Ashdown as "the Kevin Keegan of politics – someone who has reached the top through effort rather than natural ability". He even took lessons from a speech therapist once to allay the nervous squeak in his voice. In 1983 he was finally elected MP for Yeovil and five years later succeeded David Steel as leader. In 1992 his party's non-conformist stance was severely tested when he called a press conference and admitted committing adultery with a former secretary. "Paddy Pantsdown" echoed the headlines. His wife Jane loyally stood by him. They have two children, Kate and Simon, both educated at local Somerset comprehensives. He yearns for a place in Tony Blair's Cabinet.

Aspinall, John, 11th June 1926, gambler, conservationist and honorary Zulu. His pukka Mayfair casino subsidises his two private Kent zoos, Howletts and Port Lympne, where he breeds gorillas, tigers and other endangered animals. House guests are likely to find hand-reared tigers using their bath as a loo. "If I had to choose between saving a human being and a species I'd choose the species", he once insisted.

This charismatic character with the Neanderthal features was born in India where his father was an Army surgeon. He was expelled from Rugby and sent down from Oxford for being lazy and rebellious. After three years in the Royal Marines he began living on his wits in London. He would hold illegal chemmy games around Belgravia for well-heeled chums. After he was "busted" in 1958 his sprightly mother Lady Osborne fumed: "it's a poor thing if you can't have a private party in a private flat without the police coming". After his acquittal Parliament legalised gambling and in 1962 he opened his first casino, the Clermont Club, in Berkeley Square. There he held court surrounded by upper-crust toadies like the missing Earl of Lucan, Dan Meinertzhagen and Dominic Elwes. Wags say that, until the Lloyd's debacle, he probably bore more responsibility than anyone else for the redistribution of upper-class wealth.

In 1975 "Aspers" reluctantly sold the Clermont to Playboy tycoon Victor Lownes to finance his growing obsession with rearing animals. The Bunnies got a £584,000 bargain! In 1978, backed by his friend Sir James Goldsmith, he opened a smaller casino Aspinall's in Knightsbridge. In 1984 he moved to grander premises in Mayfair but sold it three years later to tycoon Peter de Savary, again to concentrate on his two zoos. These have survived, despite four fatalities among his keepers

Aspers has two children, Damian and Amanda, from his first marriage to Fifties model Jane Gordon-Hastings. His second wife was former deb Belinda Musker. He has a son, Bassa, from his current marriage to the late Earl Howe's daughter, Lady Sally Curzon. With typical bravado the couple held a spectacular ball in mid-recession for 500 guests at Port Lympne. Now back casino-keeping in Mayfair he takes life more calmly following a mild stroke in 1986. But he seems to have lost none of his robustness in wrestling with the big cats and gorillas in their cages. What news has he of "Lucky" Lucan?

Atkinson, Rowan, 6th January 1955, comedy's alien force. His trademark anteater features are, in fact, the result of years of fine Geordie breeding: he was brought up on a farm near Newcastle-upon-Tyne. After Durham Cathedral Choristers' School he went to a Cumbrian public school, St Bees, where he had a reputation for "being slightly strange, a bit of a loner".

Rowan's mother discouraged his early acting ambitions, believing showbiz was "full of cheques that bounce, homosexuals and nasty men in large velvet bow ties". He therefore spent six years at Newcastle University and Oxford, studying to be an electrical engineer. He was active in student revues, starring in pastiches of *Dud and Pete* monologues and *Monty Python*. (John Cleese has always been his idol.) He appeared in the 1979 Edinburgh Festival Fringe and at 26 became the youngest person to star in a West End one-man show.

Television has lapped up this rubber-faced comedian since the cult satire series, *Not The Nine O'Clock News*, launched him, Mel Smith, Pamela Stephenson and Griff Rhys Jones in 1979. With award-winning scriptwriter Richard Curtis he then devised the historical sitcom *Blackadder*. This sly, cringing, weaselly rogue led to another even more successful invention, the tight tweed-jacketed *Mr Bean*. The first series won a record 18 million viewers in 1990. The little nerd attracts audiences in 94 different countries and 53 airlines. With no dialogue, but much facial and physical contortions, Atkinson was able to convey the tortured life of a gormless, friendless, accident-prone wally. Before guesting in the 1997 Hollywood film, *Bean – The Ultimate Disaster Movie*, Burt Reynolds observed: "It's a real pleasure to work with someone who makes deaf children laugh!"

At his 18th century Oxfordshire rectory Atkinson enjoys a country squire's lifestyle with his Asian wife Sunetra and two children. His favourite treasure is his Aston Martin. Marriage and money have helped him to lose his childhood inferiority complex. His brilliant portrayal of a novice vicar in *Four Weddings and a Funeral* proved that *Bean* and *Blackadder* had not entirely typecast him. His secret ambition is to play a James Bond villain, "...the one who sneaks up behind and says: 'Not so fast, Mr Bond'".

Ayckbourn, Sir Alan, 12th April 1939, Britain's most commercial playwright since Shakespeare. Despite his recent knighthood some critics believe he is losing his muse and repeating himself. Even he admits he has "a writer's permanent fear of drying up". But his long-term reputation looks assured, with an entry in the *Guinness Book of Records* for having had five plays running in the West End simultaneously. He is best-known for his trilogy *The Norman Conquests*, *Absurd Person Singular* and *How The Other Half Loves*.

Sir Peter Hall dubbed this tall, shy, shambling intellectual the key chronicler of "the greed and self-interest prevalent in the Thatcher era". He has written over 50 plays (cf Shakespeare's 37) which earn him an estimated £1 million a year royalties. But he is a perfectionist. He was so horrified at one provincial revival he ran out of the theatre and punched a parking meter, gouging his fist.

Sir Alan, a former visiting professor of contemporary theatre at Oxford, is unimpressed by money or position. For over 25 years he has been an active artistic director of the Stephen Joseph Theatre-in-the-Round, in Scarborough. He has premièred all his black comedies and social farces there, from *Relatively Speaking* to the cynical *A Small Family Business* and *Sisterly Feelings* whose development is decided on stage by tossing a coin. One critic complained he was the "master of coitus interruptus" because he conveys so little love and passion in his work.

This genial bard comes from a broken home in Hampstead. His father was deputy leader of the London Symphony Orchestra and his mother wrote short stories. His plays are usually set in a complex domestic situation, rarely involving more than one set and inevitably exposing the foibles and follies of the professional middle-class. It's a social milieu he knows well. After Haileybury he was an unsuccessful actor and then spent six years as a BBC Radio drama producer. He married former actress Christine Roland at 19 and they have two sons, Stephen and Philip. But for over 20 years he has shared his quaint Scarborough vicarage with Helen Stoney, a former actress who acts as his general manager. He once labelled marriage "a rotten institution. You make promises you have no right to make – that you should be legally stopped from making."

B

Baddiel, David, 28th May 1964, the scruff who elevated laddishness to an art form. He owes his notoriety to the brash comedy series, *The Mary Whitehouse Experience* and *Fantasy Football League*. Blame him for popular "yoof" culture that promotes lager, football and ogling chesty "babes". He became chief rabble-rouser during Euro '96 and co-wrote England's hit anthem *Three Lions*.

Despite his adolescent humour this Lennon-bespectacled stand-up comic has a Cambridge double first in English. He grew up in North London, a Unilever research chemist's son. At Haberdashers Aske School he was beaten up "for being Jewish and because some people thought I was Pakistani". At Cambridge he was once arrested for obstructing the police during a demo. He was vice-president of the Cambridge Footlights, putting on a revue called *Superlads* at the 1986 Edinburgh Festival. "I became a comedian because I can't imagine doing a proper job. I don't claim to have invented Laddism, but I was doing material about it long before anyone else."

Leather-jacketed Baddiel once shared a flat with his mate and FFL co-presenter Frank Skinner. "We'd insert heterosexual caveats into our conversations, so that when a cab-driver dropped us home late at night we'd start talking loudly about our girlfriends!" He is no longer in touch with Rob Newman, whom he teamed up with while writing for the R4 comedy series, *Weekending*. Together they turned *The Mary Whitehouse Experience* into a cult success and, as Newman and Baddiel, played to packed houses of screaming teenagers at Wembley Arena.

Baddiel claims to have had only two long-term relationships. "I get very, very attached and romantic". He met his present girlfriend, record executive Sarah Bowden, after a Newcastle gig in 1993. A self-confessed sexaholic he says: "If I knew I could never have sex again I'd take my own life." He claims to have made love near a volcano in Italy ("although it wasn't erupting at the time") and during the interval in his dressing-room. He sees his future in America but could never settle there because "I couldn't live without football".

Bailey, David, 2nd January 1938, Cockney snapper and Sixties icon. This cheeky, working-class lad epitomises the Sixties ethos of beautiful women, trendy trattorias and social mobility. ("David

Bailey makes love daily" was a favourite slogan of the time). He inspired Antonioni's cult 1967 film *Blow-Up*, starring David Hemmings as a dissolute photographer. With a costermonger's cap perched over greying long hair and his squat, paunchy physique encased in denim, Bailey is no Michelangelo's *David*. But his breezy, down-to-earth chat and East End nonchalance has mesmerised the most la-di-da models. George Melly describes him as "uneducated but sophisticated, elegant but a bit grubby".

Bailey – even his wife Catherine calls him by his surname – left school at 14 to work for his tailor father. Later he sold shoes, dressed windows and dreamed of becoming a professional trumpet player. Inspired by Henri Cartier-Bresson he learnt photography during his RAF national service. He joined *Vogue* and his discovery of model Jean Shrimpton set a trend that has kept him on the covers of British and American glossies ever since.

This parrot-loving genius has been honoured with exhibitions at the National Portrait Gallery and the Victoria and Albert Museum. He remains one of our top fashion photographers and TV commercials directors. But he yearns to concentrate on serious projects. He has done photo-reportage on Bangladesh's famine victims, Mother Teresa in Calcutta and the Vietnamese boat people, has snapped Salvation Army posters and filmed Greenpeace commercials. Long before it was fashionable, he refused to photograph fur coats.

Workaholic Bailey has had four wives, although the Shrimp and his long-standing girlfriend heiress Penelope Tree were not among them. The first was his childhood sweetheart Rosemary Bramble, whom he now dismisses as "a nice girl from Clapham". She was followed by French actress Catherine Deneuve, model Marie Helvin and his present spouse, model-turned-journalist Catherine Dyer. They have three children, Paloma, Fenton and Sascha and live in a dark North London house decorated with trendy Sixties furniture and Bailey originals.

Ball, Zoe, 23rd November 1970, "yoof" presenter, once praised as "a goddess wasted on ten-year-olds". Blonde, perky and ambitious she is a younger version of Gaby Roslin and Anthea Turner. *Smash Hits* voted her "the sexiest chick on TV" and she was also described as "a hyperactive, 5ft 10in, reformed tomboy who behaves like the Dulux puppy". She became a Granada TV researcher at 17 and a BSkyB messenger girl. At 20 she began her reign as queen of tots' TV, fronting *The O Zone* and then *Fully Booked*.

In 1996 this pale-faced chainsmoker won the race to succeed Roslin as *The Big Breakfast*'s £200,000-a-year presenter. On her first day she tripped over and fluffed her lines. She could count on no support from her loud-mouthed Australian co-host Mark Little who did his best to shatter her confidence. "Try not to make 500 mistakes, Zoe", he would say before going on air. She quit seven months later, having failed to halt plummeting viewing figures. Her new rôle, co-presenting BBC1's flagship Saturday morning show *Live and Kicking*, was a doddle in comparison.

The Queen of Cute's parents split up when she was two and she did not see her mother, a former model, for 15 years. She was brought up in Beaconsfield by her father, Johnny Ball, presenter of children's programmes like *Play School*, *Star Turn* and *Think of a Number*. She was nicknamed "Big Ears" by pupils at her convent school. "I was never really a 'wild child', even at sixth-form college." Until 1996 she lived with TV producer and director Nick Poyntz, her mentor for three years. Friends joked about the "Ball-Poyntz". She announced the split on her Liberty Radio show.

Barlow, Gary, 20th January 1971, pop's Elton John-to-be? He somehow survived the junk food, Beatlemania-bedlam of Take That, when screaming fans would besiege stage doors and throw knickers embroidered with their telephone numbers from the stadium pit. After the group split in 1996 he was determined to prove he could succeed as a solo artiste, particularly in America. His debut single, *Forever Love*, went straight into the charts at No 1, as did the second, *Love Won't Wait*, composed by Madonna. Meanwhile he sacked his Svengali, Nigel Martin-Smith, and hired Spice Girls manager Simon Fuller.

Martin-Smith discovered Barlow performing around Manchester's social clubs and recognised not only his musical talents but his extraordinary songwriting prowess. He ordained the group's squeaky clean, no drugs/alcohol/sex image. "We were told what to say, how to behave, how to dress and where we could and couldn't go." In two years they had nine No 1 singles and four No 1 albums, earning some £80 million worldwide. In the midst of their energetic dance routines Barlow was always the lumpy one, surrounded by gyrating Adonises like Robbie Williams and Jason Orange. After their final Wembley concert he successfully lost two stone. "I started on a detox diet for two days and dreamt that I was sleeping on a giant Twix bar. I woke up licking the pillow."

Multi-millionaire Barlow comes from a close, working-class, Mancunian family. His parents saved up to buy his first keyboard when he was 11 and allowed him to perform in cabaret at 13. They now run a farm on his Cheshire estate. "Nobody leaves our place without some eggs from Dad's farm." His older brother Ian also lives on the estate and keeps a menagerie of owls and eagles. "It's like *The*

Beverly Hillbillies, us having moved into this place where none of us really belong." Gary met his girlfriend, Dawn Andrews, in 1995 when she was a dancer on Take That's final tour. "I used to be a terrible workaholic, but since I've met Dawn I've had some realism put back in my life." He despises the rock star lifestyle. "I've done away with the butler and the two fast cars. Now I drive a Golf convertible."

Barrymore, Michael, 4th May 1952, troubled showbiz legend. As the madcap host of shows like *Strike It Lucky* and *Michael Barrymore's Saturday Night Out* he became known as "Britain's best-loved family entertainer". But a self-destruct button almost destroyed his career in 1995. After being taunted in an East End gay pub for not being frank about his sexuality he jumped on stage and confessed. He then phoned a late-night gay radio station and demanded to be interviewed about his "coming out". After a tabloid feeding frenzy the ratings on his flagship Saturday evening show, *Barrymore*, plummeted. LWT also decided to axe his talent-spotting series, *My Kind of People*. A TV critic explained: "When Barrymore started to be seen as a homosexual with a capital H his camp style lost its ambiguity and, with it, a lot of its 'nudge, nudge, wink, wink' appeal." His public confession led to a temporary rift with his wife and manager Cheryl. He later realised he needed professional help and entered a drink-rehabilitation clinic.

Bentley-driving, beanpole Barrymore was born Michael Parker and brought up on a Bermondsey council estate. He describes his father as a "compulsive gambler and drunk" who left home when Michael was 11. "I've never met him since." While at St Joseph's RC School he had a Saturday job as a shampoo-boy with Mayfair hairdresser Ricci Burns, where he used to entertain clients with his Lulu and Shirley Bassey impressions. He played keyboards with a rock band called Fine China, wearing an old trenchcoat and velvet trousers on stage.

But he always wanted to be a comedy star like his idol Danny Kaye. After working as a Butlin's Redcoat he won a scholarship at 19 to the London Academy of Music and Dramatic Art. But, after coming first in a local talent contest, he instead chose to try his luck on the Northern club circuit. One of his early stage tricks was to stand on his head and croon Sinatra songs.

Barrymore was a bottom-of-the-bill comic when he married West End dancer Cheryl in 1976. For the next 20 years she astutely guided his career and mummied him. "Michael is a very vulnerable, sometimes very confused, man. He has always needed protection in many areas of his life. But there's also a side to him that's very strong and very stubborn."

Bassey, Shirley, 7th January 1937, Tiger Bay belter. She has become a national gay icon. Her sell-out performances are the Nineties equivalent of a Liberace concert, adored by camp and blue-rinse worshippers. With her grand theatrical gestures, spangled stage gowns and megaton voice she can out-Streisand Barbara and convey more presence than Madonna. Her songs pluck at the heart-strings: *As Long As He Needs Me, What Now My Love, No Regrets*. But any musician who gets out of synch better beware, for she has a coruscating tongue.

Like her idol Edith Piaf, this charismatic performer rose from unpromising beginnings. Her father, a West African seaman, left home when she was two. Her white mother brought up seven children in a run-down Cardiff suburb. Shirley left school at 16 to work in a factory wrapping chamberpots. "I used to write my name on them and get replies from all over the world." At weekends she performed with local bands in working men's clubs. In 1958 she had her first hit, *Kiss Me Honey, Honey, Kiss Me*. She topped the charts with *As I Love You* and *Climb Every Mountain* and headlined in variety concerts and TV shows. She did the theme songs for three James Bond films, *Goldfinger, Diamonds Are Forever* and *Moonraker*, sang at President Kennedy's inauguration and has 20 gold discs.

Shirley was Britain's first black female superstar – Diana Ross with a temper. Her private life has been less brilliant. She was an unmarried mother at 17 and her adopted son became a drug addict. Her first husband, TV producer Kenneth Hume, committed suicide. She was later cited in Hollywood star Peter Finch's divorce. She then married her Italian manager Sergio Novak. In 1985 her student daughter Samantha jumped to her death from Clifton suspension bridge in Bristol. Now single and based in Monte Carlo, Shirley depends on a series of "walkers" to escort her to film premières and parties. She admits that she is rich but often lonely. She now describes herself as having "a black belt in shopping". Her other secret vice is jelly babies.

Bath, Marquess of, 6th May 1932, the "Loins of Longleat". With his straggly grey hair, wild eyes and fustian dress he resembles Beowulf, although a high-pitched giggle rather ruins the macho image. He is best known for his "wifelets", a band of nubile young ladies who accompany him to private views, disco openings and book launches. This repertory company of pulchritude has included former starlet Cherri Gilham, rock chick Jo Jo Laine and Seychelloise actress Lucienne Camille. Retired wifelets like Jamaican singer

Nola Fontaine and former Bond girl Silvana Henriques enjoy grace-and-favour cottages on his 11,000-acre estate, an extra reward for not "kissing 'n' telling".

This former beatnik is a most unlikely product of Eton and the Life Guards. Although he belongs to an eccentric family, friends recall an incident when he was an Oxford undergraduate which may have contributed to his strangeness. After a party given by former Tory minister Alan Clark's brother Colin, he was bitten by a Great Dane. Rushed to the Radcliffe Infirmary for an anti-tetanus jab he sobbed: "I hope I don't go mad!"

The former Viscount Weymouth was an enthusiastic member of the bonking and boozing Sixties culture. His 1966 "anti-marriage" to a Sri Lankan landlady's 17-year-old daughter, Tania Duckworth, shocked his Wiltshire neighbours. Fortunately there were no anti-children. In 1969 he married Hungarian-born actress Anna Gael. The marriage survives mainly because Anna spends most of the year living in Paris. Their children, Ceawlin and Lenka both went to local comprehensives and are not at all outlandish.

Journalists often write off Alexander Bath as an amiable do-nothing buffoon. But he presides over one of the country's most profitable tourist attractions: an Elizabethan mansion stuffed with 18th century paintings and furniture. In 1993 he added a CenterParc holiday village to the famous safari park and mazes. He is an accomplished artist whose sexually-explicit murals decorating his private quarters at Longleat upset his late father. His naughty novels are less impressive. He has written over two million words of memoirs, but insists they must be published posthumously.

Beadle, Jeremy, 12th April 1948, paranoid wind-up merchant. This bearded scourge of the unwary has made a career out of embarrassing and humiliating his victims. Luckily they usually have a good-humoured, if four-lettered, reaction to his stunts and practical jokes. ITV's *Beadle's About* observes what happens when people find manure piled in their front garden, their brand new sports car reduced to scrap metal, their holiday ruined by electric drills at dawn. It takes a fiendish brain to dream up these elaborate scams which rely both on careful timing and co-operation from a close friend or relative. But viewers are perhaps beginning to suffer from Beadle-fatigue.

This wolf-grinned, roly-poly, jolly japer was the illegitimate son of a married businessman. He was brought up by his mother on a Petts Wood, Kent, council estate. He describes himself as "a friendly little freak", but perhaps we should add "prickly" to that description. At Orpington Secondary Modern School he was teased because he was

born with a deformed right hand. At 15 he was expelled for hanging
a pair of trousers, "among other things", from a flagpole. He then
travelled around Europe oddjobbing, including working as a lavatory
attendant, which may have influenced his sense of humour. He
broke into radio in the Seventies, hosting shows like *Beadle's
Brainbuster*. In 1981 he joined Sarah Kennedy, Henry Kelly and
Matthew Kelly on ITV's *Game For A Laugh*. He adapted the same
silly-stunt formula for *Beadle's About* in 1986. His other smash hit,
You've Been Framed, sees him chortling over embarrassing home-
movie clips, like an old granny tripping over the family sheepdog
and falling into the swimming pool. "My shows have the highest
laugh turnover of anything else on television. I want people to laugh
every 17 seconds!"

Beadle lives with his "sensitive, witty and wise" girlfriend Sue
near Hadley Wood, Hertfordshire. The couple have been together
since 1981 and have two daughters, Cassie and Bonnie. "I think of
us as being married." He reacts badly to criticism. A tabloid reporter
once hoaxed him, pretending to be an Australian TV producer and
offering him a new show Down Under. Beadle demanded a large fee
but later felt "deeply offended by the cheap, nasty, snide reporting
that suggested I didn't see the joke".

Bean, Sean, 17th April 1958, craggy sex symbol. A lanky, crude,
aggressive Northerner, he shares the raffish qualities of the early
Sean Connery, Michael Caine and Richard Harris. From being TV's
acceptable bit of rough he graduated to dashing leading man in
ITV's *Sharpe* and Hollywood villain. He was an IRA terrorist in
Harrison Ford's *Patriot Games* and a half-Tartar traitor in James
Bond's *Goldeneye*.

The Sheffield-born star grew up in the school of hard knocks,
working as a welder in his father's steelworks before going to RADA.
He made his professional debut as Tybalt in *Romeo and Juliet* at
Newbury's Watermill Theatre. He performed at the Citizens'
Theatre, Glasgow, the Royal Court and with the RSC in London and
Stratford-upon-Avon.

But it was television rôles like the Regency cad Lovelace in
Clarissa and the libidinous gamekeeper Mellors in *Lady Chatterley's
Lover* that turned him into a household name. His definitive part is
the swashbuckling Napoleonic hero Richard Sharpe. Life mirrored
art and Bean fell in love with Abigail Cruttenden, the Sloaney *Jane
Eyre* actress who was his screen wife in *Sharpe*. They now share his
Totteridge mansion. He has two daughters, Lorna and Molly, from
Melanie Hill, who played flighty Aveline in the hit comedy *Bread*.
They met at RADA, married in 1982 and divorced 15 years later.

"I'm fed up with being a doormat", she said. She also complained he was constantly away working and cared more about his beloved Sheffield United than their marriage. He is such a fanatic he even has "100% Blades" tattooed on his left bicep.

The screen image of a night-out-with-the-lads chauvinist who believes a woman's place is at the stove, has certain echoes in Bean's own character. It is unlikely that Abigail will turn him into a New Man. But he desperately wants a son to take to football matches.

Beaufort, Duke of, 23rd February 1928, model of a Nineties duke. Casting directors would probably reject him as not being stuffy enough. He is a leading Mayfair art dealer, can tell a Spice Girl from an It Girl and is one of the handsomest, best-dressed OAPs in Britain. In 1984 he succeeded a distant cousin, the legendary 10th duke, universally known as "Master" (as in of Foxhounds). The family is descended from Edward III's younger son, John of Gaunt, and his mistress Katherine Swynford. Before the First World War the ninth duke could boast he was related to every reigning European sovereign, except the King of Spain!

David Beaufort – worth an estimated £120 million – is only mildly interested in such details. After Eton and the Coldstream Guards he cultivated a lifelong interest in fine art. In 1950 he married the current Marquess of Bath's elder sister, Lady Caroline Thynne. He has four children, who have proved equally laid-back. His heir, the Marquess of Worcester, once sang in a Society rock band called The Business Connection and is married to former actress Tracy Ward, who sometimes embarrasses her father-in-law with her strident environmental campaigning. Weekend guests at stately Badminton House are now more Prada handbag than green wellies. Sadly, the philanthropic Duchess, once an indefatigable trekker in the Pyrenees and Himalayas, died in 1995. Well into her sixties she once abseiled down a building in aid of the Meningitis Trust.

As chairman of Marlborough Fine Art in Mayfair the duke spends millions every year buying Old Masters and Impressionists at auction. His wide contacts with aristos and the landed gentry, particularly those hit by the Lloyd's debacle, mean they often prefer to sell privately through him. The gallery also represents the estates of such notable modern painters as Francis Bacon, Graham Sutherland and Oskar Kokoschka.

Beckwith, Tamara, 17th April 1970, the Bet Lynch of the *jeunesse dôrée*. She is the ultimate trust-fund babe. She uses planes like taxis, skis at St Moritz and sunbathes in St Tropez. She shops at designer boutiques, eats in fashionable restaurants and only buys the finest chocolates and lingerie. Buying shoes is her secret fetish. This is all because her father, property tycoon Peter Beckwith, pays her a generous allowance. For her 21st birthday he gave her a swanky flat in Kensington. Her only contribution to her exchequer is the occasional modelling job to "avoid boredom".

With her swoosh of blonde hair, long legs and Jagger lips Tamara always 'makes an entrance'. She loves to show off on the dance-floor of clubs like the Hanover Grand, Tramp and Annabel's. She and fellow It Girl Tara Palmer-Tomkinson once posed naked for an advertisement, with only a handbag covering their rear quarters. "Tamara is so naff, she's cool", says one observer.

This posh tottie grew up in the family mansion beside Wimbledon Common. She attended Cheltenham Ladies' College where she played in the lacrosse team. In true St Trinians style she upset the teachers with her extra-curricular activities. She left by mutual consent after getting a punk hairstyle. At 17 she gave birth to Anouska Poppy Pearl, the result of a fling with an American Marine. She planned an adoption but her loyal parents look after her instead. This enables Tamara to continue clubbing and gallivanting round the world. "Children smear chocolate over themselves and touch your things, don't they? I'm just too selfish to have a child."

In Hollywood Tamara went to drama classes and dated Sylvester Stallone and Charlie Sheen. In 1995 she again horrified her family by announcing her engagement to Sharon Stone's brother Michael. Not relishing having this former drug-pusher 20 years her senior as a son-in-law, Daddy – worth £40 million – threatened to disinherit her. She backed down. She now claims to have put her roistering days behind her and wants to become a TV presenter or actress.

Behr, Dani, 9th July 1974, media pin-up, nicknamed Mountie because she always gets her man. She is the ultimate celebrity chick, the sort who dates soccer stars and thinks Plato is Mickey Mouse's dog. She dresses to thrill in leather trousers, plunging necklines and high heels, her Big Hair artfully tousled. Tabloid pictures of her leave little to the imagination.

The blonde, green-eyed Behr first achieved fame at 15 as Faith in the raunchy all-girl pop group, Faith, Hope and Charity. To plug their first single she pretended she was dating George Michael. Three years later she re-emerged on C4's *The Word* salivating over pop groups like Take That and Johnny Hates Jazz. She had only just left the Sylvia Young stage school and her gushing introductions and chaotic links revealed her inexperience. She moved on to present the late-night yoof show, *Hotel Babylon*. On C4's all-action series *Dani Dares* she was accidentally shot while training to be a bodyguard and stabbed attempting a high-wire circus act.

This cool young babe is a skilled networker who attends the right parties, nightclubs and restaurants. Her Filofax bulges with useful contacts in TV and the media. It also contains the names of eligible males attracted by her boisterous, direct manner. She rarely tolerates passengers, always choosing the person who will most help her career and/or image. Her conquests include footballers Ryan Giggs and Les Ferdinand. Intriguingly, she is said to have caught *ER* star George Clooney in her Behr-trap but rejected wrinkly superstar Sylvester Stallone. Her stated philosophy, "doing what I want to do when I want to do it", may not appeal to every male.

Dani comes from a close Jewish family in Mill Hill. Her South African-born father owns a North London property company. Her big dilemma is how to progress from B-list TV presenter to the new Cilla Black. She has no self-doubts: "what I have is personality and personality makes you sexy."

Bell, Sir Tim, 18th October 1941, the Cardinal Richelieu of spin doctoring. He is said to have the best contacts book in the business. "Who Tim doesn't know isn't worth knowing", whispers a co-director. Not quite true. "Tinkerbell" rose with the Thatcher Revolution and his closest allies remain those captains of industry, politicians and editors who prospered under it. Others may find him a bit brash, particularly war veterans outraged with his idea of Spam fritter-tossing to celebrate VE Day in 1995!

Charm is this master-publicist's trump card. According to legend, dogs cross the road to be patted by him, for he has an instinctive ability to make his listeners feel good about themselves. Knowledgeable, gossipy and fun he is an agreeable lunchtime or cocktail companion. Indeed that is where the serious business of Lowe Bell Communications – networking and pushing clients – gets done. His skills at political lobbying, financial PR, corporate strategy and crisis management attract clients ranging from NatWest to the Rugby Football Union.

Bell, son of PanAm's former managing director in South Africa, was educated at Queen Elizabeth's Grammar School, Barnet. His first job was as a £7-a-week chart boy at ABC TV, logging commercial-break bookings. His creative and business talents were quickly recognised in the advertising industry in the Sixties.

As chairman of Saatchi & Saatchi, Bell took personal charge of the Tory party account. His remodelling of Mrs T's image and the "Labour Isn't Working" poster helped her win the 1979 general election. She came to regard him as a lucky talisman and her "line to the British people". After further election victories in 1983 and 1987 she rewarded him with a knighthood. He forged new links with her successor John Major but under Tony Blair his company struggles to maintain its position as "the SAS of the lobbying world".

Millionaire Bell made a good recovery from cancer caused by his chain-smoking and party lifestyle. He has two young children Daisy and Harry from his Australian second wife Virginia. His secret ambition was to edit a national newspaper. But he would also like to have opened the batting for England and been a famous jazz musician. He is a great joke teller.

Bernerd, Elliott, 23rd May 1945, the Charlie Clore of the Nineties. With his hooded eyes, sleek black hair, immaculate tailoring and silky charm he resembles a Las Vegas casino mogul. He buys and sells property like Monopoly cards

He has a truffle hound's knack of rooting out undervalued or overlooked assets and then persuading partners to help buy them on advantageous terms. "Elliott has the best intelligence network of anyone other than Lord Rothschild", says an insider. "He knows where the deals are and who best to finance them". Recent coups include buying the West Midlands' Merry Hill shopping centre and Wentworth Golf Club. He describes the latter as "the most wonderful calling card". In the clubroom he can bump into anyone from Japanese electronic tycoons and Saudi oil magnates to the Sultan of Brunei and Sarah, Duchess of York. But he never dreams of lifting a putter himself.

Streetwise Bernerd, worth an estimated £175 million, came from an impoverished North London background. He left school at 16 and became a £2.50-a-week office boy. During the Sixties he worked for estate agents Michael Laurie and Partners. By 24 he had begun building his property portfolio. During the Guinness scandal he unwittingly nearly came a cropper through his friendship with banker Roger Seelig. "If you drive in the fast lane you risk smashing or scratching your car occasionally." His company, Chelsfield, was one of the few major London players to escape the recession. Among his most valued consultants is disgraced former Tory MP David Mellor who has wide contacts in the Middle East.

Music-loving Bernerd lives in a £7 million Chelsea mansion with his Brazilian-born second wife Sonia. He has two daughters from his 21-year first marriage to Susan Lynton. While chairman of the London Philharmonic Orchestra he once threatened to sue Arts Council chairman Lord Palumbo unless it received more funding. "I just had to push Palumbo to do something he didn't want to do!"

Berni, Mara, 20th August 1934, and **Lorenzo**, 11th April 1928, Knightsbridge restaurateurs. They may be growing ancient but this legendary husband and wife team still attract Britain's trendies as well as Hollywood and Euro stars. Unique among the Sixties trattorias that opened to feed the "beautiful people", this eponymous pasta joint has survived because they know how to flatter and spoil their regulars – but God help you if you are a scruffy nobody.

San Lorenzo is a fine social barometer of who is "in" or "out". A kiss and a hug from Mara means that you are among the elite of Naomi Campbell, Dustin Hoffman and Kate Moss. If she is in a bad mood everyone knows it. But her sad face soon lights up when one of her "specials" appear. For the Earl of Snowdon, Mick Jagger, Lord Lichfield and Vidal Sassoon she will always find a table: lesser-known folk are banished to the Siberia of the right-hand salon.

Quiet, moustachioed Lorenzo remains the driving-force behind the partnership, in charge of the kitchen and ruling the staff. He was a steward aboard a Norwegian yacht when he met the petite Piedmontese Mara who was an Alitalia stewardess. In 1963 they opened San Lorenzo in a cramped, tiled basement, serving the freshest spaghetti, salads, fish and meat dishes at reasonable prices. The business prospered, enabling them to send their three children, Ghigo, Paolo and Marina, to private schools, live in an elegant Georgian house 100 yards away, and have a Sardinian cliff-top villa.

The Bernis want to retire and enjoy more time abroad. Although Mara has made a good recovery from a minor stroke she is keen to slow down. But the buzz of entertaining these celebs is hard to relinquish, even if the paparazzi are more regularly stationed outside Daphne's.

Biggins, Christopher, 16th December 1948, celebrity walker. If fame was measured in restaurant lunches and dinners consumed this larger-than-life personality would be Lord Olivier. He is constantly at first-night parties, openings and charity events, often squiring a newsworthy actress or model. His smiley, bespectacled face can be glimpsed most days scanning the menu at showbiz haunts like Le Caprice, the Ivy and Joe Allen's. His circle of friends spans junior members of the chorus-line to the Very Grand Indeed. He first made his name on TV as a comic actor. He was the gay prison cook Lukewarm in *Porridge*, the 18th century Cornish vicar Ossie Whitworth in *Poldark* and the hysterical Emperor Nero in *I, Claudius*. His chirpy, camp manner made a perfect foil for Cilla Black in 1984 as co-presenter of *Surprise, Surprise*, but he was mysteriously dropped after the first series. Today, if rarely lucratively employed, he keeps himself busy – directing Shakespearean productions in Barbados, guesting on game shows and touring the provinces in pantos. He never needs a throat-mike as his voice projects like a cox's megaphone.

Raconteur Biggins, 16 stone and proud of it, trained at the Bristol Old Vic School. A Wiltshire security officer's son, he lives alone in Hackney. "I've had six relationships in my life and found them very draining." Will he have a late flowering as the millennium's new Robert Morley or Peter Ustinov?

Birley, Mark, 29th May 1930, Earl Marshal of London nightlife. This tall, aloof, sardonic Old Etonian has entertained the cream of international high society and royalty over the last three decades. Despite the crack that "Annabel's is where the middle-aged meet the Middle East" he has beaten off rivals from Regine's and Monte's to the Sultan of Brunei's Dorchester Club. He prospers because standards in food, decor and staffing are high, and membership is as exclusive as commercial common sense allows. His staff have turned away Tom Jones for not being a member and the bachelor Prince Andrew for not wearing a tie. But when Princess Diana and Fergie unexpectedly arrived with comedienne Pamela Stephenson, all dressed up in police uniforms, on Andrew's stag night in 1986, he allowed them to sit at the bar.

Birley's father was portrait painter Sir Oswald Birley and his mother Rhoda was a celebrated society hostess. He therefore learnt how to handle illustrious strangers, entertain with style, and create magnificent interiors. After only a year reading politics, philosophy and economics at Oxford he joined J. Walter Thompson's art department. He founded Annabel's in 1963, naming it after his then wife Lady Annabel, sister of the Marquess of Londonderry. As previous generations had danced to 'live' bands at the Embassy Club and the Four Hundred Club, this became London's first fashionable disco.

Birley's nightly presence there, immaculate in his dinner jacket, contributed to the break-up of his 21-year marriage in 1975. Annabel then married her long-standing lover, Sir James Goldsmith. Birley has since enjoyed a series of romances, usually with blondes decades younger than himself, but says he is "quite happy in a state of bachelorhood." He increasingly prefers a quieter lifestyle in his sumptuous Knightsbridge home, leaving it to his Old Etonian protégé Gavin Rankin to put in the long hours at Annabel's and attract the younger crowd vital for its survival. No need for a pension when he also owns fashionable Harry's Bar, Mark's Club and the Bath and Racquets Club.

Birt, John, 10th December 1944, broadcasting colossus, nicknamed Vlad the Impaler. There is something sinister-looking about the BBC's director-general, as if he belongs to George Orwell's thought-police. Perhaps it is his metal-framed specs, cropped silver hair, aquiline nose and austere manner. But friends insist he is a regular guy who plays football with TV colleagues, thinks Jimi Hendrix is "groovy" and enjoys walking in Wales and the Lake District.

Birt's 1992 appointment, after five years as deputy director-general, horrified BBC underlings. They were suspicious of his "mission to explain" philosophy and feared massive redundancies and programme cuts. He didn't disappoint them, streamlining all departments, introducing "producer's choice" and recruiting cronies. Peter Jay arrived as economics editor, Polly Toynbee as home affairs editor and Howell James as spin doctor to ensure renewal of the Corporation's charter.

Born in Liverpool, the son of a Firestone Tyres manager, Birt is your original Sixties trendy. Once an agit-prop lefty and anti-Vietnam campaigner he swapped his kaftans and long hair for designer suits, button-down collar shirts and flamboyant ties. Wags say he is the first DG to listen to R1 by choice. Ironically he made little impact at Oxford where he read engineering. He failed to win one of the BBC's coveted traineeships: "I don't think I was smooth enough". Instead he joined Granada and later London Weekend TV, producing programmes like *Nice Time*, *World in Action*, *Weekend World and The Frost Programme*. As LWT's director of programmes he introduced hit shows like *Blind Date* and *Beadle's About*. Had the BBC not poached him he would now be a multi-millionaire. The company negotiated a 'golden handcuffs' deal with senior staff prior to the 1992 ITV franchise awards.

Married since 1965 to American artist Jane Lake, Birt has two children, Jonathan and Eliza. They have homes in Wandsworth and South Wales. He hankers after a knighthood and a return to the commercial sector to make some serious dosh.

Black, Cilla, 27th May 1943, Scouse princess. This Fergie redhead with the hoofer's pins is a phenomenon. A washed-up singer without a hit record since 1974 she first tried to reinvent herself as a comedienne. But shows like *Cilla's World of Comedy* lacked finesse. In 1984 she tried a new tack as a game-show hostess, launching *Surprise, Surprise* and then *Blind Date*, capitalising on her relaxed, friendly personality. Now she is Britain's highest-paid female presenter, earning some £1.5 million a year.

Docker's daughter Cilla grew up in a tough, working-class area of Liverpool, despite being poshly-christened Priscilla Maria Veronica White. She went to St Anthony's RC secondary modern and then became a shorthand-typist. As a cloakroom attendant at the Cavern Club she met the Beatles in 1960 and began singing in local dance-halls. They introduced her to their manager Brian Epstein who rejected her. He later relented, but encouraged her to change her surname from White to Black after a music paper had boobed. For the next eight years she was never out of the charts, with hits like *Anyone Who Had a Heart, You're My World, Step Inside Love, Alfie* and *Something Tells Me*. But she remained gloriously amateur. When a TV director told her once to do a little dance in the musical break halfway through a song she did: "right past the camera – and there was a blank screen for about 10 seconds!"

In 1970 Cilla, a practising Roman Catholic, married her first (and only) boyfriend Bobby Willis whom she had met in the Cavern aged 16. He became her manager and they now have three sons, Robert, Ben and Jack. She originally wanted six children, but a hysterectomy prevented it. They live in a Denham, Buckinghamshire mansion with a Rolls Royce and five other cars in the garage. She owes her suntan to frequent trips to the West Indies and holidays at their villa near Marbella. She maintains her self-mocking sense of humour. Appearing once in *Jack and the Beanstalk* she asked the audience how she should kill the baddie. "Sing to 'im", a small boy yelled. This braying, slightly po-faced paragon will soon become Dame Cilla Black. But she must first clean up *Blind Date*.

Blair, Tony, 6th May 1953, New Labour's Moses. Single-minded and detached, he refashioned his party and is now refashioning his country. A committed Christian, he is unburdened by ideology or traditional socialist thinking. His wry sense of humour stops him from becoming priggish. Having once sung in an Oxford pop group called Ugly Rumours, he relaxes at No 10 by strumming his guitar.

Pragmatic "Bambi" is the most top-drawer PM since Sir Alec Douglas-Home and can even claim the Queen as a distant cousin. He was born Anthony Charles Lynton Blair and brought up in a Tory household in Durham. His barrister father Leo suffered a stroke at 42 and, after learning to speak again, became a law lecturer and chairman of Shrewsbury industrial tribunal. If illegitimate Leo had not been fostered by a Glasgow shipyard-worker called James Blair both men would have been surnamed Parsons. Leo's natural parents were music-hall artistes Charles Parsons (aka Jimmy Lynton) and Gussie Bridson, the black sheep of a wealthy Lancashire bleach family. The Bridsons were related to the Queen Mother's family, the

Earls of Strathmore. Tony not only inherited two Christian names from his grandfather but his excellent mimicry (of Cabinet colleagues).

After Fettes and Oxford, Blair was called to the Bar, where he specialised in trade union and employment law. He spent four fruitless years seeking a parliamentary seat, hampered by having acted for Labour against the Militant Tendency. He won Sedgefield in 1983 and quickly rose from shadow spokesman for trade and industry to home affairs. Within ten weeks of Labour leader John Smith's fatal heart attack in 1994 he took over.

Tea-aholic Blair met Cherie Booth when doing his pupillage in Derry Irvine's Inner Temple chambers. They began dating a year later when she invited him to a Christmas gathering and they played a party game which involved passing a balloon between their knees. "Tony gained a completely new impression of his driven, rather prickly colleague", recalls an insider. But she needed considerable wooing "because she wasn't quite sure whether I was what she was looking for. She felt that I'd had life too easy, with my family background, Oxford and so on". They married in 1980 and have three children, Euan, Nicholas and Kathryn. Despite living in Islington they controversially sent both sons to the London Oratory School, a grant-maintained opt-out school in Fulham. "Of all the things that ever happen to you, to be blessed with a happy family is the greatest."

Blanc, Raymond, 19th November 1949, 20th century Escoffier. His hotel-restaurant Le Manoir aux Quat' Saisons has become a French nosebag for rich and famous gourmets ready to trek (or helicopter) into the depths of Oxfordshire. His TV appearances on shows like *Ready Steady Cook* and *MasterChef* have turned him into a heart-throb. Female viewers fall in lurve with his franglais accent and dark good looks, a cross between *Jean de Florette's* Daniel Auteuil and Sacha Distel.

Besançon-born Blanc is a paean to those who maintain culinary geniuses are born not made. A watchmaker's son he was known as "Little Beaver" as a child because he was so small and hyper-active. He has never had a cookery lesson. He arrived in Britain in 1971 with an urge to show us how to prepare classic French dishes that he had learnt from watching his mother. In 1977 he opened his first restaurant, Les Quat' Saisons, in North Oxford, which became an immediate hit with trendy dons, undergraduates and food writers. He expanded with a cheaper bistro version called Le Petit Blanc in 1984. The same year he transformed a run-down 15th century manor-house, with rolling lawns and mature trees, into the

Michelin-garlanded Manoir. A Business Expansion Scheme funded it, with friends and customers like Sir Tim Rice taking shares. In 1989 he bought out his investors, although he later sold a 50 per cent share to tycoon Richard Branson. A three-acre kitchen garden supplies almost year-round organic vegetables, fruit and herbs. Every Bastille Day he holds a party with a French Revolution menu, the *Marseillaise* playing and the tricolour flying.

Since suffering a stroke at 41 Blanc has calmed down and given up smoking. "For 15 years I worked 16 or 17 hours a day. Excellence demands commitment." He owed much of his early success to his ex-wife Jenny, who became his muse and financial controller. They have two sons, Olivier and Sebastian, and divorced in 1986. His second marriage to Hungarian-born Katalin lasted five years. "I'd be a multi-millionaire by now had I not had two divorces!" He lives close to the Manoir and claims that his 500 Mercedes SL is his only extravagance.

Blandford, Marquess of, 24th November 1955, aristoprat. He once ranked just behind Princes Andrew and Edward as Britain's most eligible man. Tall and good-looking, his prospects included being heir to the Duke of Marlborough, Blenheim Palace and an 11,500-acre Oxfordshire estate. But he discovered heroin in his early 20s and – despite undergoing cures at clinics in London, Weston-super-Mare, Minnesota and Paris – it has blighted his life. In 1985 he was jailed for breaking a probation order and 12 months later received a suspended sentence for cocaine possession.

Jamie Blandford, son of Marlborough's first marriage to WH Smith's heiress Susan Hornby, followed his ancestor Sir Winston Churchill to Harrow. Aged 18 he plunged into Chelsea's fleshpots, frolicking with the older, more sophisticated Dai Llewellyn Set and bedding drifts of impressionable debs. It was a major blow when he failed to win his Army commission – what would the first Duke of Marlborough have thought? Instead he briefly worked in the City and on Wall Street before starting a course at Cirencester Royal Agricultural College. His growing addiction prevented him holding down jobs for long, but he has spent periods testing cars for glossy magazines and working in public relations.

Past amours of the frisky marquess have included schoolteacher Lulu Blacker and models Doone Murray and Louise Steel. In 1990 he married Becky Few-Brown, a blonde, horse-mad, former kindergarten teacher. The best man was her former boyfriend Paddy McNally who gave them a Range Rover as a wedding present. The Blandfords split up two years later, just before their son, the Earl of Sunderland, was born. Friends insist that Blandford's addiction problems are behind him now. He will have a tough job convincing the Duke and his trustees that he is capable of running the Blenheim estate. His Old Etonian half-brother Lord Edward Spencer-Churchill waits in the wings.

Bleasdale, Alan, 23rd March 1946, award-winning provocateur. This hairy, melancholic Scouser vies with Lynda La Plante and Jimmy McGovern as Liverpool's greatest TV dramatist. His reputation rests on three controversial series, mainly set in the bleak North of England. In 1982 he did *Boys From The Blackstuff*, featuring a gang of Scouse tarmac-layers reluctantly facing life on the dole. Bernard Hill's Yosser Hughes became famous for his catchphrase "gissa job". Then *The Monocled Mutineer* starred Paul McGann as a First World War private who led a mutiny among his harshly-treated comrades. It created a storm among Britain's war veterans for suggesting that deserters were executed by their own side. Finally C4's *GBH* in 1991 pitted Robert Lindsay's ambitious Liverpool council leader against a gentle local teacher played by Michael Palin. Bleasdale denied that it was based on former Militant leader Derek Hatton. After watching his 1997 C4 series *Melissa*, one critic accused him of suffering from Dennis Potter's Hubris Syndrome, whereby a writer becomes "so infected with plaudits that he becomes immune to criticism or advice".

Football fanatic Bleasdale was an only child brought up in Knotty Ash. His father worked in a margarine factory and his mother in a grocery store. But for the Coronation they were one of the first families to splash out on a TV set. Aged seven he tried to hang himself from the washing-line after watching a TV western. He expected the Cisco Kid to ride to his rescue! At Wade Deacon Grammar School, Widnes, a gifted English teacher inspired his writing by making him read George Orwell and John Steinbeck. Another master tried to rape him when he was 11, an experience that has "bled" right through his subsequent life. "Boy, did he attack me! He had a Crunchie Bar in one hand, his **** in the other, and he chased me all round the ******* science room. He later ended up in a mental hospital." Bleasdale went on to teacher-training college and spent eight years coaching educationally-subnormal children. At 29 he had his first novel published, based on a football-mad Merseyside teenager called Scully.

Bleasdale married his wife Julia in 1970 and they have three children. He resists lucrative offers to write in Hollywood, not only because he is "terrified of flying", but because he enjoys greater creative freedom here. "In Hollywood writers are just typists." His new ambition is "to buy a cottage in Ireland and call it 'Dunwritin'".

Blunkett, David, 6th June 1947, Labour's Stevie Wonder. He sits in Tony Blair's Cabinet like a crispy bacon sandwich in a synagogue. For this bastion of Old Labour has little time for the glossy Islington version of socialism and the black arts of media guru Peter Mandelson. But he was enough of a politician to trim his soak-the-rich, up-the-workers populism in order to achieve power. In any case as Education Secretary, with public schools at his mercy, he is now in a position to tinker with one of the great lynchpins of the Class System. As Britain's only blind MP he regards it as an insult when people pat him on the back for having achieved so much despite his disability. "I want them to admire me for doing a good job and to forget that I can't see." A loyal team in Whitehall and his constituency work hard to achieve this seemingly effortless result. "After my first year in the House I negotiated a package of essential support: the equipment for Brailling, which includes a transcriber as well as the software, and the staff to operate it." He will often work late at night and over weekends catching up on his ministerial 'boxes'. "I don't want anyone ever to say I didn't read that report or didn't answer essential correspondence because I can't see."

This tenacious, often chippy Yorkshireman went to boarding-school aged four. "My parents had no choice, because schooling for blind children was organised on a residential basis in those days." At 12 he lost his father in an accident at the Gas Board where he had worked for 47 years. "It was my anger at how my mother was treated trying to get compensation that first brought me into politics." He was already a local party activist when he attended Sheffield University to read political theory. He became a Sheffield City councillor at 22 and spent seven years as its leader from 1980. This was invaluable preparation for when he was elected MP for Sheffield Brightside in 1987.

Poetry-loving Blunkett was a Front Bench spokesman on the environment, health and education before becoming party chairman. He nearly stood for the Labour leadership after John Smith died in 1994. His punishing work schedule led to the break-up of his 1970 marriage to Sheffield lass Ruth Mitchell in 1988. "But good things came of it. I have three sons (Alastair, Hugh, Andrew), of whom I'm very proud and who I love dearly." He badly needs a new Mrs B.

Bonham-Carter, Helena, 26th May 1966, pre-Raphaelite beauty. This Pollyanna-ish English rose has at last begun to grow up. It is a sign perhaps of her boyfriend Kenneth Branagh's increasing influence on her life and career. She used to be a typical exponent of the grunge school of acting, coutured by Oxfam in long baggy overcoats, men's braces, Doc Marten boots and carrying an antique Gladstone bag. "I wear clothes that won't encourage narrow-minded men to see me for my sexuality but for my other talents." Such qualms did not prevent her removing them for a saucy bedroom scene with heart-throb Don Johnson in the US cop series *Miami Vice*.

The new Bonham-Carter dresses with more femininity, although she will never be a pouting Sharon Stone. And, finally at 30, she moved out of the family home in Golders Green into a nearby artists' studio. Since playing Branagh's leading lady in *Mary Shelley's Frankenstein* in 1995 she has loosened up and become less stridently feminist and prissy. But she remains fanatically private. While shooting *Frankenstein* she would arrive at Shepperton Studios alone, the limo having dropped off her lover to jog the last five miles. She will find Emma Thompson a hard act to follow, but is well-read, intelligent and classy enough to grip notoriously workaholic super-star Branagh's attention.

A retired banker's daughter with a French mother, Helena comes from an illustrious Whig family. Her great-grandfather was the Liberal prime minister Herbert Asquith, her grandmother was socialite Lady Violet Bonham-Carter and her uncle the former chair-man of the Race Relations Board, Lord Bonham-Carter. Even at 13 she was determined to become an actress. She spent a £25 school poetry prize on buying space in the theatrical casting directory *Spotlight* and acquired an agent. Despite achieving good A' levels at Westminster School she decided against going to Oxford. With no drama college training and a CV consisting of one TV commercial for a hi-fi company she established herself in her early-20s as the princess of period drama. She starred in Trevor Nunn's *Lady Jane* and the Merchant-Ivory films *A Room With A View* and *Maurice*. But it was their Oscar-winning *Howard's End* which turned her into a bankable Hollywood actress.

Booth, Cherie, 23rd September 1954, Britain's improved Hillary Clinton. No wonder she insists on being called "Ms Cherie Booth". She is a high-powered lady, with a better academic CV than her hus-band, Tony Blair. She won four Grade A A-levels at Seafield Grammar School, Crosby, graduated in law at the LSE with the highest first in her year and topped the 1976 bar exams. She became a QC in 1995 and then an Assistant Recorder.

An intense, driven woman, Cherie continues with her legal work, as she did when she was pregnant with each of her three children, Euan, Nicholas and Kathryn. Currently earning an estimated £200,000 a year she subsidised her husband's salary after he entered

Parliament in 1983. "Cherie is naturally brilliant, whereas I have to work at everything", he insists.

Early photographs did Cherie little justice after the media besieged their Islington home following her elevation to Shadow Norma Major. She looked like a terrified fawn caught in a car head-lamp, and she was also wont to snap at reporters. In real-life she is more feminine, maternal and soft. She lost nearly two stone and Labour's image-makers helped her to choose a more *soigné* wardrobe. Despite the power dressing, she is noticeably shy when meeting world leaders like President Clinton, Boris Yeltsin and Helmut Kohl. But backstage she has a strong, left-wing influence on policy, with important measures having to pass the "Cherie Test" before reaching Cabinet. After all, she herself contested Thanet North in the 1983 election.

Cherie retains a strident Scouse chippiness. Her mother Gale brought her up in a cramped Liverpool terrace house, shared with her sister Lyndsey and grandparents. Her father Tony Booth had left home when she was five and has always been an embarrass-ment. Once a major TV star – he played Alf Garnett's son-in-law in BBC1's *Till Death Us Do Part* – he has had three wives, including the late *Coronation Street* actress Pat Phoenix. As a child she hardly saw him but had to endure constant tabloid stories about his "crum-peteering". They were reconciled in 1979 after he suffered horrific burns in an accident when he was drunk. By the millennium she will probably be a High Court judge. She could always make a charity record as when things get stressful she bursts into football songs and sea shanties.

Boothroyd, Betty, 8th October 1929, parliamentary icon. She cre-ated history in 1992 when she became the House of Commons' first female Speaker. Thanks to Parliament being televised her gravelly, Yorkshire cries of "Order, Order" have become familiar to a world-wide audience. Her pink-cheeked, silver-haired, bespectacled face peeks out of her black silk robes. She looks like a cross between a town crier and a university vice-chancellor. Unkinder souls have likened her to Barbara Castle, Thora Hird and Mrs Merton. But she does have star quality.

The only child of Dewsbury mill-workers, Betty won a scholarship to the local technical college. In her late teens she was a high-kick-ing professional dancer and briefly a Tiller Girl at the London Palladium. For over ten years she worked as a Labour Party secre-tary at Transport House and in the House of Commons as a researcher/personal assistant. She unsuccessfully stood for Parliament four times, fighting male prejudice as much as her opponents. She was finally elected for West Bromwich in 1973 and was for two years a Euro-MP as well. Although regularly elected to the Labour party executive she was passed over for the front bench. Instead she rose from an assistant government whip to deputy speaker.

This flamboyant spinster with false eyelashes occupies a grace-and-favour apartment inside the Palace of Westminster. On public occasions she is sometimes escorted by widower John Guinery. She cannot socialise within the Commons and must be seen to be scrupulously fair in handling all parties. She successfully banned electronic pagers from the chamber. But she had "no objection to devices that vibrate", she added, amidst sniggers. On stepping down as Speaker, perhaps after her 70th birthday, Scrabble-playing Betty can expect a life peerage. Will she write her memoirs?

Botham, Ian, 24th November 1955, former wicket wildebeest, nick-named "Beefy". He is English cricket's greatest all-rounder and has a nobility of spirit to match. Record-breaking feats at 23, like scoring 1,000 runs and taking 100 wickets in 21 Test Matches, established his reputation. As did the 1981 Ashes victory which he won almost singlehandedly, despite having been sacked as captain. His charisma survived his 1993 retirement into his new career as a TV pundit, commentator and panellist. The witty asides on BBC1's quiz *A Question of Sport* prove he has other talents besides being a pantomime comic. One columnist even dubbed him the new "conscience of the nation".

The former Somerset and Worcestershire player was self-taught. At Buckler's Mead Secondary School, Yeovil, he describes himself as having been "wild, aggressive, stubborn, very hard to control. If it hadn't been for sport I'd probably have ended up in Pentonville Prison". He was never going to be normal. "If I'm any sort of hero I want to be the type who tells people to ignore everyone and go up that mountain or down that river." He has put this into practice with his marathon walks from Land's End to John O'Groats and across the French Alps in aid of leukaemia research. He is said to have raised over £3 million for charities. While accompanying the England team on their 1997 New Zealand tour he spontaneously had his head shaved to help a children's cancer fund.

Botham married his childhood sweetheart Kathy at 21. Alas, while she stayed at home looking after their three children, Liam, Sarah and Becky, he sometimes found the temptations of Test Matches abroad hard to resist. During the 1986 West Indies tour a former beauty queen sold a kiss 'n' tell story about how they had enjoyed nights of passion and had even broken the bed. Another time the

MCC suspended him for pot-smoking. Pundits wondered whether he had some self-destructive gene.

But Beefy explains his drinking, gambling and clubbing merely helped him to unwind. Today everything seems hunky dory in their North Yorkshire mansion. "My parents are the happiest I've ever seen them", reports rugby-player Liam.

Bourret, Caprice, 24th October 1973, transatlantic It Girl. Every decade has them: Koo Stark, Jerry Hall, Marie Helvin, Deniece Lewis, stunning American beauties who arrive unknown and slay Britain's eligible bachelors. This slinky, blonde Californian is the Nineties version. Best-known as the curvacious Wonderbra model, her name is on the guest-list of every smart restaurant, nightclub or film opening. Flurries of paparazzi greet her arrival as they clock who is her latest admirer. Trim as a gazelle and mischievous as a Siamese cat she has one flaw: her short-sightedness. At the 1997 World Music Awards in Monte Carlo one of her contact lenses fell out and she had to read the winners and song titles from hastily-scribbled cards. "She looked like Patrick Moore, squinting over them", one journo observed.

This 5ft 9ins supermodel arrived in New York at 18 and began a career which takes her modelling all over America and Europe. On a visit to the 1995 Monaco Grand Prix she met Iraqi-born property tycoon Robert Tchenguiz who invited her to spend the weekend in London. "I ended up staying a month, got a flat, joined an agency and, boom!, started making a life for myself over here." She denies that modelling is the bimbo's easy option. "It involves long hours and you must know how to deal with people and how to make the clothes look good." Her leap from glossy magazine covers to gossip columns happened in 1996 when she and Tchenguiz holidayed at the exclusive K Club, Barbuda. Their poolside conversation with Princess Diana provoked speculation that he was the latest royal boyfriend. More recently he defended Caprice when muggers pounced near her Hampstead home, stealing her Cartier watch. "I'll stick to Swatches in future and never wear jewellery again in public."

Bowie, David, 8th January 1947, Prince of Wails turned Swiss recluse. The lean and tanned superstar's 1992 marriage to former supermodel Iman transformed his life. Where he was moody, confused and suffering from low self-esteem, he is now positive, self-confident and sunny. "I no longer feel the need to run away from myself." Based in Lausanne and Co Wicklow he now shuns all drugs and alcohol. In 1997 he raised $55 million on Wall Street with a sale of bonds representing future profits from his back catalogue of hits. He is reckoned to be worth £100 million.

Bowie was born David Jones in Brixton, the son of a Soho wrestling-club manager and a cinema usherette. He learnt to play the saxophone and began jamming with local groups. While working as an advertising copy clerk he cheekily wrote to washing-machine tycoon John Bloom asking for financial backing. Bloom hired him to play at his wedding anniversary ball. But, after two songs, he yelled: "Get 'em off. They're ruining my party!" His first two EMI singles, with a Who-style band called the Lower Third, were flops. At 21 his name-change to Bowie (to avoid confusion with Davy Jones of the Monkees) seemed to have a magical effect on his career. His single *Space Oddity* reached the Top 10. The shaggy, dyed-blond hair was now cut Mod-style. His freaky image-changes mesmerised fans long before Boy George tried the same gimmick. He became the androgynous, extra-terrestrial Ziggy Stardust, the druggy neo-Nazi Thin White Duke and the New Romantic. In the Eighties, with songs like *Let's Dance*, he became a straight suit man.

Bowie's first wife Angie was an extrovert American hedonist. They became leading trendies on the London scene and called their son Zowie (although he now calls himself Joe). The Bowies divorced in 1980. "Living with Angie was like living with a blowtorch. She has as much understanding of the human condition as a walnut." He brought up Joe singlehandedly and even sent him to royal boarding school Gordonstoun. Today the reformed hell-raiser wants to revive his film career – he starred in *The Man Who Fell To Earth* and *Merry Christmas, Mr Lawrence*. Smoking and the Internet are his only vices.

Bradford, Barbara Taylor, 10th May 1933, golden keyboard Queen, nicknamed BTB. She is Jeffrey Archer without the trouble. Her 15 romantic sagas and their TV spin-offs have earned her an estimated £60 million. Yet she only published her first novel in 1979. Her earlier books – or "products" as she refers to her writing – had worthy titles like *The Complete Encyclopaedia of Homemaking Ideas*, *How To Be The Perfect Wife* and *How To Solve Your Decorating Problems*.

As an only child brought up in a bookish Leeds household, blue-eyed Barbara had a pampered childhood. Always ambitious she sold her first story for 7/6 to a local paper, aged 12. After attending Town Street Church of England School she joined the *Yorkshire Evening Post* as a £3-a-week secretary. She became women's editor and at 20 moved south to become fashion editor on *Woman's Own* and then a

London *Evening News* columnist. At 30 she married film producer Robert Bradford, a German-Jewish refugee who had settled in America. "I was never going to marry a local Leeds lad. I always wanted something more." She moved to New York and wrote syndicated columns for the *Chicago Tribune* and the *Los Angeles Times*. It took four unsuccessful tries before her first novel, *A Woman of Substance*, became an international bestseller – it later became a C4 mini-series.

BTB says: "If I hadn't met Bob 30-odd years ago I don't know what I'd be doing now." He masterminds publishing and TV deals which she estimates have made her worth £1 a word. Novels like *To Be The Angel* and *Dangerous To Know* feature strong, bossy heroines who make good. "But they are not feminists. They represent feminine dreams, not everyday reality." One critic dismissed her prose style as "a hybrid between Dashiell Hammett and Barbara Cartland, written in rather stiff, grammar-schoolgirl English." She has a New York apartment and an 18th century Connecticut farmhouse. Her only disappointment is that, following a miscarriage, she was unable to have children. "I just got on with my career – Bob says I can bury people half my age with my energy and drive. I never stopped to dwell on it."

Bragg, Melvyn, 6th October 1939, Aristotle of the North. His choirboy smile, bouffant hairstyle and adenoidal delivery have become trademarks on LWT's *The South Bank Show* which he launched in 1978. The series has enabled him to interview nearly all his idols, including Seamus Heaney, John Osborne and David Hockney. His unctuous, non-critical tone is in sharp contrast to his often acerbic manner on R4's *Start the Week*. One victim, novelist Kathy Lette, described him afterwards as "the thinking woman's crumpet gone stale".

This Cumbrian publican's son went to Nelson-Thomlinson Grammar School, Wigton, then to Oxford. As a teenager he was lead singer in a pop group called the Memphis 5 and still amuses colleagues with Elvis Presley impersonations. In 1961 he joined the BBC as a radio producer and began writing novels and articles for the *New Statesman*. His 16 novels have never quite won the same raves as his other work, although the sex scenes in *A Time To Dance* on television created a furore.

Bragg became a TV producer-writer on the cult BBC arts programme *Monitor* where he worked closely with director Ken Russell on biopics of famous composers. In 1973 his skill as a populariser of often complex literary subjects was recognised when he began presenting BBC2's *Second House*. He also succeeded in making books telegenic for the first time in the series, *Read All About It*. As a result of a 'golden handcuffs' deal, Mighty Melvyn, who is LWT's Controller of Arts, is now a multi-millionaire.

Bragg's first wife Lisa committed suicide in 1971 after a long illness, leaving him to bring up their daughter Marie-Elsa. In 1973 he married TV producer Cate Haste and they have two teenage children, Alice and Tom. The family divides its time between their Hampstead home, scene of many meejah parties, and a stunning Lake District "cottage". Bragg, chuffed to be elected to the Garrick Club, now hopes to become Lord Bragg of Wigton.

Branagh, Kenneth, 10th December 1960, British cultural icon. This puckish, precocious performer is the latest victim of Journalistic Jealousy Syndrome. By 36 he had directed seven films, won two Oscar-nominations for "best director" and "best actor", plus a BAFTA "best director" award and the Michael Balcon prize for "outstanding contribution to British cinema". His range as actor, director, writer and producer is extraordinary, with his screen adaptations of Shakespeare being compared to those of Orson Welles and Laurence Olivier. In the heart of the recession he also found time to start his own theatre company. Yet he regularly receives sneering notices in the British press, not least of megalomania when he published his autobiography at 29.

Working-class Branagh was born in Belfast and educated at Meadway Comprehensive, Reading. At RADA he won the coveted Bancroft Gold Medal in 1982. The same year the Society of West End Theatre named him the 'Most Promising Newcomer' for *Another Country*. He starred in RSC productions of *Hamlet*, *Love's Labours Lost* and *Romeo and Juliet*, but left after artistic differences with the director Trevor Nunn to form his own Renaissance Theatre Company in 1987. After winning rave reviews for *A Month In The Country* he then founded Renaissance Films. He directed and starred in *Dead Again*, *Peter's Friends* and *Much Ado About Nothing*. But after his award-winning production of *Henry V* he had two flops, *Mary Shelley's Frankenstein* and his over-ambitious four-hour version of *Hamlet*.

The fairytale relationship between "Ken and Em" was too like Olivier and Vivien Leigh to last. His bride and frequent co-star Emma Thompson was the only female contemporary able to match his talent, energy and brilliance. But they split up in 1995. He has since dated another up-market co-star, Helena Bonham-Carter.

Blue-eyed Branagh recently demolished a Victorian mansion near Bagshot, Surrey because he loved the view and wanted to design his own five-bedroomed home. But he spends more time in America where they admire his chutzpah, showmanship and relentless chirpiness. It can only be a few years now before we hear "Arise, Sir Kenneth". Olivier, after all, was knighted at 40.

Branson, Richard, 18th July 1950, national folk hero. At first sight this tall, dishevelled vagabond with the classless accent, hesitant grin and vague manner appears to be just another Sixties dreamer. But behind the engaging informality lurks a tough cookie who has taken on institutions from British Airways to Coutts – and won. He once turned up for an important meeting at the royal bankers in jeans. "Why the **** are you dressed like that? You know we desperately need the money," demanded a colleague. Branson replied that if he wore a suit "they'd know we were desperate and refuse the loan".

This ambitious maverick plays down his pukka background: "six generations of judges, Trinity College, Cambridge and the Blues". He left Stowe, with only three O-levels, to launch a magazine for school-leavers called *Student*. In 1971 he founded his first cut-price Virgin record shop in Oxford Street. Even though he cannot sing in tune, he made his name with the Virgin record label and its first Gold Disc-winner, Mike Oldfield's *Tubular Bells*. Never shy of controversy, he later released the Sex Pistols' album, *Never Mind The Bollocks*. His early success was nearly jeopardised when, aged 21, he was charged with Customs irregularities over the import/export of records. The case was settled before it reached trial.

Branson's luck has held ever since, whether it is launching his Virgin Atlantic airline against City advice in 1984 or surviving his hot-air balloon record attempts. He is guided by gut instinct, adding to his empire such unlikely caprices as Virgin Cola, Virgin PEPs, a private island in the Virgin Islands and the gay London disco, Heaven. A rare failure was losing the battle to control the National Lottery. He is now Britain's fifth richest man and his former cottage industry has sales worth more than £2 billion, but he still has no corporate HQ, preferring to work from a Holland Park mansion beside the family home. He married Glaswegian carpenter's daughter Joan Templeman in 1989 after a long romance. Their two children Holly and Sam have one secret wish: that Daddy stops his Boy's Own adventuring. A peerage next?

Bremner, Rory, 6th April 1961, *mimicus magnificus*. Since his entire career is built on impersonating other celebrities even he finds the real Rory Bremner hard to define. His fresh, topical impressions of Tony Blair, Gordon Brown, Prince Charles and Imran Khan make Mike Yarwood look dated. In private he is just as funny, once reducing Mrs Loyd Grossman to hysterics at a Sunday lunch party with his vowel-perfect rendition of her husband's strangulated accent. A fanatical sports fan, his favourite "victims" are Richie Benaud, David Gower, Will Carling and Bill McLaren. But critics tend to judge him on his politicians and royals. "I've a need to express my anger at some of the things that are happening in this country, through satire", he said during John Major's rule.

Edinburgh-born Bremner is the son of a retired Army officer. At eight he was sent away to prep school and then to Wellington where he began doing his "voices". While reading French and German at London University he polished his mimicry in student revues and cabaret appearances.

He made his debut as a stand-up comic at the 1981 Edinburgh Festival Fringe. While working on the London comedy pub circuit he began contributing to TV shows like *It'll Be Alright on The Night* and *Spitting Image*. In 1986 the BBC gave him his first TV series, *Rory Bremner*. He bravely bit the Corporation's hand with his take-offs of BBC personalities like Terry Wogan, Desmond Lynam, David Frost and Barry Norman. Only Bob Monkhouse and former political editor John Cole are said to have had a sense of humour failure. "But I really don't think I'm ever cruel."

In 1992 he defected to C4 because "all my ideas were being met with an air of indifference at the BBC. Suddenly from being a building full of possibilities it became a building full of problems". On C4's *Rory Bremner ...Who Else?* he is able to film sketches almost until transmission.

Bremner's private life was, well, just that – until he split up with his artist wife Susan after seven years in 1994. He blamed their inability to have children and his constant working. He seemed to find the perfect replacement in GMTV's blonde and intelligent newscaster Penny Smith. But, after nine months, she ended it because of his over-persistence.

Brewer, Liz, 6th June 1944, social Miss Fix-It. Her address books bulge with the names of the rich, famous and socially useful. As Britain's pre-eminent organiser of social events she has made a career out of introducing people and is now often better known than her clients. A BBC2 documentary, *The Fame Game*, portrayed her as an often lonely Mother Hen clucking over difficult clients. Two hundred of her closest friends became Ivana Trump's closest friends when she organised Ivana's engagement party to Italian businessman Riccardo Mazzucchelli at Syon Park in 1995.

Daughter of a Lloyd's underwriter Hugh Gansel-Brewer, Liz was brought up in rural Sussex. She claims to be descended from the Huguenot family de Briere. During the 1962 Season she was a little plumper and less sophisticated than other debutantes. Instead of marrying a debs' delight she hightailed it to Portugal where she lived for eight years. With tour operator Neville Roberts she opened the Algarve's first disco in Albufeira which attracted stars like The Beatles and Cliff Richard. She had found her métier.

Liz returned to London ready to enter public relations and to milk her contacts. British Rail chairman Lord Marsh hired her to liven up some of his hotels and set up discos. She became Queen Bee of the charity ball circuit. At one dance she put gossip columnist Nigel Dempster in the stocks and charged guests £25 for throwing rotten eggs at him.

This blonde dynamo has always had a mesmerising effect on men. She believes in love at first sight and had six fiancés before finally marrying in 1978. "Each time it was like being hit with a thunderbolt. I remember exactly where it happened: twice at a drinks party, twice in a ballroom, once in a nightclub, once in a courtroom and once in a swimming pool." Her handsome Australian husband John Rendall once lived on a Wiltshire commune with royal favourite Roddy Llewellyn. The couple divorced 10 years later but their paths constantly cross as he is a gossip columnist on *Hello!* Their daughter Tallulah is going to be a knock-out. Liz shows no sign of letting up. "I hope no-one ever asks me to give up dancing, champagne or sex because I'm not sure which would hurt the most!"

Brightman, Sarah, 14th August 1961, West End nightingale. Her extraordinary voice and stage presence have enlivened Lord Lloyd-Webber's musicals for nearly two decades. They were married for six years and she received a cool £6 million divorce settlement even though they never had children. But she just missed becoming a Lady.

This Bournemouth property developer's daughter took ballet lessons before joining the Arts Educational School to study acting and singing. She joined the sexy dance troupe Hot Gossip and at 17 enjoyed a Top 10 hit with *I Lost My Heart to a Stormship Trooper*. She met Lloyd Webber when she auditioned for *Cats and* subsequently spent 18 months as its leading lady. He claims to have fallen in love with her three-octave soprano. Their romance was complicated because both were already married: he to "Sarah One" and she to businessman Andrew Graham-Stewart. They finally wed in 1984, hours before the royal première of *Starlight Express*, enabling him to introduce her to the Queen as his wife. She inspired his first operatic work, *Requiem*, which she sang on record with Placido Domingo. She also had Top 10 hits with *Pie Jesu* and *All I Ask of You* from her leading rôle in *Phantom of the Opera*.

Life as lady of the manor at Sydmonton Court, Lloyd-Webber's 2,230-acre Berkshire estate, never quite suited this Medusa-haired vamp. Her ethnic taste in clothes and style was too bohemian for her more traditional husband. Her frequent tours and his heavy workload as a composer and impresario meant they saw each other infrequently. After their quickie divorce in 1990 he declared: "the nightingale is now free". Sarah stormed off to Los Angeles, determined to prove she could be as successful on her own. A year later she was back, starring in his new musical, *Aspects of Love*. As a solo artiste she then had a bestselling album, *Surrender*, produced by her German boyfriend, Count Frank Peterson.

Brocket, Lord, 12th February 1952, jailbird peer. He had it all and threw it away. His life story could be turned into a Hollywood mini-series, with the handsome, louche Charles Brocket cast as an aristo JR Ewing. He would own an historic English stately home, Brocket Hall, and a classic car collection worth £20 million and be besieged by eligible women. His bride (the Sue Ellen character), would be a stunning American model called Isa Lorenzo who had a mysteriously rich Cuban father. They would meet when she was doing a magazine "shoot" at Brocket and she would mistake this shabbily-dressed bachelor for a gardener. They would fall in love, marry in Las Vegas and have three gorgeous children, Alexander, Antalya and William. To relieve her post-natal depression and compensate for her husband's coldness towards her, Isa would start taking drugs. Police would arrest her for attempting to obtain drugs on a forged prescription. Meanwhile the extravagant peer's debts would be mounting up. He would arrange for three Ferraris and a Maserati to be "stolen" and then submit a £4.5 million insurance claim. Isa, now estranged from her husband, would tip off the police and he would be jailed.

Brocket's Nall-Cain family claims descent from the O'Cahans whose ancestors were the 5th century Kings of Ulster. The peerage itself is positively *nouveau*, only dating back to 1933. He succeeded his grandfather in 1967 while still at Eton. He joined the 14th/20th King's Hussars and served as a lieutenant in Northern Ireland and Cyprus. He left the Army to try to save his run-down estate. He turned Brocket into a high-security conference centre and built a championship golf course beside the lake. The family moved out into the former laundry-house.

Brocket has lost his estate, sold by his creditors for £9 million and turned into a country club by German tycoon Dieter Klostermann.

But at least the next generation may enjoy it at the end of the 60-year lease. After his 1995 divorce he observed: "My wife needed constant flattery and she didn't get it from me." Will he always be so arrogant?

Brosnan, Pierce, 16th May 1953, Irish heart-throb. Tall, elegant and debonair, he displays many of the qualities of a Cary Grant or David Niven. As the latest James Bond he is a marked improvement on his predecessor Timothy Dalton, combining some of Sean Connery's toughness with Roger Moore's comic timing. Anxious to avoid typecasting he appeared in the 1997 blockbuster *Dante's Peak*.

Born in Co. Meath, this easy-going former altar boy came to London aged 12 after his parents split up. He did not see his father again for 30 years. Contemporaries at the Drama Centre, Camden in the early-Seventies remember Pierce as "a funny-looking chap, rather overweight, with greased-back hair". While doing bit-parts on TV he worked as a mini-cab driver and developed the knack of buying elegant clothes from charity shops. He joined an experimental theatre club, the Oval House, and won West End rôles in *Wait Until Dark*, *Filumena* and *The Red Devil Battery Sign*. But critics first noticed him in the 1982 BBC series *Nancy Astor*, in which he played her brutal playboy husband. He then moved to Hollywood where he landed the lead in the long-running detective series *Remington Steele*. He also played an Irish rebel in *The Mannions of America* and Liz Taylor's toy-boy in *The Mirror Crack'd*.

Brosnan's other film credits include *The Long Good Friday*, *The Fourth Protocol*, *The Lawnmower Man* and *Mrs Doubtfire*. But these were just a prelude to the one rôle he always hankered after. In 1994 he finally made his debut as Special Agent 007 in *Goldeneye*.

Despite his chocolate-box looks he has never been a womaniser and indeed described most Hollywood women he met as "man-eating monsters". In 1981 he married former Bond girl, Cassandra Harris and had a son Sean. He also brought up as his own Charlotte and Christopher, her children from a previous relationship with Richard Harris's late brother Dermot. Cassandra died of cancer in 1991. Grief-stricken he concentrated on family and career. "No-one could ever replace Cassie – I'll always be married to her." But, at an environmental conference in Mexico four years later he met journalist Keely Shaye-Smith. She gave birth to their son Dylan Thomas in 1997.

Brown, Gordon, 20th February 1951, Britain's Calvinistic Shylock. As Chancellor of the Exchequer he has fought to end Labour's repu-

tation as high-taxers. "Fairness, decency and justice" is his mantra.
11 Downing Street is hardly conducive to romance for one of
Britain's most eligible, if ancient, bachelors. But at weekends, economic summits permitting, he can use his official residence,
Dorneywood. He has been close to PR-girl Sarah Macaulay since she
began organising Labour fund-raising dinners in 1994. Previous girlfriends include barrister Marion Caldwell and Scottish broadcaster
Sheena McDonald.

This Church of Scotland minister's son already had political aspirations as a rugby-playing teenager at Kirkcaldy High School. He
won a *Daily Express* competition for his vision of Britain in the year
2000: "A society where government enables people to fulfil their abilities and aspirations". By 19 he had a First in history from
Edinburgh University and was a left-wing student militant reading
for his doctorate. He had long hair, bell-bottomed trousers and
resembled a pop-group manager. Fellow student Princess Margarita,
the eldest daughter of exiled King Michael of Romania, became his
girlfriend for five years. "I never stopped loving him", she once
revealed. "But with Gordon it was politics, politics, politics, and I
needed nurturing."

Brown joined Labour in 1970 and within 13 years was Scottish
party chairman. He was a Glasgow College of Technology lecturer
and then a current affairs journalist on Scottish TV. He was elected
MP for Dunfermline East in 1983, rising under Neil Kinnock to
become shadow Chief Secretary to the Treasury, and Trade and
Industry Secretary.

In 1992 Labour leader John Smith promoted him to Shadow
Chancellor of the Exchequer. His only setback came in 1994 when
Tony Blair beat him in the leadership contest. Although long-time
allies, Brown had always ranked higher in the party hierarchy, but
lacked Blair's media-friendliness. As a dour-looking bachelor, with
no Cherie or little pattering feet at home, he could never play Happy
Families for the cameras. Spin doctors insist that his intense,
repressed-looking expression loosens up off-screen and he becomes
quite skittish.

Bryan, John, 30th June 1955, former royal Svengali. This oppor-
tunist Texan caused more damage to the monarchy than any other
outsider in the Nineties. For five years he was the Duchess of York's
'financial adviser', helping her to cuckold her husband. He used her
low self-esteem to manipulate and dominate her, while enjoying a
succession of free holidays in Switzerland, the South of France and
Thailand. The confused little princesses, Beatrice and Eugenie,
learned to call him 'JB'.

The lean, cocky University of Pittsburgh business graduate arrived in Britain in the mid-Eighties. He met Fergie through American playboy Steve Wyatt, who had been her previous lover. When she and Andrew were breaking up, Bryan acted as go-between. From 1992 he became a fixture at her rented mansion on the Wentworth Estate, often arriving smuggled in a car-boot.

Bryan's real rôle was finally exposed by the famous 'toe-sucking' incident. An Italian paparazzo snapped him and Fergie disporting beside a St Tropez swimming pool. Throughout their relationship the besotted Duchess bombarded him with gifts. They included Turnbull & Asser shirts with his Cheyne Place telephone number embroidered on the breast-pocket ("now you won't have to carry business cards") and Theo Fennell jewellery.

Bryan encouraged Fergie's extravagance and enjoyed hobnobbing with her showbiz friends. In 1993 they dressed up as *Grease* stars Olivia Newton-John and John Travolta to host a fancy dress party. For his 38th birthday she borrowed crystal and silver from Buckingham Palace and erected a marquee on the lawn. When he asked where the other guests were, she replied, giggling: "There aren't any, it's just us", and poured his favourite vintage champagne as Jennifer Rush's *The Power of Love* boomed out. They finally parted in 1996. Meanwhile, his Frankfurt-based construction company, Oceonics Deutschland, went bankrupt and he moved to California.

Bryer, Tania, 5th July 1962, former social butterfly, aka Tracey Sunshine. Is there life after weather-presenting? This tall blonde chatterbox is determined to follow in the wake of Ulrika Jonsson and prove there is. She belongs strictly to the no-training school of TV presenters. Armed with an international politics degree from Georgetown University, Washington DC and three years' experience as a model, she became Sky TV's weather-girl in 1991. Luckily no-one asked if she knew the difference between an isobar and an ice-cream. Her beaming personality and Valkyrie looks ensured that producers forgave the early glitches.

Tania gained three A- and nine O-levels at Queen's College, Harley Street. She had "an incredibly happy" childhood in Knightsbridge. Her South African-born father was an Oxford Rhodes Scholar and rugby Blue who became a society dentist. Her American mother received the *Légion d'Honneur* for running the European Community Youth Orchestra. But Tania's great inspiration was her grandmother, Molly Albert, a legendary Boston model agent.

Now Sky's fashion and showbiz correspondent, Tania has a trusting, even naïve, quality about her. She was among the celebrities duped by Chris Morris's spoof series, *Brass Eye*. He hired her to present an item about 'vertical farming', a revolutionary method whereby farmers used vertical plastic tubes to produce higher yields. "To my eternal shame I believed him and ended up looking a right idiot!"

Tania, well-groomed and designer-labelled, was once a fixture at film premières and restaurant launches. Gossip columnists eagerly recorded her relationships with Dodi Fayed and Australian playboy Jamie Packer and her engagement to Italian Count Gianfranco Cicogna. But in 1995 she married Lebanese-born Tim Moufarrige, vice-president of the sports management company, IMG. What will happen first, her own TV show or a baby Bryer?

Buccleuch (pronounced Buckloo), **Duke of**, 28th September 1923, Europe's largest private landowner. Nothing annoys this former Tory MP more than to be described as a multi-millionaire. He recently objected to his listing as Britain's 33rd richest man (worth £260 million), because it included works of art that were unsellable unless he paid 80 per cent death duties. These paintings hang in his four stately homes: baroque Drumlanrig Castle, Dumfries; Georgian Bowhill, Selkirk; 17th century Boughton, Northampton; and Dalkeith Palace, Edinburgh. He owns the last Titian in private hands – it accompanies him to whichever home he is staying at.

Johnny Buccleuch, Eton and Oxford, has long been a royal favourite. A nephew of Princess Alice, Duchess of Gloucester he was once tipped to marry Princess Margaret. He is descended on the wrong side of the blanket from Charles II, whose son by his mistress Lucy Walters became Duke of Monmouth. After the 1685 rebellion the duke was beheaded and his titles forfeited.

The bespectacled duke is a modest and engaging character who has four children – the Earl of Dalkeith, Lord John, Lord Damian and Lady Charlotte-Anne – from his 1953 marriage to QC's daughter Jane McNeill. He has been confined to a wheelchair since a hunting accident in 1971. But this doesn't prevent him shooting on his 300,000-acre estate from a specially converted Range Rover. He spent 13 years as Tory MP for Edinburgh North but retired in 1973 when he became ninth duke on the death of his father. In 1996 he defended himself when Labour's shadow Foreign Secretary Robin Cook attacked him for being "out of touch". His Grace gently pointed out that he had served as an ordinary seaman during World War II and had always maintained close relations with his tenants.

Bussell, Darcey, 27th April 1969, budding Margot Fonteyn. Her warm, sparkling personality and lean, elegant looks have propelled her from Covent Garden onto a wider stage. She is a TV personality, a model for de Beers diamonds and Mulberry perfume and already a CBE. Allen Jones's portrait of her hangs in the National Portrait Gallery and New York photographer Annie Leibovitz has created the definitive ballet image of her. Yet she lacks her profession's neurosis, bitchery and primadonna-dom. "She's fresh, wholesome and pretty in an old-fashioned way rather than drop-dead glamorous," observes one balletomane.

This Australian dentist's daughter grew up in Fulham. She began ballet lessons aged five because her banker mother hoped it would correct her knock-knees. It did! She went to the Arts Educational School, but at 13 transferred to the Royal Ballet School. "I was hopeless as I was a year behind everyone else." A spiteful teacher told her that she was "not cut out to become a dancer", which made her even more determined to succeed. She joined Sadler's Wells Royal Ballet and at 19 was hailed as an overnight star when Sir Kenneth MacMillan cast her in his new ballet, *The Prince of the Pagodas*. "The thing I love about Darcey is her long legs ... she has an energy and attack that are more like an American dancer", he drooled. Acclaimed performances followed in *Swan Lake*, *The Nutcracker Suite*, *Cinderella* and *Sleeping Beauty*.

Award-winning Darcey lives in Earl's Court. In 1997 she married her longstanding boyfriend, City banker Angus Forbes. Although she would like to make more guest appearances with other ballet companies she is prepared to give up full-time dancing when she has a family. "The travelling is too gruelling for a start and there is the constant fear of permanent injury." Her credo is never to take anything too seriously. "Life is about enjoying yourself."

Butler, Sir Robin, 3rd January 1938, Whitehall's real-life Sir Humphrey. As Cabinet Secretary since 1988 he has served three successive prime ministers, Mrs Thatcher, John Major and Tony Blair. He has also acted as private secretary to two more PMs, Ted Heath and Harold Wilson. No-one has a better knowledge of how power works and where the bodies are buried. Yet, outwardly at least, he shares none of the Machiavellian qualities shown in TV series like *Yes, Prime Minister*. Likened once to a giant choir-boy he has a serenity which comes from a career of unremitting achievement, plus a hint of eccentricity. In summer he often cycles to work from his South London home. At lunchtime he will stroll across St James's Park to one of his three clubs, the Athenaeum, Brooks's or the Beefsteak.

Butler's father played rugby for Lytham St Anne's and married the daughter of a local Lancashire paint manufacturer. Robin won scholarships to Harrow and Oxford where he gained a rugby blue and a First in classics. In 1961 he came top in the Civil Service exams and joined the Treasury. In 1971 he was seconded to Ted Heath's "think-tank" where he once had to make a presentation to the Cabinet on government policy. He shocked them with his conclusion that Britain "must learn to live with inflation". Ten years later Mrs Thatcher described his comment as "one of the most terrible things I ever heard". But, admiring his spunk and conviction, she appointed him her principal private secretary. Under Major he found his customary anonymity destroyed when he became embroiled in the Scott Inquiry into arms to Iraq and in the *Guardian*'s sleaze allegations against former Tory minister Jonathan Aitken.

Sir Robin married his wife Gillian in 1962. After raising three children she returned to teaching and is now deputy head of an independent school. In 1998, he will take up the Mastership of University College, Oxford, his former alma mater.

C

Cadbury, Joel, 28th July 1971, Birley Mark II. As a trendy young club owner he knows exactly what the under-30s want – the music, the cocktails, the ambience and particularly the location. Cool, elegant and friendly he remembers the names of those to court – the snobby catalysts, the big spenders, the publicity-attracters. He also knows the also-rans, the drug-dealers, the troublemakers. He discreetly informs his bouncers who to chuck out. It helps that he is a quasi-nob himself. A member of the Quaker chocolate clan, his father is multi-millionaire Peter Cadbury, who founded Westward TV. His mother is award-winning businesswoman Jennifer d'Abo. He was brought up in stately home splendour, mainly in Hampshire, with Bentleys, yachts and helicopters. No upstart Arab princeling can therefore tell him how to behave.

This rakish Old Etonian is a natural entrepreneur. At school he was already involved in running mobile discos. With his high-grade A-levels he could have gone to university. Instead he used his wide contacts among Etonians, debs and trust-fund babes, to promote one-nighters at clubs like the Café des Artistes, Embargo and the Bank. With two partners and backing from merchant banker Rupert Hambro he went on to colonise the stretch of Fulham Road, now known as "the Beach". He opened the King's Club, The Goat in Boots and the 24-hour restaurant Vingt-Quatre. In 1997 he braved fickle Battersea by launching SWX1 on the site of a former Seventies' nightclub, Bennett. Cadbury prefers to remain single. "Both my parents have been married and divorced three times. When I do reach an aisle it will be after a lot of careful thought." He remains perhaps best-known for his tempestuous relationship with tycoon Sir James Goldsmith's daughter Jemima. It finally ended after a lovers' tiff when she turfed him and his suitcase out of her convertible beside the M25.

Cadogan, Earl, 24th March 1937, benevolent King's Road landlord. Worth an estimated £500 million, he is London's second largest landowner after the Duke of Westminster. His eponymous 100-acre estate stretches from Sloane Street to Old Church Street. The previous earl, who died in 1997, had transferred it to his son to minimise death duties. In 1991 they faced a "peasants' revolt" when Walton

Street shopkeepers protested about proposed rent increases of up to 150 per cent. This followed a public row with novelist Edna O'Brien over the cost of repairs to her Georgian terrace house.

After years of dozy amateurism, Cadogan (then Lord Chelsea) transformed the estate into a go-go property company with professional managers. In 1996 it sold off fripperies like the Jermyn Street hatter Christy and a leisure park business. But it is still run on quaint lines, with, for instance, Indian and Chinese takeaways discouraged. His lordship once complained about his inclusion in a list of Britain's richest men: "It only alerts charities, beggars and conmen. It also upsets wives. They come and say: 'I didn't realise that you and your father were worth so much'." His reforms have probably ensured the estate's survival for a few more generations.

The jaunty, racegoing peer married the Earl of Portsmouth's daughter Lady Philippa Wallop in 1963. They had three children, Edward, William and Anna-Karina. But Philippa had a fatal heart attack in 1984 while driving home from Chester races where she had just watched her horse win by a neck. In 1989 he surprised friends by marrying the Jockey Club's cook, Jenny Rae, 20 years his junior. They divorced in 1994 and he immediately married doctor's daughter Dorothy Shipsey, a former matron of King Edward VII's Hospital for Officers. They live in Chelsea (natch) and Perthshire, where he owns one of Scotland's finest grousemoors.

Caine, Michael, 14th March 1933, Hollywood superstar and former Casanova. This street philosopher has made more than 70 movies, ranging from *Sleuth*, *Get Carter* and *Educating Rita* to the Oscar-winning *Hannah and Her Sisters*, *Mona Lisa* and *Dirty Rotten Scoundrels*. Asked by a journalist why he made so few artistic films he replied: "Last year I earned more than £4 million. From that I bought two Picassos and a Monet. That's art."

Caine has built a second lucrative career in catering, co-owning six restaurants, including the long-running Mayfair success-story Langan's Brasserie and The Canteen. His favourite dishes remain bangers and mash and cod and chips.

This son of a Billingsgate porter and a charlady was born Maurice Micklewhite in South London's Old Kent Road and educated at Wilson's Grammar School, Peckham. He therefore ain't no cockney! He chose his stage name after seeing *The Caine Mutiny*. Without any drama school training he had to endure ten years of badly-paid rep and walk-on parts. But thanks to his lifelong friend and agent Dennis Sellinger, in 1964 he landed the rôle of a la-di-da officer in *Zulu* and then the leads in *The Ipcress File* and *Alfie*. His tough, laconic Artful Dodger manner and horn-rimmed specs broke the mould of the smooth Cary Grant screen hero. "Caine made ordinariness look sexy", one critic said.

Although Caine was briefly married to actress Patricia Haines and had a daughter Dominique, he became the epitome of the Swinging Sixties dandy. He strutted round Chelsea bistros and West End discos, "pulling" mini-skirted "birds".

His roving days ended in 1973 with his marriage to former Miss Guyana, Shakira Baksh, and the birth of his daughter Natasha. Now back from living in Los Angeles, he accepts fewer rôles so that he can "sit back and smell the roses". The Caines live in a Wallingford, Berkshire mill-house and a Thames-side apartment in Chelsea Harbour.

Campbell, Naomi, 22nd May 1970, the black Bardot. Not since Jean Shrimpton and Twiggy has a British model achieved such mega-stardom. She is as famous for her extraordinary looks – tall, willowy and Cleopatra-ish – as her jet-setting lifestyle. She likes to think of herself not as a mere clothes-horse but as an actress, singer, even a novelist and restaurateur. The rewards for prancing up a catwalk can be £13,000 a show and for endorsing a lipstick £250,000.

Tantrum-prone Naomi was raised in Streatham. Her mother Valerie Campbell, now famous herself as a model and party creature, was then a showgirl with an international dance troupe called Exotica. She became pregnant by a white man she has never named, and whom Naomi has never met.

Valerie was determined her daughter should not suffer. She scrimped and saved and even sold her house so that Naomi could attend the Italia Conti stage school from the age of six. As a precocious disco-loving young teenager she had a Saturday job in Top Shop. At 15, while buying tap shoes in Covent Garden, she was discovered by model agent Beth Boldt. After enjoying success in teen magazines and as a catwalk model she moved to New York. Within two years she was being hailed by American *Vogue* as "the British Iman". Statuesque and oozing charisma, she now ranks alongside supermodels Cindy Crawford, Elle Macpherson and Claudia Schiffer, earns some £1.3 million a year and lives in a £700,000 Manhattan penthouse.

She is determined to use her fame to break into Hollywood, but early films like *Miami Rhapsody* displeased the critics. Naomi, 5ft 9ins, collects trophy men, like Robert de Niro, Sylvester Stallone, Mike Tyson and Eddie Murphy. She was once engaged to U2's Adam Clayton. Spanish flamenco dancer Joaquin Cortes became her boyfriend in 1996, in spite of the fact that they lacked any common language. Next man, please.

Carling, Julia, 28th February 1965, not a bimbo. She was an almost unknown PR girl before her brief 1994 marriage to former England rugby captain Will Carling. She might have remained so had he not met Princess Diana at Chelsea's Harbour Club. Their friendship led to rumours of infidelity and Julia was left facing the media at their £250,000 home overlooking Barnes Common. She behaved with great dignity, but they divorced in 1996.

This petite, fragile-looking, determined blonde – born Julia Smith – capitalised on her unwanted brush with royalty. She is now a TV presenter. Guesting on C4's *The Big Breakfast* once, she donned a surgical mask to parody Diana's bleeding heart appearance in an operating-theatre. The canny stunt garnered useful publicity and led to her replacing Anneka Rice on Carlton's daytime show, *Capital Woman*. She gained a daily show on MTV's *VH-1*, presented ITV's holiday programme *Dream Ticket* and joined Clive James co-hosting *All You Ever Wanted To Know About Formula One*. "I would never deny that I probably wouldn't be doing what I'm doing now if I hadn't married Will."

Julia admits to being "a man's woman". Her background, both personally and professionally, was in pop. She dropped out of university at 19 to live for six years with Sixties rock idol Jeff Beck, 20 years her senior. Later she dated guitar legend Eric Clapton. Mixing in that milieu she was able to found her own PR company, representing clients like Right Said Fred, Mr Blobby and Mick Jagger.

Julia is based in Maida Vale, where she lives with Biff, the black labrador she gave Will for his 29th birthday. Her boyfriend is Epic Records boss Rob Stringer. She would like to live in a large country house and be a Mother Earth figure.

Cartland, Dame Barbara, 9th July 1901, romantic novelist and royal step-great-granny. She has become our most valuable national treasure after the Queen Mother. Newspapers rely on her for instant quotes on anything from *in vitro* fertilisation to bedroom etiquette. She invites journalists to tea, receiving them in her ornate drawing-room and sending them home laden with signed paperbacks and health potions. She is good company, with a lively sense of humour. "France is the only country in the world where you can make love after lunch and people don't knock on the door asking if you're ill!"

Dame Barbara's forebears were Birmingham industrialists. But when her father died penniless in the First World War she had to work as a *Daily Express* gossip columnist. Aged 21 she wrote the first of nearly 700 pre-Mills and Boon slush. During her Sixties' heyday she wrote 23 books a year. She has also devoted her energy and flair to many good causes, particularly the St John's Ambulance Brigade. "I changed the law of England with regard to gypsy sites so that their children can go to school." She established a permanent site herself near her Hertfordshire mansion, Camfield Place.

The Dame claims to have had 49 marriage proposals. She married her first husband, Alexander McCorquodale, at 26 and produced the ever-controversial Raine (who later married Princess Diana's father Earl Spencer). After divorcing McCorquodale in 1933 Barbara married his cousin Hugh McCorquodale and had two sons, Ian and Glen. Had her "darling Dickie", Earl Mountbatten of Burma, survived she had hoped he would have become her third husband. She is determined to make her century (her mother lived to 98).

Cecil, Henry, 11th January 1943, the Ben Hur of Newmarket. In the cliquey Flat racing world this tall, wiry aristo is still tops, just. Champion trainer ten times he has had several hiccups since he and his popular first wife Julie divorced in 1990. The worst was when Sheikh Mohammed of Dubai removed 40 of his high-class thoroughbreds, following a row over whether one of them had been fit to run at Ascot's 1996 Royal Lodge Stakes. The Sheikh was also angry about the growing influence of Cecil's second wife Natalie. "When he (Cecil) allows interference to creep in from those with limited knowledge that is not good." Other leading owners, such as Lord Howard de Walden, Louis Freedman, Wafic Said and Khalid Abdulla, remained loyal.

Henry and his identical twin David were born weeks after the wartime death of their father, younger brother of the late Lord Amherst of Hackney. After Canford School, Henry went to Cirencester Royal Agricultural College. His stepfather, the Queen's racing trainer, Captain Sir Cecil Boyd-Rochfort, then appointed him his assistant trainer. In 1966 he made a useful dynastic marriage to Julie Murless, daughter of another royal trainer, Sir Noel Murless. On his father-in-law's retirement in 1973, Cecil bought his historic Newmarket stables, Warren Place. Over the next 20 years he showed a magic touch, amassing a record number of wins in the Derby, 2,000 Guineas, the Oaks, the 1,000 Guineas and the St Leger.

This laid-back dandy has two children, Noel and Katrina, from his first marriage. It ended when he met lawyer's daughter Natalie Payne, 24 years his junior, who was working as a local horsebreaker. They married in 1992 and have a son, Jake. On the plus side, she has managed to stop him smoking. On the other hand she can be unpopular with the stable lads.

Chatto, Lady Sarah, 1st May 1964, the Queen's niece. She behaves more like a Scandinavian princess than the 13th in line to the throne. She is an artist who wheels her baby, Samuel, round Hyde Park, takes public transport and goes shopping at Sainsbury's. Chestnut-haired, coltish and rather scruffy, she is a delightful, unaffected Sloane who hates the hassle of selling her paintings. With parents like Princess Margaret and the Earl of Snowdon, it is extraordinary she has turned out so normal!

As an 11-year-old Sarah was badly affected by her parents' very public separation and their subsequent choice of partners. She would yo-yo between her mother at Kensington Palace and her father's new house in Kensington. At Bedales her work suffered and she left with only one A-level. The Queen was very supportive. At Royal Ascot she insisted that her niece sat beside her in the royal box and explained the intricacies of racing. It was not Sarah's scene.

Lady Sarah inherited her artistic streak not only from Snowdon but from her great-uncle, interior decorator Oliver Messel, and another forebear Linley Samborne, the *Punch* illustrator. Her eight-year apprenticeship began at Camberwell School of Art and continued at the Royal Academy School. She was never a sex-bomb beauty like her cousin Lady Helen Windsor and was slow to start dating. Early boyfriends had one thing in common besides their non-aristo backgrounds, unusual names: Gerard Faggionatto, Lorenzo Camerana and Cosmo Fry. She met her future husband Daniel Chatto on the film set of *Heat and Dust* in India in 1982. But she only started dating this Byronesque actor turned artist five years later. The 1994 marriage was a low-key ceremony in the City. They had to overcome courtiers' misgivings that his mother, Ros Chatto, had never married his father, showbiz agent Robin Fox.

Cholmondeley (pronounced Chumley), **Marquess of**, 27th June 1960, exotic peer and squillionaire. Before succeeding his father as seventh marquess in 1990, the Earl of Rocksavage enjoyed a sybaritic lifestyle. He jetted between tax-exile homes in Monte Carlo and Paris where his contacts proved useful during his brief period working for Rothschild's. His cronies belonged to the bohemian set surrounding his mentor, the mischievous Marquess of Bristol. On his advice, David Rocksavage added to his fortune by investing in Texan oil wells. A friend described him around that time as being "an almost Wildean figure".

On his father's death, this Sorbonne-educated dilettante inherited £118 million, Britain's largest ever legacy, along with eight subsidiary titles. He had to drop his peripatetic existence to assume his dynastic responsibilities. He has two stately homes: Cholmondeley Castle, set in 12,000 Cheshire acres, which has been the family seat since the 12th century; and Houghton Hall, Norfolk, originally built for 18th century premier Sir Robert Walpole. The latter had been rescued from dereliction by his remarkable grandmother, Sybil Marchioness of Cholmondeley, a member of the wealthy Jewish Sassoon family. One of Cholmondeley's first acts was to sell off Houghton's surplus works of art at Christie's for over £21 million. He has also established a profitable sideline on its 4,000 acres breeding white fallow deer.

As the hereditary Lord Great Chamberlain of England, the piano-playing Old Etonian also assumed a key rôle at court. At the State opening of Parliament he precedes the monarch into the House of Lords, which involves learning to walk backwards without tripping over his robes. But he is no stranger to the Queen, having acted as page of honour in his teens.

A pressing need is for him to find a wife. For unless he or his bachelor cousin Charles Cholmondeley can produce an heir, the marquessate becomes extinct. He was once close to US singer Lisa B.

Clapton, Eric, 30th March 1945, the rock musicians' Messiah. This burly, bearded ladies' man is well aware of the problems associated with being hailed as the "world's greatest living guitarist". Not least because he believes that title belongs to the black blues singer BB King. "There's a danger that you're putting too much faith in your own myth", he observes. But fans continue to flock to his annual Royal Albert Hall showcase, even if the records sell less briskly.

"Slowhand" Clapton's career began in the early-Sixties when he performed in London clubs and worked as a session musician. He proved that there was more sophistication to the instrument than the twangy riffs supplied by Bert Weedon, Duane Eddy and the Shadows. His 1972 hit *Layla*, under the pseudonym Derek and the Dominoes, has become a rock classic. He was inspired to write it by his ex-wife, Sixties model Patti Boyd. During that self-indulgent decade he became a heroin addict and alcoholic. His muse almost completely dried up, as he vainly tried to sort out his life. He achieved his greatest album success with Cream, a short-lived super-group formed with fellow legends Jeff Beck and Ginger Baker. He also had a solo hit with the Bob Marley song *I Shot The Sheriff*.

Today the former beatnik wears Armani suits, trims his beard, carries a Filofax and a portable phone. Since 1987 he has regularly attended Alcoholics Anonymous meetings and believes he has conquered his chemical dependency. He admits, however, he is addicted to "beautiful women. I'm not looking for comfort or a steady relation-ship". He was briefly married to Patti Boyd whom he stole from his close friend George Harrison. In 1985 he ran off with Italian TV starlet Lori del Santo but they split up shortly after the birth of their son Conor. Ironically just as he was beginning to appreciate father-hood Conor died after accidentally falling from a window of a New York skyscraper.

Clark, Alan, 13 April 1928, Pepysian philanderer and *bon viveur*. This small, sprightly, pug-like figure could charm a piranha, not to mention the voters of Kensington and Chelsea. His arrogance, high intelligence and ready wit are great bonus in public life. "Only domestic servants apologise", he said after publication of his contro-versial *Diary* in 1993.

This Rabelaisian character was born with a golden picture-frame in his mouth. His father Kenneth Clark was a former National Gallery director and art historian who became known after his cele-brated 1969 TV series as "Lord Clark of Civilisation". Although brought up in Saltwood Castle, Kent, Alan could ill-afford to make that crack about Michael Heseltine being the sort who "bought his own furniture". For his father bought Saltwood in 1955 for £25,000 from a family fortune derived from a 19th century sewing-cotton fac-tory in Paisley.

Clark – Eton, Oxford and the Household Cavalry – is a non-prac-tising barrister. As a dilettante war historian he built up a fine repu-tation with books on the 1915 British Expeditionary Force, the fall of Crete and Hitler's war against Russia. He was MP for Plymouth Sutton from 1974 until quitting politics at the 1992 general election because he was "bored". As a junior Defence Minister he once shocked politically correct parliamentarians with his remark about "Bongo-Bongo land".

But this was tame stuff compared to the outcry which greeted pub-lication of the old goat's diaries he had kept while in office. Not only did they reveal his real opinion of old colleagues like Tom King, Nicholas Soames and John Gummer but the existence of "the coven". These were a judge's wife and her two daughters with whom he had had affairs. "I deserve to be horsewhipped", he told reporters. Clark returned to Parliament after the 1997 election. His wife Jane, whom he married when she was 16 and he 30, forgives his infidelities.

Clarke, Nicky, 17th June 1958, scissors magician. Younger and better-looking than his rivals he has become the Nineties Leonard

Lewis. A cut and blow-dry with him costs a whopping £250 and he claims to have a three month waiting-list. His salon is abounce with models, actresses, trust-fund babes and happening people, and his clients include Sarah Duchess of York, Queen Noor of Jordan, Elizabeth Hurley, Naomi Campbell, Jerry Hall and Yasmin Le Bon. He is a regular on daytime TV and maintains a high social presence at parties, film premières and launches.

Workaholic Clarke was brought up in a two-bedroomed flat in the Old Kent Road. His shoemaker father and Greek mother had six children. With two O-levels but lots of chutzpah, Nicky started as a 16-year-old junior with Mayfair crimper Leonard. "He was my mentor. He had London's most glamorous salon." He then spent nine years with John Frieda, becoming his top stylist. He persuaded Selina Scott to have a change of image with her tomboy crop and gave Fergie a more elegant style for two of her official portraits. In 1991 he acrimoniously parted with Frieda and opened his own Mayfair salon.

The trademarks of the Bee Gee-bouffanted crimper are his black leather trousers, black polo-necks and cowboy boots. His wife Lesley, a maths graduate five years his senior, has been a vital ingredient of his success. While he concentrates on the creative and publicity side she handles the salon's finances. She tied up the deal whereby Nicky Clarke Hairomatherapy and other products have become a multi-million pound business. They married in 1983 and live in St John's Wood splendour with their two children, Harrison and Tellisa. The Curse of *Hello!* nearly claimed them in 1996, with reports of them leading separate lives. He responded by throwing a star-studded 44th birthday party for Lesley at the Ritz.

Cleese, John, 27th October 1939, forever Basil Fawlty. This tortured beanpole combines the bodily inventiveness of Charlie Chaplin and Jacques Tati with the agile tongue of Lenny Bruce and Tony Hancock. The angst behind his humour probably derives from his "lower-middle-class" childhood in Weston-super-Mare. His father Reg Cheese (sic) was an autocratic insurance salesman. John, an only child, came into his own when reading law at Cambridge. He used to parody Field-Marshal Montgomery in Cambridge Footlights revues, alongside his friend Peter Cook.

The Sixties satire boom provided an ideal platform for Cleese's anti-Establishment humour in such TV shows as *The Frost Report* and *I'm Sorry I'll Read That Again*. But it was the witty sketches, insults and one-liners of *Monty Python's Flying Circus* in the early Seventies that brought him cult status. His portrayal of the hectic hotelier tyrannising his wife Sybil, the maid (played by real-life first spouse Connie Booth) and the waiter Manuel, created a TV master-piece. *Fawlty Towers* was allegedly inspired by a visit the Pythons paid to a Torquay hotel where an oafish manager threw Eric Idle's case into the street thinking it was a bomb!

The lanky 6ft 4ins frame, civil servant accent and manic delivery made Cleese instantly recognisable when he moved into films. Comedies like *Monty Python and The Holy Grail* and *The Meaning of Life* filled the vacuum left by the *Carry On* films. His box-office hit, *A Fish Called Wanda*, in 1988 created a millstone round his neck: how could he top that? Critics slammed the sequel, *Fierce Creatures*, as over-sentimental tosh This did little to help the insecu-rities exposed in his two bestselling primers, *Families and How to Survive Them* and *Life and How to Survive It*, written with psychia-trist Robin Skynner.

In 1989 Cleese sold Video Arts, the company he founded in 1972 to make training films for industry (viz *Who Sold You This Then?*), for £50 million. His £7 million share helped to finance the divorce from his second wife, American actress Barbara Trentham, by whom he has a daughter Camilla. His other daughter Cynthia is from his first marriage. He finally seems to have met his soul mate in Texan psy-cho-therapist Alyce Faye Eichelberger whom he married in 1992. "If my husband had been a racehorse they'd have shot him by now", she observes.

Clifford, Max, 6th April 1943, sleaze-broker and Establishment-basher. This grey bouffante PR-man with bushy eyebrows and a bul-bous nose invented the kiss 'n' tell agency. For 20 years he repre-sented minor showbiz figures, publicising them with embellished tabloid yarns like "Freddie Starr Ate My Hamster". In 1992 starlet Antonia de Sancha told him about her affair with a married Cabinet minister, David Mellor. He sold her story to the *News of the World*, adding titbits like Mellor's penchant for making love to her in his Chelsea football strip. Suddenly Clifford became Britain's hottest PR-man.

The guileful tabloid jackal then represented Tory MP's wife Bienvenida Buck, the mistress of defence chief Sir Peter Harding. He also helped controversial Mandi Allwood who conceived and then lost eight babies.

Sports-loving, teetotal Clifford seldom considers the effect his rev-elations will have on his victims' careers or families. "They shouldn't have misbehaved in the first place." He sees himself as a moralist who only takes on clients whose stories it is in the public interest to reveal. Insults, like "sewer rat" and "the sleazeball's sleazeball", only increase his profile, adding to his income. His power to destroy some of Britain's most powerful men has made him into the Robespierre of our media age. But he is proud too of his "cover-ups", the public figures that he deems don't deserve exposure. After "outing" Tory MP Jerry Hayes for an alleged gay affair Clifford claimed he was carrying out a vendetta against the Tories, "the hypocritical party of family values".

An electrical engineer's son, Clifford left school in Wimbledon aged 15 without O-levels. He worked in a local department store before joining EMI's press office as a trainee, representing The Beatles, Jimi Hendrix and Bob Dylan. Away from his West End office he plays the devoted, God-fearing family man rôle in suburban Raynes Park. He married his wife Liz in 1968. At night he touchingly carries their student daughter Louise up to bed because she has suffered from rheumatoid arthritis since she was seven. He drives a gold Jaguar and hopes to move into a grander house near Weybridge. He keeps his epilepsy under control with pills.

Coleridge, Nicholas, 4th March 1957, Britain's most influential magazine publisher. This lively, inspired son of a former Lloyd's insurance chairman runs Condé Nast's media empire, which includes *Vogue, Tatler, GQ* and *World of Interiors*. He has a particular rapport with female editors, whom he cossets with flowers and flattery – providing their circulation figures rise. His minimalist office contains a glass Le Corbusier desk, with nothing on it. An informal, caring boss he never shouts, preferring to rule through charm and Machiavellian means.

At school Coleridge turned the *Eton College Chronicle* into a racy *Spectator* magazine. By 17 he was already contributing satirically snobby pieces to *Harpers & Queen*. As a fogeyish Cambridge undergraduate he found university journalism so dire that he began his own literary mag. By 24 he was already an established journalist on glossy magazines and an *Evening Standard* columnist, known for his acerbic pen and intelligent overview of Sloane society. He lampooned Hong Kong's "Jardine Johnnies", once disguised himself as an Arab sheikh, grievously upset London's Russian-Orthodox monks and spent two weeks in a Sri Lankan jail on suspicion of being a terrorist. Young Journalist of the Year in 1983, he became *Harpers'* youngest ever editor three years later. In 1989 he defected to the rival Condé Nast group as editorial director.

But the industrious, deceptively shy Coleridge refused to relinquish his creative side. Having written the definitive book on the rag trade, *The Fashion Conspiracy*, he dashed off in longhand, on Saturday mornings, a volume of short stories and *Paper Tigers*, his magnum opus about Europe's press barons. His *roman à clef* novel,

With Friends Like These, caused great excitement in glossy meejah-land and inspired a cascade of sycophantic reviews. He enjoys great support from his journalist wife Georgia Metcalfe. They married in 1989, after he had enjoyed a long relationship with former fashion editor Sophie Hicks. The Coleridges have three children, Alexander, Freddie and Sophie, and maintain a high social profile, entertaining grandly at their Holland Park home.

Collins, Joan, 23rd May 1933, national treasure. When Hollywood began to overlook her for younger actresses this former "coffee-bar Jezebel" transformed herself into a bestselling novelist. Bonkbusters like *Prime Time and Love* and *Desire and Hate* drew on her racy private life, which has kept us amused for decades. Luckily she combines wit, style and star quality with a rhinoceros hide. "The thing about life is that it's one huge assorted bowl of fruit and I don't just want the cherries!"

Joan, daughter of showbiz agent Joe Collins, went to pukka Frances Holland School and then RADA. He took a full page in *Spotlight* advertising Joan's charms when she was 17. She joined the Rank charm school and made her film debut in *Lady Godiva Rides Again*. For 25 years she was a B-film actress, always in work but doing forgettable stuff. Two steamy films, *The Stud* and *The Bitch*, rescued her career in the early 80s. They led to Aaron Spelling casting her as superbitch Alexis Colby in *Dynasty*.

Joan's Achilles heels have been men and money. At 21 she wed her first husband, actor Maxwell Reed, but he proved to be a drunken womaniser who beat her up. Her second husband was Broadway and West End star Anthony Newley, by whom she has two children, Tara and Sacha. In 1972 she married No 3, record executive Ron Kass, father of her youngest child Katy. Her fourth, and most disastrous, marriage in 1985 was to an impoverished former Swedish pop singer called Peter Holm. Other past amours include Warren Beatty, George Hamilton, Ryan O'Neal and playboy Bill Wiggins.

This frisky sexagenarian has been with Robin Hurlstone, an Old Etonian art-dealer nearly half her age, since 1989. They spend three months of the year at her St Tropez villa. She is turning into a Dorothy Parker (or Mae West?) "All men are rats", she observed, "and those who aren't are boring". Even though she can draw her bus pass it is hard to imagine Joan as Norma Desmond.

Collins, Phil, 30th January 1951, self-styled ordinary bloke of pop. Songs composed by this balding South Londoner have often mirrored his tortured private life. His autocratic father worked for the Sun Alliance and his mother ran a theatrical agency. Trained at the Barbara Speake stage school, he became a child star, appearing as the Artful Dodger in the original stage production of *Oliver*. He had his first drum kit at 12 and practised in front of his wardrobe mirror. After a spell with a band called Flaming Youth he joined Genesis in 1970 as drummer, the only non-public schoolboy in the line-up.

When Peter Gabriel left five years later, Collins became lead singer. Songs like *Follow You Follow Me*, *Turn It On Again* and *Abacab* became international hits. He launched his solo career in 1981. His records *In The Air Tonight* and *You Can't Hurry Love* have become anthems of the decade, even though his croaky voice would never win choral prizes The albums *Face Value* and *No Jacket Required* have provided him with a pension for life.

Perversely this stringy, blokeish multi-millionaire is a frustrated actor. He guested in the American TV series *Miami Vice* and starred as Great Train Robber Buster Edwards in the eponymous *Buster*, in which he sang *Two Hearts* and *A Groovy Kind of Love*. But even though he finally left Genesis in 1995, he is probably too settled to switch careers.

Collins broke up with his Canadian first wife Andrea in 1982 after she fell in love with an interior decorator while he was away on a world tour. To his chagrin she took their children Joely and Simon to live in Vancouver and he dedicated a line in one of his songs to her: "if you told me you were drowning I would not lend a hand". In 1984 he married his second wife Jill and settled in a converted farmhouse near Guildford, Surrey, complete with recording studio, swimming pool and billiard-room. They had a daughter Lily.

But in 1995 that marriage ended acrimoniously after she accused Collins of dumping her by fax. The divorce settlement cost an estimated £17 million of his £105 million fortune. He now lives near Lake Geneva with Orianne Cevey, a Swiss heiress 21 years his junior. He dreams of founding a 20-piece jazz band.

Coltrane, Robbie, 31st March 1950, Highlands behemoth. He made his name as a loveable comedian. But it was his four years as a criminal psychologist in ITV's award-winning *Cracker* that opened Hollywood doors. He played a gangster in the 1995 James Bond movie *Goldeneye* and starred as a New York socialite doctor in *Buddy*. He now wants to become a film director.

Far from growing up in Gorbals tenement-block poverty, this 16-stone Glaswegian is a police surgeon's son. As a child he always tried to make people laugh. "My mum used to say: 'Robbie, you're not funny and no-one is watching.' When I got my first *Radio Times* cover I sent it to her with a note saying: 'I am and they are!'" At public school, Glenalmond, the bullying left a permanent mark. "It was a place of unmitigated cruelty, just legalised violence." Had his science been better he would have become a doctor. Instead he went to Glasgow School of Art.

But Coltrane's painting lost out to his exhibitionist nature. He joined C4's pioneering *Comic Strip* team. He starred in TV series like *A Kick Up The Eighties, The Young Ones, Blackadder* and *Tutti Frutti.* But two films, *Nuns on the Run* and *The Pope Must Die*, were less successful. By the end of the Eighties he was sick of being pigeonholed as "a Falstaff with attitude". Indeed, before landing *Cracker* in 1993 his career was in a rut. "I'll never forget walking along and hearing these kids saying: 'Look, it's the Persil Man!'" Scriptwriter Jimmy McGovern nearly vetoed him for the rôle "because he thought viewers would see me standing next to a dead body and just laugh."

Today, Coltrane resembles a reformed drug baron or sybaritic food columnist. He is friendlier and better adjusted than the sarky, hard-drinking, defensive character he was in his thirties. He describes his private pleasures as: fishing, driving, sex, eating, watching movies and jazz concerts, arguing and drinking. But he has sacrificed smoking four packs of cigarettes a day, although he still enjoys Cuban cigars. He lives with his sculptor wife Rona, 20 years his junior, in a restored barn near Loch Lomond. "I've got a shed full of cars and she's got a shed full of stone!" They have a son Spencer, named after his hero Spencer Tracy. They enjoy family outings in his vintage Cadillac.

Connery, Sean, 25th August 1930, the only credible James Bond. This ambitious son of a truck-driver and charlady, grew up in an Edinburgh tenement sharing a loo with 12 other families. He worked as a milkman, lifeguard, artists' model and coffin-polisher. After representing Scotland in the Mr Universe contest he decided to try acting. His first job was in the West End chorus line of *South Pacific*.

The rough accent and manner of this 6ft 2ins hunk – he still has "Scotland Forever" and "Mum and Dad" tattooed on his arm – made him a natural to play B-movie heavies. In 1962 he was paid just £6,000 to do the first Bond film, *Dr No*, which turned him into a superstar. He starred in six more 007 movies. Mindful of being typecast, he wisely continued with other films, such as *The Hill, Shalako* and *The Molly Maguires*. He resigned as Bond because he did not want to look ridiculous as a gnarled action man although, ironically, his successor Roger Moore was three years older.

Connery's gamble paid off. In 1988 he won a 'best actor' BAFTA award for *The Name of the Rose* and a 'best supporting actor' Oscar for *The Untouchables*. Box-office successes like *Indiana Jones and The Last Crusade*, *The Hunt for Red October* and *First Knight* enable him to maintain a glamorous lifestyle. He has homes in Marbella and the Bahamas, both conveniently near golf courses. He enjoys a combustible relationship with his Moroccan wife, Micheline, whom he married in 1975. His actor son, Jason Connery, is from his first marriage to Australian actress Diane Cilento. Notoriously careful with money he is said to have amassed a £40 million fortune. "Somebody recently told me that in Hollywood there's a group called Divorce Anonymous", he wryly observed. "It works like this: if a male member starts to feel the urge to get a divorce, they send over an accountant to talk him out of it."

Connery is a long-standing supporter of Scottish home rule and founder of the Scottish Educational Trust. His ambition is to buy a Highlands castle. Connery for First Minister?

Conran, Sir Terence, 4th October 1931, the twittering classes' Ronald McDonald. This shambling, crumple-suited genius's career began unpromisingly. He was expelled from Bryanston and left art school at 19 without finishing the course because it "bored" him. He spent a year in Paris working as a part-time chef in Les Halles. In the early Sixties he pioneered the concept of the cheap, candle-lit Chelsea bistro with the Soup Kitchen.

In 1964 the charismatic Conran opened his first Habitat, a furniture-to-household-goods store dedicated to trendy young marrieds despairing of dull post-war department stores. He made "simple good taste affordable". He was involved in the early development of Next and by 1986 was chairman of Storehouse, running British Home Stores, Habitat and Mothercare. He still dabbled in catering, launching the fashionable Blueprint Cafe and Bibendum. In 1990 he quit retailing to become a full-time foodie and designer. In a warehouse beside Tower Bridge he built the Gastrodrome complex – four restaurants and gourmet shops – and in 1992 set up the Design Museum containing everything from an electric kettle to a Le Corbusier chaise-longue. He then revolutionised the West End dining experience by launching Quaglino's and Mezzo, two artfully designed mega-restaurants.

Workaholic Sir Terence's diverse career has meant neglected relationships. His first marriage to designer Brenda Davison lasted 12 months. In 1955 he married journalist turned bestselling novelist Shirley Conran. They were together seven years and have two sons, Sebastian and dress designer Jasper. His third wife, cookery writer Caroline Conran, lasted 33 years and gave him three children, Tom,

Ned and Sophie. They divorced in 1996 and she subsequently received a record £10.5 million settlement. He had an embarrassingly well-publicised affair with Asian beauty Sunita Russell, 38 years his junior.

Punctilious, brilliant and mercurial Conran now shares his three homes – a Southwark loft, Berkshire estate and South of France villa – with divorcee Vicki Davis. His latest venture, the Bluebird Gastrodrome in Chelsea, has proved characteristically successful.

Cook, Robin, 28th February 1946, Old Labour's political conscience. The new Foreign Secretary boasted he would introduce a "moral integrity" into Britain's foreign policy. This boomeranged rather when the Press discovered that he was having an affair with his Parliamentary aide, Gaynor Regan.

He was the most unlikely-looking adulterer. His hobgoblin features, cast in stone and with a fishing rod in his hand, would look good in any kitsch suburban garden. Nonetheless in 1996 media guru Barbara Follett did persuade him to cut 3ins off his beard and comb his hair forward to make him look less intimidatingly intelligent. She reorganised his wardrobe, putting him in sleek Marks & Spencer suits. But she failed to teach him the art of the soundbite. As Foreign Secretary he has grown more regal and particularly relishes his grace-and-favour mansion Chevening in Kent.

This abrasive, Scottish headmaster's son went to Aberdeen Grammar School and Edinburgh University where he first honed his formidable debating skills. There he met his future wife Margaret. After worsting her in a student debate she thought their affair was over, until he explained that his vehement rhetoric bore no relation to his personal feelings. They married in 1969. She is now a consultant haematologist. They have two sons, Peter and Christopher.

Meanwhile the left-wing CND-marcher and English teacher progressed through the ranks of Scottish student organisations, the Edinburgh City Labour Party and Edinburgh Corporation, where he chaired the housing committee. He became MP for Edinburgh Central in 1974, nine years before Tony Blair and Gordon Brown even entered Parliament, and now sits for Livingston. He was successively Labour's front bench spokesman on EC affairs, health, trade and industry and foreign affairs.

Cook may have given the impression that he spent his spare time in sandals, smoking a pipe and studying obscure trade union magazines. But when not dallying with his mistress, he is horse-mad. Not only does he love riding – "because you have to focus so much on the horse you switch off from politics" – but the Turf. He continues to be the *Glasgow Herald*'s racing tipster.

Cooper, Jilly, 21st February 1937, Barbara Cartland with raunch. The golly-gosh brigadier's daughter from Ilkley Moor has print in her veins. Her great-great-grandfather founded the *Yorkshire Post*. After boarding school in Salisbury she was a reporter on the *Middlesex Independent*, temped in London and worked as an advertising copywriter. In 1969 she became a *Sunday Times* columnist, yacking on about her adored husband Leo, pets and neighbours' foibles. Leo, a gentleman publisher, inspired her indefatigable literary career and would occasionally tweak her grammar.

Jilly's early work was formulaic Sloaney flim-flam, with gimmicky titles like *How To Stay Married*, *Jolly Super*, and *Women and Super Women*. In 1975 she began writing Mills and Boon-style novels (with added sex), all with one-word titles: *Emily*, *Bella*, *Harriet* and *Prudence*. It was good practice for her third phase as bestselling authorine of bonkbusters like *Riders*, *Rivals*, *Polo*, *The Man Who Made Husbands Jealous* and *Appassionata*. *Riders* was turned into a 1993 TV serial starring Patrick Ryecart. "Everyone knocks my big books, saying they're crap – and, yes, they've all been deeply flawed, written too fast – but they've made me solvent."

The former Jilly Sallitt first met Leo at a children's party when she was eight and he was 12. They married in 1961 after his first marriage ended. They have two adopted children, Felix and Emma. As her career took off in 1983 they moved from "the Elysian Fields of Media-land" (Putney) to an idyllic Cotswold-stone manor-house near Stroud.

With Leo socialising all week in London, temptation soon threatened their marriage. While she "worked like a Trojan" he had a six-year affair with publishing secretary Sarah Johnson who then wrote an explicit account about it in *The Guardian*. Jilly forgave him, claiming that perhaps she had become too smug and complacent. Now an OAP she has shorn her trademark blonde hair – "it was so romantic when it was long enough to cover my nipples". Despite her flirtatiousness she has never been unfaithful. "I fall in love with my books' heroes instead."

Cowdray, Viscount, 17th June 1944, tamed Sixties' Lothario. This bearded, laid-back aristo lives in stately Cowdray Park, which he recently spent over £1 million refurbishing. He is a born-again family man, with five young children – no hardship if you have an estimated £475 million newspapers and TV fortune. He inherited his title and 17,000-acre Sussex estate, with its famous polo ground, from his father in 1995.

As playboy Michael Pearson he once had shoals of starlets, models and other totties pursuing him. His South Kensington mansion featured the ultimate bird-puller, a large swimming pool. Favoured girls were often recommended to bachelor friends as they cruised the Mediterranean aboard his aptly-named yacht, the *Hedonist*. He was known as the softest touch in clubs and restaurants, always paying for his entourage of court jesters and hangers-on.

In 1977 he married German model Fritzi Erhardt and moved into tax exile in Monte Carlo and Ibiza. This lotus-eating lifestyle continued until she fell in love with the Marquess of Northampton and they divorced in 1984. Three years later he married former Tory MP John Cordle's daughter Marina, by whom he has two sons, Peregrine and Monty and three daughters, Eliza, Emily and Catrina. He is also close to his eldest son Sebastian, from a mid-Seventies relationship with former model Barbara Ray.

The former gossip columnists' delight owes his good fortune to his great-grandfather, the first Viscount. This 19th century Bradford entrepreneur built Mexico's railroads and became MP for Colchester. The family company, Pearson, went on to own the *Financial Times*, the Westminster Press, Lazard's bank, Penguin Books, Royal Doulton China, Madame Tussaud's and Warwick Castle. As well as partying Michael dabbled in film production and property. The House of Lords will never have quite the same appeal for him as a gossip with his clubland cronies at White's.

Crawford, Michael, 19th January 1942, the world's finest song 'n' dance man. Few actors are quite so self-critical or highly-paid as this great luvvie. Before curtain-up on *Phantom of the Opera* he would spend four hours applying his 'mask' and psyching himself into the part. He received a record 7.5 per cent of the box-office, plus over £1,000-a-week salary. In the circus musical *Barnum* he risked his limbs at every performance when doing high trapeze acts. Predictably his cock-of-the-walk, finnicky attitude often upsets his colleagues. "He's an androgynous Peter Pan", sneered one journo.

Crawford was born Michael Dumbell-Smith and educated at Oakfield School, Dulwich. His father, a World War II pilot, died six months before he was born. He lived with his grandmother Edith on the Isle of Sheppey and she became a major influence on his life. She died aged 98 and he still keeps a framed photograph of her on his dressing-room table for luck.

In 1965 he married former actress Gabrielle Lewis but divorced 10 years later. They remain close friends and have two daughters, Emma and Lucy. He also has a love-child Angelique.

Crawford was a child actor, touring as a soprano with Benjamin

Britten's company in *Let's Make An Opera* and appearing in films like *Blow Your Own Horn*. During the Sixties he co-starred in *The Knack* and *A Funny Thing Happened On The Way To the Forum*. In 1971 he had his first stage hit in *No Sex Please, We're British*. But his definitive rôle was the accident-prone Frank Spencer in BBC1's sitcom *Some Mothers Do 'Ave 'Em*. It gave hope to every loser.

Crawford has never been able to repeat such telly success. But at 32 he began his transformation from light comedy star to musical superstar. After extensive voice coaching he won the lead in the West End musical *Billy*. It was followed by *Barnum* and *Phantom*, smash hits both here and on Broadway. In 1996 doctors ordered him to take a six-month rest from *EFX*, his spectacular Las Vegas one-man show. This driven man plans to leave his fortune to charity.

Currie, Edwina, 13th October 1946, former Tory MP, nicknamed "Vindaloo" and "Cruella de Vil". "Watch what that woman tells you", a fellow MP once warned, "as she has a wicked sense of rumour". During her 14-year Commons career she deployed her PR skills to promote herself and defeat her enemies. Sometimes it backfired. Within days of becoming junior health minister in 1986 she was berating "ignorant" Northerners for their unhealthy diet of chips, beer and cigarettes. Overweight former Rochdale MP Sir Cyril Smith raged: "If I was as skinny as her and looked like a banana I'd keep my mouth shut!" Sacked two years later following the salmonella-in-eggs crisis, she was ousted in the 1997 general election.

Tailor's daughter Edwina Cohen grew up in a poor Liverpool suburb. She has much in common with former mentor Lady Thatcher. They share the same birthday, attended grammar schools, won scholarships to Oxford and married richer, socially superior husbands. Edwina was a lecturer in economics and business studies when she met her future husband Ray Currie, a 16-stone, rugby-playing accountant. "It was lust at first sight", she says. Her Orthodox Jewish father boycotted their 1972 wedding because the bridegroom was a gentile. They live in a converted 17th century mill near Burton-on-Trent overlooking her former constituency Derbyshire South and have a summer bolt-hole in France. They have two daughters, mischievous TV researcher Debbie and Susie.

Edwina honed her political skills as a Birmingham City Councillor for nine years. She is remembered as a pushy, sharp-tongued, hard-working chairman of the Social Services and Housing committees. Underneath the power-suited, black stockinged veneer she still likes a good laugh. After touring a school once she remarked to the canteen manager how cold she was. "Don't worry Edwina", he replied. "You'll feel much better once you've got my spotted dick inside you!"

D

Dahl, Tessa,11th April 1957, gossip columnists' darling. She wears her heart on her sleeve, this sensitive, intuitive, kindly creature who has 21 godchildren. Her famous name ensures instant recognition and sometimes fortune-hunters and hangers-on. Her life has never been straightforward and she complicates it with an unerring ability to pick the wrong man.

This busty, 5ft 11in Amazon was christened Chantal until her parents noticed the rhyme and renamed her Tessa. She enjoyed an excellent rapport with her father, the notoriously grumpy short-story writer Roald Dahl. He raised his family almost single-handedly after his wife, Oscar-winning American actress Patricia Neal, suffered two strokes in 1965. They lived in a charming converted farmhouse near Great Missenden, where he wrote in an old chicken shed and the children played in a gypsy caravan. His only son Theo suffered permanent brain damage aged four months after a New York taxi-cab hit his pram and later his seven-year-old daughter Olivia died of measles. Tessa was expelled from Roedean for persistent naughtiness and then had teenage flings with Lord Fisher's heir Patrick and actor Peter Sellers. She became engaged to playboy Dai Llewellyn, but they soon parted.

Since 1997 this former 'wild child' has been upstaged by her daughter Sophie Dahl, a model famous for letting her 44-DD cleavage hang out on the catwalk. She was born during her mother's Seventies' romance with actor Julian Holloway. Tessa also has two children, Clover and Luke, from her first marriage, to Boston management consultant James Kelly and a fourth child, Ned from her brief marriage to Australian-born financier Patrick Donovan. She now lives in romantic semi-retirement in Shillingford, Oxfordshire.

Daldry, Stephen, 2nd May 1960, golden boy of British theatre. He put London's Gate Theatre on the map with his low-budget revivals of European classics. He proved adept at charming 'angels' and journalists into backing his projects. He then made his National Theatre debut with a stylish, award-winning adaptation of JB Priesley's thriller, *An Inspector Calls*, which even transferred to Broadway. Other long-running hits included *Six Degrees of Separation* and *Oleanna*. In 1993 he became artistic director of the Royal Court. His most important rôle was stage-managing its move to the West End while its Sloane Square premises were rebuilt. He held a trendy gala dinner at the Porchester Baths in aid of the £21 million appeal. In his speech the Court's chairman, playwright John Mortimer, jokingly compared his own "champagne socialism" to Daldry's "Hugo Boss Bolshevikism."

A long, lean cockatoo character with a flick of fair hair, Daldry was born in Dorset. As a child he would watch his mother touring as a music-hall artiste. He went to Sheffield University, via the RAF whose motto could not have been more appropriate: "through hard work to the stars". He stopped flying to go to drama school. He taught himself stilt-walking and fire-eating so that he could tour Italy with a circus. In 1984 he founded the Metro Fringe Theatre Company, running it for two years before becoming artistic director at the Sheffield Crucible's studio.

This ebullient bachelor is tipped as Trevor Nunn's eventual successor at the National Theatre, providing Hollywood does not claim him first. He enjoys building and encouraging a young team of new writers, directors and actors. His early Royal Court successes included Mark Ravenhill's *Shopping and F****ing*, Wallace Shawn's *Fever* and Doug Lucie's *The Shallow End*. Occasionally he can be a little silly, like banning critics from the 1996 first night of *Body Talk*. He is keen to escape from admin duties to direct again.

Dalton, Timothy, 21st March 1946, Shakespearian Action Man. His chiselled profile, dimpled chin and rugged Celtic features made him the Colin Firth of the Eighties. "You can see in his eyes why women are so fascinated. He's dangerous", observed former co-star Valeria Golino.

After attending grammar school in Derbyshire and RADA, Dalton joined the National Youth Theatre and toured with the RSC. This classical grounding won him leads in *Romeo and Juliet, Henry V* and *Antony and Cleopatra*. But for years he puttered along in subordinate rôles in acclaimed films like *The Lion in Winter* and *Agatha*. His metier was passionate, wild men like Heathcliff in *Wuthering Heights*. Money mattered less to him than artistic satisfaction. Indeed, in 1982 he rejected a £200,000 Hollywood offer in order to star in *Henry IV, Part 1* at the Barbican. Commercial reality took over in 1984 when he sold out to television schlock, appearing in *Mistral's Daughter*, opposite Stefanie Powers, and the Joan Collins mini-series, *Sins*.

In 1987 Dalton replaced Roger Moore as James Bond, starring in *The Living Daylights* and *Licence To Kill*. He was an unlikely choice, given his normally scruffy appearance and desire to be taken seriously as an actor and he was never entirely convincing in this macho rôle. Fortunately he was not too typecast by 007 to play Rhett Butler in *Scarlett*, the £25 million TV sequel to *Gone With The Wind*.

Dalton has always been an Oscar-winner with women. He captivated former Bond actress Ursula Andress and bonkbuster novelist Pat Booth. He then met the equally reclusive Vanessa Redgrave on the set of *Mary Queen of Scots* in 1970 and enjoyed a 16-year relationship with her. They never considered marrying. "I grew up in the Sixties when no-one gave a damn about marriage", he said. "You lived with somebody you loved." In 1997 showbiz's most determined bachelor found that his young girlfriend Ukranian actress Oksana Grigorieva was pregnant. Maybe now he will give up smoking.

Daly, Barbara, 24th March 1945 the Picasso of make-up artists. It was Big Babs who described her most famous client Princess Diana as "the loveliest natural beauty" she had ever worked with. She was so nervous before the royal wedding that she went to bed in all her St Paul's Cathedral finery, including her shoes. Her artistry has also helped to improve beauties like Faye Dunaway, Joan Collins and Mia Farrow. Photographer Norman Parkinson 'discovered' her in 1971 when he hired her for Princess Anne's 21st birthday portrait. She could even make a yak look lovely.

This friendly, rag-trader's daughter grew up in Yorkshire where her family, the Rubinsteins, had settled after fleeing Russia's turn-of-the-century pogroms. Having studied at Leeds College of Art, she joined the BBC make-up department, daubing on powder and spot-remover and learning how to feed stars' vanity. During the Swinging Sixties she went freelance, working closely with photographers Barry Lategan and Helmut Newton, hairdresser Leonard Lewis and *Vogue* fashion editor Grace Coddington. She helped to create Jean Shrimpton's and Twiggy's looks and was responsible for the weird, futuristic faces in Stanley Kubrick's film *A Clockwork Orange*.

Barbara married former heart-throb solicitor Laurence Tarlo in 1983, five weeks after being introduced by his sister, showbiz publicist Judy Tarlo. "We'd actually only spent a four-hour dinner together and gone to a movie before we got engaged!" In 1991 they sold Colourings, their hugely profitable Body Shop make-up range and retired to their Dorset farm. Both are horse-mad.

Dance, Charles, 10th October 1946, middle-aged beefcake. With his reddish-blond hair, hooded eyes and athlete's body he radiates star quality, on and off screen. But he is tired of always being the hero and jokes he wants to play a social outcast, with elements of homo-sexuality and child-molestation thrown in. "I'm over 50 now, which is over the hill to be playing leading men, and not yet old enough for interesting old wrinklies!" Had he settled in Hollywood after the award-winning ITV series *The Jewel In The Crown* turned him into a budding Robert Redford in 1984 things might have been different. "Living in Los Angeles is like being permanently on location. Everything is totally to do with the business. I refused to go there and do rubbish jobs just to maintain a luxurious lifestyle."

Instead Dance bought a large house near Hampstead Heath, with a studio for his artist wife Jo, and good local schools for his children, Oliver and Rebecca. They had originally met at art school in Plymouth and married when he was 24. Despite his drawly manner and Cavalry officer's bearing he regards himself as working-class. His father, a Birmingham engineer, died when he was a toddler and his mother was once a Lyons Corner House waitress. Raised in Devon he worked as a plumber's mate, Burton's window-dresser and graphic designer. He joined an amateur drama group and took act-ing lessons for two years behind a Devon pub, paying his two ex-RADA teachers a princely two pints of beer per lesson. In 1975 he successfully auditioned for the RSC and went on to play the leads in *Coriolanus* and *Henry V*. He starred opposite Meryl Streep in *Plenty*, and Greta Scacchi in *White Mischief*. As a contrast he played a vil-lain in Arnold Schwarzenegger's *The Last Action Hero*.

The Dances now enjoy a non-luvvie life in rural Somerset, but he continues his daily work-outs. In 1997 he gave an enthusiastic per-formance as Max de Winter in Daphne de Maurier's *Rebecca* on ITV. He badly needs another blockbuster role.

Dando, Jill, 9th November 1961, the nation's favourite older sister. As a newsreader she combines a honey-blonde elegance with friendly gravitas. The BBC is grooming her to become their new Sue Lawley/Angela Rippon. She made the ideal successor to Sue Cook as co-presenter of *Crimewatch UK*. Cheerful, unspoilt and a great gig-gler she has an appealing naturalness which transfers to the screen. But she denies reports that she earns £750,000 a year.

Brought up in Weston-super-Mare, Jill began as a *Western Mercury* cub reporter. She migrated to BBC local radio stations in Devon and Bristol. She was then chosen to present BBC Southwest's nightly news programme *Spotlight*. She became a BBC1 newscaster in 1987 and transferred to *BBC Breakfast News* two years later. In 1993 she made the vital leap from newsreading to presenting when she joined BBC1's *Holiday* as host and reporter. She has also pre-sented *Children in Need* telethons, *Safari UK* and *Songs of Praise*

This independence-loving former BBC Personality of the Year admits to being "a good flirt". She prefers dating older, more successful men. "They have a calmness and lack of naïveté about certain things. I don't like being the guide, I like to be guided". She had a seven-year relationship with her former *Breakfast News* boss, Bob Wheaton, but always refused to move in with him. She partly blames their 1996 split on "pressure of work, particularly my constant travelling". On the rebound she enjoyed a four-day fling with game warden Simon Bassil, whom she met while filming in South Africa. Jill worries about the future. "If I keep on putting work first I'm going to be like one of those women on the postcards who turn round at 40 and say: 'Oh my God, I forgot to have children!' Ideally I'd like to have a big house in the country, roses round the door, be working whenever I choose and have two children."

Davidson, Jim, 13th December 1953, Casanova of Comedy. His thin, crumpled, vulnerable face splits open like a naughty cherub when he laughs. His humour is Cockney cabbie, filthy with right-wing overtones. He may top the bill at end-of-pier variety shows, pantos and Christmas TV specials, but it is his rackety private life that keeps him famous.

The "Nick, Nick" comic grew up in Blackheath. Before his discovery on ITV's *New Faces* he worked as a window cleaner and fork-lift truck driver. At 24 he was the youngest ever comedian to appear at the London Palladium. He then appeared on TV shows *What's On Next?*, *Tiswas* and *Make 'em Laugh* and headlined in two sitcoms, *Up The Elephant* and *Round The Castle*. He now presents *Big Break* and *The Generation Game*.

The Lilliputian wise-cracker has been less successful in dealing with the pressures of stardom and has spent periods in drink-rehabilitation clinics. He has never lost his penchant for fast cars, flash nightclubs and chatting up chorus girls. It is a lifestyle that destroyed his four marriages. "Jim rampages through people's lives like an out-of-control child", observes one of his ex-wives, TV presenter Alison Holloway.

Laddish Davidson enjoyed a fling with former call-girl Pamella Bordes in 1987 and married topless model Tracy Hilton in 1990. They had three children, before he decamped with Page 3 girl Deborah Corrigan in 1997. Which number wife will he be with at 50?

Davies, Andrew, 20th September 1936. Dennis Potter with slightly fewer kinks. Our most controversial dramatist revolutionised TV costume drama, transforming the stodgy and reverential into the racy and unmissable. *Emma, Pride and Prejudice, Middlemarch, Moll Flanders* and *Persuasion* have all recently received his bold treatment. He managed to have Moll involved in 17 rumpy pumpy scenes, including a censored lesbian one. Purists were horrified when he added a happy ending to Jane Austen's *Persuasion*.

The man with the vitriolic pen had his first play broadcast in 1967. His track record has included award-winning series such as *To Play The King, Anglo-Saxon Attitudes* and *Harnessing Peacocks*. Despite being so prolific he only became a full-time writer at 50, when he gave up teaching at Warwick University, bought a Mercedes and had a vasectomy. "It was my version of a mid-life crisis."

A teacher's son, brought up in South Wales, Davies constantly rowed with his feisty mother, who was frustrated at giving up teaching to be a housewife. In 1989 his award-winning drama, *Mother Love*, featured Diana Rigg as a pathologically obsessive mother. "My mother could create an extraordinarily tense atmosphere, without making it clear exactly what you were supposed to have done wrong." His thorough grounding in English literature came from studying it at London University.

Feline Davies has never allowed his "rather flexible" marriage – he and his wife Diana have two grown-up children – to interfere with his social life. "Both of us have fallen in love with other people. But, although we're lower-middle-class, we take the upper-class view that what started off as a love affair between us has developed into a very close friendship and can't imagine anything separating us." In a 1994 Royal Television Society lecture he attacked his BBC and ITV paymasters for "attempting to narcoticise the viewing population with a diet of of tired, formulaic drama". He plans to continue being a thorn in the side of those in authority for at least 20 years. "I also still hope to have women 30 years younger falling in love with me".

Day-Lewis, Daniel, 29th April 1957, Marlon Brando with Richard Gere overtones. This class act is one of Britain's most bankable Hollywood stars. Lanky, craggy-faced and brooding he represents the classic leading man.

The vagabond actor resented his toff's background, but not enough to change his name. His late father Cecil Day-Lewis was the Poet Laureate, his mother the actress Jill Balcon and his grandfather Sir Michael Balcon managed Ealing film studios. Aged 13 he ran away from Sevenoaks School because he hated the tough boarding-school regime. He was discovered camping in the grounds of Bedales, the co-educational school where his devoted older sister Tamasin was a pupil. He moved there and began writing and acting in school productions. In 1973 his first play, *Breakout*, transferred to the Hampstead Theatre Club.

Day-Lewis trained at the Bristol Old Vic Theatre School and then made his West End debut in Julian Mitchell's award-winning play, *Another Country*. A small part in *Gandhi* led in 1985 to the cult low-budget movie, *My Beautiful Launderette* and Merchant-Ivory's *A Room With A View*. In 1989, while playing Hamlet at the National Theatre, he left the stage in mid-performance claiming "nervous exhaustion".

This tortured soul blames his emotional problems on not having really known his father who died when he was 15. But his career has never suffered. He was praised for his rôle as a Czech neuro-surgeon in *The Unbearable Lightness of Being* and won an Oscar for the crippled Irish genius Christy Brown in *My Left Foot*. He bared his chest in the politically-correct *The Last of the Mohicans* and looked debonair in *The Age of Innocence*. To prepare for his Oscar-nominated rôle in *In The Name of the Father* he slept in a prison cell, slopped out and ate prison food.

Despite relationships with Hollywood leading ladies like Winona Ryder, Juliette Binoche and Julia Roberts this complex superstar managed to stay single until he was nearly 40. For six years he had an on-off affair with Isabelle Adjani but left her two months before she had their son Gabriel in 1995. The following year he married actress-painter Rebecca Miller, whom he had just met while starring in her father, Arthur Miller's, film *The Crucible*.

Deayton, Angus (pronounced Dee-tonn), 6th January 1956, King of the ad-libs. He is that rare species, a comedian as funny in real-life as on screen. As host and co-writer of *Have I Got News For You* since 1990 he can do what he does best – insult people with masterly disdain. Described as "John Cleese with more hair and dimples" he displays a faintly pedantic charm that trips up the unwary. The award-winning show has earned him the unexpected title of 'TV heart-throb'. But his doting Scots mother, a cookery teacher, brings him down to earth. She rings up after the show and berates him: "your jacket was disgusting", "your father said you spoke too fast", "why have you parted your hair like that?"

This Surrey insurance man's son was given a trial for Crystal Palace FC at 12 . He had no interest in performing or writing when at Oxford studying modern languages. But his scriptwriter friend Richard Curtis finally persuaded him to join the Oxford revue at the Edinburgh Festival with fellow undergraduates Tony Slattery and Clive Anderson. He spent a year in Paris as an English tutor, planning to work for the British Council abroad. But at 22 he sold his first script to Dick Emery for £40. He wrote another sketch about a spoof pop group called the Hee Bee Gee Bees and formed a Barron Knights-style pop band. They toured Australia after their first record, *Meaningless Songs in Very High Voices*, went gold there.

Deayton toured with *The Rowan Atkinson Stage Show*, as Mr Bean's straight man, did voiceovers and scripted radio shows. In 1989 he joined the cult BBC1 sitcom, *One Foot In The Grave*, as Victor Meldrew's frustrated next-door neighbour. He also appeared in the BBC2 sitcom *KYTV* as Mike Channel and in C4's comedy series *Who Dares Wins*.

This eligible but ageing bachelor spent nine years with former Sixties singer Stephanie de Sykes, sharing a rambling vicarage and looking after her children from an earlier marriage. It ended acrimoniously in 1993 with her jolting his clean-cut image by selling a kiss 'n' tell story about his mean behaviour towards her. He now lives in Islington with American scriptwriter Lise Meyer, a long-time friend who previously dated his old mate Rik Mayall.

de Cadenet, Amanda, 19th May 1972, patron saint of It Girls. As a teenager this nifty blonde exhibitionist easily out-Tamara-ed Tara. She left posh Benenden and was put into care at 15 because of her 'wild child' lifestyle gallivanting round nightclubs with unsuitable men. At 17 she became a *Playboy* centrefold and the stumbling co-presenter of ITV's pop series, *The Word*. At 19 she turned down would-be lover Jack Nicholson and married Duran Duran star John Taylor. The following year she had their baby, Atlanta.

Having 'conquered' London, this relentless networker and glamour-junkie high-tailed it to Los Angeles in 1994 to try acting. She hung out with controversial rock star Courtney Love. Paparazzi once snapped them kissing each other full on the lips at the Oscar ceremony. "The best career move I ever made was *not* sleeping with Jack Nicholson." For he introduced her to Hollywood's leading acting coach and other key names. If she is not yet Sharon Stone she is well on the way. In her first two years as an actress she appeared in *Four Rooms* with Madonna, the Fifties-inspired musical *Grace of My Heart*, *Valley Girls* with Rosanna Arquette and the comedy-thriller *Fall*.

Pouting Amanda grew up in South Kensington, the daughter of trendy Swinging Sixties parents. Her father is former racing-driver Alain de Cadenet and her mother Anna is an ex-model and born-again Christian. In LA she has become a leading member of the British ex-pat community. Estranged from her husband she has dated heart-throb Keanu Reeves and George Hamilton's pop singer son Ashley. She tantalises men with the gold ring she wears through her belly-button ("great for keeping your stomach in shape"). She will continue being outrageous even as a granny.

de Chambrun, Comtesse Raine, 9th September 1929, earls' delight. This gushing, prattling dowager wears her hair coiffeured like a bewigged Lady of the Bedchamber. Her ensemble is invariably politically incorrect: mink coat, tortoiseshell spectacles, crocodile handbag with matching shoes. She is Lady Docker with class.

She was born Raine McCorquodale, the eldest of bestselling author Dame Barbara Cartland's three children. Taught by governesses until the age of eight, she was evacuated to Canada during the war. Despite a keen brain she never had a proper education. She was 'deb of the year' in 1947 and at 19 married the future Earl of Dartmouth. Ambitious, dynamic and persuasive, she enjoyed a long career in local politics. She was a Westminster City councillor and served on the LCC and GLC. She chaired the GLC's Historic Buildings Board and the Covent Garden Development Committee.

The Dartmouths divorced in 1976 so she could marry Northamptonshire landowner Earl Spencer. She became stepmother to his four children who included the future Princess of Wales. They nicknamed her "Acid Raine" because of her overbearing manner and "vulgar" redecoration of their stately home, Althorp. But her cosseting of Johnny Spencer after a stroke in 1978 prolonged his life until 1992. The following year she surprised friends by marrying an impoverished Frenchman, Comte Jean-François de Chambrun. They had only met five weeks before at a Monaco dinner party and she had no idea that he sometimes rented out his château near Cannes for soft-porn shoots. "Raine can't stand being alone", explained Dame Barbara. But three years later the marriage was quietly dissolved.

Dempster, Nigel, 1st November 1941, doyen of diarists. This one-time scourge of the upper class now seems more Establishment than most of his victims. He could pass for an ageing Bolivian playboy and relishes friendships with the aristos he once pilloried. His homes in South Kensington and Richmond are stuffed with his wife Lady Camilla's family treasures, and he holidays in South Africa, the Caribbean and the South of France. He remains loyal to his friends and not materialistic, spending rather than saving his estimated £150,000 a-year *Daily Mail* salary.

This Australian mining engineer's son was born in India and educated at Sherborne. He became a doorman at New York's El Morocco nightclub and in 1958 joined Lloyd's and later the London Stock Exchange. He gained his first social contacts working for Mayfair publicist the Earl of Kimberley. A debs' delight, he began tipping off newspapers about scandals before the *William Hickey* column hired him fulltime in 1963. He was briefly married to Countess Emma de Bendern, granddaughter of the Marquess of Queensberry. He moved to the *Daily Mail* in 1971 and began his Mail Diary two years later, adding the *Mail on Sunday* diary in 1986. He married the daughter of the late Duke of Leeds, Lady Camilla Harris, in 1977 and they have a daughter Louisa on whom he dotes.

A keep-fit fanatic, Dempster regularly plays squash at the RAC Club and runs round St James's Park and Hyde Park. A rather touching sight is to see *Private Eye*'s former "Greatest Living Englishman" exercising his five pekes round Kensington Gardens while frantically picking up last night's gossip on his mobile. His raconteur skills should have earned him his own TV chat show or at least a British version of Robin Leach's *Lifestyles of the Rich and Famous*.

This Antipodean charmer is impeccably outfitted in Savile Row and Jermyn Street. He constantly diets and watches his drinking (except on Friday lunchtimes when he lunches "with the boys" in Chelsea). His biggest hang-up is his galloping baldness for which he has contemplated a hair-transplant. He has a relaxed manner, photographic memory and an innate ability to make whoever he is with feel important. He carefully ensures he has no obvious successor.

Dench, Dame Judi, 9th December 1934, Britain's Julie Harris. Her rôle in BBC1's gentle sitcom, *As Time Goes By*, as near as dammit portrays her own cosy character. Never a raving beauty she nonetheless epitomises all the decency, charm and sweetness of Middle England. "Before filming began I was told that everybody loves her and so I thought I'm bound to find something wrong", recalls co-star Geoffrey Palmer, "But I couldn't! She's just such fun to be with". The series reprises her gentle Eighties' comedy, *A Fine Romance*, in which she starred with her real-life husband, Michael Williams.

This small, plumpish Quaker was educated at the Mount School, York and the Central School of Speech and Drama. She spent four years with the Old Vic company, playing major rôles like Ophelia in *Hamlet*. One critic wrote of her performance, "She stepped out into the limelight, tripped over her advance publicity and fell flat on her pretty face". But she went on to win many theatre awards, including for *Juno and the Paycock* and *Antony and Cleopatra*. Her film career was partly delayed as a result of a producer's caustic comment at an audition when she was 23. "You've every single thing wrong with your face", he declared. She later won BAFTA awards for *A Room With a View* and *A Handful of Dust* and became 007's politically correct spymaster in *Goldeneye*. "I got to call Bond a sexist, misogynist dinosaur and a relic of the Cold War". Although she admits she cannot sing she won a 1996 Olivier award for the stage musical, *A Little Night Music*.

Doctor's daughter Judi and her husband are one of showbiz's most devoted couples. He sends her a red rose every week. They married when she was 37 and have an actress daughter Finty. "My only big regret is that I didn't have five or six children." They live in a converted farmhouse on the Surrey-Sussex border and an 18th century Hampstead house. Curiously she has never lost her first-night nerves. "The stress is like being involved in a multiple motorway pile-up."

Dent-Brocklehurst, Henry, 6th May 1966, toff with Hollywood style. He is a handsome dandy with David Niven charm and impeccable manners. For his 30th birthday he threw a black-tie hooley beside the Thames attended by all his trendy showbiz and aristo friends. It also celebrated his inheritance of Sudeley Castle near Cheltenham, once owned by Henry VIII's wife Catherine Parr. This magnificent Tudor mansion, together with its 1,200-acre estate, is worth £50 million. After the premature death of his stockbroker father Mark in 1972, it was held in trust for him and his sister Mollie and looked after by their American-born mother Elizabeth, now married to multi-millionaire building heir Lord Ashcombe.

Life is on the up for this laid-back bachelor. As a teenager he became hooked on solvent abuse and after leaving Stowe acquired a £200-a-day coke habit. For four years he was a heroin addict. His stepfather sent him to a succession of rehabilitation clinics and he has been drug- and alcohol-free since 1988. He then moved to Los Angeles to try his luck as an independent film producer. A long-time friend of actress Elizabeth Hurley he became a bit-part player in the "Liz and Hugh Show" when her boyfriend Hugh Grant was caught with a prostitute in his car off Sunset Strip. She took refuge at Sudeley and provoked rumours that she was switching boyfriends. In 1995 Henry was falsely accused of rape by a would-be actress whom he had dated twice. It hastened his decision to spend more time in Britain where he hopes to establish his castle as a corporate events venue.

Porsche-driving D-B keeps fit with daily yoga sessions and has grown quite blasé about drugs. "I get offered them all the time, but I find it really easy to say 'No'". He has never been a lady-killer. He once even attended a £2,000 "Get Laid" workshop in Los Angeles aimed at teaching men the art of seducing women. It seems to have worked, as in 1997 he announced his engagement to Hawaiian-born model Lili Maltese.

de Paul, Lynsey, 11th June 1948, North London socialite, dubbed "Looney de Small" by Spike Milligan. This glamorous blonde singer-songwriter is better-known for her boyfriends than her hit records. In her youth she dallied with Ringo Starr, Dudley Moore and James Coburn – and Prince Charles once played footsie with her at a charity dinner. A more recent admirer was Sean Connery. Their romance might have continued had he not already been married. It was Sky TV presenter James Bellini who dubbed her the Basque Separatist because of her penchant for tightly-waisted dresses. "I'm either nymphomaniac or nun. When it's around I go mad for it. When it's not, I don't miss it."

This teetotal, non-smoking vegetarian was born Lynsey Reuben in Cricklewood. Her father was a property developer who abused her and called her "Tube-Train nose". It gave her such a complex that she has since had three nose jobs. She twice tried running away from home. Finally at 18 she enrolled at Hornsey College of Art, moved into an £8-a-week flat and began to reinvent herself. She shed two stone, dyed her hair blonde and changed her name to the more melodious de Paul. She even lost her virginity to a businessman 30 years her senior. Her first job was as a commercial artist, designing record covers. At 22 she made her Top 10 debut with her song, *Sugar Me*. Her schmaltzy style continued with *Won't Somebody Dance With Me* and *Rock Bottom* from the Eurovision Song Contest. She composed TV signature tunes for Seventies series like *No Honestly* (another hit single) and, more recently, *Hearts of Gold*.

Lynsey is a life-enhancer who can even laugh at her Essex Girl meets Barbie Doll image. She remains resolutely single, living in an imposing Chalk Farm house, with a white Mercedes outside (numberplate LDP II). "My best friends are my cats. Animals don't betray you". In recent years she has starred in the West End musical, *Pump Boys and Dinettes* and made a TV documentary on women's self-defence. Although only 4ft 11ins she can chuck a six foot male over her shoulder.

De Savary, Peter, 11th July 1944, Gordon Gekko with a soft centre. This international deal-maker, yachtsman and exhibitionist has had more comebacks than Jeffrey Archer. A mystery man raised in

Essex, he claims to be descended from one of Napoleon's generals. At 16 he was expelled from Charterhouse after being found frolicking with a maid, and started his wheeler-dealing career. By 32 he was a millionaire, having made his fortune trading in the Bahamas, Africa and the Middle East. Inspired by his girlfriend, Lord Hanson's stepdaughter Karen Hanson, he acquired a penchant for Montecristo cigars, yachts, fast cars and grand houses.

De Savary was little known until he founded the St James's Club in 1980, a showbizzy haunt behind the Ritz Hotel. He repeated the formula in Paris and Antigua, where he gave the cash-challenged Prince Michael of Kent a building plot overlooking the sea. Such PR coups were helped by his long friendship with publicist Liz Brewer. In 1983 he became a national hero when he funded the British challenge for the America's Cup yacht race.

In 1986 this bearded, Kojak-domed capitalist bought historic Littlecote House and tried to turn it into a Berkshire Disneyland. But, like many of his ambitious schemes, it failed. He lost £50 million in the Nineties property slump. His present dream is to open a series of worldwide Carnegie Clubs based on Skibo Castle in Sutherland which he has turned into a swish golf and sporting club.

Buccaneering de Savary has two daughters, Lisa and Nicola, from his first wife Marcia, a sculptress. In 1985 he jettisoned South Carolina belle Lana Paton to marry his secretary, Alice Simms, in Gibraltar. Within weeks he was back wooing Lana whom he married the next year. They now have three daughters, Tara, Amber and Savannah, and at last his roving eye seems to have settled.

Dettori, Frankie, 15th December 1970, superstar jockey. Forget Lester Piggott and Willie Carson this lithe, joke-cracking livewire has become horseracing's first telegenic legend. His sleek appearance on chat shows and sports quizzes seems far removed from the sweat and straw of his equestrian livelihood. He has brought much-needed glamour and excitement to a sport long dominated by dour, stuffy, monosyllabic champions. This effervescent, articulate practical joker is Superman on a steed. His ejector-seat style of dismounting may upset bowler-hatted race stewards but enthrals ordinary fans. As does his habit of spraying the losers, Grand Prix style, with champagne and shouting "fantastico, I love you" to the TV cameras.

The defining moment in this iron-willed, 5ft 4ins jockey's career came on 28th September 1996 when he won all seven races at Ascot. The odds against this were 25,095 to 1, earning punters £500,000 on a £20 stake! William Hill declared it the "worst day in bookmaking history", with losses of £18 million. As Sheikh Mohammed of Dubai's No 1 jockey he is assured of riding only the best mounts. By 25 he had already won five domestic Classics, the French Derby, the Irish Derby and the Prix de l'Arc de Triomphe.

Lanfranco Dettori is the son of Gianfranco Dettori, a Sardinian peasant who arrived penniless in Milan and became champion Italian jockey 13 times. He married a beautiful young circus acrobat, but the marriage failed. Riding prodigy Frankie, wanting to escape from his father's shadow, came to Britain. His talent and extraordinary self-discipline were quickly recognised by Newmarket trainer Luca Cumani. After an early brush with the police over cocaine possession his career has never looked back.

Champion jockey in 1994 and 1995, dandyish Dettori lives near Newmarket with his new wife, Cambridge professor's daughter, Catherine Allen. A freak paddock accident at Newbury in 1996, in which he broke his elbow, shows the high risks involved in winning £2 million-a-year prize money. His victory in the 1996 Japan Cup alone earned £430,000.

de Varela, Marquesa, 21st March 1948, Society fixer, known as Neneta by friends. Through her international contacts she chronicles the lifestyles of the rich and famous. Everyone from Princess Anne and Sarah Duchess of York to Paula Yates and Koo Stark have succumbed. "I'm very good at persuasion. It's a gift, like a painter!" She has an annoying habit of beginning sentences "my friend the president/king/prime minister". But she never betrays confidences, even for a "scoop".

This "silken enabler" was born Maria Julia Marin in Uruguay, daughter of a wealthy Spanish colonial farmer and an Italian mother. "I was terribly spoilt. I remember as an eight-year-old refusing to take my medicine unless my pony was brought to my bedside – and it was!" At the British School in Montevideo she learnt to speak five languages.

When she was 18 her father refused to lend her $3,500 to start a jewellery business. "He thought women were inferior. He said that if I wanted money I should marry a rich man." So she did. Her first husband was an Italian playboy, Julio Cesar de Montenegro, by whom she has two daughters, Natalia and Valeria. Her second was the Marques de Varela, a womanising Spanish nobleman and "the sexiest man I've ever met". She produced an heir, Bruno.

Alas, these jet-setting marriages gave her the right social introductions but no alimony. To finance her lavish lifestyle and children she had to work. She booked celebrity guests for a Spanish TV chat show and did "at home" interviews with the rich and famous for a new Spanish glossy magazine called *Hola!* In 1988 she helped to launch the UK version, *Hello!*

The husky-accented Marquesa threatened to resign in 1996 after a row over her tycoon-sized telephone bills and entertaining expenses. ("How am I supposed to woo these celebrities? Over a Big Mac?"). Eventually the magazine's Spanish publisher, Eduardo Sanchez Junco, smoothed her bruised ego.

Easily bored, she leads a gypsy life between homes in London, Madrid, Montevideo and Uruguay's Punto del Este where she looks after stray dogs that she has rescued. She is a lonely soul who needs another macho male in her life.

Devonshire, Duke of, 2nd January 1920, quintessential English grandee. Modest, conscientious and eccentric, this Old Etonian former Coldstream Guards officer combines most human virtues with an other-worldliness that has sometimes landed him in trouble. At Chatsworth, his magnificent 175-room Derbyshire seat, he potters round the landscaped gardens with his labradors, hunts for rare rock specimens and gloats over his collection of modern first editions. In St James's he owns his own dining club, Pratt's, where all servants are traditionally called George.

The tall, slender, slightly stooping 11th Duke has always seemed slightly older than he is. If his tweed suits and sports jackets look comfortably battered it is because he allows his head gardener to wear them in first. His lifelong passion is the Turf. A former Jockey Club steward and member of the Tote board his pale yellow racing colours are the oldest registered in Britain. He can recite the winner of every British classic since the war – a party game he sometimes plays with the Queen – and has written a biography of his most famous racehorse, Park Top.

The Cavendishes have served the country since before the first Duke was created in 1694. The present incumbent twice failed to win his local Peak District constituency, Chesterfield, but was rescued by his uncle, Harold Macmillan, who appointed him a junior minister in the Commonwealth Relations Office in 1962. "It was nepotism without any doubt", admits His Grace. Later he defected to the SDP.

Andrew Devonshire married in 1941 and has three children, who include Ascot supremo, the Marquess of Hartington. His wife Debo, the cleverest and most normal of the Mitford sisters, loyally stood by her husband in 1985 when it was revealed he had lavished large sums on young mistresses. But then he had a fortune estimated to be £390 million. Land holdings comprise 70,000 acres spread over Derbyshire, Yorkshire and Eastbourne, and his art collection is so outstanding that in 1984 he could sell off surplus Old Master drawings and prints to raise £21 million.

Dimbleby, David, 28th October 1938, political heavyweight. His headmasterly approach suffers in comparison with his late father Richard Dimbleby, who ranks alongside the great Walter Cronkite. Richard was the BBC's top wartime correspondent, commentated at every State occasion from the Coronation to the funeral of Sir Winston Churchill and launched *Panorama*. But the lad hasn't done badly and may yet win the knighthood curiously denied his father.

David made his broadcasting debut aged 12, compering the Boxing Day edition of *Family Favourites*. He received an eclectic education: Charterhouse, Oxford, the Sorbonne and the University of Perugia. He joined the BBC in Bristol in 1960, where he nearly dried up on his first job. Interviewing a local headmaster whose school had just burnt down "all I could think of saying was: 'how sad!'" His passion for politics enabled him to become a presenter on *Panorama*, *Nationwide* and *24 Hours*. In 1971 his controversial documentary *Yesterday's Men* infuriated the Labour party after he quizzed former prime minister Harold Wilson about profits made from his memoirs.

Dimbleby is noted for his meticulous research, unflappability and photographic memory. During his live coverage of Prince Andrew's wedding in 1986 he even discovered how many mulberry leaves were needed to feed the silkworms responsible for Fergie's dress! But he is proudest of having been the BBC's commentator at every general election since 1974. For three years he quizzed politicians on *The Dimbleby Talk-In* and since 1994 has chaired *Question Time*. Alas, John Birt beat him to the BBC director-generalship in 1992.

Cigar-chomping Dimbleby has run the family's Surrey newspaper group since his father's death in 1965. Domestically his life is less settled. He has been married to cookery writer Josceline Dimbleby since 1967 and they have three grown-up children, Lisa, Henry and Kate. But, while making the 1988 documentary series, *An Ocean Apart*, he fell in love with a production assistant Belinda Giles. Will she become the second Mrs Dimbleby?

Dodd, Ken, 8th November 1927, Squire of Knotty Ash. This hilarious, coal-merchant's son is the last of Britain's great vaudeville stand-up comics. His Street-Porter teeth, pop eyes and wild hair make him look as if he has one hand permanently plugged into an electric socket. He packs theatres throughout Britain with his one-man show, four hours of non-stop jokes. "I reckon there are 27 different types of humour, ranging from straight gags and the surreal to the bottom end of satire and sarcasm." He keeps a "giggle-map" of which gags go down best where. He writes new jokes down on the back of his hands as they occur: "there's some good ones there, but some are a bit near the knuckle." (Geddit?) "Slaving over a hot audience is my idea of heaven! I'm completely stage-struck. Every night is like a party for me."

This proud Liverpudlian was educated at Holt High School. He lives in the same Georgian farmhouse in Knotty Ash where he was born and used to give childhood Punch and Judy performances. After working as a door-to-door salesman he made his professional debut at the Empire, Nottingham aged 22. He billed himself as 'Professor Yaffle Chucklebutty, Operatic Tenor and Sausage-Knotter'. Snobs may jeer at his schmaltzy records, but he has the last laff: *Tears* topped the charts for six weeks in 1965. He rations his TV appearances but boasts that he wants to star in every theatre in Britain. In 1997 Kenneth Branagh cast him as Yorick in his film version of *Hamlet*. "As Shakespeare said of Yorick, Doddy 'set the table a-roar'", recalls Branagh. "He reduced fellow actors Derek Jacobi, Brian Blessed and Julie Christie to tears. We had to re-touch their make-up after every take!"

A lifelong bachelor, Dodd's constant companion is former Bluebell dancer Anne Jones. The only blip on his career happened when the Inland Revenue prosecuted him in 1988. He was acquitted after a five-week fraud trial involving £800,000, during which it emerged that he hid wads of cash under his bed. Now he jokes about the Revenue in his act.

Donohoe, Amanda, 29th June 1962, cat-eyed vamp. She had to up sticks to Hollywood in 1990 and hack off her long blonde tresses to relaunch her career. As bisexual English attorney CJ Lamb in *LA Law* she had TV's first on-screen lesbian kiss. "Love is a profound human experience, no matter who you're doing it with." She has had much practice defending sexually explicit rôles. She pranced naked on a desert island with overweight Oliver Reed in *Castaway*, bared her boobs in the first ten seconds of *Diamond Skulls*, writhed naked with snakes in *The Lair of the White Worm* and seduced actress Sammi Davis in *The Rainbow*. "My rôles have all been strong women, not male playthings."

The provocative star's exotic looks come from her Irish-Russian civil servant father and Swiss mother. As a seven-year-old living in North London she was sexually abused by a neighbour ("the emotional scar has been with me ever since"). She hated her Catholic convent and rebelled against the nuns. At 16 she was a scruffy, skinny punk, hanging around Chelsea and partying with bands like The Clash. She went to the Central School of Speech and Drama and briefly lived with "glam rock" star Adam Ant, but had to wait a decade for her "first profound love experience". "Before I'd always wanted to change the guy I was with. By the time I'd helped to sort out their problems, they would say: 'bye, bye, I'm well now and don't need you anymore!'" For five years British film director Nick Broomfield provided a stabilising influence in California, but she likes her independence.

Amanda has come out of therapy now, eats only organic food and drifts round downtown LA in jeans, tee shirt and cowboy boots, a Marlboro Light usually dangling from her long, unpainted fingers. Her ambition is to live on a farm "with lots of kids" – when she finds the right man. Meanwhile she has become a Hollywood TV producer, starred in Strindberg's *Miss Julie* at Manchester's Royal Exchange and been paid "lots of silly money" to star in *The Thorn Birds: The Missing Years*.

Driver, Minnie, 31st January 1971, rising Hollywood actress. With her lopsided features and frizzy hair she has become famous despite not being classically beautiful. She exudes such luminous class and such a sparkling personality that, like Barbara Streisand, her unusual features have become an asset. Daughter of millionaire Sixties *boulevardier* Ronnie Driver, she grew up in Sloaney luxury, dining in fashionable restaurants, shopping at Harrods, mixing with the stars.

Versatile Minnie – ex Bedales and Webber-Douglas drama school – won early success on television. She played Trevor Eve's mistress in *The Politician's Wife* and opposite Bill Paterson and Sinead Cusack in C4's *God on the Rocks* ("a brilliant film that should have got a cinema release").

Her breakthrough came in 1995 with *Circle of Friends*, a small independent movie adapted from Maeve Binchy's novel, which became a worldwide hit. She moved to California. "If you want to make cars, go and live in Detroit, and if you want to work in films, go to Hollywood!" Alas, she adds, "people at home just think 'snooty old cow, she's just making Hollywood films now'".

Minnie's moneyed background helped because, if producers ignored her or she chose the wrong rôles, she could afford to fail. Instead, in 1996, she was chosen as leading lady in *Sleepers*, opposite Dustin Hoffman, Robert de Niro and Brad Pitt. "I would love to have started shaking with lust when I met Brad, but I've discovered Hollywood stars are not like their projected image." With typical cheek she ordered de Niro to "eat up" in the studio canteen because he was too thin!

This smart, sparky bachelor girl enjoys a giddy social life in LA. She dated heart-throbs Matt Le Blanc and John Cusack, and another, even more famous, Hollywood name (she is very discreet). "But I had my heart shredded."

Duffield, Vivien, 26th March 1946, party-giving philanthropist. Beady and benevolent, she is Britain's Lady Bountiful. Every year she gives millions of pounds to children's causes, hospices, museums and art gallery appeals. "I'm a sucker for hand-written letters from vicars whose steeples are falling down." Her permanent memorial will be the modernist Clore Gallery she had built to house the Tate Gallery's Turner Bequest. But she uses her estimated £45 million fortune for sybaritic purposes too. For her 40th birthday she flew 110 friends to Venice where they boarded the "Sea Goddess" and enjoyed a luxury Mediterranean cruise.

Educated at the French Lycée and Heathfield, Vivien grew up like a pampered oriental princess, with palatial homes in Mayfair and Newbury. Her parents, self-made Jewish tycoon Sir Charles Clore and French Resistance heroine Francine Halphen, divorced when she was 11. He owned Selfridges, shoe shops, jewellers, bookmakers and property. He was also a celebrated *roué*, giving his young girl-friends a chargecard to buy frocks and underwear at his stores. Vivien would co-host his annual pre-Ascot ball, sumptuous affairs designed to curry favour with aristos who were wont to snigger behind his back at his pretentiousness. For her coming-out ball he transformed the Savoy Hotel's River Room into the Forest of Arden, with champagne flowing until 3am.

Rumbustious Vivien inherited Clore's brains, flair and energy, but not his ruthlessness. After reading languages at Oxford she married playboy financier John Duffield, but her father boycotted the cere-mony on religious grounds. They have two children. Her "significant other" for nearly two decades has been boisterous English Heritage supremo Sir Jocelyn Stevens. Based in Chelsea and the Swiss Alps they have a combustible relationship and have never married. To celebrate his 50th birthday in 1982 she flew 130 friends by private jet to Gstaad for three days' non-stop partying. "People say Vivien is vulgar," says a friend. "But then so are other people who don't do half the good that she does."

E

Ecclestone, Bernie, 28th October 1930, King of the pit stops. In 1997 he stunned the City by announcing plans to float Formula One on the international stock market, with a £1.5 billion price tag. He had the vision to transform this minority spectator sport into a worldwide media phenomenon beating the Olympic Games and World Cup. In 1996 he forced ITV to pay £70 million for the Grand Prix TV rights, ten times more than the BBC previously paid.

For over 20 years this much-admired but feared multi-millionaire has masterminded F1's every detail, from hot dog stand concessions to sponsorship and merchandising rights. His mobile HQ, a dark grey coach with one-way tinted glass, is discreetly parked inside the paddock at every Grand Prix. A friend says: "everyone recognises the power he yields and few people would want to cross him."

This Suffolk trawler captain's son had a tough South London upbringing. He made his first fortune in the Fifties as a secondhand car-dealer. In 1970 he bought the Brabham team and won two world championships.

Ecclestone, the archetypal Medallion Man in tinted glasses, relishes the trappings of his success. He owns a Chelsea mansion and a Gstaad chalet. In 1996 he bought Biggin Hill aerodrome in Kent, mainly so he could park his two jets. But he can afford to indulge his whims as in 1993 his £29.7 million salary was allegedly the highest ever recorded in Britain. His hi-tech Knightsbridge headquarters once belonged to the equally flamboyant Saudi arms dealer Adnan Khashoggi. "Basically I'm a dealer. I've no hobbies, I just do deals." If he were granted one wish, it would be extra height. His second wife, Croatian-born former model Slavica, towers 10ins above his chunky 5ft 4ins. They have two daughters, Tamara and Petra.

Edmonds, Noel, 22nd December 1948, telly's court jester. With his chummy manner, hobgoblin beard and loud sweaters he is a softer version of Jeremy Beadle. His silly pranks, hidden camera stunts and schoolboy gags have helped him become one of Britain's richest performers. Many viewers believe he really does live at Crinkley Bottom, his spooky Gothic studio.

This mischievous only child of an Essex headmaster and art-teacher attended fee-paying Brentwood School. He was a trainee teacher before becoming a Radio Luxembourg newsreader and DJ in 1968. A year and a half later he moved to the new "wunnerful Radio One". He hosted the Saturday afternoon show and became the proto-type breakfast DJ. But he soon outgrew radio, appearing increasing-ly on *Top of the Pops* and yoof programmes. His big break was the anarchic *Multi-Coloured Swap Shop*. He has dominated Saturday schedules ever since, with live shows like the *Saturday Roadshow* and *Noel's House Party*. In 1986 he learnt how stunts can go badly wrong. A volunteer Whirly Wheeler died during rehearsals and the BBC closed Edmonds's top-rated *The Late, Late Breakfast Show*.

Off-screen Edmonds has little in common with Mr Blobby. He is a workaholic would-be Branson who runs Crinkley Bottom theme parks and a helicopter hire business. This enables him to live on a 840-acre Devon estate and yet still be able to commute to TV studios. He is a devoted family man with two daughters Lorna and Olivia and a step-daughter Charlotte from his second wife Helen, who is 14 years his junior.

Speed-freak Edmonds is baffled that he has never been able to export his *Gotcha*, *NTV* and *Cash For Questions* formula to America. His chat show there was not a success. Now he should mature into a Wogan figure, introducing the BBC's top variety shows and live broadcasts. It would be embarrassing if he were still ambushing celebrities at 60.

Edward, Prince, 10th March 1964, royal luvvie. Much rests on the seventh in line to the throne if, finally, he marries PR-girl Sophie Rhys-Jones. His three siblings have had failed marriages: can he buck the trend? His reticence with the opposite sex before meeting her had led some misguided hacks to speculate he was gay. Beneath that meek veneer Edward can be arrogant and feisty. Once during a pheasant shoot at Sandringham he deliberately shot over the heads of journalists who he claimed were ruining his 'sport'.

The youngest of the Queen's brood was always the most sensitive and vulnerable. His condition was not helped by having to wear metal braces to straighten his teeth. He received the traditional royal education: private tutors, Heatherdown prep school and Gordonstoun. While reading archaeology and anthropology at Cambridge he appeared in university plays and revues, organised Cambridge Rag Week and was frequently bashed in college rugby scrums. Instead of choosing an arts career, he was "persuaded" by Prince Philip to join the Royal Marines. Trying on his new cap he said to an NCO "How do I look?" The NCO winked at his colleagues and replied: "You look lovely, Sir, just lovely" and kissed the embar-rassed Prince on the cheek. He quit after only four months.

Stagestruck Edward Windsor (*sic*) joined Andrew Lloyd Webber's Really Useful Company as a dogsbody working backstage in his West End musicals. He then co-founded a rival production company which collapsed in the 1991 recession. Two years later, having lost his Civil List entitlement, he set up Ardent, an ambitious TV production company which lost nearly £1 million in its first three years. Although he had promised not to take advantage of royal connections, its most profitable series was on the Duke of Windsor narrated by the Prince himself. "I'm in a no-win situation. If I devote all my time to public duties I'm criticised for being a sponger and if I do my own thing they say I wouldn't be doing any business if I was not who I am." Poor lamb!

Elton, Ben, 3rd May 1959, stand-up comic and comedy scriptwriter. He defined the tone of Eighties humour. He was "the smug git in the shiny suit" who used to yell anti-Thatcher invective on *Saturday Live*. But there are signs that "Bolshie Ben" has mellowed.

The Catford-born motormouth was raised in stockbroker Guildford. He comes from a long line of Jewish immigrant academics. His scientist father, Professor Lewis Elton, and uncle, Professor Geoffrey Elton, the Tudor historian, were originally named Ehrenberg. After Godalming Grammar School, Ben did drama studies at Manchester University. He described himself as "a little twit with specs" compared to his glamorous contemporaries Ade Edmondson and Rik Mayall. At 21 he became the BBC's youngest ever scriptwriter.

Elton made his professional debut as a stand-up comic at London's Comedy Store in 1981. He developed a bombastic line in political and social abuse. But it was his scriptwriting skills that first made his reputation. He has created or contributed to *The Young Ones, Happy Families, Filthy, Rich and Catflap* and *Blackadder*. But his 1996 hit sitcom *The Thin Blue Line* made critics wonder whether he had gone soft. "I'd had ten years of being told I was a bigoted, loud-mouthed, left-wing yobbo. Suddenly, it's 'where's his claws?'"

Elton has written four bestselling novels, *Stark, Gridlock, This Other Eden* and *Popcorn*, as well as scripting three West End plays, *Gasping, Silly Cow* and *Popcorn*. Cynics may ascribe the success of these ventures to his telly fame. Unlike other comics he refuses to cash in and do TV commercials.

This quintessential pub politician lives in Primrose Hill, but still drinks beer at his local with cronies like Chris Evans. In 1994 he married his longstanding Australian girlfriend, Sophie Gare, who once played bass guitar in a group called the Jam Tarts. Off-screen he is polite, clean and courteous and enjoys going on country walks.

Enfield, Harry, 30th May 1961, reformed Bollinger Bolshevik and Dick Emery wannabe. This brilliant inventor of comical stereotypes has found a lucrative way of giving them extra shelf-life – as TV commercials. Loadsamoney has sold Sekonda watches, Mr Cholmondeley-Warner (Mercury), DJ Nicey (Fab Ice Creams), Frank Doberman (Hula Hoops) and Only Me (British Gas).

Enfield was brought up in a Conservative middle-class household in Billingshurst, West Sussex. He quickly developed rebellious left-wing tendencies (or so he claims). But his father, a former local government officer, dismisses this as bunkum. He went to the Roman Catholic public school Worth and "scraped into York University" to read politics. *Spitting Image* producer John Lloyd saw his comedy act at a Dalston pub and hired him to impersonate Jimmy Greaves, Douglas Hurd and David Steel. His big break came when he did a sketch about Prince Philip visiting a Greek kebab shop where the owner was his "cousin". A talent-scout from *Saturday Night Live* was watching and the gabby Stavros became Britain's favourite foreigner since *Fawlty Towers'* Manuel.

This TV chameleon has showcased a wide range of topical, wacky characters in *Harry Enfield's Television Programme* and *Harry Enfield and Chums*. But the invention of Loadsamoney and other monstrosities owes much to the inventive genius of his writing partner Paul Whitehouse. When Harry's mother objects to the coarseness he blames his fellow scriptwriters. "They taunt him, telling him he shouldn't be frightened of his mother", explains Enfield Snr, "but he's too wet to say 'Yes, I am frightened of my mother, so let's take it out. It's my show!'"

The Regent's Park-based comic seems to be returning to his Establishment roots. He poshly announced his engagement to fashion consultant Lucy Lyster in the *Daily Telegraph* and they married in 1997. He likes large families. He was a doting step-daddy to his previous girlfriend Alison Allen's three children.

Evans, Chris, 1st April 1966, Ginger Prince of yoof TV. This scruffy, loud hysteric looks like a WH Smith assistant who thinks he is a star. He has always attracted strong emotions, being variously described as a witty genius comparable to Michael Barrymore or an unpredictable, obnoxious creep heading for burn-out. Even he has admitted he is sometimes "a complete prat".

Evans was raised on a Warrington council estate. He lost his hospital clerk father at 14 and was brought up by his no-nonsense mother. After leaving Padgate High School he worked as a shop

ABOVE Naomi Campbell and sometime boyfriend, flamenco dancer Joaquin Cortes
BELOW LEFT Lord and Lady Lloyd-Webber
BELOW RIGHT Tamara Beckwith and her daughter Anouska

ABOVE LEFT Sophie Rhys-Jones
ABOVE RIGHT Marquess of Blandford
BELOW Tara Palmer-Tompkinson, Mogens Tholstrup and Normandie Keith
OPPOSITE PAGE Michael Flatley

ABOVE Andrew Neil and Tony Blair
BELOW LEFT Darcey Bussell
BELOW RIGHT Duke of Beaufort

ABOVE LEFT Gary Rhodes with his children Samuel and George
ABOVE RIGHT John Galliano
BELOW Sting

ABOVE David and Catherine Bailey with their children Paloma and Fenton
BELOW LEFT Elle Macpherson and ex-lover Tim Jefferies
BELOW RIGHT Liam Neeson
OPPOSITE Prince Edward and an actress from Starlight Express

ABOVE LEFT Jerry Hall
ABOVE RIGHT Cherie Booth and Lesley Joseph
BELOW Kate Moss, Rachel Hunter and Naomi Campbell

assistant, Tarzan-o-gram and forklift truck-driver. His first radio job was as Timmy Mallett's gofer on Manchester's Piccadilly Radio. As a DJ at London's GLR, he began perfecting the zany, in-yer-face style that made his reputation. Sky gave him his first TV pop series, *The Power Station*. In 1992 Channel Four poached him to attract a yoof audience to their new *The Big Breakfast*. Its mixture of wacky spoofs, celebrity interviews and *Down your Doorstep*-style foolishness soon beat the staid BBC Breakfast Time and GMTV.

Throughout his short career Evans has proved adept at leaving just when the ratings are about to slide. He quit *The Big Breakfast* to concentrate on his Saturday night show, *Don't Forget Your Toothbrush*, a frenzy of chaos that was in fact carefully scripted. In 1996 he reshuffled the formula for another live C4 series, *TFI Friday*. For 18 months he was also Radio One's £1.4 million-a-year breakfast host, constantly in the news for his lewd jokes, on-air humiliation of staff and insults to the station's controller Matthew Bannister. He finally walked out in January 1997, ironically just as Virgin and Capital Radio were winning back their lost listeners.

Evans, millionaire boss of his own company Ginger Productions, has homes in Kent and Holland Park. He once famously confessed that he had just bought an eight-seater dining table – and then realised that he didn't have seven friends! He has a Jack the Lad reputation, usually having several girlfriends on the go. He has a daughter, Jade, from childhood sweetheart Alison Ward. He left his wife, radio presenter Carol McGiffin, after two years in 1993. "You gotta realise he was never interested in settling down. Chris loves Chris, that's all you need to understand", observed a friend. Recent girlfriends have included model Rachel Tatton-Brown, singer Kim Wilde and TV assistant Suzy Aplin.

Everett, Rupert, 29th May 1959, the English Rock Hudson. Youthful success led to a period of overweening arrogance when this archetypal luvvie put two fingers up to Hollywood. He dropped out, writing trashy novels like *Hello Darling, Are You Working?* and mixing with the *demi-mondaines* of St Tropez. His scene-stealing performance as Julia Roberts' gay pal in *My Best Friend's Wedding* led to his 1997 rediscovery. He horrified the film's publicists by revealing that he had once spent two years as a rent-boy. "I didn't set out to hustle but, like a lot of upper-class people, I had no money. Any actor worthy of the name should get back to the spirit of Shakespeare's day when many turned out to be criminals, prostitutes or sex addicts!"

This tall, flamboyant, stockbroker's son has always been a rebel. He left the Roman Catholic public school Ampleforth at 15 because he despised his Hooray Henry contemporaries and wanted to act. After two years at the Central School of Speech and Drama he was expelled for insubordination. Undeterred he joined the Citizens' Theatre, Glasgow. In 1980 he won rave reviews for his West End debut in *Another Country*. He then starred in films like *Dance With a Stranger*, *Duet for One* and *The Comfort of Strangers*. Although he turned down a mega-buck rôle in the American soap *Dynasty* he accepted two TV pot-boilers, *The Far Pavilions* and *Princess Daisy*. He also starred in *Hearts of Fire*, described as so bad that "its very mention is guaranteed to invite hoots of derision" among cineastes.

Feckless Everett has always had a confusing private life. At 21 he was Bianca Jagger's toy boy. Always a loner, he hunted in New York with the Andy Warhol social pack and the Sabrina Guinness crowd in London. Once he was invited to dinner by Princess Margaret at Kensington Palace. "I had a panic attack because I didn't own a suit. In the end I wore a jumper and a pair of chinos". Before his recent 'coming out' he was romantically linked with Cher, Madonna and Lord St Just's daughter Natasha Grenfell. His self-parodying performance as Prinny in *The Madness of King George* showed he could be a Great Actor if only he applied himself.

F

Faithfull, Marianne, 29th December 1946, pop's ultimate survivor. During the Sixties she abused heroin and alcohol and was the archetypal rock chick. For four tempestuous years she played Patsy Kensit to Mick Jagger's Liam Gallagher. They were pop's golden couple. She had a No 1 hit with his song *As Tears Go By*, beguiling audiences with her reedy Francoise Hardy voice, doll-like face and fragile innocence. Things began to go badly wrong when Chelsea police "busted" them and found her wrapped in just a fur rug. Later she had a miscarriage and during a Rolling Stones tour 'Down Under' botched a suicide attempt. She spent most of the next 20 years trying to cure her addiction. Despite these tribulations, she still has the battered charisma to fill concert halls round the world.

Marianne has always been potent combination of 'U' and bohemian habits. She was raised in Reading and educated at convent school, but her Austrian mother, Baroness Erisso, was a great-niece of kinky Victorian novelist Leopold von Sacher-Masoch. Her father, Dr Glyn Faithfull, was a respected philologist. At 18 she married her first love, Cambridge graduate John Dunbar, who ran a trendy Mayfair art gallery. They had a son Nicholas, but unfortunately she then discovered the forbidden delights of London's pop scene. In 1979 she had a brief marriage to fellow heroin addict Ben Brierley, a punk musician whose stage name was Ben E Ficial. During this period she recorded two albums, *Broken English* and *Dangerous Acquaintances*, which brought her a new generation of fans. Years of heavy smoking and brandy have created a sexy, theatrically husky voice, and in 1997 her tribute to Kurt Weill and Bertolt Brecht, *An Evening in the Weimar Republic*, played to packed houses in America and Europe.

This damaged grandmother still has a tiny swallow tattooed on both hands, a vestigial Jagger memento. She enjoys her new healthy, unaddicted life deep in the Irish countryside.

Farrell, Terry, 12th May 1938, Geordie masterplanner. This lively and controversial post-modernist is the junior member of that trendy architectural trio, led by Lord Rogers and Sir Norman Foster. His most visible monuments are TV-am's former studios in Camden Lock with its giant boiled eggs on top and MI6's new, not terribly discreet, terraced pyramid besides the Thames in Vauxhall. He has stamped his personality on many other high-profile sites, including the redevelopment of Charing Cross station and the Henley Royal Regatta HQ. His work is usually on a Cecil B deMille scale. Of course he is too brash for traditionalists like Prince Charles, preferring to be judged as an innovator rather than a classical revivalist like Quinlan Terry. But Farrell forced former Royal Institute of British Architects' president Max Hutchinson to retract a comment that his South Bank rehab scheme was "bimbo architecture".

This burly, bushy-browed, genial fellow grew up in Newcastle's Irish Catholic community, the son of a Civil Service clerk. At St Cuthbert's Grammar School he developed a precocious gift for draughtsmanship and passion for buildings. He could have become a painter but his mother insisted that he must get "a proper job" as an architect and he won a First in architecture at Durham University. In 1962 he landed a visiting fellowship to study at the University of Pennsylvania. He then had a long partnership with architect Nick Grimshaw before starting his own practice in 1980.

Farrell has five children from two marriages. Despite his acclaim and fortune he still lives in the Maida Vale semi that he bought in 1973 when he married his second wife Sue, though the house has been much extended. His family call it "the Tardis" because "you think it's only a little box but it keeps taking you into fantasy". Inside is a phantasmagoria of bright colours and kitsch objects found in local junk shops. A penchant for Art Deco has influenced his use of Egyptian and Aztec styles in his designs.

Fellowes, Sir Robert, 11th December 1941, the Queen's eyes and ears. This Duke of Gloucester lookalike is the epitome of the buttoned-up, Civil Service type of royal courtier. As HM's Private Secretary and Keeper of the Palace Archives, he ranks one rung below the Lord Chamberlain, the Earl of Airlie, as head of the Royal Household. He advises on policy, drafts speeches, deals with correspondence, controls the press office and liaises with 10 Downing Street. His run-ins with the Duchess of York led to her dubbing him "Robert Bellowes". He would enter her Buckingham Palace apartment bearing the morning papers and say: "We've not done very well today, have we, Ma'am?" Ironically, they are cousins.

This slim, bespectacled clubman (Athenaeum, White's and Pratt's) imbibed royal service with his mother's milk. His father, Sir William Fellowes, was Land Agent at Sandringham from 1936 to 1964 and lived in a grace-and-favour house there. During school holidays from Eton he would join Prince Philip and other royals on shooting parties. Meeting the young Prince Charles he learned to behave as an equal but to be deferential. He followed his father into the Scots Guards on a short service commission. On his demob in 1963 he worked in the City. He always knew that he could have a royal career but needed to build up some capital first. The Queen appointed him assistant private secretary in 1977, deputy private secretary in 1986 and secretary in 1990.

Sir Robert married the late Earl Spencer's daughter Lady Jane in 1978 and has three children, Alexander, Laura and Eleanor. They live in Nottingham Cottage (*sic*), a grace-and-favour house in Kensington Palace, only a bread roll throw away from her late sister Diana Princess of Wales's home. Their proximity caused embarrassment. Diana dubbed him "the enemy" for plotting against her during her marriage. Many royal-watchers blame him for the disastrous series of 'anni horribili' involving the young royals. Will this prevent him achieving his dearest wish to become Lord Fellowes?

Feltz, Vanessa, 21st February 1962, Britain's answer to Oprah Winfrey. She is a Big Lady succeeding in a sexist medium where size (and beauty) can count as much as talent. "If viewers are thinner than I am they love me and, if they're as fat, they're thrilled because I've become a TV presenter!" On her thrice-weekly talk show, *Vanessa*, guests share their deepest secrets with her. "But I'm no Oprah, as I haven't got a lot to confess in return. When Oprah broke down in a show about cocaine-abuse crying 'I did your drug!' to an addict, I thought blimey! What can I say? 'I did your cake!'"

On C4's *The Big Breakfast* this witty, flamboyant Mother Earth interviews celebrities like Bo Derek and Goldie Hawn while reclining on a king-size bed. "The sight of me, with all my numerous poundages, at 7.15 am wearing full evening dress covered in sequins and feather boas, is one of life's tonics – even for me!" No wonder she is a gay icon. "Apparently I'm the acme of high camp, whatever that means!" Her coiffeur is her Achilles heel. "It's like public hair and takes hours of blow-drying to make it look like Ulrika Jonsson's!"

After Cambridge, Vanessa worked as a stand-up comic. This experience enables her to cope with hecklers and guests who 'dry' on her show. Her rock is her marriage to orthopaedic surgeon Michael Kurer. They live in "splendid suburban Finchley in a house with columns". Every night they try to have a sit-down family dinner with their two daughters, Allegra and Saskia. It is a strict Orthodox Jewish household, with a traditional Friday dinner attended by other members of the family, and no newspapers or TV allowed on the Sabbath. She has Beattie-like leanings, with two telephones in her kitchen and a mirror opposite "so that I can talk to several people at once while looking at myself doing so!"

Fennell, Theo, 8th August 1951, jewellery's Kevin Costner. Handsome and flirtatious, he wows the girls while designing some of London's most innovative jewellery. Clients include Elton John, Viscount Linley and Joan Collins. Record companies often commission miniature gold pianos, guitars and other instruments to schmooze their artistes. The most romantic present he ever made was a silver pair of klipspringers, a type of antelope. "They are monogamous and once they have mated they never move more than five feet apart."

Earls Court-based Fennell keeps a high social profile. He loves partying and the attentions of beautiful women. He plays golf with the Duke of York and has a weekend cottage near Newbury. He and his glamorous wife Louise have two daughters, Emerald and Coco.

Fennell describes his Fulham Road emporium as "the unstuffy alternative to Bond Street". But his unofficial title used to be "jeweller by appointment to HRH the Duchess of York". There was no accounting for her taste. Among the 'lurve' tokens she gave former boyfriend, John Bryan, were gold cufflinks symbolically shaped like cherry trees and gold collar-stiffeners inscribed "Linky" (Bryan's pet name for her). A rival once described Fennell's shop as "an Aladdin's Cave of vulgarity". Maybe they were thinking of the silver ketchup holder or the silver pepper and salt shakers shaped like cowboy boots.

This elegant Old Etonian, a personification of almost every film rôle Hugh Grant has ever played, comes from ancient Irish stock. He spent his formative years being dragged round the world with his Army officer father. He trained as a portrait painter at the Byam Shaw School of Art before serving his apprenticeship at a Hatton Gardon jewellers. He opened his first Fulham Road shop in 1982, conveniently close to his down-market rivals Butler & Wilson. In 1996 his backer, former DIY tycoon Richard Northcott, floated the company on the London stock exchange, valuing it at £19 million. The showroom moved to swanky new premises a few doors away and the name will now be franchised round the world. He sincerely wants to be the new Pierre Cartier.

Fiennes, Ralph (pronounced Rafe Fines), 22nd December 1962, Humphrey Bogart with Class. *Schindler's List* catapulted this intense, brooding thespian to superstardom. Like Rudolph Valentino he has a ravaged, famished look women find irresistible. "If laid out on a marble plinth he would be a dead ringer for an Arthurian knight", drooled one writer obsessed with his "ardour, nobility and courage". But he refuses to be sucked into the Hollywood system. In 1997, rather than accept another £6 million rôle, he took the £200-a-week lead in Chekhov's *Ivanov* at the Almeida Theatre, Islington.

This cousin of explorer-baronet Sir Ranulph Twisleton-Wykeham-Fiennes, comes from a talented upper-middle-class Catholic family. His late mother Jini was the novelist Jennifer Lash, his father Mark is a photographer. He had a suitably bohemian upbringing, with the family moving home 15 times. He studied at St Kieran's College, Kilkenny and Bishop Wordsworth School, Salisbury. Although obsessed with acting he spent a year at Chelsea School of Art before going to RADA.

Fiennes' early work was in the theatre, notably with the RSC. Apart from two plays, *Lawrence After Arabia* and *The Cormorant*, he has rarely bothered with television. His film breakthrough came in 1992 when he played Heathcliff opposite Juliette Binoche in *Wuthering Heights* and later the American game-show cheat Charles van Doren in *Quiz Show*. A sci-fi movie, *Strange Days*, flopped. His portrayal of the Nazi prison camp commander in *Schindler's List* led to comparisons with Laurence Olivier and Alec Guinness. In the 1997 Oscar-winning epic *The English Patient* he spent half the film wearing a facial prosthetic resembling an unhusked coconut.

Fiennes' marriage to Moll Flanders star Alex Kingston lasted two years although they spent ten years together. "I don't know why he bothered to marry me as it was a decision he almost instantly regretted." In 1995 he ran off with actress Francesca Annis, 18 years his senior, who played Gertrude to his Hamlet in the acclaimed Hackney Empire production. "Does he have to kiss his mother so passionately?", an observant critic grumbled.

Finney, Albert, 9th May 1936, rebel superstar. Laurence Olivier dubbed him "the greatest actor of his generation". His personality has been magnetic, capricious and overbearing enough to sort out even the most difficult directors. His wide-ranging performances since 1982 include films like *Annie*, *The Dresser* and *A Man of No Importance*, stage plays like *Orphans* and *Sergeant Musgrave's Dance* and TV series like *The Green Man*, *Karaoke* and *Nostromo*. As a multi-millionaire bachelor he can afford to be choosy.

This jovial, cigar-chomping, bookie's son admits he was a dunce at Salford Grammar School. He likes to romanticise his rags-to-riches story. But his mother showed a journalist round her semi once and said: "Look, it's quite nice around here, isn't it? Not crumbling to bits? Albert has always had a house like this!" After RADA he worked with the RSC and at the Royal Court. He exemplified the new "angry young man" style of Sixties Northern working-class heroes. Critics hailed his portrayal of a stroppy factory-worker in *Saturday Night and Sunday Morning* as "electrifying". Hollywood producer Sam Spiegel then offered him *Lawrence of Arabia* before Peter O'Toole, but characteristically he refused to sign a seven-year contract with the studio. Instead he starred in the cult West End play, *Billy Liar*, seduced Susannah York over a lobster dinner in Tony Richardson's film *Tom Jones* and headlined on Broadway in John Osborne's *Luther*. He formed his own production company, Memorial Enterprises (Memorial as in Albert!) and starred in its first two films, *Charlie Bubbles* and *Gumshoe*. Twice at peaks of his career he has "disappeared" for 12 months, to South America and the South Seas, to recharge his batteries. His cussedness may explain why he has never quite achieved the knightly eminence of contemporaries like Sir Derek Jacobi and Sir Ian McKellen.

Racing-mad Finney continues to live in his old Sixties stomping ground, Chelsea. Although barrel-chested and jowly now, his deceptively slow Lancashire accent and cheeky grin have always helped "pull the birds". At 21 he was briefly married to actress Jane Wenham and had a son, Simon. His 1970 marriage to French actress Anouk Aimee ended after five years when she ran off with Hollywood actor Ryan O'Neal. He then spent seven years living with *Brideshead Revisited* star Diana Quick and three years with rising actress Cathryn Harrison. "Albert has a pure animal magnetism", quoth an admirer.

Finnigan, Judy, 16th May 1948, nanny to the nation. Lively, streetwise, intelligent and with piercing blue eyes, she has a knack of asking the questions the viewer wants answered rather than relying on autocue banalities. Unlike many interviewers she really listens to her guests and has an appealing vulnerability beneath that brisk professionalism. The on-screen chemistry with her husband Richard Madeley helped them to win the so-called "Battle of The Sofas" in 1996 against rival BBC1 presenters Anne Diamond and Nick Owen.

But the responsibility of presenting five shows a week, plus caring for four children, puts a tremendous strain on Judy. "At the end of the week I'm so tired I sometimes just flop into bed without even taking off my make-up." Few couples could survive seeing each other 24 hours a day. "The advantage is they can keep an eye on each other so that neither can have an affair!", joked a studio insider.

This flaxen-haired milliner's daughter had a *Coronation Street* upbringing in a two-up, two-down Manchester terrace. She styles herself as "working-class, hauled up by the highlights". She won a scholarship to Manchester High School where genteel teachers insisted she took elocution lessons to lose her Mancunian accent. She read English and drama at Bristol University before becoming a Granada TV researcher and then a news reporter. She met Madeley in 1982 when both were married to other people. On his first day on the regional news programme, *Granada Reports*, she was assigned as his 'minder'. "I'm your mummy", she said, touching him lightly on the shoulder.

They married in 1986 and have two children, Jack and Chloe. She also has twins Dan and Tom from her 12-year first marriage to TV producer David Henshaw. Always self-conscious about her weight she was horrified in 1990 when a tabloid featured her sunbathing on a South of France beach with the headline "Blancmange in a Bikini". The Madeleys moved to Hampstead in 1996 when *This Morning* transferred to London because superstars refused to schlepp up to Liverpool for interviews.

Firth, Colin, 10th September 1960, the new Jeremy Irons. Few actors could have filled Mr Darcy's breeches better than this dark, dashing, brooding heart-throb. BBC1's *Pride and Prejudice* confirmed his position as telly's most romantic superstar. *Smash Hits* even sold out of his posters. All very perplexing for a man claiming to be a Serious Actor, whose grandparents were missionaries.

Hackney-based Firth cannot understand this Austen-mania. "*Pride and Prejudice* wasn't my cup of tea. I felt like a drug-dealer who doesn't get high on his own supply." Hollywood offers were immediately forthcoming. Instead, he played yet another repressed Englishman in BBC2's adaptation of *Nostromo* and Kristin Scott-Thomas's screen husband in *The English Patient*.

Firth had a peripatetic childhood because his history teacher father worked in Nigeria and America. His mother, a lecturer in Eastern religions, would meditate cross-legged in front of a candle. Eventually they settled in Winchester and his old drama teacher at nearby Barton Peveril College says: "Colin had this huge presence on stage and of course that amazing voice." He quit the London Drama Centre in his final year after being offered his first West End rôle in the gay public school drama, *Another Country*. "Fans would send me soiled Y-fronts in the post." On TV he then played the embittered Falklands War casualty Robert Lawrence in *Tumbledown* and John McCarthy in *Hostages*.

"It is a truth universally acknowledged that a single man in possession of a good fortune must be in want of a wife." Firth long evaded Jane Austen's dictum. In 1988, while filming Milos Forman's period drama *Valmont*, he met Hollywood actress Meg Tilly. Afterwards he chucked his career and spent four years living with her in the wilds of Canada. After their son Will was born, they split up because he found her too controlling. While playing Darcy he enjoyed a brief romance with his leading lady Jennifer Ehle. "I don't think actors have a greater predilection for bonking each other than any other profession." In 1997 he finally married Livia Giuggioli, an Italian production assistant he met while filming *Nostromo* in Colombia. "I find it quite funny that Colin is a sex symbol", she says.

Fitzgerald, Tara, 18th September 1967, a sexy Helena Bonham-Carter. She leapt to fame with her strip-off performance as nubile Polly in C4's *The Camomile Lawn*. She played Ophelia in *Hamlet* on Broadway where she complained her body was constantly bruised by her leading man Ralph Fiennes hurling her to the ground. She then co-starred with Peter O'Toole in the West End production of *Our Song*. She again injured herself when opening a wardrobe door on stage and O'Toole had to ad-lib: "oh darling, shall I get you a plaster?" Intriguingly, she claims to have "potato picker's hands!"

Despite her Irish name, Tara and her two sisters grew up in a poky, rented South Kensington flat. Their posh photographer mother Sarah Fitzgerald worked as a waitress to support them, their artist father Michael Callaby having left home when Tara was three. "He used to send me tapes from the Bahamas. I just thought he was going on long holidays." He committed suicide when she was eleven.

Tara went to a Clapham comprehensive school and North London's Drama Centre. She made her film debut in *Hear My Song* two weeks after graduating but was rejected by the RSC. While 'resting' she worked as a sales assistant in the Mayfair boutique Browns. Drama rôles like the pious Helen in BBC1's serial *The Tenant of Wildfell Hall* and the cult film, *Brassed Off*, opposite Ewan McGregor have consolidated her reputation as an Emma Thomson going-to-be.

Tara has a quiet Celtic beauty, with big, wide-set dark eyes and prominent cheekbones. She is the very opposite of a Elizabeth Hurley. She dresses down, almost in grunge, and hates film premières and schmoozing. She does smoke Marlboro Lights incessantly, though. She lives in Barnes with her "very best mate", *Soldier, Soldier* actor Dorian Healy. She likes painting still lifes and once found herself in *Private Eye's* Pseud's Corner when she said her ideal dinner companions would be Dorothy Parker and Oscar Wilde.

Flatley, Michael, 16th July 1958. Lord of the Prance. Not since Nijinsky has a dancer enjoyed such a phenomenal overnight success.

Nor has one stirred such strong emotions, ranging from drooling wonderment to impotent fury at such vaunting arrogance. He was unknown until 1994, when a seven-minute interval-filler of Irish jigs during the *Eurovision Song Contest* in Dublin captured viewers' imagination. As a result he created and choreographed the stage show *Riverdance* which won rave reviews in Dublin. Alas, on the eve of the 1995 London première, he was sacked by the producers in a furious row over billing, artistic control and egos.

Mercurial Flatley's career seemed washed-up. But within 12 months, he had reworked the same formula of high-kicking Irish dance, Gaelic folk songs and ballet solos, into *Lord of the Dance*. Typically he insisted on choosing every hoofer himself and overseeing tiny details like the colour of each one's tights and the shape of their hairstyle. "He was manic", recalls an insider. "He drove them 12 hours a day and anyone who wouldn't or couldn't do it his way was out!" Four days before its world première he tore his calf muscles but insisted on dancing through "the excruciating pain". One critic described the show as "a fusion of *Finian's Rainbow* and the Village People". He sold eight million videos worldwide and went on to earn £50,000 a week touring America.

The Chicago-born dancer has always driven himself like a leprechaun on moonshine. At 17 he was Irish dance champion of the world. He has since divided his life between Ireland, Britain and America. At a Chieftains concert in London in 1985 he met his Polish wife Beata, a make-up artist, and with characteristic dynamism proposed three weeks later. They parted in 1996, following rumours about his close friendship with Irish dancer Kelley Byrne. With his legs allegedly insured for £25 million he is determined to become a major Hollywood song-and-dance man.

Follett, Ken, 5th June 1949, Socialist Midas and would-be John Grisham. Bright, industrious and sparky he belongs to the superleague of popular airport authors. Less predictable than Jeffrey Archer he actually harbours literary ambitions though he is likely to join the House of Lords before he wins the Booker Prize.

Chunky Follett went to Harrow Weald Grammar School before Poole Tech and London University. In the Seventies he was a news hack on the *London Evening News* and then a paperback publisher. He therefore knew how to write commercial fiction. Early thrillers like *Eye of the Needle*, *The Key to Rebecca* and *The Man From St Petersburg* became international bestsellers. With the Cold War over he has moved into period fiction.

This frustrated Jimi Hendrix – he plays a mean bass guitar when his creative energy is flagging – has two children from his first marriage. He wed his dynamic present wife Barbara in 1985 and they became leading Labour luvvies. Before the 1992 election she was the party's image-consultant. She so improved the appearance of shadow ministers Jack Cunningham, Harriet Harman and Robin Cook that a new word "folletting" was coined.

Ken and Barbie (MP for Stevenage since 1997) see no dichotomy between their political beliefs and their extravagant lifestyle. Their 18th century Cheyne Walk mansion overlooking the Thames is the scene of lavish dinner parties, with liveried servants and fine wines. They spend the winter at Jumby Bay, their island villa off Antigua. To protect baby turtles from drowning in the swimming pool they have built special barriers. But he cannily prevents TV crews from filming inside his homes. Instead he borrows a book-lined chamber at Chelsea Public Library.

Forsyth, Frederick, 25th August 1938, superstar author. This poker-faced royalist and Spanish bullring *aficionado* is determinedly low-key compared to rivals Jeffrey Archer and Ken Follett. He rarely does chat shows, newspaper interviews or film premières. Instead he prefers life as a gentleman farmer, raising prize-winning lambs in Hertfordshire, plus the company of his second wife Sandy.

Forsyth, a Kent furrier's son, went to Tonbridge School. He then trained on a local paper. As a Reuters foreign correspondent he specialised in Africa and became emotionally involved with the Biafran cause during two years covering the Nigerian civil war. While reporting from East Berlin during the Cold War he committed a major gaffe after a night out on the tiles. On his way home he found the road was blocked by six divisions of Soviet tanks, rocket-launchers and troop-carriers. He filed a report to Reuters predicting that an attack on West Berlin was imminent. Unfortunately the battle force was merely rehearsing for the annual May Day Parade!

In 1970, the solidly built, crew-cut Forsyth became a full-time novelist. He meticulously researched *The Day of the Jackal*, about an assassination attempt on General de Gaulle. The manuscript took him just four weeks to write – and was rejected by four publishers! Two more bestsellers, also made into Hollywood films, followed: *The Odessa File* and *The Dogs of War*. By his seventh book, *The Fourth Protocol*, he was receiving £1 million for the paperback rights before having written a word!

This Nineties Alastair Maclean tried tax exile in Spain and Ireland, but found he missed his friends and the "English way of life". He has two sons, Stuart and Shane, from his first wife, Irish former model Carrie. During that marriage he would escape from his St John's Wood mansion to write in a starkly-decorated flat nearby with blinds tightly drawn and no telephone. He has always found the process of inventing credible new plots difficult and, following publication of his ninth novel, *Icon*, in 1996, threatened to retire.

Franks, Lynne, 16th April 1948, would-be shaman. Thanks to her former best friend Jennifer Saunders's *Absolutely Fabulous* she has become Britain's most famous PR lady. Yet it is no use to her now since she sold her company for £6 million in 1993. She has "downsized", swapping her fully-staffed Maida Vale mansion for a smaller maisonette nearby, and "finding herself" with ever more curious adventures. Her journey of self-enlightenment introduced her to crystal and spiritual healing, hallucinogenic drugs, women's sexuality groups, celibacy, re-birthing and sacred geometry. Having initially hated *AbFab's* wicked portrayal of her lifestyle she could laugh enough to call her 1997 autobiography *Absolutely Now*.

This Buddhist-chanting whirlwind swept through the materialistic Eighties in power suits, brimming with enthusiasm, self-confidence and wacky ideas. She had blue-chip clients like Next, Jean-Paul Gaultier and Katharine Hamnett. She helped promoter Harvey Goldsmith to fill stadia with *Carmen* and *Aida*, and even promoted Neil Kinnock's Labour party. At her peak she had 50 employees.

Lynne was born into a North London Jewish family. Her father was a butcher who suffered from manic depression, and her mother was "funny, bright and supportive". She left school at 16 with four O-levels and took a Pitman's typing course. Her first job was as a secretary on *Petticoat* magazine and her second editing a magazine for Freeman's mail-order catalogue. Then Katharine Hamnett persuaded her to set up her own PR company in 1971. She had just married Australian fashion designer Paul Howie. They had two children, Joshua and Jessica, but split up during her Nineties reappraisal. American engineer-turned-psychology writer Tom Blakeslee became his replacement. He appears to fulfil her CV for the Perfect Man: "Someone happy with himself who loves travelling, is intelligent, fun and sexy, can cook, already has grown-up children and is practical enough to know what to do when the washing-machine packs up."

Fraser, Honor, 18th December 1974, heather supermodel. She is one of the new breed of aristo models who are beautiful without being stuffy and street-cred without being cor blimey. She has worked for Isaac Mizrahi, Ralph Lauren, Nina Ricci, Guy Laroche and Ungaro. She owes her striking looks and unusual intelligence to her Celtic and Norman-French ancestry. Her forebears have been clan chieftains since time immemorial. Her late grandfather, Lord Lovat, was the World War II hero described by Sir Winston Churchill as "the handsomest man who ever cut a throat". Her great-aunt is the biographer and novelist Lady Antonia Fraser.

Prancing on the catwalk for Christian Lacroix and Valentino, haughty Honor looks like a pedigree Afghan Hound. But she objects to fashion mavens describing her as "shudderingly skinny". She "went ballistic" when she saw the "tasteful" nude shots taken by photographer Richard Avedon for the 1997 *Pirelli Calendar*. She wrote in *The Spectator* they made her look anorexic and flat-chested. "I don't want to boast but at 34C I've got bigger breasts than Helena Christensen, Cindy Crawford or Eva Herzigova – who are held to be three of the sexiest models". Her Audrey Hepburn looks caused Alexander McQueen to select her as the "face" of Givenchy in 1997.

Feisty Honor worries about the so-called "Curse of Fraser". In 1994 her uncle, boulevardier Andrew Fraser, was gored to death by a buffalo while on safari in Tanzania. Four days after his funeral her father Simon, the Master of Lovat, suffered a fatal heart attack. Six months later she lost Lord Lovat, supposedly devastated by the death of his two sons. The family seat, Beaufort Castle, therefore had to be sold, along with most of their Inverness-shire estate which they had owned for over 500 years.

French, Dawn, 11th October 1957, award-winning mirth-creator. She is the dominant member of the comedy team French and Saunders. She does the slog while the butterfly-brained Jennifer Saunders supplies the crazy flights of fantasy. When critics wondered if she had exhausted her ammo-belt of creativity she reappeared in *The Vicar of Dibley*. The title-role fitted her like a surplice, enabling her to make sly digs at trendy clerics, randy churchwardens and atheist parishioners.

The dumpy, delightful Dawn worked as a schoolteacher before training at the Central School of Speech and Drama where she met Jennifer. They began doing sketches at the Comedy Store, the seminal nursery for aspiring Eighties' comics. This spawned C4's cult series *The Comic Strip Presents*, starring unknowns like Robbie Coltrane, Rik Mayall and Alexei Sayle. She appeared in such classics as *Five Go Mad in Dorset*, *Slags and Spaghetti Hoops*, as well as the film *Supergrass*. She then played the bossy feminist Amanda in *Girls on Top*, ITV's sitcom about four incompatible flatmates. She also starred in the creepy black comedy series, *Murder Most Horrid*.

Laughter is seldom absent from Château French, actually a converted farmhouse near Reading. She and husband Lenny Henry occupy separate studies but try their jokes on each other at mealtimes – he generally cooks.

The couple try to avoid being too competitive. "We have humungous egos, like asteroids, clashing everywhere in the house. Boom!" jokes Lenny. Critics blame her for making his sketches more serious and political. "Nonsense", she says, "I've merely purged them of sexist and racist overtones".

Since their 1984 marriage they have suffered from racist behaviour themselves. Yobs have smeared their front door with excrement and sent poison-pen letters. They further annoyed extremists by adopting a mixed-race baby, Billie.

Frieda, John, 5th July 1951, the Nineties Vidal Sassoon. He originally wanted to be a doctor but lacked the academic qualifications. His father owned a hairdressing salon in Ealing and his grandfather one in Fleet Street.

Frieda left school at 16 and became a £4-a-wcck trainee at Leonard of Mayfair. One of his first jobs was to shampoo Twiggy's hair. Within three weeks he became Leonard's personal assistant. After nine years he was promoted to creative director, but left in 1976 to set up his own business with a colleague. Three years later he founded the first John Frieda salon, in New Cavendish Street, which fashion editors, photographers and stylists soon made the most fashionable in town.

This slim, fit and tanned maestro was named 'Hairdresser of the Year' in 1989. He has proved to be as brilliant a businessman as a stylist and schmoozer. He now owns three London salons and, since 1990, one in Manhattan's Upper East Side. His product range of shampoos, conditioners and other lotions began in Boots and are now bestsellers in America. In 1989 he published *The Precision Styling System*, which was dubbed "the most important educational book to come out of this industry in the last decade". His star clients include Diana Ross, Glenn Close, Joan Rivers and Barbara Walters.

Creative and dynamic Frieda has an easy, friendly, instantly likeable manner. He used to be resident hair guru on ITV's *This Morning*. Overwork had already given him an ulcer at 35. "When business expansion is this meteoric it's all-consuming. Life is 100 per cent work." He is a perfectionist who believes a crimper's artistic ability is as important as his technical prowess.

In 1976 Frieda married Sixties pop singer Lulu. Their Mayfair apartment was pure *Dynasty*, with giant crystal chandeliers, Old Master paintings and serious period furniture. They are now divorced and he lives mainly in America. They sent their son Jordan to Eton and Cambridge.

Friel, Anna, 12th July 1976, acting's Little Red Riding Hood. This delectable beauty is living proof there is life after Soap. As feisty lipstick lesbian Beth Jordache in C4's *Brookside* her willowy presence and soft Scouse accent kept all red-blooded males glued to their TV sets. Indeed she horrified the Mary Whitehouses when Beth enjoyed an infamous gay kiss with Margaret (Nicola Stephenson). Still only 20, she left the series to avoid being typecast.

If anyone still doubted her sex symbol status she achieved it by stripping off in the film, *The Tribe*. Anxious to be accepted as a serious actress she accepted rôles in a wartime epic, *Land Girls*, and in two period classics. She is in BBC2's adaptation of Dickens's *Our Mutual Friend*, playing the heroine Bella, and in a film version of RL Stephenson's Napoleonic epic, *St Ives*. If her talent matches her energy and ambition she could be one of Britain's hottest actresses by the millennium.

Rochdale schoolteacher's daughter Anna has a serenity about her reminiscent of a young Natasha Richardson. Friends are still puzzled why she spent two-and-a-half years with egotistical TV personality Darren Day. The couple rowed about her refusal to give up her career to look after him. Early in 1997 he boasted: "Anna is the first girlfriend I've ever been faithful to and I'm pleasantly surprised by that." Within weeks the romance was very publicly over. He humiliated her by parading through the tabloids his new love, actress Tracy Shaw, who plays *Coronation Street*'s man-eating Maxine. Anna was then dumped by former Take That singer Robbie Williams. She kept a dignified silence throughout.

Frost, Sir David, 7th April 1939, TV inquisitor. "He rose without trace", according to the late Kitty Muggeridge. But this ambitious, ever genial Gillingham grammar schoolboy has become almost as Establishment as his father-in-law, the Duke of Norfolk. Yet he used to be a left-winger who sneered at private education and inherited privilege. Shortly before his 1983 marriage to Lady Carina Fitzalan-Howard, the duke asked her whether he was religious. "Oh yes," she replied, "he thinks he's God".

Although now coasting on his old reputation, no star has made such an impact on British television as Frost. He has interrogated every British premier since Harold Macmillan and the last eight US presidents, notably the disgraced Richard Nixon who wept during his interview. Like a cerebral Forrest Gump he seems to have been present at every notable event for more than a generation. He also found time to help found London Weekend Television and TV-am.

A Methodist minister's son, Frost read English at Cambridge where he edited *Granta* and appeared in Footlights revues alongside Jonathan Miller and John Cleese. He won a year's traineeship with Redifusion TV and in 1962 fronted the BBC's controversial satire show, *That Was The Week That Was*. It is hard to imagine now the clawings he once gave to drug doctor John Petro and insurance fraudster Emil Savundra – for his style has become so non-confrontational. But he still attracts every major politician to BBC1's *Breakfast With Frost*.

The demands of his busy television career, crossing the Atlantic twice a week, wreaked havoc with Frost's personal life during the Seventies. He dated a string of beautiful women including actresses Janette Scott, Jill St John and Jenny Logan. He was engaged to singer Diahann Carroll and US model Karen Graham. In 1981 he was briefly wed to Peter Sellers's widow, actress Lynne Frederick.

Happily married at last, he has three sons, Miles, Wilfred and George, all at private schools. The family lives in baronial style in Hampshire and Chelsea, where their annual Summer party has become a social highlight. Can it be long before he becomes Lord Frost of Beccles?

Frostrup, Mariella, 12th November 1962, TV's Nordic vamp, known as Mazza. She has the dirtiest laugh in showbiz. Her husky voice turns newspaper editors and TV producers into quivering blancmanges. But her considered utterances and jottings never quite fulfil their potential. With her short blonde hair she parades through the swinging *boîtes* of Notting Hill, near her wackily-decorated maisonette. She is in touch with all the right people.

This former Dublin waitress was born in Oslo, the daughter of a Norwegian shipping heir and a Scottish artist mother. When she was six, the family up sticked to Ireland. Her parents then divorced. As a result she moved house 13 times in ten years and went to ten different schools. The experience has left her with perpetually itchy feet. Her eccentric father, an *Irish Times* journalist, died of a heart attack at 44.

Precocious Mariella immediately left home and moved into a Shepherd's Bush squat. She worked as a recording technician for the Rolling Stones. She then became a rock PR, using her blarney to organise press coverage for *Live Aid* and representing Dire Straits, Tears for Fears, UB40 and Spandau Ballet. With her cute looks and Page 3 girl figure she was an immediate social hit. At 18 she briefly married TV presenter Richard Jobson, then a punk rocker with The Skids. Another smitten swain was West End impresario Nick Allott. But with men she generally adopts a take-it-or-leave-it attitude.

As a TV presenter many critics believe that Mariella's talents lie in weather forecasting. "She's living proof that a *soufflé* can only rise so far", one journo wrote after she briefly hosted a chat show. She made her debut in 1989 on C4's music show, *The Big World Café* and later presented Carlton's *The Little Picture Show* for four years. "She made an ideal film critic because she looks like a film star – a blissful mix of Greta Saacchi and Pussy Galore", drooled one fan. She takes herself very seriously. "I actually long to be 50 because then nobody will accuse me of being 'a sexy, blonde bombshell' anymore."

Fry, Stephen, 24th August 1957, multi-talented celibate mummer. This highly intelligent, quixotic character has excelled as an actor, comedian, playwright and novelist. But he possesses a fatal flaw which baffles friends and fans.

Fry was born in Norfolk to a scientist father and Viennese mother. By 13 he had already passed nine O-levels. He was then expelled from three schools, including Uppingham, for schoolboy japes which included stealing. He was finally jailed at 17 for credit card fraud. "My great fortune was getting caught. I screeched to a halt before going off the rails."

Stephen won a scholarship to Cambridge where he met his future comedy partner Hugh Laurie. He won a First and began his career in the theatre. His first starring rôle in 1984 was as a schoolmaster in *40 Years On*, opposite Sir John Gielgud.

On television this lofty young fogey starred in long-running series like *Blackadder* and *A Bit of Fry and Laurie*. He was perfectly cast as the calm, resourceful Jeeves to Laurie's silly ass Wooster in ITV's eponymous series. As an author he has won literary praise for two bestselling novels, *The Liar* and *The Hippopotamus*. But his real bonanza was writing the West End and Broadway musical, *Me and My Girl*, which has earned him an estimated £3 million.

Fry's personal life has invariably been tortured. He suffers from depression and low self-esteem and, despite his flamboyance, is a loner. He has beaten a £1,000-a-week cocaine habit and admits to being "90 per cent homosexual". "I've been in love, not recently, but I keep myself open to the possibility."

In 1995 he walked out of the West End play *Cell Mates* after experiencing poor reviews, a rare experience for him. As suicide rumours grew he issued a statement from his Belgian hideaway saying he had suffered "a dreadful attack of what golfers call the yips".

Fry's Eeyore-ish charm and satirical manner has largely reclaimed his reputation. His voice, redolent of port being passed round the senior common room, is highly persuasive. But he can also be heavy-handed. He lives regally in St James's and Swaffham, Norfolk.

G

Gallagher, Liam, 21st September 1972, the Nineties' Johnny Rotten. His 1997 marriage to actress Patsy Kensit seems to have calmed Oasis's lead singer and chief troublemaker. Once he revelled in controversy, trashing hotel rooms, brawling with his elder brother Noel, bingeing on cocaine and alcohol. Lewd and foul-mouthed, he even swapped punches with INXS star Michael Hutchence backstage at the MTV awards.

Liam belongs to a large working-class Catholic family from a Manchester council estate. Talent, hype and luck contributed to Oasis' rapid rise from a £100-a-night band to mega-stardom. In 1991 Oasis played their first professional gig at the Boardwalk, Manchester. They were discovered by Creation records boss Alan McGee who predicted they would become bigger than The Beatles. Their sartorial style – Adidas trainers, Harrington jackets, Kangol sun-hats and Fred Perry shirts – created a cult.

Oasis' 1994 first album, *Definitely Maybe*, became Britain's biggest selling debut album while their second, *Morning Glory*, out-sold even The Beatles' *Sergeant Pepper*. Their first No 1 single, *Some Might Say*, looks like being the *Hey Jude* of the Nineties. Noel describes their sibling relationship as a "classic case of hating the one you love. Liam wishes he was me 'cos I can write songs and I wish I was as brassy and cocky as him." Immature Liam is an avid Manchester City fan, with a typically chauvinist attitude towards females. "If a bird wants a shag I'll do it. I'm in the music business for the birds" he once said. In 1995 he began dating Patsy Kensit, four years his senior. They were dubbed the "President and First Lady of Britpop". To her surprise he proved to be a gentle stepfather to her son James, although she often wonders "who needs mothering more?" Will his excessive habits eventually cause Oasis to implode or will he mellow like David Bowie?

Galliano, John, 28th November 1960, Vivienne Westwood with extra class. In 1996 this exuberant, plumber's son became Gibraltar's most famous export since duty-free. He became Maison Dior's chief designer. It placed this former *enfant terrible* of British fashion ahead of all his American and Italian contemporaries. His style was markedly different from his staid predecessor Gianfranco

Ferre. He favours nostalgia, borrowing designs from the Twenties' flapper girls, the Thirties' bias-cut and the Forties' New Look. A huge influence was his former partner, Jasper Conran.

Galliano's appearance resembles a mad pirate with a faintly Rastafarian air. He was brought up in Streatham, the son of a Gibraltarian father and a Spanish mother. He went to Wilsons Grammar School and then studied at St Martin's School of Art. He made his name in the Eighties with outrageous and provocative designs, including tulle tutus teamed with pointy bodices and a Marseilles-inspired "matelot-meets-smart-signora orgy of ruffles and stripes". In 1990 he became the first Brit to show at the Louvre during Paris Fashion Week. Tina Turner, Kylie Minogue, Marisa Berenson and the Ballet Rambert are now among his clients. In 1995 he began designing couture and ready-to-wear for Maison Givenchy. Madonna insisted on wearing his designs in *Evita* and at its world première.

The endlessly creative Galliano maintains separate identities for his own and Dior's collections. A 20-minute show, with supermodels Carla Bruni, Naomi Campbell and Kate Moss wearing 45 outfits, may cost £2 million. His collections are themed and scintillatingly theatrical. An ear-shattering soundtrack of winds blowing and wolves howling began one collection. Supermodels, high on champagne, will disport on giant Fragonard-style swings or impersonate *Wuthering Heights* maidens in distress. The bandana-wearing bachelor is a born schmoozer, particularly with the fashion press. He relaxes in his Paris studio by dancing the flamenco.

Galvin, Daniel, 7th April 1944, Sultan of the Subtle Streak. Princess Diana called him her guru and so do dozens of household names who would rather keep their hair-dyeing a secret. His success enables him to drive a Bentley Turbo, ski in Aspen and scuba-dive in Jamaica. "I'm the world's most expensive hairdresser." As well as his Marylebone HQ he has salons in America, Japan and the Middle East and sells his shampoos, conditioners and colouring products world-wide. But he hasn't cut hair for over 25 years. "If I did you wouldn't come back!"

Galvin left his Kensal Rise secondary modern aged 16 without O-levels, but with distinctions in football, boxing and swimming. His first job was sweeping floors at his father's North London barber's shop. In 1965 he joined Mayfair crimper Leonard where he tinted the locks of trendy photographers, models, actresses and Society gels. In 1978 the master colourist opened Europe's first salon to specialise in hair-colouring. "With perms going out of fashion the industry needed something new." He has since helped tint the tresses of clients like

Mel Gibson, Mandy Smith, Tom Cruise, Nicole Kidman and Cher. Among films he has worked on are *Cry Freedom, The Living Daylights, Braveheart* and *First Knight*.

Of mixed Polish, French and Spanish ancestry, Galvin resembles a gypsy dancer. He dresses down, in black jeans, black tee-shirt and Gucci loafers. He and Mavis, his wife of over 30 years, live in a Jacobean manor house near Elstree, Hertfordshire. They have three children, Louise, Daniel Jnr and James. In 1995, acute stress caused by overwork and Daniel Jnr's temporary defection to rivals Michaeljohn, caused a nervous breakdown. He spent two weeks in a rehabilitation clinic in Harrow. He is now obsessed with his diet and keep-fit regime, working out four times a week and running the London Marathon. His next goal is to learn to fly.

Gambon, Michael, 19th October 1940, theatrical colossus, dubbed the "Great Gambo" by Sir Ralph Richardson. This distinguished Dublin-born mummer possesses all the skills of Derek Jacobi or Ian McKellen, but no knighthood yet. A recent highlight was his portrayal of a roistering restaurateur opposite Lia Williams in David Hare's West End hit, *Skylight*. He then made his Broadway debut in it, but "couldn't wait to get back home". He has been married since 1962 and, like his wife Anne, hates showbiz socialising. His non-theatrical life is dominated by an unlikely passion – precision engineering.

The raddled-looking thesp spent seven years with Vickers as an apprentice engineer after leaving St Aloysius School, North London. He spends hours tinkering in the machine room of his Kent home. He is also a liveryman of the Gunmakers' Company and a trustee of the Royal Armoury, honours which mean more to him than his shelves of BAFTA awards.

For a man with size 13 feet Gambo moves with a surprisingly panther-like grace. He ascribes this to his fascination with ballet. "The best night I ever had in a theatre was watching *Romeo and Juliet* at Covent Garden with Baryshnikov and Lynn Seymour. I'd love to have been a dancer."

Gambon's earliest stage successes were in Alan Ayckbourn's *The Norman Conquests* and *Just Between Ourselves*. Later he won awards for *Galileo* and *A Chorus of Disapproval*. On television he is best-known for Dennis Potter's surreal drama, *The Singing Detective*. More improbably he was also cast as the eponymous Parisien flic in ITV's revival of *Maigret*. Although Maigret's pipe, raincoat and trilby were reassuring accessories for his predecessor Rupert Davies, Gambo merely looked sinister. But then portraying sly, complex, edgy individuals is his forte, like the MI5 blackmailer in *The Heat of the Day* and the Mafia godfather in *Mobsters*.

Garrett, Lesley, 10th April 1955, opera's sex-bomb. Her natural, fun-loving temperament is as different from the haughty grandeur of Maria Callas as a Spice Girl from Cilla Black. On record covers and on stage with the English National Opera she loves to flaunt her curvaceous, 5ft 4ins charms. She has sung on Kenco coffee and Renault car ads, appeared on Esther Rantzen's schmaltzy TV series *Hearts of Gold* and been "gotcha'd" by Noel Edmonds. She even tried to teach *Birds of a Feather* stars Pauline Quirke and Linda Robson how to become opera singers in their BBC series, *Jobs For The Girls*. It is all part of her "crusade to bring opera to the people".

The Doncaster-born warbler grew up in a musical household. One grandfather was a classical pianist and the other ran a skiffle group. At family gatherings she would sing excerpts from Gilbert & Sullivan and Verdi with her father, a railway signalman turned schoolteacher. At Thorne Grammar School she was nicknamed "Gobby Garrett" and "Have-a-go-Les". She sang and acted in school productions like *My Fair Lady*. But it was only when she saw her first opera, *Madame Butterfly*, at 15 that she knew what her vocation would be. After studying at the Royal Academy of Music and winning the 1979 Kathleen Ferrier Memorial Prize she continued training at the National Opera Studio. Her first break was singing in Handel's *Orlando* at the Wexford Festival. She has since used her unique gifts of popularising opera in productions ranging from *La Boheme* to *Don Giovanni*.

Lesley was briefly married to a music teacher, but they parted in 1982. "I was travelling so much it was eventually a choice between my marriage or my career. Partly through guilt I lost my voice." She needed years of coaching and psychoanalysis to restore it fully. She now lives in Highgate with her second husband GP Peter Christian and their two children Jeremy and Chloe. "We met on a blind date. It was love at first sight and we've never looked back!"

Gascoigne, Paul, 27th May 1967, Britain's Maradona, aka Gazza. Every generation has them: George Best, John Conteh, Hurricane Higgins. Brilliant sportsmen, flawed characters. This chunky England and Glasgow Rangers superstar constantly provokes negative headlines and never learns. He goes on drunken sprees with bad influences like Chris Evans and Danny Baker, dallies with Page 3 girls in discos, threatens to "f***ing have" journalists. He admitted beating up his wife Sheryl for two years, mainly because "she wasn't paying me enough attention, so I thought she didn't love me. I've been a violent bastard and a coward." He would certainly win top prize for being Britain's naffest man. His clothes, cars, houses, even his wedding ceremony shriek Yuck! But his fans love him: "Gazza's boys are here...shag women, drink beer", read one stadium banner.

Gascoigne grew up in a clannish, working-class family in Gateshead. At Heathfield Senior School he revealed a remarkable football talent. He joined Newcastle United at 18 and transferred to Tottenham Hotspur in 1988. Two years later he became a national hero when he wept after England lost the World Cup semi-final to West Germany in Turin. His £5.5 million transfer to the Italian club Lazio in 1992 was plagued by injuries and further scandals.

This clowning Geordie surrounds himself with sycophants who encourage his boorish behaviour on pub crawls and lads' nights-out. He hates solitude, except when he goes fishing. "When you're alone you have to think a lot and I don't like to think a lot." He met blonde ex-model Sheryl in a wine-bar in 1991. Their stormy relationship was punctuated with her walking out half a dozen times and being enticed back with gifts, including a £25,000 Toyota Celica. They finally married in 1996, four months after the birth of their son Regan. A year later he moved to Scotland while she remained at their Wates-style home in Hertfordshire. Will Gazza dissipate his estimated £10 million fortune and end up like George Best?

Geldof, 'Sir' Bob, 5th August 1954, Saint but sinner. This high-struttin', articulate Irishman is Mick Jagger with a cause. In 1984, inspired by TV pictures of fly-blown, matchstick-thin Ethiopian children, he produced a fund-raising single sung by his pop friends. "I thought it would take a week organising and then I'd get back to hyping our new single", says the former Boomtown Rat. The song *Do They Know It's Christmas?* raised £8 million for famine relief, selling 11.7 million copies world-wide. He then organised simultaneous Live Aid concerts in London and Philadelphia, raising over £50 million and a similar sum with Sports Aid. His honorary knighthood was a just recompense for missing the Nobel Peace Prize.

This Dublin commercial traveller's son was known as "Liver Lips" at his Catholic boarding school, Black Rock College. He enjoyed "winding up the Fathers" with tricky questions about church dogma and the Vatican's wealth. Despite his intelligence he never bothered to pass an exam after 11.

On leaving school Geldof worked as a road-mender, meat-packer and photographer's assistant. But he found his real vocation as a journalist on the *New Musical Express* and *Melody Maker*. Ever the activist he joined anti-apartheid and CND marches and later performed in Polish Solidarity concerts. In 1975 he co-founded the Boomtown Rats who had No 1 hits with *Rat Trap* and *I Don't Like*

Mondays. By the time he became Saint Bob his rock credentials were waning.

Sanctity sits uneasily on the bony shoulders of this gangling, greasy-haired, big-swearing raconteur. Much publicised squabbles with his wife, TV presenter Paula Yates, reflected badly on both. In 1996 she became pregnant by her lover, INXX lead singer Michael Hutchence and left the family home in Chelsea with their three children. His girlfriend, French starlet Jeanne Marine, moved in.

Geldof runs a lucrative TV production company, Planet 24, whose output includes C4's *The Big Breakfast*. He spends most weekends at his converted medieval priory in Kent with his angelic-looking children. He blames Paula for their names: Fifi Trixibelle, Peaches and Pixie.

George, Eddie, 11th September 1938, bank manager to the nation. With his silver hair, ruddy complexion and tubby physique he resembles an old-fashioned GP or school bursar. But he could never have risen to Bank of England governor had he also not had a steely ability to deal with Euro-Scrooges and obdurate central bankers. His background is quite pedestrian for the Bank's top dog. His predecessor Robin Leigh-Pemberton, now Lord Kingsdown, was an Old Etonian former Grenadier Guards officer complete with Kent stately home. A wag once described George as "a market technocrat with ice-cold convictions and an ever-glowing Rothmans".

George – note the matey "Eddie" – was a scholarship boy at Dulwich College. He read economics at Cambridge, winning a 2:1, rather than the expected First. He has spent almost his entire career in Threadneedle Street, rising to the governorship in 1993. Under Chancellor of the Exchequer Kenneth Clarke he became known as "Steady Eddie" for his benevolent control of the money markets. Labour's new Chancellor Gordon Brown gave the Bank more power by allowing it to fix interest rates, but removed its supervisory rôle of banking, insurance and pensions. This followed the roasting he received over the disastrous BCCI collapse and failure of Baring's.

Bridge-playing George and his wife Clarice have three children. A passionate Aston Villa supporter, he expects to retire in 1998 and begin a lucrative private sector career. A life peerage will follow.

Getty Jnr, J Paul, 7th September 1932, Britain's greatest philanthropist. Like Fort Knox the very name is synonymous with money. He is the antithesis of his Scrooge-like father, American oil tycoon J Paul Getty, who fitted payphones in the guest rooms of his Tudor stately home, Sutton Place. Getty Jnr's charitable donations totalling over £100 million earned him an honorary knighthood in 1986. "I simply have no use of an income of over £100 million a year." Gifts included £50 million to the National Gallery and £3 million for a new stand at Lord's cricket ground.

The altruist Anglophile is paying the price for past excesses. During the Sixties he was the Sean Penn of Rome's Dolce Vita set. He was a swinging playboy who drove fast cars, drank heavily, experimented with drugs and squired raunchy starlets. His sybaritic lifestyle enraged Getty Snr, who wanted him to concentrate on the family oil business. In 1971 the fun stopped when his second wife Talitha Pol died of a heroin overdose. The shocked widower vowed to reform his ways. Two years later his eldest son, J Paul Getty III, was kidnapped by Calabrian bandits. They later released him, having cut off his ear after his grandfather initially refused to pay the £1.25 million ransom. In 1981 the boy suffered a massive stroke, caused by drug and drink abuse, from which he has never recovered.

Getty himself developed phlebitis, which left him fat and weak. He grew a beard, sold his £3 million Cheyne Walk house, scene of wild showbiz parties, and became a recluse. His philanthropy – including £100,000 to the striking miners in 1984 – was largely conducted from the London Clinic. He spent a total of three years there, with prime minister Mrs Thatcher one of the few visitors allowed. He now commutes between a St James's penthouse and his 3,000-acre Buckinghamshire estate, Wormsley Park. His passions are collecting medieval illuminated manuscripts and watching cricket and old movies. Friends praise his third wife, former model Victoria Holdsworth, for bringing him out of his shell.

Giggs, Ryan, 29th November 1973, the new George Best? Britain's handsomest and most gifted young footballer has all the accoutrements of a Hollywood idol: a silver Aston Martin DB7, designer wardrobe and bevvies of beautiful women. He might have achieved the same wizardry in rugby league had his British trial not coincided with the start of his Manchester United apprenticeship. Having captained the under-15s, he could equally have played for England instead of Wales. But would he have become the multi-millionaire superstar he is today?

The 5ft 11ins Cardiff-born Romeo grew up in Salford, Manchester. His father Danny Wilson was a former rugby league international, whose career was wrecked by alcohol. Young Ryan's precocious talent led to his early signing by Manchester United. But manager Alex Ferguson soon recognised a dangerously sybaritic side to his character. Giggsy's shyness, modesty and decorum seems to evaporate in the proximity of nightclubs, girls and booze. He has become a lucrative target for kiss 'n' tell girls. He picks them up in discos or lap-dancing venues, spends a few passionate nights with them and then dumps them. His most enduring relationship was with *Hollyoaks* TV star Davinia Murphy. Their fraught 18 months together contrasts with a fling he had with TV presenter Dani Behr, who nevertheless describes him as "one of the very few men I've ever loved".

In 1996 Giggsy finally moved out of his mother's Salford home into an executive estate on the city's outskirts. He receives over 1,000 fan letters a week. The spin-offs – calendars, books, TV series and endorsements – should keep him in Ralph Lauren for many years. It remains to be seen whether he has the strength to resist Best's path to self-destruction.

Gilbey, James, 4th October 1957, London's favourite spare man. This velvet-tongued, former Lotus car salesman became Princess Diana's close confidant during her marriage. They would yack for hours about Prince Charles's peccadilloes and Gilbey's convoluted love-life.

The so-called Squidgygate tapes in 1992 inadvertently made them look as if they were having an affair. Intimate conversations between them were illegally recorded and the lovey-dovey transcript reprinted in the *Sun*. It coincided with Andrew Morton's bestselling book, *Diana: Her True Story*, in which he was named as a primary source. Gilbey revealed that the royal couple were no longer sleeping together and that Diana "thinks the prince a bad father". After this furore Dame Barbara Cartland said of her step-grand-daughter's friend: "His behaviour is extremely common and vulgar. He should be thrown out of his club."

Gilbey belongs to the prominent Roman Catholic family that produced not only his saintly great-uncle Monsignor Alfred Gilbey but Gilbey's gin. Since leaving the RC school Ampleforth he has devoted his life to cars. Although attentive, well-connected and smartly-groomed, he is something of a *dummkopf*. When trying to escape from journalists quizzing him about Squidgygate he crashed his car outside the Lotus team offices near Norwich, leaving embarrassing documents in the back seat.

Women tend to mother him or cry on his shoulder, rather than experience James Hewitt-style palpitations. He consoled model Lisa Butcher after her brief first marriage to superchef Marco Pierre White. He was briefly engaged to the Earl of Mexborough's daughter Lady Alethea Savile, who later died of a drug overdose. One girl-friend complained he only had one topic of conversation, Princess Diana. Some say he is a social climber.

Gilbey, Tom, 19th May 1939, *bon viveur* tailor. He is a rare survivor of those who supplied the plumage for the dandies swaggering
through the Swinging Sixties. Names like Mr Fish, Tommy Nutter
and Deborah and Clare long ago hit the cutting-room floor. But this
flamboyant character remains, thanks to his professionalism, drive
and ability to adapt to changing styles and financial circumstances.
He was one of the first tailors to offer a range of cheaper, computer-
cut Italian-made suits, dispatching an army of "killer bimbos" to
measure up City customers. He foresaw the return of the waistcoat,
as a flashy addition to a dinner jacket and as a female accessory
with jeans.

Cockney Gilbey began as a window-dresser and pattern-cutter. He
opened his first shop off Piccadilly in 1968, making frilly brocade
jackets and silk bell-bottoms for pop stars like Paul McCartney and
Elton John, who are still clients. He persuaded sceptical aristos,
publishers and bankers to wear safari jackets and elastic-waisted
blousons. He was less successful in getting them to commute to the
City in tailor-made jackets with matching shorts!

This trilby-wearing extrovert has a talent for making parties
swing. Indeed Society hostess Liz Brewer uses him as her "warm-up
man". Witty, lively and outrageous, he has been known to get up at a
black-tie stag night and start jitterbugging with the stripper. His
legendary exploits as a "bird-puller" could have done for tailoring
what Warren Beatty's film *Shampoo* did for hairdressing. Women,
particularly orientals, were beguiled by his camp manner. In 1985
prime minister Margaret Thatcher's daughter Carol briefly fell for
his well-practised charms, but found him too indiscreet. It took a
determined Polish blonde, 30 years his junior called Isabella, to lure
him to Marylebone register office in 1993. Alas, they parted in 1997.

Glenconner, Lord, 1st December 1926, Caribbean and Scottish
grandee. He is best known as Princess Margaret's lifelong friend
Colin Tennant, who turned a small, mosquito-infested island into
glamorous Mustique. But, despite his air of aristo disdain, this
imposing former Irish Guards officer has quite recent bourgeois origins. His great-grandfather was a Glasgow bleach manufacturer.

Flamboyant Glenconner – ex-Eton and Oxford – operates well
below his intellectual capacity. His skills as a property developer,
interior decorator and party organiser could have made him a cross
between David Mlinaric and Lady Elizabeth Anson. But his family
fortune and sybaritic character have enabled him to enjoy a life
without too much responsibility. His flair manifests itself in the

fancy-dress "jump-ups" he has organised in the Caribbean, usually with Princess Margaret as guest of honour. His 60th birthday celebrations on Mustique continued for seven days of limbo-dancing, barbecues and fireworks.

Recent family misfortunes have led many people to wonder if there is a Tennant Curse. In 1996 Glenconner's disinherited heir Charlie died after a long battle with heroin addiction, during which he sold stolen family holiday snaps to a Sunday newspaper. Second son Henry died from AIDS in 1990. The third son Christopher was in a coma for four months in 1987 following a motorcycle accident in Belize. The two younger children, twins Amy and May, have so far proved luckier. All hopes now rest on Henry's teenage son Euan, from his marriage to Tessa Cormack. He will eventually inherit the bulk of the 9,000-acre Peebleshire estate and an estimated £14 million fortune. But the title will go to Charlie's son Cody from his brief marriage to former drugs counsellor Shelagh Scott.

Glenconner's saintly wife Anne, daughter of the late Earl of Leicester, is Princess Margaret's long-standing lady-in-waiting. During 40 years of marriage she has accepted his long absences in the West Indies with close friends. As he relaxes in his latest development on St Lucia he probably reflects how lucky he was to have resisted marrying Margaret in the early-Fifties.

Glitter, Gary, 8th May 1940, self-styled Leader of the Gang. Despite his slide from the Top 10 and those dreadful bouffant wigs, he has become truly a cult figure.

This illegitimate former Banbury Teddy boy was born Paul Gadd in an Oxfordshire workhouse. As "Paul Raven" he was a run-of-the-mill pop singer until 1972, when he changed his name to Gary Glitter and became the "King of Glam Rock". Teenyboppers mobbed this gyrating geriatric in the diamanté jump suit and Cuban heels as he yelled hit songs like *I'm The Leader of the Gang* and *Do You Wanna Touch Me*. His saving grace has always been his ability to send himself up. He admits that he has "garage mechanic's eyes, a truck-driver's body and cannot sing, but I'm a great shouter and can pull marvellous faces". Few realised that at the height of Glittermania he had a wife, Anne, and two children.

Sadly Glitter enjoyed his idol Elvis Presley's lifestyle without having the King's cash. His "toys" included two Rolls-Royces, a Jensen and a helicopter. But the hits fizzled out and in 1980 he was declared bankrupt and had to sell all his glitter to repay debts. Today this exuberant bachelor has become a Quentin Crisp figure, enlivening chat shows with his high camp performance. He is a vegetarian, teetotal and a Buddhist. Having lost his driving licence for 15 years after repeated drink-driving convictions he now drives a Mercedes and has a 40-foot yacht. He has homes in London and Somerset.

Gold, John, 25th June 1932, club owner with bezazz. For nearly 30 years he has presided over London's grooviest nightclub Tramp. Rivals like Regine, Dai Llewellyn and Peter Stringfellow have unsuccessfully tried to topple the man who practically invented the discotheque. Regulars have included Michael Caine, Roman Polanski, Joan Collins, sundry aristos, millionaires and men-about-town. Today their children carry on the tradition and they can be confident that "Johnny will look after them", protecting them from unsuitable company, drugs and too much alcohol. But he still attracts the current trendies, from Liam Gallagher and Patsy Kensit to Dani Behr and Tamara Beckwith. The paparazzi hang outside in Jermyn Street as if Tramp is still the trendiest club in town.

The Golden formula is his continued presence every night – he often dines with celebrity friends at his ringside table. Cool and intuitive he has a photographic memory for people who matter and bans gossip columnists (except Nigel Dempster). He acts as favourite uncle to the models, starlets and trust-fund babes who flock there.

This Brighton bookie's son opened his first West End disco, Dolly's, in 1963. Six years later he founded Tramp, with two partners, Bill Ofner and Jackie Collins's late husband Oscar Lerman, in the former Society Club. It was there that Lotharios like Warren Beatty, Jack Nicholson and Mick Jagger did their courting.

Cauliflower-eared Gold has wisely been cautious about expansion. He briefly opened a Los Angeles Tramp but closed it when he found Hollywood stars preferred to be in bed by 9pm. He founded Rags, a Mayfair dining-club, and owns the Belvedere restaurant in Holland Park. Unusually for this business, he remains steadfastly faithful to his wife, Sixties model Jan de Souza, whom he married in 1971. They have two children Nick and Claire. Newspapers have offered him a fortune to write his memoirs. "I never would. I don't want to live in Tibet!"

Goldsmith, Lady Annabel, 11th June 1934, the Tina Turner of Ham. She is immortalised as the lady who lent her Christian name to the world's finest nightclub. Gassy, dynamic and outspoken, she was never going to be a wallflower. Her youthful energy still ensures she has a wide circle of friends of all ages. She latterly became one of Princess Diana's closest confidantes.

The former Lady Annabel Vane-Tempest-Stewart belongs to a distinguished Anglo-Irish family. Her father was the eighth Marquess of Londonderry and she was raised in stately grandeur at Wynyard Park on Teesside. The family fortune was derived from North Country coalmines. Educated at Southover, she was clever enough to have gone to university and had a career. Instead, at 19, she married man-about-town Mark, then a trainee adman. They had three children: Rupert who was later to drown off the West African coast aged 30, City sandwich tycoon Robin and painter India-Jane. In 1963 Birley founded the Berkeley Square nightclub Annabel's which quickly became the trysting-ground for Britain's smart set. His well-connected wife's early influence in persuading aristo friends to come boogeying is often overlooked. But his anti-social hours had a disastrous effect on their marriage. They divorced in 1975 and three years later she married the charismatic Sir James Goldsmith, her lover for over ten years. They already had two children: Jemima and Zacharias, who is being groomed to take over his late father's business empire. In 1980 they had another son, Benjamin.

Lady A, based in an exquisite Georgian mansion overlooking Ham Common, Surrey, took a patrician *laissez-faire* view when Goldsmith acquired a new mistress, French journalist Laura Boulay de la Meurthe. He divided his time between Ham and his Paris villa where Laura raised their two children, Jethro and Charlotte. Both women had to plan their visits to his Burgundy *château* and Goldfinger-style Mexican *palacio* carefully in case they bumped into each other. Ironically his final few years fighting pancreatic cancer brought this extended family closer.

Goldsmith, Harvey, 4th March 1946, rock's anonymous superstar. Stubby, balding and bearded, this philanthropic impresario possesses all the charisma of a baked potato. But his power and prestige equal Cecil B deMille. He has presented nearly every major star in concert over the last quarter-century: the Rolling Stones, Bruce Springsteen, Bob Dylan, Phil Collins, Wham! and Michael Flatley. He organises concerts for the Prince's Trust and persuaded Prince Charles and Princess Diana to attend the 1985 Live Aid concert in London which helped to raise over £140 million for famine relief. He has diversified into opera, presenting the Three Tenors in Hyde Park and productions of *Aida*, *Carmen* and *Tosca* at Earl's Court.

This chirpy, East End tailor's son originally trained as a pharmacist at Brighton College of Technology, where he organised Student Union balls. From hiring pop groups at £15 a night and laying on the beer and sausage rolls he became a full-time concert promoter. In 1968 he held the first open-air, free concert at Parliament Hill

Fields headlined by Fleetwood Mac. "This job is like having a gamble on the three o'clock race every day." He needs to be a lawyer, accountant, PR man, psychiatrist, drug counsellor and transport manager. While Elton John and Led Zeppelin may be instant sell-outs, lesser names may cost him a fortune. He has become inured to artistes with stage fright, drug overdoses and prima donna demands. The Stones once insisted on him supplying crates of 100-year-old tequila in their dressing-rooms, while Van Halen wanted boxes of American smarties, but only ate the green and yellow ones!

Bentley-driving Goldsmith lives in St John's Wood. He married his wife Diana in 1971 and they have a son, Jonathan. At concerts he is invariably the most soberly clothed person backstage.

Grade, Michael, 8th March 1943, showbiz colossus. Relaxed, friendly, witty, he was once TV's highest paid boss, earning £600,000 a year. Yet he had no actual programme-making experience. At the BBC he launched *EastEnders* and screened award-winning series like *Tutti Frutti*, *The Monocled Mutineer* and *The Singing Detective*.

During nine years as C4's chief executive, Grade succeeded in beating BBC2's audience share, attracting ten per cent of viewers. His greatest successes were *GBH*, *Lipstick On My Collar*, *Drop The Dead Donkey* and the films *Trainspotting* and *Four Weddings and a Funeral*. But columnist Paul Johnson dubbed him "Britain's pornographer-in-chief" because of his screening of programmes like *Dyke TV*, *The Girlie Show* and *The Red Light Zone*. Melvyn Bragg once said: "Michael puts out a sober mask of public service, while up in the attic his real expression is one of commercial lust."

Grade was raised by Olga Winogradsky, the formidable mother of showbiz barons Lords Grade and Delfont and his father, showbiz agent Leslie Grade. His mother left home when he was six months old and has never seen him since. He briefly went to Stowe but found it hard to fit into the public school ethos. At 17 he arrived for his first job, as a *Daily Mirror* reporter, in Daddy's chauffeur-driven Bentley. There he wrote a sports column by-lined 'Mike Grade'. In 1966 he joined the powerful Grade Organisation as an agent.

Michael was then head-hunted to become LWT's deputy light entertainment chief, but left to become president of Embassy TV in Hollywood. His hopes of making "mega-bucks" were not realised and family friend Bill Cotton rescued him in 1984. He was appointed BBC1's youngest ever controller and quickly promoted to director of programmes where his brilliance as a scheduler enabled the BBC to start catching up ITV. Annoyed at John Birt's appointment as deputy director-general, he moved to Channel 4 in 1988, horrifying the chattering classes because of his philistine background. As First

Leisure chairman he now runs a less controversial business: bingo halls, bowling alleys, nightclubs and Blackpool Tower.

In his private life, Grade, the darling of the media, finds it hard to sustain a lasting relationship. His 1967 marriage to former BBC librarian Penny Levinson ended after 14 years. They had two children, Alison and Jonathan. In 1982 he married Lord Burnham's daughter Sarah Lawson, a TV producer, but they divorced nine years later. He has since had on-off romances with TV producer Pati Marr and couturier Lindka Cierarch.

Graff, Laurence, 13th June 1938, Lord of the Rings. This Harry Winston of the Nineties has sold some of the world's most spectacular diamonds: the Paragon, the Idol's Eye, the Emperor Maximilian and the Empress Rose. "As soon as I pick up a valuable stone I feel a power stirring inside me and I've just got to own it." Potentates and superstars flock to his Bond Street emporium because they know he is discreet. At Sotheby's 1987 sale of the Duchess of Windsor's jewels he paid £1.3 million for her emerald engagement ring. In 1995 he bid £5.1 million for the Begum Blue diamond, belonging to the Aga Khan's ex-wife Sally.

The son of a Russian-Jewish schmutter merchant, Graff grew up in Hackney. He left school at 13 determined to make his fortune. He worked in an East End factory assembling costume jewellery before beginning his Hatton Garden apprenticeship. "I didn't have any big break. It was a long haul of buying and selling smaller stones and slowly building the capital to retail larger ones." During the Sixties his workshop became a mecca for the super-rich, but he never advertised or sought publicity. After winning the Queen's Award for Industry he moved to swish new premises near Harrods in 1974.

This chunky, immaculately-suited Cockney radiates elegance, probity and calm. He is devoted to his French wife Anne-Marie, who brilliantly entertains jet-set clients who have become friends. They have three children, François, Stephane and Kristelle, and live in a sumptuous mansion next to Sir Winston's old home in Hyde Park Gate. They have a South of France villa, an ocean-going yacht and a LearJet.

The astute Graff thrives in an industry which is entirely built on trust. "If you break your word you're out. I do millions of dollars of business on the telephone and every deal finishes with two Hebrew words: mazel (luck) and brocha (blessing), whether the dealers are Chinese, Lebanese, Catholic or Jewish". It can be a high risk business too. In 1993 his Hatton Garden workshop was the scene of Britain's biggest jewellery robbery when thieves grabbed diamonds worth £7 million.

Grant, Hugh, 9th September 1960, boyish Cary Grant wannabe. In 1994 the Oscar-winning *Four Weddings and a Funeral* transformed him from a virtual unknown into a superstar. The film fed the prevailing Hollywood myth that all English gentlemen are effete, bumbling, diffident charmers. Unfortunately, since the hype he has failed to demonstrate a wider repertoire. He feels "embarrassed" about his rôle as a child psychologist in *Nine Months* and *Extreme Measures*, the first film produced by his own company, also flopped. He badly needs another blockbuster.

Grant achieved notoriety following his £700 conviction for lewd conduct with Sunset Strip hooker Divine Brown in 1995. But his grandmother understood the situation completely: "What I tell people, darling, is that you had a few drinks with the boys and got a bit fresh with the girls."

Hugh Mungo Grant was brought up in Chiswick, the son of a carpet salesman and a primary-school teacher. He made his acting debut aged nine as the White Rabbit in *Alice In Wonderland*. He was a teenage Don Juan, using chat-up lines like: "God, you're clever as well as beautiful. I think I'm going to kiss you." He acquired his foppish mannerisms at Oxford, where he mixed with a fast crowd. With his hair flopping over his forehead, lisping accent and tweedy clothes he fitted in, even though he had only been to a minor London public school, Latymer.

Grant then enrolled in rep at the Nottingham Playhouse. He spent six years in minor rôles, modelled for teen magazines and even worked as a waiter in a London pâtisserie. In 1987 he co-starred in Merchant-Ivory's adaptation of E M Forster's gay love story, *Maurice*. The rave reviews led to the B-movie *Rowing With The Wind*, a Byron biopic notable only because he met a 21-year-old model called Elizabeth Hurley on the set. They made a golden couple and have lived together in Earls Court and Los Angeles ever since. Their relationship has survived because she acts as his mother, sister and occasional lover. "Hugh knows he's hen-pecked but likes bossy women", says a friend.

Green, Michael, 2nd December 1947, small screen Napoleon. Although one of Britain's most influential media tycoons he is not interested in the creative side, only the profits. He is determined to build Britain's first international multi-media company, to rival Rupert Murdoch and Silvio Berlusconi. Insiders fear that this will mean producing lowest common denominator programming rather than more cultural offerings.

Handsome, publicity-shy Green grew up in North London. His father owned the Tern shirt company and his mother was a child psychologist. Instead of pocket money his parents put a set amount of cash into his bank account every January. "I could spend it in a week, but it had to last me a year. I learned about budgeting!" He left Haberdashers Aske School with just four O-levels. He was already a mini-tycoon at 20 when he bought a loss-making printing firm. He sold its headquarters at a profit and invested in new equipment and staff. He then bought a photographic firm called Carlton. He diversified into video and in 1988 bought the film-processing and video-duplication company Technicolor. With strategic investments in several TV companies, Carlton Communications became a major media force. In 1991 he ousted Thames from its London weekday franchise and two years later bought Central TV

This low-key, reclusive deal-maker – now worth an estimated £90 million – has always been skillful at networking. He is close friends with Michael Grade, Gerald Ratner and Charles Saatchi and they used to hold regular poker sessions. In 1972 he wed Lord Wolfson's daughter Janet, thereby marrying into one of Britain's richest and most prominent Jewish families. They had two daughters, Rebecca and Catherine. After the marriage broke up he romanced Irish actress Jeananne Crowley. She claimed that during their three years together he only read two books, Bob Geldof's autobiography and Tom Wolfe's *Bonfire of the Vanities*.

In 1990 he married Tessa Buckmaster, a titian-haired barrister specialising in medical negligence cases. Grade quipped: "This must be the only deal Michael has ever done in which he will not have control." The couple live between homes in Mayfair, Berkshire and the South of France and have three sons, Oliver, Theodore and Jack.

Greer, Fergus, 8th May 1961, Hollywood celebrity-snapper. He is the first Guards officer since the Earl of Lichfield to choose this jazzy profession. And his sights – viewfinders – are set equally high. He is determined to join the David Baileys and Patrick Demarcheliers who are as celebrated as their subjects. His first coup – illustrating royal cad James Hewitt's newspaper reminiscences about his relationship with Princess Diana – was a double-edged one. Lucrative but dangerous for his credibility.

Ambitious Greer, not quite as grand as he seems, was born in Aldershot, the son of a tobacco company executive. He went to Cranleigh School before entering the Irish Guards. At 27 he resigned his commission to work with royal photographer Terence Donovan. There he learnt how to flatter women with subtle lighting and an airbrush. Within two years he was shooting fashion for glossy magazines and working as a party paparazzo. Cannily he always had his by-line removed from any compromising gossip column shots.

Raven-haired Greer's metamorphosis into Californian snapper owes much to his skilled networking. His relationships with beautiful, influential women have provided contacts and raised his social profile. The white master-bedroom at his Hollywood home is covered with portraits of ex-girlfriends. They include royal biographer Robert Lacey's daughter Scarlett, US actress Molly Ringwald and Mrs Merton's *alter ego* Caroline Aherne – plus a naughty shot of TV weather girl Sally Faber cartwheeling on a beach in a nightie. Were he not so suave and eligible people might accuse him of operating a casting couch!

Grossman, Loyd, 16th September 1950, foodie turned TV personality. This favourite punchbag of telly critics and linguistic pedants suddenly descended on us in the early 1980s. One moment he was *Harpers & Queen*'s restaurant critic ("my companion, a well-known film producer's daughter, tried the frog's legs with fig sauce"), and the next he was hosting BBC1's *Masterchef* and ITV's *Through The Keyhole* with Sir David Frost.

Grossman's stealthy showbiz rise began in his hometown Marblehead, Massachusetts. Aged eight he showed his entrepreneurial ability by putting on puppet shows for fellow pupils. After Boston University he did a postgraduate course at the London School of Economics. He settled here and made a pop record under the pseudonym Jet Bronx which failed to make the top 100. He also wrote his first book, *A Social History of Rock*. His early articles for *Harpers* were mainly about style, covering architectural, culinary, sartorial and behavioural matters. A fellow scribe nicknamed him "Gross Loyd Man".

Critics lovingly try to recreate this sensitive and unassuming Bostonian's idiosyncratic accent, once described as "Irritable Vowel Syndrome". On *Masterchef* he will dig his silver spoon into a dish of mushroom and cheese ravioli and exclaim: "Eeeogh, gawsh! An intorksikating cormbinayshun. Time for a refreshing glorse of worter, then orn to the corve's liver".

The garrulous gastronaut raises almost as many hackles as Jeremy Beadle and Chris Evans. This is not only due to his strange manner, but because he is a cocky Yank lecturing us on our food and manners. He first became a lifestyle snoop when he began secretly filming celebrities' homes for a weekly slot on TV-am's breakfast show. With Frost's backing he expanded the concept into a half-hour panel-game now watched by 11 million viewers. Alas they are running out of sacrificial victims prepared to have their diabolical taste exposed and treasures advertised to possible burglars. Grossman is married to *Chariots of Fire* producer Lord Puttnam's daughter Debbie. They live unostentatiously in Fulham with their two daughters Florence and Constance.

H

Hague, William, 26th March 1961, the Yorkshire Nipper. This Mekon-domed 'unknown' beat off political heavyweights like Kenneth Clarke, Michael Howard and Peter Lilley to become Tory leader in 1997. Though many MPs were unsure of his political convictions he had the advantage of making Tony Blair look old. He was the party's youngest leader since Pitt the Younger, who was 24 when he became prime minister. Keen to dispel the notion that he is "John Major with a shiny head" he stresses his right-wing convictions on Europe and law and order. He supports capital punishment and, in his youth, even urged the return of the birch.

William Jefferson Hague (the same Christian names as President Clinton) was brought up in an imposing house outside Wentworth. His father ran the family soft drinks business and hoped his only son would play cricket for Yorkshire. But William (never Bill) hated sport and became hooked on politics during the two 1974 general elections. As a nerdy 16-year-old pupil at Wath-upon-Dearne Comprehensive he made his precocious political debut at the Tory party conference in Blackpool.

At Oxford Hague was voted President of both the Union and the Conservative Association. Armed with a First in politics, philosophy and economics he became a graduate trainee at Shell. He then joined the go-go American management consultants McKinsey. He moonlighted as one of Foreign Secretary Sir Geoffrey Howe's speech-writers and won the Yorkshire seat of Richmond in 1989. He quickly rose through the ministerial ranks to become, in 1995, Britain's youngest Cabinet minister since Harold Wilson.

It was while he was Welsh Secretary that this workaholic bachelor met his fiancée, Ffion "Jolly" Jenkins, then his private secretary. She taught him after-hours how to sing the Welsh national anthem before the National Eisteddfod and "we just clicked". Their 1997 engagement not only halved the bookies' odds on him becoming Tory leader but scotched the gay rumours that had dogged him. He has long been a keen *aficionado* of transcendental meditation.

Hall, Jerry, 2nd July 1956, supermodel turned proud Mama. This golden go-getter is the epitome of the small-town American gal made good. She was born in a rodeo-town on the Tex-Mex borders, her

father a long-distance lorry-driver and her mother a librarian. Aged
14 she was already telling her four sisters: "Ah'm goin' to be real
famous and real rich one day!"

In 1972 this leggy, determined blonde arrived in Paris, staying in
youth hostels and clutching her *Europe on $10 a Day* guidebook. She
was discovered by a model agent on a St Tropez nudist beach.
Despite being 6ft she became one of Europe's top cover-girls and catwalk models. In 1976 Bryan Ferry booked her for his album cover
having fancied her picture in French *Vogue*. And so began a seemingly idyllic relationship which ended two years later when she
dumped him for Mick Jagger. Foxy Jerry knows how to please a
man. "As long as aah have a maid and a cook ah'll do the rest
myself." The affair worked well until he was photographed outside a
New York night-spot with teenage American heiress Cornelia Guest.
After further infidelities she retaliated by dating racehorse-owner
Robert Sangster. Jagger won her back and in 1990 they were finally
married in a Hindu-style ceremony in Bali. They have three children, Elizabeth, James and Georgia, with, a fourth on the way in
1997. They flit between between palatial homes in Richmond, New
York, the Loire Valley and Mustique. She remains upset by her husband's dalliances with models Carla Bruni and Nicole Kruk.

Jerry loves moving in smart circles. She still dabbles in modelling,
earning £150,000 for a recent Bovril ad, and has diversified into
books and health videos. She sees herself as a new Mae West but
cameo rôles in *Batman* and *Princess Caraboo* were disappointing.
Which aristo will she choose if and when she finally decides to trade
in her unfaithful husband?

Hall, Sir Peter, 22nd November 1930, showbiz polymath, nicknamed Genghis Khan and Fu Manchu. This misleadingly cherubic-
looking whirlwind has done it all. He is an award-winning stage
director who has also been fêted at Covent Garden, Glyndebourne
and the New York Met. On TV he presented the Seventies arts programme *Aquarius* and later directed a steamy TV version of *The
Camomile Lawn*. Only in the cinema has he failed, directing the forgettable *Work is a Four Letter Word* and *Three Into Two Won't Go*.

But in the theatre *"Il Principe"* has probably exerted a greater
influence on British drama than any other producer-director this
century. Aged only 30, he founded the RSC and was then director of
the National Theatre. He succeeded in encouraging contemporary
drama as well as reviving the classics and built up an outstanding
côterie of actors, directors, producers and writers. Glenda Jackson
once said: "I do wish Peter would stop pretending to be so bloody
nice when he's really a dictator!"

Sir Peter's published *Diaries* reveal how he had to combine the skills of diplomat and businessman with his creative role, cajoling successive arts ministers for more subsidies. Unlike rival director-producer Trevor Nunn, he has rarely reaped the financial rewards of his productions, although his percentage of Peter Shaffer's award-winning play *Amadeus* was said to have exceeded £1 million.

Hall's success grew out of the cultural wasteland of Suffolk where his father was a local station-master. He won a scholarship to the Perse School, Cambridge and then moved to St Catharine's College where he acted and directed with the Cambridge Footlights. At 24 he directed the first English-language version of *Waiting for Godot*.

Hall's topsy-turvy marital record began promisingly in 1956 when he married France's leading actress Leslie Caron. He was then married for 16 years to his PA, Jacqueline Taylor, and for eight years to American soprano Maria Ewing. In 1990 he married his present wife, former National Theatre publicist Nicki Frei, 29 years his junior. There are a total of six Hall sprogs, including actress Jenny Hall who closely resembles her mother Leslie, and Emma from Nicki. A seat in the House of Lords must surely await him.

Halliwell, Geri, 6th August 1972, pop icon, known as Ginger Spice. She is the sparkiest, most brazen Spice Girl, the one in the button-popping Union Jack mini-dress. She once astonished Prince Charles by telling him "I think you're very sexy" and kissing him on the cheek backstage at a Prince's Trust concert. In this notoriously fickle teenage market she will be the singer who survives if and when this phenomenally successful group breaks up.

Rebellious Geraldine Estelle Halliwell went to Watford Grammar School. Her late father Laurence was a car dealer who made (and lost) a small fortune selling black market goods after the Second World War. Her mother Anna was a former Spanish *au pair*, 23 years younger than him. They divorced when Geri was ten, but she remained devoted to Laurence who encouraged her musical interests and often drove her to auditions. At home in Watford she would sing her anthem: "I wannabe a nightclub queen, the most exciting you've ever seen." As a struggling 18-year-old model she posed for nude shots which a tabloid published after she became famous.

In 1993 this brassy redhead faced a dilemma: should she join the unknown Spice Girls or accept producer Janet Street-Porter's offer to present a new children's cable show? "The chances of the band hitting the big time were pretty slim but Geri took the gamble", explains her brother Max. She found herself part of a slick, pre-packaged group, designed as a female alternative to Take That and Boyzone. In Summer 1996 *Wannabe* became the most successful debut single ever made, selling over four million copies worldwide. Their first album, *Spice*, sold 12 million and their next three singles, *Say You'll Be There*, *Two Becomes One* and *Mama* topped the UK charts. Geri's chutzpah sells the group.

Hamilton, Paula, 23rd January 1961, fragile beauty. This complex, creative creature achieved instant fame in 1987. She played the jilted lover in the VW commercial who threw away the ring and fur coat but kept the Golf GTi. She has rather reversed the ad rôle in her private life. "Men are attracted to this colourful, free, rebellious woman. But as soon as I fall for them they want to change me." It happened with cameraman Danny Mindel, to whom she was married for three years, and her 1994 fiancé, Old Etonian film director Henry Cole.

Paula only discovered that she was a love-child when she was 13. She spent her early childhood in South Africa before settling in Chalfont St Peter, Buckinghamshire. Dyslexia meant she was unable to read or write until she was 11. She left her private school at 15 and drifted into modelling. Her first job, posing in swimwear at a Spanish villa, proved to be a con. The photographer forced her to do nude shots which were republished after she became famous.

As an impressionable teenage cover-girl earning £1,000 a day Paula soon became an active participant in the jet-set world. But her growing addiction to alcohol and cocaine destroyed her marriage and nearly her career. She underwent treatment at four rehabilitation centres here and in America. To prove that she wasn't a "brainless bimbo model" she co-founded the elephant charity, Tusk Force. But she had to resign following a drunken relapse in a London taxi when she spent the night in a police cell and was charged with criminal damage. She finally "dried out" in a Florida recovery centre in 1991. Today she religiously attends Alcoholics Anonymous meetings. "Sometimes the thought pops into my head that it would be nice to have a shandy down by the river, but then I remember where that shandy could lead me."

Paula lives with her West Highland terrier Titchy Piglet T-Pot in Brixton. She hopes to become the new Julie Christie, but her film debut in *Mad Dogs and Englishmen* was panned. She has reached that dangerous stage of merely being famous for being famous.

Hampshire, Susan, 12th May 1937, goody two-shoes actress. Telly zealots revere her as gentle Fleur in the award-winning Sixties serial *The Forsyte Saga*. When contemporaries were playing bed-hopping dolly birds on screen she earned her acting spurs on the stage.

She appeared in classics like *The Ginger Man*, *A Doll's House*, and *Miss Julie*. The image was always twinset and pearls and soft perms – perish the thought of mini-skirts, kinky boots and beehive hairstyles. She was the nation's favourite older sister.

Susan made her film debut aged ten opposite Jean Simmons in *The Woman In The Hall*. She then went to ballet school and spent a year with the Festival Ballet. During school holidays she partnered clod-hopping Hooray Henries at her mother's Knightsbridge dancing academy. When she grew too tall for ballet she switched to acting. At 22 she was the leading lady in a West End musical, *Expresso Bongo*, and on television played Andromeda in the cult BBC sci-fi series, *The Andromeda Breakthrough*. *The Forsyte Saga* was followed by Fleur-clone rôles in *The First Churchills* and *The Pallisers*. Although she has made countless films and stage appearances (notably in the musical *The King and I*) she has never quite managed to repeat those early glories.

This saccharine actress was first married in 1967 to French film director Pierre Granier-Deferre. They had a son, Christopher, but divorced in 1974. She then went into a delayed-rebellion mode. Hunky actor Nicky Henson became her toy boy and she took to wearing black catsuits and roaring around Chelsea on the back of his Harley-Davidson. When they broke up she surprised her friends by marrying bear-like Greek shipowner and theatrical impresario Sir Eddie Kulukundis in 1981. Her book, *The Maternal Instinct*, tells how she made a pilgrimage to Lourdes to pray for another child. Recent Lloyd's losses have forced her to work with renewed vigour, taking the lead in ITV's hotel drama series, *The Grand*. She is also a bestselling gardening author and president of the Dyslexia Institute.

Hanover, The Prince of, 26th February 1954, wacky European potentate. A prince of Great Britain and Ireland he is head of the Royal House of Hanover which ruled Britain during the 18th century. If Germanic rules of succession prevailed here he would be King today: Salic law ordains that the throne cannot pass through the female line and therefore Victoria could never have become Queen.

Hugely wealthy and very generous Ernst has a family seat, Schloss Marienburg, outside Hanover. Euro-royals and aristos flock to his lavish parties where liveried servants serve champagne by the magnum. He hosted one where guests came dressed in nappies and drank cocktails from bottles with teats. With characteristic vigour he is fighting for the restoration of his family estates and castles confiscated by East Germany after the war. Based in a Fulham mansion, he could also petition the House of Lords to have his title Duke of Cumberland and Teviotdale restored after its forfeiture during

World War I.

The suave, very private Ernst is the great-great-grandson of the last King of Hanover, blind King Georg, who lost his throne in 1866. Ernst succeeded his father in 1987. His mother is the grandly-titled Princess Ortrud of Schleswig-Holstein-Sonderburg-Glucksburg. He had a wide education, first at Box Hill in Surrey, then Salem in Germany, the University of Guelph near Lake Ontario and Cirencester Royal Agricultural College. During the Seventies he was an energetic Lothario on the London scene and dabbled with film-making. "He was great, great fun in a racy, somewhat childish way – he never stopped!", a contemporary recalls.

In 1981 the boar-hunting Prince surprised royal matchmakers by marrying a commoner, Swiss architect's daughter Chantal Hochuli. Beautiful, clever and mischievous, she has given him two sons, Prince Ernst and Prince Christian. In 1996 rumours started about his growing friendship with Princess Caroline of Monaco. They were spotted on holiday in Thailand and Burma, although her office later explained it was "just a cultural trip".

Hanson, Robert, 3rd October 1960, bachelor magnifico. Heir to an estimated £50 million fortune, this tall, immaculately-dressed Old Etonian could become the Rocco Forte of his generation. He is already a director of Hanson plc, the industrial colossus founded by his father, Lord Hanson, in 1965. But his social life and unending selection of nubile women keep him equally busy, much to the amusement of White's Club cronies. Once he was driving down the M4 to a wedding in Wales when his companion, American model Normandie Keith, suddenly realised she had forgotten her dress. He reached for his carphone and arranged for it to be flown down to their destination by helicopter.

This non-academic playboy was an undergraduate at St Peter's College, one of Oxford's more obscure colleges. He compensated for it with his tireless membership of the Assassins, an exclusive dining-club famed for its well-heeled members and riotous dinners. In 1982 he was bound over to keep the peace by Thame magistrates after one of their celebrations ended in a local restaurant being wrecked.

Hanson is a legendary Romeo. His former loves include PR-girl Jenny Halpern, Lord Braybrooke's daughter Cazzy Neville, model Brenda Schad and playgirl Tara Palmer-Tomkinson. His relationship with American heiress Normandie Keith lasted a lengthy (for him) two years but ended in 1995 because of his reluctance to make a commitment.

Former Rothschild trainee Hanson has a flat overlooking the Thames in Cheyne Walk and a £3 million country pad in the

Cotswolds where he hosts jazzy house parties. Contemporaries still sneer that "if he hadn't been his father's son, Robert might be selling shirts at Hackett."

Harry, Prince, 15th September 1984, third in line to the throne. "Great! We've almost got a full polo team!" enthused Prince Charles on the birth of his second son. From the age of five he has followed in the footsteps of Prince William, first to Mrs Mynors's kindergarten and then to Wetherby School, experiencing for the first time mass media attention. "Harry is a real flirt, absolutely charming and great fun", says an insider. But the death of his mother, Diana Princess of Wales, a fortnight before his 13th birthday, put a huge damper on his spirits.

Cheekier and more extrovert than William, Harry proved to be a plucky sportsman at prep school, Ludgrove. He is also a daredevil on the ski-slopes at Klosters. But his lack of academic progress led to fears that he might be dyslexic. If he is unable to pass the stiff Eton entrance exam he will probably go to Radley or Charterhouse. Diana's hopes that sensitive Harry would become the first royal to abstain from bloodsports seem to have been dashed. He is already an enthusiastic shot on the royal estates at Sandringham and Balmoral. Hopefully he will be able to choose his own further education. A course at Cirencester Royal Agricultural College would equip him to become a landowner, with an estate later kindly supplied by the Queen.

Providing William stays healthy Harry will be able to enjoy the 21st century while being spared most of the traditional royal commitments. Gossip persists that he bears a striking resemblance to dashing former Cavalry officer James Hewitt. But his birth happened over a year before Princess Diana began their affair and the supposedly telltale red hair is a family characteristic shared by her brother Earl Spencer and sister Lady Sarah McCorquodale.

Haslam, Nicholas, 27th September 1939, Society decorator. A late developer, he sincerely wants to be the new John Fowler. He specialises in the rich dowager market, but nostalgic Sloanes and the aspirational newly-rich also vie for his services. His trademark "faded *nouveau pauvre* look" has developed from Seventies gimmickry.

Cousin of the Earl of Bessborough and grandson of a former Mayor of Bolton, chain-smoking Haslam was once described as "a blend of Liberace and Danny La Rue". He startled fellow Etonians at 16 by decorating his room with tiger-skin curtains and ostrich-plume pelmets. As a budding designer he once arrived at a fancy dress ball clad in black body-paint and festooned with ropes of pearls. Black leather became his uniform and he used to tinge his prematurely silver hair with pink. Under the pseudonym Paul Parsons he once wrote a bitchy gossip column for *Ritz* newspaper. An early protégé of his was Princess Margaret's former lover, Roddy Llewellyn.

This laid-back, convivial bachelor has designed for Charles Saatchi and Bryan Ferry and is in great demand as a black-tie "walker". He lives in a tiny South Kensington flat and at his exquisite National Trust property, the Hunting Lodge in Hampshire, where he dotes on his three Pekineses. He has never allowed a lack of business acumen to interfere with his flamboyant lifestyle. His legendary parties combine the best of Café Society with the trendiest aristos. For his 40th birthday he gave a ball *"en tenue de chasse"*. Among the 450 guests was the venerable Lady Diana Cooper carrying a huge bow and quiverful of arrows. Another year he threw a purple dinner-party, with every course dyed purple and the men in purple satin shorts. "Well, you're only middle-aged once."

Havers, Nigel, 6th November 1952, gentleman player. With his chiselled Greek god looks, he was a mini-Tom Cruise in the Eighties, playing heroic figures. It began with the Oscar-winning *Chariots of Fire* – he still won't reveal how many champagne glasses he spilt during the garden party hurdling scene. He was in David Lean's *A Passage To India* and Steven Spielberg's *Empire of The Sun*. Younger actors like Ralph Fiennes and Hugh Grant almost buried him in the early-Nineties. Even his rôle as a Battle of Britain pilot in *A Perfect Hero* bombed. But he rallied in the BBC1 drama *The Heart Surgeon*, in which he was an adulterous cardiologist. It even shamed him into giving up smoking!

Havers can trace his lineage back to a 15th century East Anglian duke's equerry. His father, Lord Havers, was Mrs Thatcher's Lord Chancellor and Attorney General, his aunt is Lord Justice Butler-Sloss and his grandfather Sir Cecil Havers was a judge. He went to boarding-school at six and then turned down Eton to study drama at the Arts Educational School. At 16 he joined the cast of R4's *Mrs Dale's Diary* and then worked as a researcher booking guests for R2's *The Jimmy Young Show*. On stage he appeared in *Richard II*, *Conduct Unbecoming* and Alan Ayckbourn's *Season's Greetings*. But it was the title rôle in the TV series *Nicholas Nickleby* that launched him. He displayed a talent for playing effete English aristos in the TV series *Upstairs, Downstairs* and *The Glittering Prizes*. But he received most fan mail for his title rôle in *The Charmer*.

The old smoothie met his first wife Caro after double-crossing a chum who asked if he could look after his girlfriend for the evening. He so bewitched her that they ran off together and married in 1974. They had a daughter, Kate. But then he fell in love with former model Polly Bloomfield who became his second wife in 1989. They live in Barnes.

Helvin, Marie, 13th August 1952, Britain's first supermodel. This delicate-looking Siamese pussy-cat has a remarkable ability to keep re-inventing herself every decade. During the Seventies she and her photographer husband David Bailey were the golden couple of British fashion. He was less fat in those days, thanks to her insistence on a macrobiotic, low-booze diet. In the Eighties she split up with Bailey (never "David") and diversified into television and writing. She presented ITV's *Frocks On The Box* with Muriel Gray, wrote for *The Independent* and compiled a self-help guide to modelling. She continued on the catwalk, modelling for Armani, St Laurent, Valentino, Lagerfeld and Calvin Klein. Her Nineties have all been about health and exercise videos, capitalising on the fact she is over 40 and looks ten years younger. She ascribes this to "a very healthy sex life", plus 20 vitamins a day, yoga, champagne and no red meat.

Canny Marie has posed for nearly every top photographer from Helmut Newton to Barry Lategan She comes from a wealthy Hawaiian family and keeps a home near Honolulu. She owes her exotic looks to her Danish-American father and Japanese mother. She first modelled in Tokyo and came to London when she was 19. She met Bailey on a plane, flying back from a job in Paris. He raced royal photographer Lord Lichfield to sit in the empty seat beside her. In 1975 she became the third Mrs Bailey, following French actress Catherine Deneuve. They lived in chaotic splendour, sharing his North London house with an Old English sheepdog, three cats and 25 parrots. They divorced in 1985 and she settled with her two cats in a minimalist flat in Pimlico. Discreet and discerning, her great love was writer-explorer Mark Shand, Camilla Parker Bowles's macho brother. Ironically, Princess Diana's boyfriend Dodi Fayed was another ex.

Hempel, Anouska, 13th December 1941, social-climbing hostess and hotelier. With her Brigitte Bardot looks, guile, cheek and limitless ambition, how could Anouska fail? Of Russian-German ancestry she arrived in Britain from Australia in 1962 with £10 in her backpack. Two years later she married journalist turned property developer Constantine Hempel. He died in a car crash in 1973, leaving her with two young children, Julian and Sasha, and a run-down South Kensington b&b. She transformed it into Blake's Hotel, which became a much-admired celebrity haunt.

It is easy to embarrass Anouska – born Ann Geissler – who takes herself very seriously. Never mention her shortlived acting career. It included the X-rated film *Slaves*, *The Scars of Dracula* and her appearance as Lust in *The Magnificent Seven Deadly Sins*. It peaked as a Bond girl in *On Her Majesty's Secret Service*. She is also ashamed of her whirlwind 1978 marriage to *Coronation Street* actor turned impresario Bill Kenwright – "not grand enough".

But this petite *dictatrice* has found her match in insurance tycoon Sir Mark Weinberg who takes no nonsense from anybody. They married in 1980 and have a teenage son Jonathan. In 1986 he encouraged her to diversify by launching her own range of couture clothes. Ten years later, backed by Japanese investors, she launched the minimalist Hempel Hotel and was ridiculed for trying to re-name Craven Hill Gardens, Hempel Garden Square.

The Weinbergs are tireless hosts, in both their London and Wiltshire mansions. Guests are mainly chosen for their social credentials, with Princess Margaret an old favourite. Pretentious, tireless and talented, Anouska should learn to relax. Even close friends are puzzled why such a stunning-looking woman should feel the need to lop six years off her age.

Henman, Tim, 6th September 1974, shy Superman. The first Briton to reach the Wimbledon men's quarter-finals for 23 years, he also won a silver medal in the Olympic men's doubles. This nonchalant six footer quickly learned to accept all the attention being showered upon him, behaving with dignity and gentlemanliness. His "Mr Cool" image has only been dented once when in a fit of pique he accidentally hit a ball-girl with a ball during Wimbledon 1995 and was disqualified.

Aged three Henman was already playing tennis on the family court with his solicitor father and costume-designer mother. His grandfather Henry Bellingham regularly competed at Wimbledon in the early Fifties. Tim was trained from the age of 11 by David Lloyd, winning the national under-18 singles and doubles in 1992. He left Reeds School, Cobham with 10 GCSEs and in 1994 joined the Davis Cup squad. He became British champion in 1996, surprising even the most hard-bitten commentators. After his early-1997 victories in Qatar and Sydney his singles ranking rose from 25 to 14. Tennis buffs noted that this was just three points away from the highest ever placing by a British man since Roger Taylor.

Clean-cut, blue-eyed "Henners" is a marketing executive's dream:

handsome and articulate, magnanimous in victory, self-effacing in defeat. These qualities attract some £1 million a year from sponsors like Adidas sportswear, Slazenger racquets, Kellogg's Sustain and the Midland Bank. But one misery-guts labelled him "a robot with a key in its back". Bjorn Borg is his idol.

Iron-willed, foible-free Henman lives in Chiswick. He met his girl-friend, Hampshire surgeon's daughter Lucy Heald when she was working on a C4 sports documentary in 1996. He would like to become another Fred Perry but is fearful he will prove yet another false British dawn, like Buster Mottram and John Lloyd.

Henry, Lenny, 29th August 1958, Dudley's best export since coal. This 6ft 4ins black genius is Britain's answer to Bill Cosby and Eddie Murphy. He can do impressions, tell jokes, sing, dance and even be a straight actor. Hollywood, Broadway, Las Vegas here we come! Yet something prevents him leaving the safe old BBC. But should his ego needs massaging he can always drop into the National Portrait Gallery and admire his portrait.

He was born Lenworth George Henry in the West Midlands. His Jamaican-born father Winston worked for British Leyland and his mother Winifred was a hospital cook. He first found that he could make people laugh as a slightly overweight pupil at Bluecoat Secondary Modern School, where he was nicknamed "the Suntanned Kid". He did Elvis Presley impressions and mimicked his class-mates which stopped him being bullied.

Lenny left school at 16 to be an apprentice engineer. In 1975 he won ITV's *New Faces* talent contest and became a stand-up comic on the Northern club circuit. The BBC's *Black and White Minstrel Show* hired him as their first genuinely black member. ("I got loads of stick and racist remarks.")

Henry was a manic host of *Tiswas* and its adult offspring, *OTT*, and starred opposite Tracey Ullman and David Copperfield in *Three of a Kind*. In 1981 he began *The Lenny Henry Show*, inventing char-acters like PC Ganja, the Rastafarian community police officer, and the streetwise Delroy. Its four series, together with *Lenny Henry Tonight*, made his reputation as a loveable, mainstream comic who was neither lewd nor unkind. In 1987 he became the ever-smiling face of *Comic Relief*, with its infuriating Red Nose days!

Henry's portrayal of the temperamental chef Gareth Blackstock in the BBC1 comedy series *Chef!* has fully occupied him since 1992. The right next career move is a topic often discussed at Château Henry – the converted farmhouse near Reading which he shares with his wife since 1984, comedienne Dawn French, and adopted daughter Billie.

Henshall, Ruthie, 7th March 1967, West End skylark. In the cut-throat showbiz world it is no drawback to have had a royal love affair. During the early Nineties she was linked with Prince Edward although she was too much of a lady to reveal its platonic nature. She handled the "Prince and the Showgirl" publicity with self-assured aplomb. But you would expect this from the daughter of David Henshall, a former *Evening Standard* executive editor.

Youngest of four daughters, Ruthie grew up in suburban Bromley, Kent. She was determined to go on stage and took ballet lessons after school. At 21 she was performing in the West End chorus line and won her big break in Andrew Lloyd Webber's hit musical *Cats*. She took singing lessons and found her vocal abilities matched her dancing. She won the lead in the musicals *Crazy For You*, *She Loves Me* and *Oliver*. In 1997 she toured Britain giving sell-out concerts.

This slender, 5ft 4ins former waitress keeps a humidifier beside her bed at home in Surrey to keep her vocal chords moist. She describes herself as typically Piscean: "artistic, very loving, very giving". She has had a long engagement to TV star John Gordon Sinclair, her co-star in *She Loves Me*. He towers nearly a foot over her. After their marriage she hopes to have "two or three children". Has she told him there are twins in her family? She is a poor sleeper and once slept-walked into her kitchen instead of the loo, with embarrassing consequences.

Heseltine, Michael, 21st March 1933, Prime Minister who never was. "Tarzan" enjoys the life of a country grandee at his 18th century Northamptonshire mansion surrounded by a 400-acre estate that squawks with his prized waterfowl. Forget politics, he wants to be remembered for planting Britain's greatest arboretum.

Heseltine, aka Goldilocks and Michael Philistine, was born in Swansea. His father was a structural engineer and his grandfather a coal-merchant. As a first-generation public schoolboy (Shrewsbury) he found the smart set at Oxford hard to infiltrate. But his passionate oratory and determined networking eventually helped him to become President of the Union. He was said to have sketched out on a napkin his future political career, ending with "prime minister".

The would-be politician invested a small legacy in a run-down Notting Hill boarding-house. Within five years he owned a Bayswater hotel and property in South Kensington and was being driven around by a chauffeur. He also co-founded Haymarket Press, a publisher of technical and trade magazines that would eventually be worth £120 million.

Military service briefly interrupted Heseltine's money-grubbing but cannily he was able to resign his commission from the Welsh Guards early in order to stand for Parliament. He won Tavistock for the Tories in 1966. Over the next 30 years he climbed the slippery pole under Ted Heath, Margaret Thatcher and John Major, even though none of them entirely trusted him. He was too sleek, ambitious and vain. Nonetheless he became Environment Secretary, Defence Secretary, President of the Board of Trade and Deputy Prime Minister. He resigned from the government over the Westland affair in 1986 and four years later stood against Mrs Thatcher in the 1990 leadership contest. A heart attack on holiday in Venice revealed he was actually human.

"Hezza" has been married since 1962 to the huntin' and art-lovin' Anne and has three children: Annabel, Alexandra and Rupert. His name was once closely linked with the Countess of Shelburne, but, despite his handsome features and aura of power, journalists have never caught him straying. "He's a classic example of 'PGL' (pointless good looks) – not remotely sexy", observed one Tory lady.

Hewitt, James, 17th January 1958, bounder and cad. This handsome former Cavalry officer is nicknamed "Red Setter". It refers not only to his russet hair but to his powerful ability to sniff out vulnerable women. This brilliant horseman and boulevardier could melt the heart of the iciest ice-maiden. But conquest is for him always more fun than the actual relationship.

Hewitt infiltrated the royal circle when he gave the horse-shy Diana riding lessons. As her marriage to Prince Charles crumbled he became her confidante. He claims she seduced him after dinner at Kensington Palace. He would visit her at Highgrove when Charles was away and sometimes invited her for the weekend to his mother's remote cottage in Devon. Diana would even help with the washing-up there. In her 1995 *Panorama* interview she admitted that she had "loved and adored him". She also told friends that she had "decked him out from top to toe" at Turnbull & Asser.

The lovers were parted while this fearless, Millfield-educated stud served as a tank commander during the Gulf War. The Princess wrote to him almost daily. He will never be able to sell those letters because her estate holds the copyright. But he had no qualms in 1994 from revealing the secrets of their five-year romance by co-operating with Anna Pasternak's bestseller, *A Princess In Love.*

Hewitt has all the appearance of a gentleman without actually being one. His mother ran a riding school which paid for his fees at Millfield and Sandhurst. He joined the Life Guards even though he lacked the private income that defrayed his brother officers' polo ponies, tailor's bills and entertaining. Despite an Errol Flynn tally of beautiful blondes – they include polo-playing singer Maggie Moone and TV announcer Sally Faber – he has always preferred to live with his mother. They have an impressive manor house in Devon, bought from the proceeds of his royal disclosures.

Hill, Damon, 17th September 1960, racetrack wizard. He has the coolness of James Bond, the dark satanic looks of Chris de Burgh and the ambition of Juan Fangio. But success was late in coming. Compared to James Hunt, who was 29 when he became world motor-racing champion in 1976, Hill was 36 when he finally beat arch-rival Michael Schumacher. Although he describes racing as "a bit like drug addiction" he plans to retire by 40.

This terribly serious former despatch rider has always carried the extra baggage of his late father. The glamorous extrovert Graham Hill was twice world champion in the Sixties but died in a plane crash in 1975. "My father didn't want me to become a racing-driver. He said I was too intelligent!" Damon – he hates his Christian name – was brought up in St Albans and went to nearby Haberdashers Aske School. He started a polytechnic business degree but left after a year to race motorbikes. He became a Formula One test-driver for the Williams team before starting in Formula Four. Fellow drivers nicknamed him "Secret Squirrel" because he was so buttoned-up. He entered his first Formula One race at Silverstone in 1992 and the following year won the Hungarian, Belgian and Italian Grand Prix. After winning the world championship in 1996 he was horrified when racing team boss Frank Williams dumped him.

Hill is very family-minded and unflash. In 1994 he chose to live in tax exile near Dublin rather than join other Formula One champs in the warmer, more congested climes of Monte Carlo. He met his wife, former fashion designer Georgie, at a Bonfire Night party and married her in 1988. They have three children, Oliver, who was born with Down's Syndrome, Josh and Tabitha. His relaxation is singing Elvis Presley songs very loudly, accompanying himself on his classic 1968 Gibson guitar. His bravery and persistence finally triumphed, but he lacks the charisma to become a true British hero.

Hirst, Damien, 17th June 1965, genius or conman? This greasy-haired controversialist delights in his notoriety. He has earned a £1 million fortune from exhibiting the carcasses of sheep, cows and rats preserved in tanks of formaldehyde. Not to mention a 14-foot shark entitled *The Physical Impossibility of Death in the Mind of*

Someone Living. He has become the Andy Warhol of his generation, as assiduous in cultivating his publicity as his melancholy art.

The wild-eyed, gregarious *bon viveur* first attracted attention when he was runner-up in the 1992 Turner Prize with that pickled shark. Three years later he came first, with a cow and a calf sliced in half in two tanks. "I haven't killed anything for art. If I hadn't taken these animals for exhibits they would have ended up as dog food."

Hirst was born Damien Brennan, the result of a brief affair his mother had with a photographer while working as a secretary in Jersey. In 1966 she married a secondhand car salesman who adopted him. He went to a Catholic school and was brought up in a Leeds semi. "Damien was a lovely little boy who was always messing around with paints. He only started doing all those weird things when his parents split up and he found out he was illegitimate," a relative explains.

Equipped with an E in A-level art and lots of chutzpah, he was rejected by St Martin's School of Art. He worked on building sites for two years and in 1986 was accepted by the Goldsmith's School. His originality and marketing genius drew him to the attention of art-loving adman Charles Saatchi who exhibited him at his St John's Wood gallery and at the Tate Gallery. With price tags of up to £150,000 Hirst was soon able to swap his 14th floor tower-block flat in Rotherhithe for a Covent Garden flat. He has a son, Connor, from his girlfriend, Californian jewellery designer Maia Norman, whom friends describe as "pure *Baywatch*".

Hislop, Ian, 13th July 1960, national jokesmith. This quick-witted, multi-creative iconoclast is in danger of becoming the Alan Coren of his generation. Television, radio, Fleet Street and publishers constantly call upon his services for clever, soundbite humour. Yet former colleagues refer to him as "a pushy little midget" and "a balding, pug-faced fogey" who has 'sold out'.

Hislop, a Scottish civil engineer's son, was head boy at Ardingly. As an undergraduate studying English he appeared in satirical revues with the Oxford University Dramatic Society. He founded a self-indulgently witty magazine called *Passing Wind*. After interviewing *Private Eye* editor Richard Ingrams he was offered a job. But first he spent a year teaching at a South Kensington crammer. He joined the *Eye* full-time, mainly contributing to the jokes section. After two years Ingrams took a rare holiday and made him 'guest editor' ("more in a spirit of mischief than anything else"). In 1986 Ingrams unexpectedly announced his retirement at Auberon Waugh's leaving lunch. The appointment of his protégé as successor infuriated resident gossip-mongers Nigel Dempster and Peter

McKay. The latter likened it to "the Archbishop of Canterbury passing on his job to a 24-year-old."

The "evil Eye" now lacks the bitchiness, cruelty and vindictiveness
of the previous regime. There is less public school humour, investiga-
tive journalism or controversy. ("Ian lacks fire in his belly", one critic
says). After losing a rare libel action brought by the Yorkshire
Ripper's wife he complained: "If this is justice, I'm a banana."
Lacking Ingrams' private income the ambitious Hislop has always
moonlighted as a comedy scriptwriter, working with Maureen
Lipman, Harry Enfield and *Spitting Image*. He is a popular TV performer. BBC2's *Have I Got News For You* thrives on his ingenious ad
libs, bad puns and mental dexterity. He even has an unexpected
pious side, presenting the C4 religious series, *Canterbury Tales* and
delivering R4's Lenten address.

Hislop grows increasingly Establishment. He lives with his wife
Victoria in Clapham and has a country retreat in Somerset. They
send their children, Emily and William, to private schools.

Hockney, David, 9th July 1937, Pop Art Leonardo with a touch of
Picasso. With Francis Bacon dead, this quirky Bradford legend unas-
sailably became our greatest living painter. So it can only be because
he has spent the last 30 years living in California that he remains
unknighted. Mr Blair should honour this prolific, wise old owl of
British art.

Audit clerk's son Hockney went to Bradford College of Art and the
Royal College of Art, where he won a gold medal for life drawing.
Mayfair dealer John Kasmin 'discovered' him and held his first one-
man show in 1963. Hockney has since exhibited at nearly every
major gallery, including the Tate, the Hayward, the Louvre and the
Museum of Modern Art in New York. He has designed operatic sets
and costumes for Covent Garden, Glyndebourne, La Scala and the
Met, illustrated Grimm's fairy tales and Langan's Brasserie menus.
He was one of the first public figures to "out" themselves as gay, but
lacks a permanent soul mate.

Hockney's early work – lonely vases of yellow tulips, naked boys
on unmade beds and stark windowscapes – dominated the Sixties
art movement. His canvas *A Bigger Splash* made the same dramatic
impact as Andy Warhol's soup tins. Yet his work was the antithesis
of the abstract art then so fashionable. After suffering from
"painter's block" he entered a less satisfactory experimental period
in the Eighties with photographic collages in the Cubist manner and
images created by photocopiers, faxes and computers. He lives in Los
Angeles, where he finds the sunlight invigorates him and his canvas-
es. He deserted Britain in 1964, because he found it "boring and

stultifying, weighed down by bureaucracy and philistinism". But he misses his octogenarian mother, a down-to-earth Yorkshirewoman, who has always had a strong influence over him.

This flamboyant bachelor has aged considerably in recent years and suffers from deafness. He now resembles a slightly frail, absent-minded professor.

Hodge, Patricia, 29th September 1946, quintessential Noel Coward heroine. Despite her cut-glass English accent Patricia – never Pat – grew up on Humberside and went to Wintringham Girls' Grammar School. Her parents ran the Grand Hotel, Grimsby, but Patricia was largely raised by her stern grandmother in Cleethorpes. "She put the fear of God in me. Every time they visited I used to cry: 'please take me back with you.'" Consequently, with her own children, she has tried to be at home during the daytime, sacrificing plum TV and film rôles in favour of the theatre.

Beneath that elegant, haughty exterior, LAMDA-trained Patricia has a bawdy sense of humour and generous spirit. She has been married since 1976 to music publisher Peter Owen, 15 years her senior. Their first child Alexander was born when she was 42 and the second, Edward, at 44. She describes the births, after years of trying, as "a miracle". "Having children has freed all sorts of emotions within me as an actress." They live in a Barnes house straight out of *World of Interiors*, with no need of a nanny because Owen acts as house-husband.

As an actress Patricia will never go hungry. She made her name on TV: as Leo McKern's plummy barrister pal in *Rumpole of the Bailey*, as a bestselling author in *The Life and Loves of a She Devil* and as the eponymous TV presenter/detective, Jemima Shore. On stage she is best-known for *The Mitford Girls*, *Noel and Gertie*, *Separate Tables* and *The Prime of Miss Jean Brodie*. She will gradually develop into a delicious stage *grande dame* like Edith Evans.

Holm, Ian, 12th September 1931, the actor's actor. Critics compared his 1997 *King Lear* at the National Theatre to Lord Olivier's. His triumph followed his return to the stage after he "dried" during a preview of Eugene O'Neill's *The Iceman Cometh* in 1976. He blamed a traumatic period in his personal life and an exhausting four months filming *Jesus of Nazareth* in the Tunisian desert.

Ian's father was a psychiatrist. After Chigwell Grammar School and RADA wee Ian's first rôle was the Fool opposite the legendary Sir Charles Lawton's Lear. He went on to become one of the leading classical actors of his generation, appearing with the RSC in rôles like Puck, Ariel, Richard III and Prince Hal. His award-winning portrayal of Lennie in Harold Pinter's *The Homecoming* transferred to Broadway in 1966. "Doing Pinter is far harder than all that 'Once more unto the breach' stuff. It's the discipline you need, the stillness, the focus." During his stage absence he established a new reputation, with films like *Alien*, *Chariots of Fire*, *Greystoke*, *Dance With a Stranger* and *The Madness of King George*. On TV he was Lech Walesa in *Strike*, the cuckolded classics master in *The Browning Version* and the careworn spy in *Game, Set and Match*. "Let's face it, if you dry while filming you can at least have another take!"

This stocky, 5ft 6ins scene-stealer has been married three times and has five children. He met his third wife, actress Penelope Wilton, when she appeared opposite him in *Laughterhouse*. They have acted together in two Pinter plays, *Landscape* and *Moonlight*, and in the TV series, *The Borrowers*. Their 1991 marriage played a crucial part in his recovery.

Holmes, Eamonn, 3rd December 1959, the housewives' choice. He is the man who restored the fortunes of GMTV. The station was being trounced in the ratings by C4's *The Big Breakfast* when he joined in 1993. It's so-called dream-ticket of Michael Wilson and Fiona Armstrong lacked the spontaneity and fun of Chris Evans and Gaby Roslin. But Holmes' friendly Irish charm and professionalism helped to recover its predecessor TV-am's healthy viewing figures.

Holmes had a long-running feud with his co-presenter Anthea Turner whom he nicknamed "Miss Tippy-Toes". He accused her of throwing off-screen tantrums and sulking. On one occasion he reduced her to tears after telling Noel Edmonds on air that her interviews were so dull they sent him to sleep. Eventually he threatened to resign, unless she left. Fortunately for him she grew tired of the early-morning starts and quit in 1996. He then signed a new three-year £1.5 million contract and enjoys a better relationship with her successor, Fiona Phillips.

This Ulster carpet-fitter's son had a strongly Catholic upbringing. Brought up in a council house he continued to share a bedroom with his younger brother until he was 26. By that time he was a 'face' on Irish television. He moved to the BBC in Manchester, presenting a programme called *Open Air*. In 1987 he married his childhood sweetheart Gabrielle whom he had begun dating at 16. They moved to a smart new home in the stockbroker suburb of Gatley. Marital problems arose when he joined GMTV and she refused to move to London. Instead, she insisted they buy a house near Belfast. For three years she and their three children, Declan, Rebecca and Niall only saw him at weekends. Alone all week at his Putney home, he began dating TV weather girl Ruth Langsford in 1996.

Hopkins, Sir Anthony, 31st December 1937, forever Hannibal Lecter. Not since Sir Laurence Olivier has an actor been able to submerge himself so brilliantly in different rôles. They range from the misogynist Oxford don CS Lewis in *Shadowlands* to the womanising artist in *Surviving Picasso*. Films like *The Bounty, 84 Charing Cross Road, The Silence of the Lambs* and *The Remains of the Day* have won him more prizes than any other living British actor. He was deservedly knighted in 1993.

Bullet-headed Hopkins grew up as an only child in working-class Port Talbot where he went to Cowbridge Grammar School. He still claims to be "a bundle of sweating Welsh neurosis" but it didn't stop him beating the system and being accepted by RADA. He was first known as a stage actor, making his debut in *Julius Caesar* at the Royal Court in 1964 and then moving to the National Theatre. He won glowing notices for *Juno and the Paycock, A Flea in Her Ear* and *The Three Sisters*. Post-Hollywood he returned to the theatre, winning awards for his portrayal of a megalomaniac media tycoon in *Pravda* and starring in the tragic musical *M Butterfly*. On Broadway he triumphed in *Equus* ('best actor' award) and *Old Times*.

Baker's son Hopkins used to be in the Richard Burton league of carousers. But actor John Stride warned him that "unless you stop drinking you'll end up in the gutter like the rest of them." Teetotal since 1975 he is a zealous Alcoholics Anonymous supporter. He has a daughter, Abigail, from his brief first marriage to Peta Barker. In 1973 he married Jenni Lynton, a production assistant on his film *When Eight Bells Toll*. She spends most of the year at their Kensington home while he lives quite modestly in California. In 1995 he had a fling with starlet Joyce Ingalls whom he met at AA. But he returned to Jenni, a born-again Christian. He admits he hates being tied down: "I'm a devious bag of trouble."

In 1996, after completing six films over 14 months, the exhausted superstar hired a Jeep and drove 5,000 miles all over America. "I just kept going, staying in motels, talking to the people I met in cafés. It was like a therapy. I became at ease with myself again."

Hucknall, Mick, 8th June 1960, pop stallion. He took the Rôd Stewart/Mick Jagger route to fame, becoming almost as notorious for his bedroom antics as hit records. He hung out in nightclubs with supermodels, went carousing with his Manchester United pals and showed an unshakable self-belief when in the recording-studio. But at 35 he began to show signs of bedroom fatigue. "My head and my body clock are giving me very definite signals – I want to settle into a long-term relationship and have children and a family life." With homes in Manchester, Weybridge, Milan and Miami he will have no shortage of nurseries.

This hyperactive former art student enjoys a close relationship with his father, a retired barber, who raised him single-handedly. His mother, a spirited Irish redhead who married four times, walked out of their Manchester home when he was just two years old. At Audenshaw Grammar School, Mick refused to do his homework and was regularly thrashed by a master with a cricket bat. He read fine art at Manchester Poly but spent four years on the dole before founding Simply Red, named after the colour of Man United's shorts. Their first No 1, *Money's Too Tight To Mention*, in 1985, led to a string of hit singles here and in America. They have had five multi-platinum albums and sold more than 30 million records worldwide. This mixture of soul, reggae and re-worked classics has earned him an estimated £25 million.

Dreadlocked Hucknall had a flingette with Sylvester Stallone's lofty ex-wife, Danish model Brigitte Nielsen. "She was my type, big and domineering. Her silicone breasts are very sexy." He has also dated singer Kim Wilde, supermodel Helena Christensen, tennis champion Steffi Graf and many models and Stringfellow's waitresses he would rather forget. He blames his short romantic timespan on his work. "You're forever moving from aeroplane to concert-hall to hotel-room." He sees himself as a "politically incorrect feminist": "the things I want from women are friendship, companionship and loads of sex!"

Humphries, Barry, 17th February 1934, a distinguished immigrant from the world's cultural armpit. This brilliant impersonator lifted the drag queen into new respectability. His egocentric, social-climbing, violet-haired Dame Edna Everage has become a national stereotype and will live on like Scarlett O'Hara and Ena Sharples. His other creation, the grossly offensive Oz cultural attaché Sir Les Patterson, panders more to pre-existing preconceptions.

Their alter ego is a prosperous Australian builder's son, a right-wing, art-loving bibliophile and reformed womaniser. His grandfather emigrated to Australia from Manchester in the 1880s. After attending posh Melbourne Grammar School and the University of Melbourne Barry became an actor. He moved to Pommie-land in 1959. He played Fagin in the West End musical *Oliver* and drew *Private Eye*'s Barry McKenzie strip cartoon. His party pieces around

"Kangaroo Valley" in Earl's Court led to the birth of Dame Edna in 1965. From guest appearances on TV variety shows the "housewife megastar from Moonie Ponds" graduated to one-woman shows, with titles like *A Night With Dame Edna* and *Last Night of the Poms*. Humphries blames the breakdown of his first two marriages on overwork, alcoholism and his eye for the Sheilas. But he has been a teetotaller and non-smoker for nearly 30 years now. From his first wife, actress Rosalind Tong, he has two daughters and from his second wife, artist Diane Millstead, two sons. In 1990 he married poet Sir Stephen Spender's daughter Lizzie, a writer 16 years his junior, and seems more settled.

Humphrys, John, 17th August 1943, Mr Verbal Punch-up. This early-morning scourge of politicoes resembles a Wild West gunslinger. His *Today* programme confrontations with government ministers and other heavyweights invariably set the daily news agenda.

Humphrys is the son of a French polisher and a hairdresser. He left Cardiff High School at 15 because he felt "duty-bound to help out the family financially". He wishes he had gone to university. He bears the scars of a lifetime's news hackery on his prematurely-aged face. White-haired and wiry he worked as BBC TV's Washington correspondent, Southern African correspondent and Diplomatic correspondent before landing the plum job of presenting BBC1's new-look *9 o'clock News* in 1981. Six years later he replaced John Timpson as co-presenter of *Today,* a baptism of fire since he was unused to live interviewing. He quickly learnt. He has also presented BBC1's *On The Record* and *You Decide.*

This cello-playing Rottweiler of the Airwaves can display a friendly aspect, appreciated by listeners to the "JY Prog" when he stands in for Jimmy Young. A farmyard fantasist, he bought a dairy farm in Pembrokeshire in 1981. "I was insane. I thought I could stand around watching the animals, but I actually just wrote a lot of cheques." The experiment failed, but he still retains a holiday cottage where he unwinds by going on long coastal walks.

Humphrys has two children, PR girl Catherine and cellist Christopher, from his 26-year marriage to his former childhood sweetheart Edna. "I was a dreadful husband, away for months on end as a BBC foreign correspondent, but a good provider."

Hunniford, Gloria, 10th April 1940, Queen of Blarney, nicknamed "Grievous Bodily Hunniford" by Terry Wogan. This twinkly, wholesome Belfast mother-of-three achieved stardom in the nick of time.

She was over 40 when she landed her first national radio series. In Northern Ireland her warm personality and witty professionalism was already apparent as presenter on local radio series like *A Taste of Hunni* and *Good Evening Ulster* on TV. In 1981 she deputised for Jimmy Young and her merry repartee and sexy badinage about wearing black silk stockings impressed R2 chiefs. Success meant a permanent move to London and the eventual break-up of her marriage to TV producer Don Keating in 1985.

Gloria was born in Portadown, Co Down, the daughter of a newspaper advertising manager and amateur magician. She left school at 17 to pursue a singing career in Canada. There she fell in love with a local boy, but just as she was about to lose her virginity she received a letter from her mother "warning me her not to misbehave". She was therefore "proud" to be able to wear a white wedding dress "without blushing" when she married Keating in 1962. By then she was a BBC production assistant in Belfast but still continuing to sing Irish ballads at private parties.

Today the Honeybun is a female Wogan, constantly popping up in TV light entertainment shows, usually a little over-dressed. She is a regular on the party scene: restaurant openings, premières and private views. As a sideline she models clothes for Littlewoods catalogues. But it is her sense of humour that keeps her in work.

Home is a £500,000 neo-Georgian mansion near Sevenoaks which she shares with her three dogs and a collection of Royal Doulton china. After a spell dating a toy boy she now lives with Mayfair hairdresser Stephen Way. She remains very close to her sons Michael and Paul and daughter TV presenter Caron Keating. With Gloria what you see is what you get.

Hurley, Elizabeth, 10th June 1965, *femme fatale* with attitude. She is one of Britain's most glamorous models, actresses and girlfriends. In Noel Coward's words she adroitly "uses sex as a shrimping-net". Yet despite her lustrous brown hair and pneumatic cleavage she has trouble proving she can act. Critics mauled *Samson and Delilah*, comparing her Delilah to an "an anaemic Jackie Bisset who preened and leered before the camera". They said worse things about her erotic thriller *Dangerous Ground*, in which she played a stripper.

If *Four Weddings and a Funeral* made Hugh Grant's career in 1994 it also kick-started Elizabeth's. She memorably stole its London première, arriving in a Gianni Versace gown held together with giant safety pins. They were soon Hollywood's most glamorous couple. She became the new face of Estée Lauder and alternated with Princess Diana on nearly every glossy magazine cover. Ambitiously she and Hugh set up their own production company,

called Simian Films "because I think Hugh looks like a chimpanzee".
Things began to go wrong in 1995 when Grant was arrested in
Hollywood for consorting with a prostitute. She loyally stood by him,
jeopardising her £3 million cosmetics contract which contained a
morality clause. Their first film, *Extreme Measures*, was a flop.

Despite her posh vowels Surrey-born Elizabeth went to a comprehensive school. She has one A-level in sociology. Known as "Hurley
Burly" she rebelled against her suburban background – father was
an army major and lived in Basingstoke – and became a punk, complete with holey fishnets and a nose-ring. She has always liked to
shock. She was a model when she met the equally unknown Grant
on a Spanish film-set in 1987. He encouraged her to try acting and
the next year she made a much-praised TV debut in Dennis Potter's
Christabel. Alas, she has never quite fulfilled that promise. She
received scalding reviews for *Mad Dogs and Englishmen, Aria* and
Passenger 57. But the 1997 spy spoof *Austin Powers: International
Man of Mystery* has helped to restore her credibility.

Grant put these setbacks into perspective: "We've been deep in the
bunker, me and Eva Braun." While filming and schmoozing they
have spent long periods apart. But bossy, chain-smoking Liz swears
she has always been faithful. "I'm not against marriage, only it's not
something that I see for myself in the near future."

Hurt, John, 22nd January 1940, tortured genius. He displays all
the character flaws of superstars Richard Harris and Peter O'Toole.
But, unlike them, he has never quite managed to conquer his boozing. He remains one of our finest actors. From movies like *Scandal*
and *Nineteen Eighty-Four* to children's TV series like *The Storyteller*
and the poignant *Journey to Knock* he invariably steals the notices.

This rumbustious, Cleethorpes-born son of an Anglican vicar was
educated at Lincoln School. "My parents didn't allow me to play with
boys they considered to be common – they were the only ones I really
liked!" After RADA he starred in seminal Sixties plays like Arnold
Wesker's *Chips With Everything* and John Osborne's *Inadmissible
Evidence*. He also co-starred in the films *A Man For All Seasons* and
10 Rillington Place,

But it was his showy TV rôles as the purple-rinsed poseur Quentin
Crisp in *The Naked Civil Servant* and the evil Caligula in *I,
Claudius* which first won him Hollywood recognition. He received
BAFTA awards for *Midnight Express* and *The Elephant Man* and
starred opposite Greta Scacchi in *White Mischief*.

Chain-smoking Hurt's tendency to enjoy life near the precipice is
etched on his creased face. It has embarrassed him in public and
damaged personal relationships. The irrepressible thespian

promised to go on the wagon in 1990 when he married his third wife, Jo Dalton, a production assistant whom he had met on the set of *Scandal*. They drank mineral water at their wedding and similarly toasted the arrival of their son Alexander a fortnight later. Yet soon afterwards he received a drink-driving ban for a year after crashing his Toyota Landcruiser into a Dublin lamppost.

This marriage broke up after five years and a second son, Nicholas. Hurt then briefly returned to his beautiful blonde second wife of six years, Donna Peacock, with whom he had lived in an idyllic £1 million Kenyan villa overlooking the Indian Ocean. Based in County Wexford, he has since enjoyed a series of girlfriends, including Dublin PR-girl Sarah Owens. A fourth wife? "Highly unlikely, but do you know what makes God laugh? People who make plans!"

Hytner, Nicholas, 7th May 1956, the Nineties' Peter Brook. By 40 he was already an acclaimed stage, opera and film director, being tipped as a future National Theatre or RSC supremo. His creative energy powered the hit musicals *Miss Saigon* and *Carousel* and the National's adaptation of *Wind In the Willows*. He directed Janacek's *Cunning Little Vixen* in Paris.

Hytner has none of the flamboyance and luvviness often associated with great directors. Slim, balding and undramatic in appearance, he can appear solemn. He commands with a rigorous intellect that insists on finding motivations for all his leading characters. The son of Benet Hytner QC, he went to Manchester Grammar School and Cambridge, where he directed undergraduate plays. He began his career in opera, working with Kent Opera and winning awards for his 1985 ENO production of *Xerxes*. The same year he became associate director of the Royal Exchange Theatre, Manchester, where he directed shows like *As You Like It* and *The Country Wife*.

In 1993 Hytner tried his hand at film-directing. His debut, adapting Alan Bennett's *The Madness of King George*, won four Oscar nominations, despite having few star names. He then directed another period piece, Arthur Miller's *The Crucible*, about the Salem witchcraft trials, starring Daniel Day-Lewis and Winona Rider. Critics praised his ability to reinvent a famous stage play for Hollywood without making it feel too stagey. "I just loving making movies. As a film-director you feel that what you eventually put before an audience contains more of you. But I never want to churn out mega-buck studio movies." After a four-year absence he returned to the National, directing *The Cripple of Inishmaan* at the National. He now keeps an apartment in New York where he is the Lincoln Center's associate director. A friend said of this single-minded bachelor: "If Nicholas had to marry to become US President, he would."

I

Irons, Jeremy, 19th September 1948, poseur superstar. That languid, pretentious manner sticks in many a craw. He claims to have accepted his lucrative baddie rôle in *Die Hard III* only in the interests of "broadening his audience". "You do a series of repertory plays you *know* they want to see and then slip in a Pinter or Ionesco hoping they will like that too."

Irons failed his A-levels at Sherborne because he was starring in the school play, but won a place at the Bristol Old Vic Theatre School. "You've got the right qualifications for acting, i.e none", murmured his accountant father. He played John the Baptist in the original West End production of *Godspell*. But, despite his consumptive Byronic looks and hypnotic voice, he had to slave away in minor rôles with the RSC until he was 33. "An actor must do theatre in order to build the right muscles", he observes. In 1981 he won the first of many romantic, brooding rôles in ITV's *Brideshead Revisited* and *The French Lieutenant's Woman*.

Irons married actress Sinead Cusack in 1978 following his divorce from actress Julie Hallam. Appropriately Sinead's first baby Sam was conceived when both were appearing in *Wild Oats*. She delicately broke the news while they were on stage, whispering: "Darling, I'm with child." He forgivably fluffed his next few lines! They now have a second son Max. "My husband is a great hoarder", she says. "He hates throwing things away, so I suspect I'll be around for a long time." They live in Oxfordshire and County Cork.

Irons won rave reviews on Broadway for Tom Stoppard's *The Real Thing* and in 1986 spent a year with the RSC at Stratford-upon-Avon. He has since won an Oscar for his portrayal of Claus von Bulow in *Reversal of Fortune* and further plaudits for Josephine Hart's tragic novel *Damage* and playing a near-corpse in Bertolucci's *Stealing Beauty*. The irony is that he fancies himself as an Olivier but producers rate him as a Redford.

Irvine of Lairg, Lord, 23rd June 1940, Labour's fairy godfather. A youthful Tony Blair first met fellow pupil Cherie Blair at Irvine's King's Bench Walk chambers. As a leading QC specialising in industrial tribunal work he could earn £15,000 to £20,000 a brief, plus £1,800-a-day 'refreshers'. Ironically on becoming Blair's Lord

Chancellor he attacked "fat cat lawyers" who earned up to £1 million a year. He has a key rôle advising the government on its controversial constitutional reforms. His plans to overhaul legal aid and civil justice are also likely to provoke m'learned friends. But "there's nothing Derry likes better than being in the thick of an intellectual battle".

This indefatigable, roof slater's son was educated at Inverness Academy and Hutchesons' Boys' Grammar School, Glasgow. He is said to have inherited his brilliance from his doting mother, a Lairg builder's daughter. He read law at Glasgow University and then at Cambridge where he won the university's top jurisprudence prize. At 37 he became Britain's youngest silk. A lifelong Labour supporter, he unsuccessfully stood for Parliament in Hendon North in 1970. As a reward for finding a legal way to oust Militant from the party Neil Kinnock recommended him for a life peerage in 1987.

A buffalo of a man, Irvine married Ayr butcher's daughter Margaret Veitch in 1962. Although married for 11 years, he curiously omits her from his *Who's Who* entry. Scottish Secretary Donald Dewar still bristles at how nearly three decades ago Irvine "stole" his wife Alison. The pair finally married in 1974 and have two sons David and Alistair. Both went to State schools because he believes private education is socially-divisive. His London home is filled with a valuable collection of 18th and 19th century British paintings. "He can drive a very hard bargain", reports a dealer. He has a 16-bedroomed Scottish mansion where he enjoys playing the Highland laird and entertaining friends with the finest malt whisky and claret. He is certainly a lot more human than his predecessor, Lord Mackay of Clashfern.

Izzard, Eddie, 7th February 1962, voted Britain's top stand-up comic and transvestite. In an age ruled by television he is remarkable for having built his audience mainly through his stage shows. His 1993 West End debut, *Live at the Ambassadors*, made his name. His performance is as uninhibitedly camp as Boy George and as outrageous as Danny La Rue. Yet he shares with Barry Humphries a solidly upper-middle-class background. His father was a high-powered BP accountant in the Middle East and its chief auditor before retiring to pukka Bexhill. His son only dared to reveal his cross-dressing secret when he was 23. "I can't say I was best pleased, but then what really was there to be displeased about? I looked at Eddie and realised: he's my son, I love him and this is who he is. There are so many worse things he could be."

Aden-born Izzard was sent to a Welsh boarding school aged six after his mother died of cancer. At Eastbourne College his early acting attempts were as third spear-carrier. "I was always too short or not good-looking enough." He failed to win a Cambridge place where he dreamed of joining the Footlights. Instead he went to Sheffield University, nominally to read accountancy, and devoted his time to writing, producing and acting. He dropped out after a year and took a student revue to the Edinburgh Fringe Festival. He spent the Eighties establishing himself as a stand-up comic on the comedy club circuit, often earning just £20 a night. But his superb timing and topical ad-libs were eventually rewarded with guest TV spots and one-woman shows.

Even in his butch jeans and leather jacket this beefy-looking Goon fan never entirely sloughs his female alter ego. The tell-tale make-up and nail varnish give him away. His threat one day to turn up at a Crystal Palace game wearing a frock, remains – for the moment at least – just a threat. No wonder he has trouble convincing journalists he is entirely heterosexual.

J

Jackson, Cindy, 30th June 1955, self-styled "bionic beauty". She floats around London's Café Society, a blonde vision of loveliness. Yet something jars slightly, something not quite natural. She is a human sandwich-board for cosmetic surgery. She has had almost every sinew of her magnificent body resculpted, from her nose, cheekbones and lips to her jawbone, breasts and bottom. Its purpose – to transform her into the glam lady that she wishes she had been born. "My new look is based on Leonardo da Vinci's theory of the classically-proportioned face." This relentless quest to reset nature's clock has cost her nearly £60,000. But her high social profile is helpful to the Cosmetic Surgery Network, an advisory service she founded in 1991.

This witty, outgoing pig farmer's daughter arrived in Britain as a 21-year-old art student from Cincinnati, Ohio. She studied at the Heatherley School of Art and became a rock singer, fronting a band called Joe Public before going solo. "I was kinda Blondie mixed with Suzi Quatro." She has had a string of broken romances. For 12 months she managed to keep up with that indefatigable partygoer, baronet-to-be Dai Llewellyn. Unfortunately she never quite managed to persuade him to undergo liposuction on his portly frame. In 1997 she romanced Alexander de Cadenet, a handsome toy boy 19 years her junior. She has already had three facelifts and has booked a fourth for 1998. "Before all the surgery, I couldn't find a man who'd treat me decently. No matter how I felt inside or who I was as a person I wasn't given the feedback that I craved for. But beautiful women are deferred to." At 60 will she resemble Zsa Zsa Gabor?

Jackson, Glenda, 9th May 1936, Oscar-winning MP. No actress has immersed herself so thoroughly in politics since Vanessa Redgrave. Indeed she sacrificed her acting career in 1992 to concentrate on her greatest role: as Labour MP for the chattering classes of Hampstead and Highgate. In 1997 Tony Blair appointed her junior Transport Minister, with special responsibility for the London Underground. Insiders already talk of promotion.

This cerebral, bricklayer's daughter has capitalised on her working-class, Merseyside background. It was particularly useful during the era of "kitchen sink" drama, when cut-glass accents were Out. It also helped her street-cred when she became one of former Labour leader Neil Kinnock's "luvvies-for-Labour" campaigners. Born in Birkenhead she went to West Kirby County Grammar School and then spent two years selling cough sweets and laxatives at Boots. She won a RADA place and became a member of the RSC for four years. Her intense stare, lank hair and stolid build have meant that she could never compete for glamour rôles. One critic described her as having "a face that could launch a thousand dredgers". This ordinariness, coupled with an ability to immerse herself in very different rôles, enabled her to stay constantly in work for 30 years. Her film credits range from *Women In Love*, *A Touch of Class* (both won her Oscars), *The Music Lovers*, *Sunday Bloody Sunday*, *Bequest To The Nation*, *The Romantic Englishman* and *The Rainbow*. But her reputation is solidly based in the legit theatre – Ibsen, Shakespeare, Marlowe, Chekhov.

At 22, honest, down-to-earth Glenda married theatre director Roy Hodges and had a son Daniel, who works as her parliamentary aide. They divorced in 1976 after she fell in love with lighting designer Andy Phillips on a world tour of *Hedda Gabler*. After this relationships ended she has kept a low profile romantically. Spinsterhood does not worry her. "If you fail the first time it's odds-on you're going to fail again." Ironically, she was in line to be a Dame before politics intervened.

Jackson, Michael, 11th February 1958, the Peter Pan of TV moguls. No sooner was this bouffant-haired bachelor appointed C4's new chief executive in 1997 than he was railing against his former employers. Its output suffered from being too middle-aged, masculine and southern-based, complained the former BBC1 and BBC2 controller. Ironically, he had recently described C4 as "the lager channel" because of its "obsessive desire to appeal to upwardly mobile young males". C4 programme director John Willis had retaliated by branding him "the copycat criminal of British television" who "cloned" C4 ideas. Jacko's more immediate problem is to dissuade the government from privatising his hugely profitable station.

Jackson is unusual as a senior TV executive because he does not come from a sophisticated metropolitan or Oxbridge background. He was brought up in Macclesfield where his father ran a long-established family bakery. As a child he claims to have spent hours poring over the *Radio Times* rearranging its TV schedules. "For people like me television brought the world right into our living-rooms and I was fascinated by exactly how that happened." After attending the local King's School he read media studies at the Central London Poly where he wrote a thesis on the urgent need for a radical, innovative, minority channel. At 21 he organised the Channel 4 Group which lobbied for independent production companies to play a key rôle when the new station finally began transmission in 1981. As an independent producer himself he made C4 programmes like *The Sixties*, *Open The Box* and *The Media Show*. The BBC head-hunted him in 1987 and he won awards for *The Late Show* and *Tales From Prague*. At 33 he became the Corporation's youngest ever department head, running music and arts. In 1993 he succeeded his mentor Alan Yentob as controller of BBC2, where he launched hit series like *Absolutely Fabulous*, *The X Files*, *Mrs Merton*, *Middlemarch* and the fly-on-the-wall Covent Garden documentary, *The House*.

As a workaholic, the phlegmatic Jackson has little time for relationships. A female colleague once described him as having "a melancholic, monastic air about him which women find irresistible".

Jagger, Mick, 26th July 1943, rock's grand ole daddy. The funky guitar riffs of *I Can't Get No Satisfaction*, have become pop's equivalent of the opening bars of Beethoven's Fifth Symphony. Such is the awe in which Jagger and the Rolling Stones are now held, it is hard to visualise that in the Sixties their loutish, foul-mouthed behaviour was worse than Liam and Noel Gallagher's.

The swivel-hipped possessor of what Joan Rivers described as "child-bearing lips", has always dominated the Stones, both physically and intellectually. Hits like *It's All Over Now*, *Little Red Rooster*, and *Jumping Jack Flash* depend so fundamentally on him that it is almost unfair to share the royalties. His screechy vocals and jerky antics are what sells their songs on stage and television.

The Stones first toured Britain over 30 years ago. Two of their first gigs were Bunty Lampson's coming-out dance in Hastings Caves and the Magdalen Commem Ball in 1963. Both were booked before the Stones became famous and paid less than £50. Today's tours earn over £70 million and are increasingly elaborate, with massive stage sets and sexy female dancers to distract from the Creaking Bones.

Educated at Dartford Grammar School and the LSE, this Kent PT instructor's son has always exaggerated his yobbish manner and Estuary accent. He is a frightful snob, enjoying hobnobbing with the Guinnesses in Ireland, stately house parties and what he once described as "upper-crust crumpet". The Earl of Lichfield was best man when he married Nicaraguan-born Bianca in St Tropez in 1971. Cannily he insisted on her signing a pre-nuptial agreement. The marriage lasted eight years and their daughter Jade has already made him a grandfather twice.

The list of Jagger ex-girlfriends include Marianne Faithfull, heiresses Sabrina Guinness, Natasha Fraser and Cornelia Guest, and sundry starlets, models and waitresses. He has a daughter Karis from his fling with Sixties actress Marsha Hunt. In 1990 he finally married lofty Texan model Jerry Hall after they had spent over ten years together.

Despite his well-publicised dalliances with actress Uma Thurman and supermodel Carla Bruni they have managed to stay together. Not least, perhaps, because of the difficulty they would have agreeing who should have which house: the family has a mansion in Richmond, Surrey, a Loire *château,* a villa in Mustique and a New York brownstone.

James, Baroness, 3rd August 1920, the Nineties Agatha Christie. This formidable, taxman's daughter is better-known as PD James, our foremost crime writer. Her award-winning creation Inspector Dalgliesh rivals detectives Morse and Wexford as one of TV's most original characters. She has only once veered away from this genre in *The Children of Men.* "The great satisfaction of a whodunnit is all there in the title. You are secure in the knowledge that, at the end of the book, the mystery will be solved – and you'll know for sure who really ran amok with the lead piping in the library."

Phyllis Dorothy James left Cambridge Girls' High School at 16. Her father persuaded her to join him at the Inland Revenue rather than study for university. Apart from a short interlude, having her daughters Jane and Clare, she has worked all her life. This was partly the result of her tragic marriage at 21 to Irish medical student Connor White. After serving in the Army Medical Corps he returned from the Second World War with such severe mental damage that he was unemployable.

To gain academic qualifications Phyllis attended evening classes at the City of London College while administering five psychiatric outpatient clinics by day. She rose to become a senior Home Office civil servant, retiring in 1979 as a principal in the Criminal Policy Department. Such experience was perfect for her other, early morning and weekend, occupation. For she had published her first novel, *Cover Her Face,* in 1962.

This shrewd, mild-mannered widow represents Middle England at its most altruistic. She received her 1991 life peerage after serving as a BBC governor, chairman of the Royal Society of Authors, a member of the British Council Board, a Booker Prize judge and as a lay magistrate.

Even now in her late seventies she is one of the Church of England's leading lay advisers, "The spiritual dimension is very important in my books." She remains a passionate campaigner against the decline in the use of English.

James, Clive, 7th October 1939, Australian humorist, Whicker wannabe and former royal confidante. This fiendishly erudite broadcaster spent the first ten years of his career as an academic and journalist. He honed his punning exaggerations, sarky asides and bitchy pay-offs writing for the *New Statesman* and *Listener*. But his ten-year stint as *Observer* TV critic convinced him that the medium desperately needed his brilliance. He fronted ITV's *Cinema* and *Saturday Night People* before landing the talk show bragathons that made his name: *The Late Clive James, Saturday Night Clive* and *Sunday Night Clive*. But he is proudest of documentaries like *Clive James and the Calendar Girls,* which enable him to polish those trademark *mots justes* rather than worry about his ad-libs.

Less successful have been James's forays into literature. In 1975 he composed a contrived epic poem called *The Fate of Felicity Fark in the Land of Media* which featured Lord "Larry" Polaroid, David Dross and Bob Skunkhouse. The royal sequel about Charles Charming and Lady Diana See-Through Spiffing was also unworthy of him. But his 1980 autobiography, *Unreliable Memoirs*, while heavily embroidered, was a deserved bestseller.

The self-styled "bad boy from Kogarah" was christened Clive Vivian Leopold James. Having attended Sydney University he moved to Cambridge where, as president of Footlights, he was able to indulge his penchant for satirical revue. It was there that he met his wife Pru, a retiring Aussie don who hates self-promotion as much as he revels in it. They still live near the university, although he is usually travelling or enjoying his bachelor life in London. Princess Diana became an occasional lunch guest.

That cheery grin and glinting cranium are seen to best effect in his travelogue *Postcard From...* series. He has filmed in nearly all the world's most exotic capitals, including Rio de Janeiro, Rome, Paris, New York and Berlin. A common theme is him flirting with local girls or exposing his whale-like physique either on the dance floor or in some dangerous sport. Journalist Peter McKay once described him as "an ill-natured fellow who writes like a man who wishes he was invited to more parties."

Jason, David, 2nd February 1940, forever "Del Boy". This Billingsgate fish porter's son has been described as having "a face like a pickled walnut, a voice lacking theatrical resonance and a workman's physique". Yet he is Britain's best-loved and most bankable television star. Almost 25 million viewers watched the Christmas 1996 edition of *Only Fools and Horses*. If South London wide boy "Del Boy" Trotter has become a national institution, then so too has rural roisterer Pa Larkin in *The Darling Buds of May* and sombre Detective Inspector Frost in *A Touch of Frost*. Versatility is Jason's middle name.

Despite this eminence Jason has always shunned showbiz glitz and indeed is almost a recluse. "As an actor you have to communicate all the time. So when I get home I'd rather dig the garden or take the dog for a walk than, say, go out to lunch and start communicating again." For 18 years he lived with former Welsh actress Myfanwy Talog. He was devastated when she died in 1995 after he had nursed her through a long battle with breast cancer. "She was the great love of my life." He now shares his Buckinghamshire home with Gill Hinchcliffe, a location manager 19 years his junior, whom he met on the set of *A Touch of Frost*.

Jason – born David White – adopted his stage surname from his favourite film, *Jason and the Argonauts*. After leaving school in Finchley at 15 he became an apprentice electrician while doing local amateur dramatics. At 25 he joined Romney Repertory Theatre and for nearly 20 years worked in stage productions like *No Sex Please...We're British* plus making appearances in TV series like *Z Cars*. He first made his name in 1976, playing second fiddle to his hero Ronnie Barker, as the naïve Yorkshire shop assistant, Granville, in BBC2's *Open All Hours*. In Tom Sharpe's *Porterhouse Blue* he won a BAFTA award for his brilliant portrayal of a Cambridge college servant.

This most private of men has many hidden talents. As well as a keen do-it-yourselfer he is a qualified glider pilot and scuba-diver and a former award-winning gymnast. If insurers would allow it he would do all his own TV stunts.

Jefferies, Tim, 6th November 1961, the yuppy Richard Gere. This handsome owner of Hamilton's Gallery continually sets female hearts racing. Unfortunately the £50 million it was said he would inherit from his grandfather, Green Shield stamps founder Richard Tompkins, turned out to be folklore. Slim, sociable and fashionably-dressed, he is a permanent fixture at glitterati parties and premières. Underneath the bezazz he has proved to be a valuable patron of David Bailey, Patrick Lichfield and many talented new photographers.

Jefferies's mother, Hilary, split up with little-known artist Richard Jefferies when Tim was seven. He lived a sheltered, provincial life in West Sussex, attending a minor public school. He once worked as a hi-fi salesman in East Grinstead. He received £500,000 on his 21st birthday: the party ended with his pals covered in chocolate cake.

Jefferies was only 23 when he married former soft-porn actress Koo Stark against his family's wishes. She was too worldly-wise for him and on the rebound from her great love, Prince Andrew. Their marriage lasted 16 months.

He then dated American models Deniece Lewis and Terri May. But his most enduring relationship was his three years with Australian supermodel, Elle 'The Body' Macpherson. They were the Mick Jagger and Jerry Hall of the early Nineties, dazzling at all the right parties, nightclubs and restaurants. But, despite sporting a massive diamond engagement ring, she decided to leave him in 1996. He replaced her with the Spanish model Ines Sastre and later Belgian cover-girl Ingrid Seynhaeve.

Predictably, this lanky boulevardier also has a penchant for Ferraris and other fast motors. He once received a year's driving ban after smashing up four cars in an accident. His first girlfriend, Judy Hughesdon, remains unimpressed by all this gallivanting. "When God gave out brains he gave Tim marbles", she rasped.

John, Elton, 25th March 1947, the Liberace of rock 'n' roll. Born Reginald Kenneth Dwight, this former pub pianist chose his stage name because he had played in a blues band with Elton Dean and the legendary Long John Baldry. Tubby, short and bespectacled, he was the most unlikely pop idol material. But such was his vocal and song-writing talent that he became an almost overnight success in 1971 with the single *Your Song*. Hits like *Rocket Man, Crocodile Rock, Daniel, Goodbye Yellow Brick Road, Candle in the Wind* and *Song For Guy* have become anthems of the Seventies.

The exuberance of John's stage performances have helped to sell his records throughout the world. He will kick over his piano stool and pound the keyboards like Jerry Lee Lewis, even if his wig is sometimes knocked skewwhiff. He has wasted thousands of pounds on transplants and toupees, but the results fool nobody. In 1976 he fulfilled his greatest fantasy when he bought Watford Football Club and saw it leap from fourth to first division.

Despite being the first rock star to admit to being bisexual, John married German recording engineer Renate Blauel on Valentine's Day 1984. She announced that she wanted to have "lots of children", although cynics sneered that Elton had found "a cover, not a lover!" The marriage ended shortly afterwards and he recorded the song *Understanding Women*, joking "it's a very long single!"

The star's current relationship with former Canadian adman David Furnish seems to have helped to bury many of the insecurities which left him suicidal in the Seventies. Despite his fame, fortune and friendship with royals like Princess Margaret and Fergie, he

needed the outrageous costumes and stage *braggadocio* to disguise
weedy little Reg Dwight. But now he seems to have found peace of
mind in doing less. He rarely performs on TV or in concert, campaigns endlessly for his AIDS charity and writes Oscar-winning
scores for Disney films like *The Lion King*. He has been drug and
drink-free since 1991.

Today he is worth an estimated £150 million, paying himself a
salary of £13 million a year. He has sold off his collection of Cartier,
Fabergé and other works of art because he felt he was "being pos-
sessed by his possessions". But Furnish's hilarious ITV profile,
Tantrums and Tiaras, showed that he can still shop for England. He
deserves to become Sir Elton.

Jones, Vinnie, 5th January 1966, self-styled "hard man of football".
He would never win a prize for political correctness, chivalry or elocution. He has been sent off 12 times. He once bit a journalist's nose
and was fined £20,000 by the Football Association for participating
in a video giving tips on how to foul players behind the referee's
back. He was therefore amazed when American ballerina Cynthia
Harvey described him as "one of the most loyal, sensitive and generous men I've ever met". "I can't think why she said that", he replied.
"I only slept with her once!"

The Wimbledon Football Club skipper goaded the normally mild-
mannered Gary Lineker enough to brand him a "self-hyped personality". But amidst the sheep, pigs, cattle and hens on his 68-acre
Hertfordshire farm he loses his pugnacious Sean Penn image and
becomes a gentle Mel Gibson.

He is very supportive of his wife Tanya, whom he married in 1994.
She had a heart transplant after the birth of her daughter Kaley
during her first marriage and has since suffered serious health problems. "Unfortunately Tanya can't have any more children. We did
talk about the possibility of adopting, but in her condition it would-
n't be fair. It would put too much pressure on her." Kaley now treats
Vinnie as her father. He also has a son Aaron from his former girlfriend Mylene Elliston.

Builder's son Jones first kicked a football around on a Watford
council estate. His parents split up when he was 14 and he left
school at 15. After working on building sites he signed with
Wimbledon at 21.

"Yeah, I've probably got more rough edges than most players. But
when the fans know you're earning five or six grand a week you can't
let them down. If you're not sparking, then you're cheating yourself,
the fans, your manager and the other players." Meanwhile he fancies
himself as a film star or chat show host.

Jonsson, Ulrika, 16th August 1967, Scandinavian scatterbrain.
This bubbly, blue-eyed blonde with a cheeky smile and penchant for
posing in saucy underwear is the *Carry On* version of the classic
Swedish *au pair*. She rose to fame as TV-am's weather girl, was
voted 'Rear of the Year' and there it could have ended. But in 1993
LWT hired her to present *Gladiators*, a show that required her ad-
libbing talents as much as her looks and yelling ability. She finally
shed her "bimbo" tag in 1996 when she joined BBC2's game show
Shooting Stars. As a team captain she developed a naughty line in
repartee and learnt to down a pint of lager in under a minute. Her
off-screen *tendresse* for its host, Vic Reeves, inspired him to write her
a comedy series called *It's Ulrika!*

Coquettish Ulrika was born on a housing estate outside
Stockholm. Her Swedish parents divorced when she was a child.
Aged 12 she came to live in Berkshire with her mother, who had
married film mogul Michael Brodie. She was teased at Burnham
Grammar School because she could barely speak English. Having
failed to land a place at drama school she did a secretarial course
and became PA to TV-am supremo Bruce Gyngell. She badgered him
for a screen-test and eventually left to join a London-based
Scandinavian TV channel. But she returned to TV-am in 1989 as
weather girl. "Leos get what they want."

Ulrika describes herself as "a very passionate person" and a
"man's woman" with few close female friends. In 1990 she married
TV cameraman John Turnbull, but three years later had an affair
with *Gladiators* cameraman Phil Piotrowski. She returned to her
husband and a year later had their son Cameron. In 1995 they
divorced and she began an 18-month affair with James Crossley, *aka*
Gladiator Hunter, who was six years her junior. She claims to have
had "the best sex I've ever had" but unfortunately his brainpower
could not keep up with his stamina.

K

Keith, Normandie, 2nd February 1972, American adventuress. This petite, blonde cover-girl will enter a party and guests stop talking. She has graduated with three 'M's: money, modelling and men. She grew up in New York, daughter of Norman Keith, a Vermont sawmill heir who founded his own oil company. Spoilt and cosseted, she attended Foxcroft, an East Coast boarding school where she excelled at riding and socialising. By 17 she already had her own apartment on New York's Park Avenue. While taking drama lessons she was voted "deb of the year". At 19 she married Texas sugar heir Jonathan Avery, ten years her senior, but split up three months later. Back in New York she began modelling, made TV commercials and was an extra in Al Pacino's *Scent Of A Woman*.

Normandie stormed London in 1993, briefly working behind Christie's front counter. Her Ursula Andress looks made her a founder It Girl. She became as ubiquitous at Café Society *soirées* as Tara Palmer-Tomkinson and Tamara Beckwith. "I love going to parties because I love meeting people." She began a transatlantic relationship with tycoon Lord Hanson's jet-setting son Robert, 12 years her senior. His reluctance to settle down prompted their break-up two years later. Within months she was dating an even more eligible bachelor, his handsome polo-playing friend Lucas White. Younger and greener than her, he proposed three months later. She now dreams of becoming a jet-set wife and an actress ("more Goldie Hawn and Meg Ryan than Sharon Stone"). London socialites are divided into those who brand her an "air-head" and a "girl on the make" and those who think she is "a caring, life-enhancing delight". She neither smokes nor drinks. "My one vice is telling dirty jokes", she says. But she is a shopaholic too.

Kendal, Felicity, 25th September 1946, a cerebral Shirley Maclaine. Tiny, fragile-looking, slightly *distrait*, she fizzes with enthusiasm and nervous energy. Perennially popular on television she is now a busy member of Sir Peter Hall's Old Vic repertory company, starring in Granville Barker's *Waste* and Chekhov's *The Seagull*. Critics generally adore her. But they disliked her hamming it up with an American accent in TV's *Honey For Tea* and slammed two stage productions in which she starred, Anthony Minghella's

Made in Bangkok and more recently Feydeau's stage farce, *Mind Millie For Me.*

Birmingham-born Felicity moved to India aged three months to join her parents' travelling theatre company. She played the changeling boy in *A Midsummer Night's Dream* while still in her cot, Puck at nine years and Ophelia in *Hamlet* at 17. Educated at local convents, she returned to Britain in 1965. She made her TV debut opposite Sir John Gielgud in *The Mayfly and the Frog*. At an audition in front of Sir Laurence Olivier she chose Ophelia's mad scene and two other bits. "I don't know how I thought I'd get away with it! Then someone shouted: 'okay, get to the end of it'. I burst into tears and fled home. But I got the job!"

Felicity quickly established herself as a stage actress in *Henry V*, *Kean* and *Romeo and Juliet*. But it was Alan Ayckbourn's trilogy, *The Norman Conquests*, in 1974 that created her brand image as a scatterbrained, vulnerable, sexy character. In BBC1's batty sitcom, *The Good Life*, she fuelled men's fantasies in the unlikely rôle of a formerly conventional Surbiton housewife who turns her back garden into a farmyard. Another sitcom, *The Mistress*, cast her for the first time as a *femme fatale*, with a pink suburban boudoir, a florist's shop and a married lover.

Award-winning Felicity lives in Chelsea, working out daily in her home gym. She has a son, Charley, from her first marriage to actor Drewe Henley. In 1983 she converted to the Jewish faith to marry theatre director Michael Rudman. They have a son, Jacob, but divorced following her close friendship with Sir Tom Stoppard. Although they keep separate homes she has long been the playwright's muse, starring in seven of his plays, including *The Real Thing*, *Jumpers*, *Indian Ink* and *Arcadia*. In 1998 she finally hopes to complete her autobiographical book about her "Shakespeare Wallah" upbringing.

Kennedy, Nigel, 28th December 1956, the cor blimey fiddler. Every generation has one – an oddball who breaks the classical music mould: James Galway in the Seventies, Vanessa-Mae Nicolson in the Nineties and our Nige in the Eighties. With his spiky hair, urchin manner and busker's clobber he is as different as can be from the virtuoso stereotype. "When Keith Richards is expected to wear tails on stage then maybe I'll consider it."

The gimmicks got him noticed and luckily he had the talent to repay the attention. His rendition of Vivaldi's *Four Seasons* became his signature tune. "Audiences would be annoyed if I didn't play it, but it became a millstone." Critics, though, rate his Elgar *Violin Concerto* rather higher.

After joining the Yehudi Menuhin School at eight and studying at New York's Juilliard School this punk prodigy made his concert debut with the Philharmonia Orchestra at the Royal Festival Hall in 1977. A five-year BBC documentary on the development of a soloist kept him in the spotlight. He has since played with every major British orchestra and at every leading UK and European festival.

Kennedy's popularity with jazz and pop fans shot his career in several directions. The old guard predicted his penchant for heavy drinking and all-night partying would lead to "burn-out" by 40. Indeed, following an operation to remove a cyst from his neck in 1992, he took a five-year sabbatical from "live" performing. He still practises three to five hours daily, beginning with Bach "because his music reaffirms in my mind the reasons why I play the violin".

This laddish Aston Villa and Jimi Hendrix fanatic became a father for the first time in 1996. He lives with his girlfriend Eve and baby Sark near Malvern. With his Worzel Gummidge outfits and frugal lifestyle no-one could accuse him of acting like a pop star. He refuses to become "a media darling". "I'd never let showbiz mess up my private life." He keeps a North London bolt hole for when he becomes "insufferable" and needs space.

Kensit, Patsy, 4th March 1968, rock chick and tantrum-prone actress. She is cute, blue-eyed and beautiful, but her turbulent relationship with laddish Oasis singer Liam Gallagher has detracted from her career. She has been constantly in the news, whether photographed kicking his car after his late return from a drinking spree or karate-punching him after he dallied with supermodel Kate Moss. Her thick bleached blonde hair and leather outfits are all vintage Marianne Faithfull, but without the drugs or Mars bars. She once boasted that her big ambition was to be "the kind of woman men dream about when they go to bed".

Convent-educated Patsy is the daughter of an East End gangster and a posh Dior PR-lady. As a toddler she starred in a Bird's Eye frozen peas commercial. She then became Britain's answer to Shirley Temple, appearing aged four alongside Robert Redford in *The Great Gatsby* and Elizabeth Taylor in *The Blue Bird*.

Her first pop star boyfriend was Spandau Ballet's Gary Kemp when she was 15. "All I want to be is more famous than anyone or anything." Her big break came in 1986 with the movie *Absolute Beginners*, but it flopped. She developed another career as a member of a pop group, Eighth Wonder. Aged 20 she married her first husband, Big Audio Dynamite keyboard-player Dan Donovan, but they parted three months later. Patsy's Hollywood career briefly revived with *Lethal Weapon 2* opposite Mel Gibson and *Angels and Insects* in which she stripped. In 1992 she married Simple Minds singer Jim Kerr, from whom she has a son, James. Their marriage ended four years later, after she met Gallagher, then a rising Britpop star. They married in 1997 and share a Primrose Hill mansion.

Kent, Princess Michael of, 15th January 1945, former royal black sheep. When Princess Diana and the Duchess of York stole the title "Her Royal Naughtiness", the spotlight largely deserted this incorrigible social-climber. She now attracts headlines for her riding and hunting rather than her social gallivanting and freebies. Even her old nicknames, "Our Val" (for Valkyrie) and "BTL" (Billiard-Table Legs) are largely forgotten.

The Queen once dryly remarked that the Princess was "more royal than we are". She was born in Bohemia, the daughter of Baron Gunther von Reibnitz, a wartime member of Hitler's SS, who later became a Mozambique fruit farmer. But Marie-Christine's parents split up when she was three and she moved to Australia. Her proud but impoverished mother ran a Sydney beauty parlour and later married a Polish nobleman, Count Tadeusz Rogala-Koczorowski. After leaving the Sacré Coeur convent she "escaped" to Europe. "I always hear my mother's words: '900 years of breeding must be worth something'". She studied art in Vienna and Florence before arriving in London in 1967 to do a diploma course at the Victoria and Albert Museum. With little experience she founded an interior-decorating business, Szapar Designs.

Amazonian MC's formidable presence and discreet name-dropping soon gained her a place at the most select dinner parties, and she was seen in the right company at Ascot and Wimbledon. In 1971 she married merchant banker Tom Troubridge, whom she had met on an Austrian boar-hunt. But the marriage lasted only two years. Their divorce was followed by a papal annulment on the eve of her second marriage. Because of her religion the Queen's second cousin, Prince Michael of Kent, renounced his right to the throne. To save further embarrassment the ceremony took place outside the country, in Vienna Town Hall.

The royal pair soon became the white-tie whales of Café Society. "We'll go anywhere for a free dinner", she jested. She once persuaded British Airways to lay on a special aircraft to ferry her from Manchester to London for a private engagement. Tycoon Peter de Savary gave her a £150,000 building plot on Antigua and an American admirer presented her with a £115,000 racehorse. She found time to have two children, Lord Freddie Windsor and Lady Ella Windsor. But an unwise friendship with Texan oil heir J Ward Hunt almost led to a divorce.

Kenwright, Bill, 4th September 1945, latter-day Binkie Beaumont. This former child star began as a producer of 'safe' provincial tours, reviving classic plays and West End musicals, usually starring major TV stars. In the early Eighties he had 11 shows running simultaneously. From these slightly tacky beginnings he has taken the theatrical establishment by storm. He is now respected as a brilliant, innovative impresario, unafraid to take risks.

A Liverpool brickie's son, Kenwright attended the Liverpool Institute with the Beatles' Paul McCartney and George Harrison. Aged 12 he was already working as a stagehand on *Toad of Toad Hall*. He then became the bumptious Gordon Clegg in *Coronation Street* and made pop records (unsuccessfully). He turned part-time stage producer in 1968, producing *Billy Liar* at the Buxton Theatre because he wanted the lead part. His first success was *The Miracle Worker*, starring his former leading lady Pat Phoenix. He lost a fortune on his West End revival of *West Side Story*, but recouped it on *Joseph and the Amazing Technicolor Dreamcoat* which toured Britain for eight years in the Eighties.

Teetotal Kenwright claims that his hair turned grey aged 17. But it has only had a positive effect on women. For 25 years he was a Scouse Peter Stringfellow, bedding starlets, Page 3 girls and dolly birds He has a daughter, Lucy, from a relationship with actress Virginia Stride, but his great love was actress Shirley Anne Field.

In 1978 Kenwright married Anouska Hempel whom he barely knew. Friends surmised that she was attracted to his legendary amorous skills while he was *bouleversé* by her posh image. Two years later they were divorced and she refuses to discuss him, even obliterating their marriage from her *Who's Who* entry. He subsequently wooed three miniature beauties: Elaine Paige, Lynsey de Paul and Koo Stark.

This easy-going, multi-millionaire lives in Maida Vale and is proud of being an Everton FC director. He is poised to achieve his final ambition of becoming a Hollywood producer. Early in 1997 he provoked cries of nepotism by casting his girlfriend, actress Jenny Seagrove, in his first film, *Us Begins With You*.

Khan, The Aga, 13th December 1936, racehorse-owning philanthropist, known as "K". Anglophile Karim is a serious improvement on the late Aga, his grandfather, who married four times and when caught drinking alcohol replied: "I'm so holy that when I touch wine it turns to water!" He disinherited his son Prince Aly Khan because he was a playboy, best-known for his amatory gifts. Karim therefore became the 49th Imam in 1957 and was accorded the title "His Highness" by the Queen.

K, a short, balding double billionaire, claims direct descent from the Prophet Mohammed. He is treated as a "living god" by his estimated four million Ismaili Muslim followers, spread over Pakistan, East Africa and Britain. But he is no longer ceremonially weighed in gold and diamonds on his birthday, which was a costly tradition when his portly, long-lived predecessor ruled. His business empire covers insurance, banking, hotels, newspapers and Sardinia's Costa Smeralda development. His charities fund Muslim schools, hospitals and housing projects. But his greatest interest is racing: he was part owner of Shergar which won the Derby an unprecedented three times in the Eighties. "Horses are not just a gentleman's hobby but big business." In 1990 he removed his 90 horses from British stables in protest against the Jockey Club's disqualification of his 1989 Oaks winner, Aliysa.

The Le Rosey and Harvard-educated Aga married his beautiful Begum, former British model Sally Croker-Poole, in 1969. At the wedding pearls were thrown on the bridal pair instead of rice. They have three children, Princess Zahra, Prince Rahim and Prince Hussain. But their 1995 divorce cost him an estimated £50 million. He has enjoyed long friendships with Italian industrialist's daughter Milena Maffei and Austro-American former model Pilar Goess. He lives like a 20th century emperor, whisked by private jet between his principal homes in Paris and Geneva, his Chantilly and Irish stables and his Sardinian palazzo.

Khan, Jemima, 30th January 1974, trustafarian beauty. Marrying heart-throb Imran Khan was akin to winning the great lovers' Grand National. She managed to edge ahead of a field that contained some of Britain's most eligible runners, including painter Emma Sergeant, society belle Susannah Constantine and Earl Cawdor's sister Lady Liza Campbell. Jemima had a victorious combination of youth, willowy blonde looks and a sunny manner. Brought up in stately Ormeley Lodge beside Richmond Park, she is surprisingly unspoilt. She has inherited her mother Lady Annabel's good manners and ability to impress people from all backgrounds. Cushioned by her late father Sir James Goldsmith's billionaire fortune she has sadly never bothered to develop her own career.

Jemima's birth created a minor scandal because both her parents were, nominally at least, still married to other people: Jimmy to his French second wife, Ginette, and Annabel to Mayfair club owner Mark Birley. Jemima's parents finally married in Paris in 1978. She absorbed some of her father's shrewdness, toughness and charm.

She has always had a busy social life, but refused to become a deb.
She sat on the membership committee of Kartouche and revelled in
her trust fund babe lifestyle. She rejected most suitors, but trendy
club owner Joel Cadbury was an exception.

The demurely-robed bride converted to Islam on her 1995 marriage to Khan but finds it hard to eschew alcohol. The wedding
guests at Ormeley Lodge were an intriguing mixture of big business,
Sloane Rangers and trendydom. Nine months later she dutifully produced an heir, Sulaiman, who bears his father's distinctive Pathan
features. Early married life in her husband's Lahore compound was
uncomfortable and rather fraught. While campaigning in the
Pakistani general election they received death threats. A bomb
exploded in the cancer hospital that Khan had set up in his mother's
memory. Jemima also had to cope with heiress Sita White threatening him with a paternity action. Even with adjustments on both
sides will the Khans still be married after the Millennium, given her
genes and his wanderlust?

Kidd, Jodie, 25 September 1978, superskinny cover-girl. Many
fashion pundits consider her the Face of the Nineties. Ordinary folk
wonder what all the fuss is about: "Poor lass, feed her up and send
her home to mum."

She lacks the refinement of Jean Shrimpton but shares many of
the qualities of Twiggy. An inch over six feet tall, with racehorse
legs, she is gawky and grungy, with lips reminiscent of Van Gogh's
Potato Pickers. But her debby voice reveals her toffish origins. She is
the great-grand-daughter of the first Lord Beaverbrook, owner of the
Daily and *Sunday Express*. Her father is millionaire ex-showjumper
Johnny Kidd who owns palatial homes in London, Gloucestershire
and Barbados.

Jodie owes her fame to fashion photographer, Terry O'Neill, who
'discovered' her in Barbados. Although she was only 15 he saw the
potential in her extraordinary cheekbones, cat's eyes and natural
poise. "Jodie was breath-taking. She looked like Grace Kelly, Kim
Basinger and Bardot rolled into one." He introduced her to top model
agent, Laraine Ashton, and within 18 months this new discovery
was rivalling Kate Moss and Naomi Campbell.

Blue-eyed Jodie was always a winner. At St Michael's, Petworth
she may have only achieved a GCSE in art but she was an international showjumper at 13. Her high metabolism makes it impossible
to put on weight however many pizzas and Chinese takeaways she
eats. At the 1995 Milan fashion shows even flinty-faced fashion editors gasped at her skin-and-bones appearance and she subsequently
dropped out of New York fashion week to recuperate in Barbados.

This freckled, waif-like mannequin has stayed close to her family and avoided the drug-pushers and Romeos who chat up supermodels. They accept her relationship with Jersey politician's son Joel Chinn, with whom she has lived since 16. "He looks after me. I go out and get the money and he cooks and washes."

Kirwan, Dervla, 24th October 1971, Ireland's Meg Ryan. She is as delicate-looking as a cameo brooch. But her vulnerability conceals an ambitious, highly motivated actress. The TV series *Ballykissangel* turned her into a household name, winning her a BAFTA 'best actress' award in 1996. As Assumpta, the pub landlady with a crush on a handsome English priest, she fulfilled everyone's fantasy image of a feisty Irish colleen. British Telecom hired her for the "it's good to talk" commercials because she "looks the sort of person you could confide in".

Willowy Dervla grew up in Dublin, youngest of three daughters. Her father was an insurance man and her mother a teacher. When she was 16 *Brideshead Revisited* director Charles Sturridge chose her to appear in the TV drama, *Troubles*. She combined school with theatre work before moving to London. She made headlines in 1992 as the teenage lover of elderly roué Ronald Pickup in TV's controversial adaptation of Melvyn Bragg's novel *A Time To Dance*. Asked what she thought of the torrid sex scenes she replied that she would watch them in three months "with a bottle of whiskey and from behind a pillow". She then played Phoebe, the publican's innocent daughter, in BBC1's wartime sitcom, *Goodnight Sweetheart*.

Dervla's real-life affair with *Drop the Dead Donkey* star Stephen Tompkinson began on the set of *Ballykissangel*. It was kept secret until a tabloid discovered them on holiday together. "We're a team and laugh a lot. It's a wonderful relief to have found someone to go home to and talk to, who knows you and understands your work." She is fearful of working in Hollywood. "You get chewed up and thrown out after the first wrinkle appears." Instead she plans a long career as an actress, screen-writer and producer.

Knopfler, Mark, 12th August 1949, scruffbag genius. Since Dire Straits folded in 1991 this £50 million troubadour has been indulging his musical fantasies. He records in Nashville and plays small venues with his group, the Notting Hillbillies (named after his funky former stomping-ground). He seems content that his 1996 solo album *Golden Heart*, sold a fraction of the 85 million worldwide sales Dire Straits notched up. But his mournful guitar solos remain as distinctive as those of his idol Jimi Hendrix. His career can move in several directions: as a composer – he wrote the *Local Hero* film score; as a record-producer – he produced Bob Dylan's comeback album *Infidel* and, of course, as a performer.

Mark Freuder Knopfler was born in Glasgow, the son of a Hungarian-born architect. When he was seven the family moved to Newcastle where his teacher-mother grew up. Before he was given his first guitar at 15 he used to pretend with a tennis racquet. He started neglecting his studies at Gosforth High School for music, but eventually scraped into Leeds University to read English literature. While performing in pub bands he worked as a journalist on the *Yorkshire Evening Post*. In 1977 he founded Dire Straits, named after its members' financial situation. With triple platinum albums like *Brothers in Arms* and classic singles like *Sultans of Swing* they became the country's most popular "live" band. Their most ardent fan Princess Diana even dragged Prince Charles to a concert, although he insisted on wearing earplugs.

The notoriously reserved Knopfler was briefly married in 1972 to his old schoolfriend Kathy White. He then had twin sons, Benji and Joseph, from his 1983 marriage to American recording executive Lourdes Salomone. They seemed to be soul mates but broke up in 1990, mainly because of his constant touring. On Valentine's Day 1997 he married actress Kitty Aldridge in Barbados. They live in Chelsea, with few of the usual pop star accoutrements. Indeed a woman once accosted them in the street: "You look just like Mark Knopfler". Jovially he replied: "Wish I had his money!"

L

Lambton, Lady Lucinda, 10th May 1943, architectural harridan. Her haughty manner and Niagara of opinions have turned this eccentric, grandee's daughter into TV's tame toff. Her impeccable contacts enable her to gain unique camera access to stately homes and other treasured sites. On series like *Lucinda Lambton's A to Z of Britain*, her formidable personality drags the viewer along with pithily expressed observations. She is not the sort of person to displease in a medieval dungeon – she might slam the door!

Her Ladyship seems to have inherited none of the sleazy characteristics of her multi-millionaire father, "Lord" Lambton, who had to resign as junior defence minister in 1973 after being caught with a call-girl. Earlier, he had disclaimed the earldom of Durham in order to stay in the House of Commons. Intelligent, original and fun, Lucy has always refused to be the traditional huntin', shootin' wife and mother. She began taking architectural photographs for interior decorating magazines during her 20-year marriage to economist Sir Roy Harrod's son Henry. They have two sons, Barnaby and Huckleberry. In 1986 she became chatelaine of a Warwickshire stately home, Charlecote Park, when she married baronet Sir Edmund Ramsay-Fairfax-Lucy. In 1991 she settled down with her third husband, former *Sunday Telegraph* editor Sir Peregrine Worsthorne. They live in her Victorian Gothic Buckinghamshire rectory where she collects weird objects.

Lucy is passionate about her dogs: two mongrel collies Thistle and Clover and two dachshunds Florence and Violet. She is an authority on the history of the loo. For her latest book, though, she has been traipsing round the country visiting graveyards where famous people are buried. Prepare for ghostly jokes.

Lane, Carla, 5th August 1937, telly wordsmith and animal rights campaigner. Normal scriptwriters are content to let directors and stars hog all the off-screen glory. But this scatty Scouser believes in using her fame to publicise more serious matters. She campaigns against hunting, fur coats and animal-testing and maintains a sanctuary on her Hayward's Heath estate. A vegetarian for over 30 years, she won't wear leather shoes or suede coats and claims to feel "real pain" when she sees a squashed pigeon on the road. Once while dining in a snooty Los Angeles fish restaurant she chose four live lobsters from the tank and released them in the ocean.

Comedy series like *The Liver Birds*, *Bread* and *Butterflies* have made this self-confessed "crank and nut" a rich lady who is able to indulge almost any caprice. She once kept in her Grade I-listed West London home a menagerie of eight cats, two rabbits, two tortoises, one dog and some 90 birds. In 1990, together with Linda McCartney and Rita Tushingham, she founded the pressure group Animal Line. She turned an island off North Wales into a nature reserve. "It's going to be an animals' paradise where even rats can live in peace."

Carla – born Romana Barrack – remains close to her two sons Carl and Nigel from her former husband, naval architect Arthur Hollins. She ascribes her obsession with preserving all forms of life to her childhood. Twice she nearly died: the first time from meningitis and the second when she needed emergency resuscitation after being given the wrong injection for an appendix operation. "Experiences like these change your life."

La Plante, Lynda, 18th September 1946, drama diva. This titian-haired Dennis Potter specialises in gritty heroines, like bank robber's widow Dolly Rawlings in *Widows*, Detective Superintendent Jane Tennison in *Prime Suspect* and prison chief Helen Hewitt in *The Governor*. She has suffered only one major flop: BBC1's *Lifeboat* series. Petite and gloriously funny, she is a meticulous researcher, visiting prisons, watching criminals at work, going on the beat with police officers. She denies that her scripts suffer from gratuitous violence. Ciggies and black coffee fuel her restless brilliance.

RADA-trained Lynda began as an actress (stage name Lynda Marchal), doing stand-up comedy and appearing in TV series such as *The Gentle Touch* and *Minder*. She turned to writing after realising she would never be Vanessa Redgrave. She made a major impression in 1983 with her first TV drama *Widows*. But it was the award-winning *Prime Suspect* that made her one of Britain's five highest-paid scriptwriters. She has also written a slew of thriller novels, including *Cold Shoulder* and *Cold Blood*. Often writing 15 hours a day she admits "I can't go on at this rate. But I'm driven by that old worry about unemployment from years ago".

The Liverpool sales rep's daughter – born Linda Titchmarsh – suffers from dyslexia. In 1978 she married Richard La Plante, a superfit American hippie who rode a Harley-Davidson. "I wouldn't be anywhere the success I am without him. He gave me the confidence in myself." Unfortunately they were unable to have children or to adopt, and divorced acrimoniously in 1996. She kept the baronial Kingston-upon-Thames house and the two wolfhounds while he returned to America with a generous financial settlement. Unaccustomedly single she told the first man who invited her out: "That would be wonderful. Can you call Liz (her PA) and find out when I've got a free..."

Laurie, Hugh, 11th June 1959, reluctant comic. Most actors who play upper-class twits are in real-life nothing like their screen characters. But this closet toff is everything Hugh Grant aspired to be in *Four Weddings and a Funeral*. It is not just the well-polished brogues, plummy accent and languid manner: the son of a country doctor, he was educated at Eton. His finest rôle was as PG Wodehouse's eponymous gentleman in ITV's *Jeeves and Wooster*, opposite his chum Stephen Fry. They could easily have switched parts and nearly did.

Modest, Oxford-born Laurie inherited not only his LSE-educated mother's brains but his father's rowing prowess – Laurie senior had been an Olympic gold medallist. At Cambridge Hugh rowed in the 1980 boat race and starred opposite Fry, Emma Thompson and Tony Slattery in Footlights revues. But he has always been "too scared" – or perhaps too pukka? – to do stand-up comedy. His professional partnership with Fry continued on graduation, in ITV's sketch show *Alfresco* and later in *A Bit of Fry and Laurie*. Both were regulars on those influential Eighties comedy shows, *The Young Ones*, *Happy Families* and *Saturday Live*. In *Blackadder*, Laurie was cast as drawling George, Prince of Wales. Like all comic actors he yearns to prove himself in straight parts. He appeared in LWT's drama *All Or Nothing At All*. In 1996 he forsook his Squire Nice Guy image to take on the rôle of Cruella de Vil's nasty sidekick Jasper in Hollywood's *101 Dalmatians*.

Blue-eyed Laurie is a mega-worrier and has had ulcers to prove it. His vagueness is such that one interviewer counted 32 "I don't know" replies in 90 minutes. He has three children, Charles, Bill and Rebecca, from his wife Jo, a former theatre administrator. "I used to be a terrible sulker, but after I married Jo I had to give up because she turned out to be an even better sulker than me!"

Le Bon, Yasmin, 29th October 1964, Britain's Linda Evangelista. Her deep, dark eyes could beguile the most militant misogynist. She is no flibbertigibbet but a caring wife and mother who fights for green causes. Her strong bone-structure, plus hours working out in the gym, maintain her luminous beauty. "You can smoke, drink, party as much as you like but lack of sleep makes you old." Alas, her husband Simon Le Bon, once voted Britain's sexiest pop star, shows signs of beauty fatigue.

Yasmin juggles motherhood with being an international model. She has three daughters, Amber, Saffron and Tallulah. "No-one ever told me how difficult it was having babies. I certainly wasn't prepared for the sheer exhaustion." She continues her career because as the main bread-winner she can earn up to £20,000 a show.

The former Yasmin Parvaneh grew up in Oxford, the daughter of an Iranian academic and a British mother. Aged 14 she had a Saturday job working in a local boutique "where I learned the art of being asleep on my feet with my eyes wide open!" She claims she "drifted" into modelling when she was 19, snapped up for her exotic looks by top agency Models One. Her romance with playboy Le Bon began in 1984 when he spotted her picture in a fashion magazine. He bombarded her agency for her 'phone number and eventually tracked her down. "I was very suspicious at first because I didn't know this guy. But one of the other models did and so I grilled her before I agreed to talk to him." Their first date was to the world première of *Indiana Jones and The Temple of Doom*. He jilted his long-standing girlfriend, Canadian model Clare Stansfield and married Yasmin in 1986. The Le Bons would now dearly love a son.

Legge-Bourke, Tiggy, 1st April 1965, royal jolly hockey sticks. This tall, bouncy banker's daughter managed the rare feat of upsetting both Princess Diana and Camilla Parker Bowles. Diana felt she was becoming over-familiar with Prince William and Prince Harry by hugging them in public and calling them "my babies" while Camilla suspected she was having an affair with Prince Charles. As his PA for three years she organised his huntin', shootin' and other social activities, as well as acting as surrogate mother to the princes during school holidays. She joined them at Sandringham and Balmoral, but her biggest perk was the skiing trips to Klosters. An ill-judged comment from Diana once reduced her to tears at the palace Christmas staff party and in 1996 she finally resigned. But the Princess's death saw her return as a surrogate mother.

Tiggy first met the princes in 1993 and established an immediate rapport. Charles has known her since she was a child when he used to shoot on her father's 6,000-acre Glanusk Park estate in South Wales. Her mother, Shan, and aunt Victoria, are both ladies-in-waiting to Princess Anne and her younger brother, Harry, was a Page of Honour to the Queen.

The fun-loving, indefatigable Tiggy – christened Alexandra – achieved only four O-levels at Heathfield. After a Swiss finishing school she took a Montessori course in 1985 and taught at a private kindergarten in Wandsworth. In 1987 she founded her own school in Battersea, named after her Beatrix Potter nickname, "Mrs Tiggywinkle". Parents were a little worried by her chain-smoking Silk Cut, which is her only vice.

This rural trust-fund babe hates smart London society, designer labels and most status symbols. She lives in Battersea where she gives noisy dinner-parties. Her house is so small that friends have to bring dining-room chairs. At the weekend she heaves her beloved black Labrador, Hercules, into the car and heads for the country.

Lichfield, Earl of, 25th April 1939, photographer and Queen's cousin. Confronted with this grey-maned, ravaged face, it is hard to imagine he was once a pivotal member of the Sixties "beautiful people". He had the sleek looks and glamour of a Hugh Grant, plus the extra allure of a stately home, E-type Jaguar, title and cash. Even his mother was a Princess, following her second marriage to Prince Georg of Denmark.

Never has an Earl had more fun selecting his Countess. Debutantes, dolly-birds and actresses conspired to lure Patrick Lichfield to the altar. But as far as he was concerned, bed would do nicely. His lady friends included Britt Ekland, Joanna Lumley, Gayle Hunnicutt, Alana Hamilton and scores of nudie models who aspired to be in his Unipart calendars. He became inured to the kiss 'n' tell newspaper stories ("I bonked Queen's cousin").

Lichfield's only attempt at matrimony was in 1975 when he married the Duke of Westminster's sister Lady Leonora Grosvenor. The Queen Mother was said to have observed: "what a pity, we were saving her for Charles." Divorced in 1986 they have three children, Viscount Anson, Lady Rose and Lady Eloise. His wife accused him of spending too many months away on photographic assignments, particularly his calendar work. He was devastated by the break-up, losing two stone and aging ten years. "If I'd settled down in the country with her I'd probably still be married."

The Old Harrovian playboy took his first professional photographs snapping fellow pupils for ninepence a portrait. After Sandhurst and the Grenadier Guards, he stunned stuffy contemporaries by turning his hobby into a career. Despite great success, as a royal photographer, author and Burberry fashion model, people still confuse him with Lord Snowdon.

Warm, charming and reluctantly middle-aged, Lichfield finally seems ready to settle down, leaving it to other peripheral royals to create the scandals. Based at his West London studios, he spends most weekends pottering at his Staffordshire stately home, Shugborough Hall, which is now overrun by tourists.

Lilley, Peter, 23rd August 1943, political gunslinger. With former Cabinet colleagues John Redwood and Michael Portillo he was dubbed a "bastard" by John Major. But, unlike them, he has always managed to avoid appearing too rabidly right-wing. He once discombobulated *Newsnight* interviewer Francine Stock with his trick of giving swift, concise answers to questions followed by silence. In 1997 he failed to become Tory leader, partly because he comes across as a passionless bureaucrat. In private he is warmer and funnier. Despite being in his mid-50s and spending five hassled years as Social Security Secretary he remains curiously unlined.

This small, neat, BBC personnel officer's son grew up in suburban Kent. He went to Hayes County Primary School and then Dulwich on a scholarship. At Cambridge he watched future colleagues Michael Howard, Norman Lamont and Kenneth Clarke star in Union debates, but confessed to being "too shy" to speak himself. He then worked as an economic consultant in under-developed countries and as a City stockbroker. A political activist, he became Bow Group chairman, worked in the Tory research department and in 1983 became MP for St Albans. His financial skills helped him to become Nigel Lawson's parliamentary private secretary at the Treasury, then Economic Secretary, Financial Secretary, and Trade and Industry Secretary. At Social Security he introduced the controversial Child Support Agency and learnt the truth of his mentor Lawson's dictum that "as a politician you must never be interested in being loved".

Lilley proposed to his artist wife Gail at a Cambridge May Ball while walking beside the Cam at dawn. "People think I can't be all that boring if I'm married to such an attractive and interesting lady." Shortly after their 1979 marriage she had a miscarriage and was unable to have more children. "It drove us together", he says. "It's a disappointment, but one has to find what recompenses there are." Friends say she "mothers" him. They have homes in Islington, Normandy and his constituency. Now shadow Chancellor of the Exchequer, he is still determined to lead the party.

Lindsay, Robert, 13th December 1949, stage and TV star. He sprang to fame as Teddy boy Jakey Smith in the 1975 sitcom *Get Some In* and as Tooting revolutionary Wolfie in BBC1's *Citizen Smith*. He had an adaptability that made him popular with casting directors. In 1985 he switched to stage musicals, starring in *Me and My Girl* in the West End and on Broadway. He also appeared as Henry II in Anouilh's *Becket* and in the lead rôle of *Cyrano de*

Bergerac. He was brilliant as the scheming city council supremo in Alan Bleasdale's award-winning satirical drama *GBH*. More recently he starred in TV's *Jake's Progress* and won a 1997 Olivier award for his rôle as Fagin in Lionel Bart's musical *Oliver*.

Lindsay was born in Ilkeston, Derbyshire and went to RADA. His career began at the Manchester Royal Exchange but he headed south in 1971 to star as Jesus in the West End hit musical *Godspell*. Unfortunately his well-developed ego clashed with co-star Jeremy Irons who played Judas and on one occasion they came to blows. His first film was a forgettable 1974 musical called *Three For All*. Lindsay married his co-star Cheryl Hall the following year. "Unfortunately Bob wanted a wife to be barefoot, pregnant and in the kitchen", she recalls. But she refused to give up her career or to tolerate his close friendships with various leading ladies. The marriage finally collapsed in 1980 when she was away touring with the RSC and he was starring in *The Three Musketeers* in Manchester. She discovered that he was dating actress Diana Weston. This romance continued for 15 years, during which she became the leading lady of ITV's hit sitcom *The Upper Hand*. Despite having a daughter, Sydney, they never married. In 1994 he dumped her for Rosemarie Ford, BBC1's *Come Dancing* hostess. The couple share their Buckinghamshire home with two dogs and a cat.

Lineker, Gary, 30th November 1960, the Queen Mother of football, nicknamed "Big Ears". Who says nice guys never win? The former England captain prospered in a yobs' environment where the Ten Commandments teach you how to crush your opponent rather than love your neighbour.

He has cleverly prolonged his professional career by moving into TV, as a commentator and as a model crunching Walker's crisps. Women viewers fall for his rich brown eyes, boy-next-door, goofy good looks and ripping thighs. Jealous rivals brand him "a wimp" and "Mr Squeaky Clean".

Lineker went to Leicester Grammar School and made his debut as a professional footballer with Leicester City aged 18. He transferred to Everton in 1985, represented England in the 1986 and 1990 World Cups and captained England in 1991-2. He was once described as "the Muhammed Ali of football – floating like a butterfly around his opponents and stinging like a bee in the back of the net". Playing for Barcelona in the late Eighties he characteristically learnt to speak Spanish and immersed himself in the culture. A toe-injury finally forced his retirement in 1994.

In 16 years' playing no referee ever had to book him or send him off. His happy 1986 marriage to childhood sweetheart Michelle adds to his goody-goody image. Their son George survived leukaemia at eight weeks and now has three siblings: Harry, Tobias and another boy born in 1997.

This Nineties Stanley Matthews may describe himself on Desert Island Discs as "a boring sort of person". But as a BBC pundit, commentator and presenter he has transformed himself into a cross between Paul Merton and Desmond Lynam.

With slots on *Radio 5 Live*, *Grandstand's Football Focus*, *Match of the Day* and *They Think It's All Over* Lineker's holier-than-thou image is slowly disappearing.

Linley, Viscount, 3rd November 1961, royal carpenter and Harley-Davidson freak. Although 12th in line to the throne he won't let this cramp his style. He even has a stake in a chain of hamburger restaurants called Deals. His mother Princess Margaret once explained he was *not* royal: "you just happen to have the Queen as your aunt."

The artistic genes of his photographer father, the Earl of Snowdon, and interior decorator great-uncle Oliver Messel, have proved stronger than the Windsors'. He has also inherited his father's slight build, monkey features and unforgiving nature. As one of Britain's top cabinetmakers, Linley's marquetry desks, tables, chairs and other pieces now adorn the Savoy Hotel and many private collections. When Princess Margaret spied a £75,000 four-poster designed for Elton John she quipped: "that's not a bed, it's a room!"

Shy and pampered David Linley's bohemianism began at co-educational Bedales where pupils are allowed freedom of expression: he was considered too dim to go to Eton. He did a two-year course at the John Makepeace woodwork school in Dorset and then set up a carpentry co-operative with three fellow pupils in Dorking. Linley now has an impressive showroom in Pimlico and a factory. But does Mrs Snooks from Weybridge buy his overpriced bookcases for the name or their artistic merit? He has hired Elton John's manager John Reid to help his expansion in America and Japan.

Speed-freak Linley – the title derives from his ancestor, the *Punch* illustrator Linley Samborne – was once quite a heart-breaker. He had an on-off relationship for five years with tycoon's daughter Susannah Constantine and was also much smitten by blonde model Nicola Formby. But in 1993 he married the Earl of Harrington's grand-daughter, Serena Stanhope.

The Linleys enjoy being social leaders, with heiress Serena provoking excitement with her Hervé Leger dresses. They live in a converted Battersea school and spend long holidays at Princess Margaret's former villa on Mustique. But he grafts away at his drawing board, anxious to prove he can make his own fortune.

Lipman, Maureen, 10th May 1946, Jewish Momma. She has won countless BAFTA, SWET and Variety Club awards but one rôle has eclipsed them all: Beattie in British Telecom's TV commercials. This stereotypical Jewish housewife and chatterbox both infuriated and intrigued viewers. But it left her agent begging her to stop before she became irredeemably typecast.

In real-life Maureen is the antithesis of the scatty, self-deprecating creature that turned her into our busiest character actress. The public image encompasses neuroses, chicken soup, nerve-jangling edginess and, of course, her mother. The reality is more calculating and a great deal more organised. She claims it was not until she was 40 that she finally learned self-confidence. "I wasn't very comfortable with the idea of sexuality for a long time and then I became more laid-back about myself." Every experience becomes more material for her bestselling books, magazine columns and stage appearances.

Maureen left home at 18 after attending Newland High School for Girls in Hull. She trained at LAMDA. In 1969 she made her debut in *The Knack* at the Palace Theatre, Watford and appeared in Nell Dunn's film *Up The Junction*. She worked under Sir Laurence Olivier for three years at the Old Vic. She has since won acclaim for plays like *Messiah*, *Outside Edge* and *See How They Run* and the comedy film *Educating Rita*. She starred in two TV series, *Agony*, in which she played an agony aunt, and *All at No 20*, in which she was a hard-up landlady. Her one-woman show, *Live and Kidding*, defined her talent even more.

This willowy 5ft 7ins luvvie has made a career out of poking fun at her looks. "People used to look in my pram and jump back in horror. I was sallow and piggy-eyed and they thought I was a Korean refugee." She recites her physical defects: "The buck teeth, chicken neck, spaghetti legs, too-wide hips and too-narrow bust." She met her future husband, playwright Jack Rosenthal, in a Manchester pub. "I'd just had a distressing perm that sat on my head like a dead beaver." It clearly did not bother him because they married five years later in 1973 and enjoy one of showbiz's strongest marriages. They have two children, Amy and Adam. Quirkily, she allows herself one cigarette a day.

Llewellyn, Dai, 2nd April 1946, a posh Peter Stringfellow. His life is as dissolute and rackety as his forebears' was chapel-going and sober. His grandfather, Sir David, was the owner of the largest coalmines in South Wales.

After Eton, David St Vincent Llewellyn went to Aix-en-Provence

University. He describes himself as "a dark, hairy-chested Welsh goat, with a fatal attraction for long-legged blondes." A debs' delight during the Sixties, he sometimes bedded three gels a week. He has worked as a travel agent, journalist and even a male model in Australia under the pseudonym "David Savage". In 1974 he found the perfect vocation that combined a life of women, late nights and entertaining. But his first nightclub, Rufus, lost money, mainly because he insisted on ordering fresh flowers daily and entertaining his chums free. Later he became 'greeter' at Wedgie's and Tokyo Joe and ran the Dorchester Club for the Sultan of Brunei. His charm, wide contacts and energy keep him in PR jobs.

Publicity, no matter how embarrassing, has always powered the Llewellyn rocket, raising his profile in "William Hickey" and Nigel Dempster's column. In one 12-month period he was engaged three times: to Isabel Richli, Beatrice Welles and Tessa Dahl, all lively, beautiful and well-connected. Other early conquests included Lady Charlotte Curzon, Princess Ala Auersperg and Lady Jacqueline Rufus-Isaacs. He found marriage to the Duke of Norfolk's beautiful niece, Vanessa Hubbard, curbed his freedom. They divorced in 1987 after seven years but have two daughters, Olivia and Arabella.

Dai will inherit the family seat in Gwent, but unless he produces an heir, his more sober younger brother, Roddy, will eventually succeed him as baronet.

Lloyd-Webber, Lord, 22nd March 1948, composer, impresario and restaurant critic. He revolutionized the 20th century stage musical, with songs carrying the whole narrative instead of dialogue.

Chipmunk-featured Lloyd-Webber and his cellist brother Julian were brought up in South Kensington. His organist father, William, was director of the London College of Music and his mother was a music teacher. He wrote nine musicals at Westminster School and then moved to Oxford as an organ scholar. But he left early after collaborating with EMI trainee Tim Rice on *Joseph and The Amazing Technicolor Dreamcoat*. Friends told them that Bible stories were uncommercial but producer David Land put them both on a £25-a-week retainer. The show's 1968 debut was followed by two even greater hits, *Jesus Christ Superstar* in 1970 and *Evita* in 1976. But temperamental and artistic differences broke up this budding Gilbert and Sullivan partnership.

The maestro's first solo musical *Jeeves*, with lyrics by Alan Ayckbourn, was his first flop ("a witless travesty", *Guardian)*. But he then enjoyed world-wide hits with *Cats, Starlight Express, Aspects of Love, The Phantom of the Opera* and *Sunset Boulevard*. "Andrew changes lyricists like gardeners", observes his some-time collaborator Don Black. Not generally noted for his sense of humour, Lloyd-Webber once observed: "It's easy to become a millionaire theatrical producer, all you have to do is to start out a billionaire."

Lloyd-Webber's over-developed work ethic contributed to the failure of his first two marriages. He has two children, Nicholas and Imogen, from his childhood sweetheart Sarah Hugill. In 1984 he married *Cats* leading lady Sarah Brightman ("I fell in love with her three-octave soprano"). But she proved to be too hippy and too busy touring. His third wife, three-day eventer Madeleine Gurdon, has revolutionized his life. As well as producing three children, Alistair, William and Isabella, she has added a successful stud farm to his Berkshire mansion, Sydmonton. She also gave him a full makeover, re-styling his pudding-basin haircut, making him slim and replacing his naff wardrobe with Doug Hayward finery.

The composer's estimated £550 million fortune includes an unrivalled pre-Raphaelite art collection. His homes include a Trump Tower apartment in New York, a South of France villa and Kiltinan Castle in Co Tipperary.

Lumley, Joanna, 1st March 1946, a Sloane Goldie Hawn. BBC1's award-winning comedy *Absolutely Fabulous* rejuvenated this luscious Sixties survivor's acting career. Her sell-by date was fast approaching when she became the outrageous Bolly-drinking, drug-taking, nymphomaniac Patsy. Her over-the-top performance brought TV commercials, modelling contracts and other leading rôles.

Joanna was never one of your cor blimey dolly-birds. A retired Indian Army major's daughter she has the carriage and style of an Oscar Wilde heroine. Born in Kashmir, she was brought up in Hong Kong, Malaysia and Singapore. She left her Hastings convent with just one A-level. But her rangy, long-legged physique and full-lipped smile made her a natural model. "Mini-skirts were in and anything above the knee could cause a car crash. I'd buy anything extreme and then turn it up a bit shorter!"

Eligible bachelors like the Earl of Lichfield and war hero's son Brian Alexander chased Joanna. But in 1967 she bravely chose to have a love-child, Jamie. Only recently did she reveal that he was the result of a fling with a little-known Cockney photographer called Michael Claydon. She paid for her son to go to prep school and on to Harrow. In 1970 she married *Are You Being Served?* writer Jeremy Lloyd, sometimes described as London's wittiest man. But they broke up after four months. She had romances with Rod Stewart, backgammon champion Philip Martyn and actor Michael Kitchen. In 1986 she married Stephen Barlow, a conductor eight years her junior, and now lives in Stockwell.

Joanna had no theatrical training. Early films like *Some Girls Do* and *Don't Just Lie There Say Something* were instantly forgettable. She was a Bond girl in *On Her Majesty's Secret Service* but her 1976 rôle as the karate-chopping Purdey in ITV's *The New Avengers* transformed her into a household name. She once spent a week on a desert island for the TV documentary *Girl Friday*. She has also written a weekly diary for *The Times* and published her memoirs, *Stare Back and Smile* which revealed she never wore knickers.

Joanna doesn't bother with gyms, hairdressers or fancy clothes, cars or holidays. "I did all that in the Sixties." She will now progress into becoming a Very Grand Actress and follow Diana Rigg into Damehood. She should give up smoking.

Lynam, Desmond, 17th September 1942, the James Bond of the gogglebox. This white-maned, moustachio-ed Irishman enjoys a following way beyond the sports ghetto. Popular with female viewers he is smart enough to have rejected entreaties to cross over to mainstream TV. Remember what happened to his old colleague Frank Bough? He has also rejected £1 million-a-year bags of swag to defect to Sky. TV professionals value his chatty, unhysterical style. After Gareth Southgate missed his vital penalty in the 1996 European football championship Lynam observed: "You can come out from behind your sofas now!"

This suave ratings-winner was brought up in Brighton and went to Varndean Grammar School. After leaving Brighton Business College he spent six years as an insurance salesman. He began broadcasting on BBC Radio Brighton in 1969, mainly doing boxing commentaries. His TV break came in 1978 with *Nationwide*'s Friday night sports coverage. He gravitated to *Grandstand*, *Sportsnight* and *Match of the Day*, gradually eclipsing David Coleman and Frank Bough. He now acts as anchorman for every major sporting event. His only diversifications have been as *Holiday* presenter and co-host of *How Do They Do That?* His strengths are a laid-back style, laconic delivery and merry quips, plus an encyclopaedic knowledge. Above all he comes across as a decent bloke.

Keen racegoer Lynam has a son Patrick from his nine-year marriage to beautician Susan Skinner which ended in 1974. He has been with his girlfriend, interior decorator Rose Diamond, since 1981: trainer Jenny Pitman once chided him publicly at Aintree for not making an honest woman of her. Rose shares his Chiswick and Brighton houses. His four-year BBC contract is said to be worth an annual £500,000. Cannily he handles all his business affairs himself, resenting the agent's ten per cent. Alas, that trademark striped blazer and club cravat can make him appear a bounder.

Lyndhurst, Nicholas, 21st April 1961, reluctant heart-throb. As plonker Rodney Trotter in *Only Fools and Horses* he became Britain's most popular young comedy star. Viewers loved this 20-year-old Hampshire lad's freshness, naïveté and hangdog expressions, particularly when dealing with spivvy Del Boy. But he became so typecast that when he played another rôle, such as a gay kitchen-fitter in *Straight and Narrow*, fans came expecting to find Rodders. "We've come all the way from Bolton expecting a bloody good night out," complained one theatre-goer. "You've made my daughter cry and we've missed the coach back!"

Only Lyndhurst's hands were visible in his first professional engagement, aged ten. For a TV commercial he pushed a toy car, opened its bonnet and removed a chocolate bar. He subsidised his fees at the Corona stage school by working as a film extra. He then starred in children's programmes such as *The Tomorrow People*, *Heidi* and *The Prince and the Pauper*. His first adult rôle was as Wendy Craig's wayward son Adam in Carla Lane's 1978 sitcom *Butterflies*. To his surprise *Only Fools and Horses* became the Eighties' most successful sitcom and continues to attract a record 24 million viewers with its Christmas specials. In the Nineties he has developed another, almost equally well-loved, character. As Gary in the time-travel sitcom *Goodnight Sweetheart*, he is a married TV engineer who falls for a wartime barmaid in an East End pub.

In real-life Lyndhurst is surprisingly shy, avoiding first nights, fashionable restaurants and discos. He lives alone near Chichester with his cat Mark. He has been engaged twice but claims to be "terrified" of marriage. His first fiancée was beauty therapist Gail Parr. He then became engaged to an Italian translator called Alexandra, but got cold feet. "I've seen too many divorces and too much unhappiness to risk that kind of involvement." His fear of commitment probably stems from his childhood in East Wittering. His father was a married businessman and his mother a holiday camp dancer. "He treated my mother very badly. He told her he'd marry her and she thought for a long time that he would." Lyndhurst is now said to be "head over heels in love" with girlfriend Lucy Smith.

M

Macauley, Mark, 10th April 1956, reformed rake and mischief-maker. This exuberant nephew of former *Daily Telegraph* proprietor Lord Hartwell was brought up in County Wicklow. He hunted with the Blessington and his father owned racehorses. After Ampleforth and Sandhurst he spent six years in the Blues and Royals. He enjoyed a rackety social life mixing with a crowd of zany, hard-drinking, coke-sniffing, dance-to-dawn socialites. His vintage Bentley, nicknamed Bertie, proved a great "bird-puller". Two major influences were "disco dowager" Lady Edith Foxwell and the flamboyant owner of the Embassy Club, Stephen Hayter.

In 1981 this aristo Dai Llewellyn was carpeted after he staged an SAS-style raid on the Embassy with three fellow officers. Shortly afterwards he resigned his commission. He decided that his handsome features and dashing manner would help him to become the new Rex Harrison. His acting career proved shortlived. By the mid-Eighties cocaine and vodka had caused him to become "a complete zombie". Helped by Alcoholics Anonymous, he finally managed to face up to his addiction in 1988.

Belgravia-based Macauley now helps other addicts and is a budding TV producer and scriptwriter. His independent film company, Ballyward, produced *A Gypsy In Africa*, a profile of legendary white hunter Bunny Allen. Other projects include *Scramble For Africa,* a documentary series about the economic development of Africa and *Hangover Hall*, a drama series set in Ireland during the early Sixties. "I wanna win an Oscar within five years."

Mackintosh, Sir Cameron, 17th October 1946, the world's most successful impresario. He pays himself an estimated £10 million a year, yet he is personally very frugal. "I still compare prices when I go shopping in the supermarket." Over Christmas 1996 he had a record six West End musicals running: *Cats, Les Miserables, Phantom of the Opera, Miss Saigon, Martin Guerre* and *Oliver*! But poor notices for *Moby Dick* and *Martin Guerre* show that even he is fallible.

The son of a Scottish timber-merchant and jazz trumpeter and a Maltese mother, Mackintosh grew up in North London. He went to Prior Park College, Bath and, after seeing *Salad Days* aged eight, he wanted to join the theatre. He went to the Central School of Speech and Drama but lasted only a year. He became a £14-a-week stagehand at the Theatre Royal, Drury Lane on *Camelot*. He began producing low-budget touring shows of safe West End and Broadway musicals. They were often slow to make a profit. On bad weeks he made a point of being first in the dole queue. "I wanted to avoid bumping into any of the actors I was working with. I knew they didn't wake up until after 9.30am!" The Andrew Lloyd Webber musicals *Cats* in 1981 and *Phantom of the Opera* in 1986, changed his luck.

Boyish, plumpish, ordinaryish Mackintosh – no-one calls him Sir Cameron except tradesmen – still cannot sing in tune. He mainly invests his estimated £320 million fortune in property. He owns homes in Regent's Park, Somerset, New York and Provence, plus a log cabin with no electricity or telephone set in 12,000 scenic acres beside Ben Nevis. He has inaugurated a visiting theatre professorship at Oxford University. Intensely loyal to family and friends, he has enjoyed a close relationship with photographer Michael Le Poer Trench since 1982.

Madeley, Richard, 13th May 1956, TV's best-pressed interviewer. His chocolate-box looks have been both his fortune and a millstone round his elegant neck. They helped him to leapfrog rivals and become Britain's top daytime TV host. But they also mean he is taken less seriously as a journalist. For inside him is a demon saying: "why aren't you presenting *Newsnight* or *Cutting Edge* documentaries?" Part of his success is that women empathise with him while men find him sexually unthreatening.

Guitar-playing Madeley found his niche on ITV's *This Morning*, a rare survivor of the chat show format. His relationship with his wife and co-presenter, Judy Finnigan, is daily paraded. He clearly dotes on her and leaps to the rescue if he senses an interview floundering. A perfect relationship is said to be where the man is slightly more in love with the woman. It seems to be true of them. In 1990 it was he who needed her support after he was arrested near their home in Didsbury for allegedly stealing soap powder and alcohol from Tesco's. Fortunately magistrates accepted his plea that it was caused by absent-mindedness. The scandal still haunts him. After asking Bob Geldof during an interview why the singer had been declared bankrupt for a day, Geldof replied: "It's like shoplifting, Richard. I couldn't believe that either."

This Essex-born matinee idol began on his local newspaper and radio station. In 1978 he joined Border TV as a reporter and then moved to Yorkshire TV where he read the news. He was nicknamed "the Mannequin" on account of his well-preened appearance. In 1982

Granada TV headhunted him to work on their regional magazine programme, *Granada Reports*. There he met Judy Finnigan. He was soon spellbound by her blonde looks and strong, sensual personality. She may have been eight years older but he had the energy and ambition to drive both their careers. He finally married her in 1986 after the divorce from his first wife, Lynda. The devoted couple now live in a £1 million house near Hampstead Heath.

Mandelson, Peter, 21st October 1953, Minister for Meddling. Every unkind cliché from "Rasputin" to "Prince of Darkness" has been thrown at Labour's legendary spin doctor. But, without his modernisation blueprint and presentational skills, New Labour would never have trounced John Major so effectively in 1997. As Tony Blair's campaign manager he daily advised on policy and tactics, a rôle he continues as Minister Without Portfolio. "Peter has an ability to see a problem a week or a month ahead", says an insider.

The grandson of former Labour deputy leader Herbert Morrison Mandelson grew up in Hampstead Garden Suburb. His father was advertising manager of the *Jewish Chronicle* and a local Labour activist. After Hendon County Grammar School he spent a year in Tanzania, teaching and helping in a village hospital. He read PPE at Oxford and then worked for the TUC and British Youth Council. He first entered politics as a Lambeth councillor under left-wing leader Ted Knight. For three years he was an LWT producer on Brian Walden's *Weekend World*.

Labour leader Neil Kinnock then appointed Mandelson director of campaigns and communications to fight the 1987 general election. He smartened up Kinnock and invented the rose-bud logo and pastel backdrops to party conference platforms. He became MP for the tough Teesside constituency of Hartlepool in 1992 and was made a junior whip. During John Smith's leadership his influence waned, but he reinforced his rapport with Blair and Shadow Chancellor Gordon Brown. His dumping of Brown during the 1994 leadership election showed ruthlessness plus an ability to spot a winner. One of his most enduring coups was to make Labour heavyweights Robin Cook, David Blunkett and John Prescott more media-friendly.

The witty, Chardonnay-loving Mandy shaved off his moustache because it made him look camp. A confirmed bachelor, he lives alone in an interior-designed Notting Hill house, but is much entertained by influential friends of all political persuasions. He is an *aficionado* of smart Islington and Westminster restaurants. But he denies that he once ordered "guacomole" in a Hartlepool fish 'n' chip shop, only to be told by the owner that he had just pointed at mushy peas. He is said never to forget a slight.

March and Kinrara, Earl of, 8th January 1955, ducal democrat.
He was happy being a simple photographer in Fulham called
Charles Settrington. He found the "Lord" Settrington handle rather
an embarrassment. Now he is lumbered with running his father's
18th century stately home – Goodwood House, Sussex, with its
12,000-acre estate, racecourse and art treasures. Eventually he will
succeed him as 11th Duke of Richmond and 6th Duke of Gordon.

Car-freak Charles grew up with a nagging social conscience. His
father was a senior Church of England layman and had taken the
then revolutionary step for an aristo of adopting two black girls. One
of them, Nimmy March, became a leading soap actress. Young
Charles was expelled from Eton after leading a classroom revolt.
Undeterred he went to Ireland to work on Stanley Kubrick's film
Barry Lyndon as a stills photographer. After snapping houses and
their contents for estate agents he then set himself up as a commercial photographer. He became as adept at making cheese, scarves
and jewellery look tempting in a Harrods catalogue as David Bailey
did with models in glossy magazines. His hi-tech Fulham house contained a bizarre collection of Fifties dentists furniture and a brand-
new Belgian racing-bike hanging like a sculpture.

The bashful peer's confidence was boosted by his marriage to the
late Viscount Astor's brainy daughter Janet. She quickly supplied
the vital heir, Lord Settrington, plus a 'spare', William. He already
had a daughter, Lady Alexandra, from his first wife, former Pan's
People dancer Sally Clayton. Meanwhile he tries hard to dream up
new scams to lure visitors to Goodwood.

Margaret, Princess, 21st August 1930, former royal 'wild child'.
She is the Palace court jester. Witty, intelligent and sophisticated,
she captivates friends with her mimicry, anecdotes and Lady
Bracknell asides. On being told Prince Rainier was contemplating
marriage to the buxom Princess Ira von Furstenberg she observed:
"Such a big girl for such a small country!" She is dubbed "the house
party guest from hell" because of her "call me Ma'am" imperious-
ness, but sometimes redeems herself with spirited renditions of *Red
Hot Momma* on the drawing-room piano.

As a child this spoilt, wilful, tantalising princess was always prettier and cleverer than her older sister "Lilibet". Unable to go to
boarding school, university or even art school she was brought up "in
a gilded cage" at Buckingham Palace. The death of her devoted
father George VI in 1952 removed her only restraining influence.
She embarked on a doomed affair with his former equerry, Group

Captain Peter Townsend, 15 years her senior. In those Neanderthal days, his divorce and inferior social status were sufficient barriers to a royal marriage.

Maggie then flung herself into a frivolous life of nightclubbing and party-going. Had today's paparazzi been around she would have been dubbed another Fergie. At 30 she married photographer Antony Armstrong-Jones, who shared her wild social habits and artistic interests. He was created Earl of Snowdon so that any offspring would not be born commoners. A Welsh baronet observed that the title had "made a mountain out of a molehill." They divorced in 1978, having had two unusually talented children, Viscount Linley and Lady Sarah Chatto.

Margaret began flaunting her latest boyfriend, Roddy Llewellyn, 17 years her junior, who lived in a Wiltshire commune. During their five-year affair they frequently visited her Mustique villa. One riotous evening there she met East End crook John Bindon who performed his party trick for her – balancing a number of beer mugs on his manhood! She was heartbroken when Roddy deserted her to marry Tania Soskin in 1981, but characteristically observed that she could no longer afford him.

After a health scare Margaret has finally given up smoking and cut down on her whisky. She surrounds herself with amusing "walkers" like Ned Ryan and Ben Holland-Martin. No longer on the Civil List, she carries out few public duties.

Marlborough, Duke of, 13th April 1926, Oxfordshire landowner. How ironic that this pin-striped giant should be nicknamed "Sunny", for he is famed for his haughtiness. But it derives from his subsidiary title, Earl of Sunderland. His Grace has lavished millions on restoring Vanbrugh's masterpiece Blenheim Palace and commercialised it by expanding his Churchilliana rooms, adding boats to the lake and opening a garden centre. Kenneth Branagh's *Hamlet*, in which the duke had a cameo role, is the latest of many film and TV projects to use Blenheim as a location. But he has rejected offers to open a theme park or safari park.

A Japanese tourist once asked a tour guide: "Marlborough. He live here, yes?" When assured that this was so the visitor enquired: "He make cigarettes, yes?" In fact, the duke and his third wife Rosita spend most of the time at their nearby home, Lee Place, or their Mayfair townhouse.

Marlborough, descended from our greatest war hero, loves all the pomp associated with his position. He can even style himself Prince of the Holy Roman Empire and Prince of Mindelheim. Perhaps he should remind himself that he is descended from a humble blacksmith! Ex-Eton and the Life Guards he is happiest when gossiping with cronies at White's Club or at race meetings.

Marlborough was one of five grandees who could have married Princess Margaret, but she needed a brighter, more stimulating husband. In 1951 he married stationery heiress Susan Hornby, who produced his wayward heir the Marquess of Blandford and interior decorator Lady Henrietta. His second wife was Greek heiress Tina Livanos, the former wife of tycoon Aristotle Onassis. He only achieved marital harmony in 1972 when he married his present wife, Swedish count's daughter Rosita Douglas, who has taken total charge of his life. Alas, primogeniture will prevent their well-qualified son, Lord Edward Spencer-Churchill, from succeeding him as duke. But who will take charge of the 11,500-acre estate?

Mayall, Rik, 7th March 1958, self-confessed purveyor of "filthy juvenile humour". As the sneering revolutionary poet in the Eighties TV series *The Young Ones* he became a cult success at 24. "Rick" was based on his own nerdish character at Manchester University. He and his comedy partner Adrian Edmondson first performed in university revues with an act called 20th Century Coyote. On graduation they competed against rising comics like Alexei Sayle and Keith Allen at London's Comedy Store. "They were all big grown-ups being really cool and very dangerous and telling jokes about Mrs Thatcher. We were the ones saying 'Hello, we're ****holes'".

C4 then bagged all four for *The Comic Strip Presents*, which became a nursery for alternative comics. *The Young Ones* spawned BBC2's *Filthy, Rich and Catflap*, with Mayall playing a failed TV star trying to keep up with "Brucie and Tarby". In BBC2's 1991 sitcom *Bottom* he and Edmondson played seedy flatmates. ("It's video sales have just gone platinum.") But his most defining rôle was the shifty Tory politician Alan B'Stard in *The New Statesman*, which he now hopes to revive under New Labour. About his rôles he says: "There's a quality about me that you don't quite trust. So one of the things that I can get laughs off is dissembling badly."

Gangling Mayall grew up in Essex and was educated at the King's School, Worcester. His drama-teacher parents would encourage him to perform on stage with their students. "I found I could make people laugh and enjoyed that feeling." Today, despite his manic screen rôles, he enjoys a normal un-luvvie life in West London with his wife Barbara, a former BBC make-up artist. "I like everything about her. She's an enormously wise, instinctive person who understands all the problems of being an actor." They have three children, Rosemary, Sidney and Bonnie. "For so long I've been living a schizoid existence, pretending to be a wild man when really I'm Mr

Mortgage, Mr Two Cars." Between series he gets restless at home. "I don't have any hobbies and am happiest working." He fancies himself as a straight actor.

McAlpine of West Green, Lord, 14th May 1942, eccentric *bon viveur*. Alistair McAlpine is credited with having miraculously raised £100 million towards Mrs Thatcher's three election victories. During the 1983 election he sent a marked copy of Labour's manifesto to Britain's 500 top industrialists with the message: "When you've had a look at this, perhaps you'd like to send us some money!" Mrs T was his heroine, and her successor John Major could never quite cut the mustard. McAlpine deserted the Tories in 1997 to campaign for Sir James Goldsmith's Referendum Party. But it was his irreverent memoirs, *Once A Jolly Swagman*, which probably did more damage.

This friendly, cultivated, Bollinger-loving multi-millionaire was born with a silver trowel in his mouth. His grandfather Sir Robert – "Concrete Bob" – McAlpine founded the family building empire in the 19th century. Alastair, known as "Roly Poly" at Stowe, left school at 16 with just three O-levels. As clerk of the works on McAlpine's South Bank development he soon had his smooth edges roughened. On his 21st birthday he joined the board. In 1964 he took charge of their new Western Australian subsidiary, developing a lifelong passion for the Outback, particularly its old pearling villages, wildlife and wine.

This pink-cheeked multi-millionaire – ennobled in 1984 – invariably wears a crumpled pale linen suit with a Garrick Club tie. He is now based in Monte Carlo and Venice. He used to live at West Green House, a National Trust property near Basingstoke, where he bred rare waterfowl and collected antique dolls, truncheons and duck decoys. There he would cook banquets for Cabinet ministers and other weekend guests deemed useful for fund-raising activities. His speciality was to stuff four different game birds inside a pheasant.

Dilettante McAlpine has two daughters, Mary and Victoria, from his first wife, tobacco heiress Sarah Baron. In 1980 he married silk-stockinged temptress Romilly Hobbs, who owned a Mayfair delicatessen. She refused to marry him unless he agreed to follow a "tiresome" fig diet – he lost two stone. They have a daughter, Skye, and dote on each other. More bitchy memoirs, please.

McCartney, Paul Sir, 18th June 1942, the 20th century's towering musical genius. Despite his estimated £420 million fortune this legendary singer, song-writer and bass guitarist has always refused to go into tax exile. Like Queen Marie-Antoinette he prefers to lead a "simple" life on his 220-acre farm near Rye, forsaking the rock star glitz. He and his wife Linda grow their own organic vegetables, drive a battered Range Rover and go shopping in the village. Their children Mary, Stella and James went to the local comprehensive and Paul buys a season ticket to commute to his West End office. As dedicated vegetarians they ban hunting and shooting at their Sussex home and on their Mull of Kintyre estate.

This witty, baby-faced composer of classics like *Yesterday*, *Hey Jude* and *Penny Lane* was always the most upwardly-mobile Beatle. Teachers at the Liverpool Institute expected him to go on to university. But, instead of revising for his A-levels, he played with skiffle groups, the Quarrymen and the Moondogs. The Beatles were already Merseyside prodigies when they had their first hit, *Love Me Do*, in 1962. No pop band has ever emulated their musical, financial or cultural success. Today, without fanfare, the McCartneys plough the profits from their back catalogue into charitable causes.

During Beatlemania Macca was never the groupie-bedding pop stereotype. For most of the Fab Four's eight years, his girlfriend was actress Jane Asher, a Harley Street doctor's daughter. But he ditched her in 1969 to marry American rock photographer Linda Eastman who already had a daughter from an earlier marriage. He has remained touchingly loyal to her, both when critics attacked him for letting her perform with his supergroup Wings and during her long battle with breast cancer.

McCartney's 1996 knighthood might have happened earlier if he had not boasted that The Beatles had smoked a joint in the gents at Buckingham Palace when collecting their MBEs. His Tokyo conviction for possession of cannabis in 1980 also didn't help. But his clutch of over 60 gold discs, Grammies and other awards, plus his endowment of the Liverpool performing arts centre, finally tipped the balance. He still has two major ambitions: to become pop's first life peer and to buy back The Beatles' music copyrights from superstar Michael Jackson.

McDonald, Trevor, 16th August 1939, Trinidad's greatest export since Hasely Crawford. His clipped Oxbridge accent sounds very un-West Indian. Indeed, he is chairman of a government committee set up to encourage the use of better English in schools. He enjoys singing calypsos, but only when he is very merry. He originally strove to be as British as possible "so that I'd avoid being labelled a black commentator".

McDonald was raised in a poor Trinidad fishing village. His father worked in the local oil refinery and his devoted mother, Geraldine, insisted that Trevor grew up to "speak proper". He would try to copy the announcers on the BBC World Service. "She taught us old-fashioned values like playing the game, never blowing your own trumpet and treating success and failure just the same."

This inveterate high-achiever began reading news bulletins on local radio stations. He came to Britain aged 30 to join the World Service. In 1973 he became ITN's first black news reporter and was then a sports correspondent. He became a relief newsreader in 1982 and later read the C4 News for two years. He shared *News at Ten* duties with Sir Alastair Burnet until promoted to main presenter in 1992. Among his scoops was the first British TV interview with South African president Nelson Mandela after his release from prison and a half-hour exclusive with Saddam Hussein just before the Gulf War. His secret fear is "not being properly briefed". The shambles of ITV's 1997 monarchy "debate", of which he was co-presenter, horrified him.

Behind McDonald's austere expression is a tiger waiting to escape. He is a convivial companion who enjoys good Burgundy and Cuban cigars. His other passion is watching the Test Match and he has written biographies of the West Indian cricketers Viv Richards and Clive Lloyd. He married his English first wife in 1964 and had two children, Joanne and Tim. From his 1986 marriage to ITN production assistant Josephine Goode he has a son Jamie. "At home I've a kind of Dickensian thing about cleaning and tidying up", he says.

McDonald has never quite managed to become the Walter Cronkite figure he desires. But soon, on retirement, his wide knowledge of politics and world affairs would prove useful in the Lords.

McKenna, Paul, 8th November 1963, modern Merlin. At his sell-out roadshows this slick, charismatic hypnotist will turn a quiet factory worker into Mick Jagger singing *Can't Get No Satisfaction* or a nerdish bank clerk into a chicken clucking round the stage. He describes his act as "3D karaoke".

McKenna rivals Cilla Black and Michael Barrymore as one of Britain's highest-paid performers. As well as ITV's *The Hypnotic World of Paul McKenna*, he has a lucrative line in Stop Smoking/Overeating/Worrying/Failing books and cassettes. He rejects criticism that he is bastardising his gift by using it as a form of entertainment. He enjoys the high-profile and helps showbiz stars and sportsmen reach their full potential. He cured Spike Milligan's insomnia, stopped *EastEnders* star Michelle Collins smoking and helped Frank Bruno win a fight. Yet before his fame he was so miserable that he once contemplated suicide.

This cocky, designer-suited bachelor comes from Enfield, the son of a building contractor and a teacher. He went to a local Jesuit boys' school where he claims his teachers "bled all my self-confidence away". He became a Capital Radio disc jockey. But his interests always lay in the paranormal. His greatest influence was the American psychotherapist Milton H. Erickson, who did healing from a wheelchair. He would get close to patients by "mirroring", exactly matching their movements, even down to their rate of breathing. McKenna learned that a hypnotist should be a soothing communicator rather than an authoritarian figure ordering patients "you won't smoke anymore". In 1987 he made his first public performance in a Cambridge pub to a crowd of 50. A year later he was 'discovered' by impresario Harvey Goldsmith.

Kensington-based McKenna is more a Stringfellows person than a Billy Graham. His former fiancée was *Gladiator* Zodiac's leggy blonde sister Clare Staples, whom he helped cure of bulimia. Although they split up in 1995 she continues to be his personal manager. He insists that his powers don't include forcing a woman to fall in love with him. When he starts a family he plans to hypnotise his wife so that she feels no pain in childbirth.

McNally, Paddy, 20th December 1937, fun-seeker tycoon. He will always be remembered as the owlish-looking playboy who passed on Fergie to the Duke of York. She married him on the rebound after McNally ungallantly rejected her "marry me or else" ultimatum at the 1985 Italian Grand Prix following a three-year romance. Undaunted, this RAF doctor's son went to the royal wedding and remains her closest and most reliable friend.

Educated at Roman Catholic public school Stonyhurst, former racing-driver McNally was a familiar Sixties figure. He was a journalist on *Autoroute* magazine before becoming involved with Marlboro which sponsored James Hunt's McLaren team when he won the 1976 Grand Prix. He was briefly former world champion Niki Lauda's manager. He has since built an estimated £20 million fortune from providing advertising space and hospitality facilities on the Grand Prix circuit.

McNally has two sons, Sean and Rollo, from his 1968 marriage to heiress Anne Downing. Both are keen amateur racing-drivers. After her death from cancer in 1980 he set a frenetic social pace at his Verbier chalet, nicknamed "the Castle". The frisky, former Sarah Ferguson had to cook for his raffish circle of friends, who included the Marquess of Blandford, Nigel Pollitzer and numerous hangers-on. A stolen photograph of her lying in the bath there smoking a herbal cigarette was once sold by a "friend". McNally later went out with kindergarten teacher Becky Few-Brown who went on to marry Blandford, and heiress Lucinda McAlpine. He may lack Tom Cruise's sex appeal but his riches ensure that he is never short of beautiful female admirers.

McQueen, Alexander, 17th March 1969, Norman Hartnell with attitude. This 1996 Designer of the Year is the physical antithesis of his Hollywood namesake Steve. He is tubby, grubby, oddly-proportioned and sometimes wears red contact lens that make him resemble a sci-fi monster. He will design trousers specially so that he can expose his bum cleavage at fashion shows. His gaucheness upset the Paris fashion establishment when he succeeded arch rival John Galliano as chief designer at Maison Givenchy in 1996. A *Nouvel Observatoire* journalist berated him for his personal "style": "The slightly soiled, open-neck shirt, the chic way he carries a can of beer and that haircut, très football-club de Liverpool". Patrician Hubert de Givenchy was horrified by his protégé's observation that "*haute couture* should not be a jacket so over-embroidered and beaded that it looks like someone has thrown up over it".

This East London taxi-driver's son was bullied at school because he was not interested in girls or sport. He is proud of his Scots ancestry. Highland battles sometimes provide the inspiration for his shows and he is keen to revive the 'auld alliance' with France. His muse is funky baronet's daughter Isabella Blow, a freelance stylist and writer. Aristo model Honor Fraser leads a loyal band of supporters who bond with his "cute, real sweetie-pie" personality and witty asides. His suspicion of journalists means that he now almost expects criticism. An American fashion writer, arriving to interview him, found a note pinned to his studio saying: "Not in. Don't want press in your magazine anyway." He has sometimes perversely sited his London shows in semi-derelict warehouses in no-go areas.

The brilliant, self-destructive McQueen's styles – bumster trousers, asymmetric longline jackets and fan-tailed pencil skirts – generally only suit customers on a strict diet. Still under 30 he could, if given the right financial backing, develop into another Giorgio Armani or Yves St Laurent.

Mellor, David, 12th March 1949, broadcaster and ex-politician, known as Mellorphant Man. He was the archetypal Thatcherite who triumphed from a humble background to become a cabinet minister. After Swanage Grammar School he went to Cambridge where he was president of the university's Conservative Association. He was called to the Bar in 1972 and became Tory MP for Putney seven years later. He served as a junior minister in the Home Office, Foreign Office and Department of Health.

The formidably ambitious Mellor is living proof of the truism that you can turn even the most tacky publicity to your advantage. He began the Nineties as John Major's blue-eyed boy, rapidly winning promotion from Treasury minister to National Heritage Secretary where he impressed with his wide knowledge of the Arts. It was he who warned newspaper editors that they were "drinking in the Last Chance Saloon" if they ignored people's right to privacy.

In 1992 a Sunday tabloid revealed that Mellor had had an affair with would-be starlet Antonia de Sancha and even made love to her wearing a Chelsea strip. The revelations were all the more surprising given that he resembled a Sixth Form swot rather than a lusty Romeo. He tried to bluff it out by posing for a "united family" photo-opportunity with his wife Judith and two children. But it failed to save his Cabinet post. He then reinvented himself as a media personality and influence peddler. His trademark specs and gap-toothed grin was constantly seen on TV and he became a regular sports presenter on *Radio 5 Live*. His earnings from journalism soon far exceeded his ministerial salary while he became known as "king of the consultancies" particularly for his services to British arms companies selling to the Middle East.

The Mellors divorced in 1995 after 21 years of marriage. David moved into a £1 million Georgian house overlooking the Thames, only a bellow away from his old newspaper persecutors in Wapping. Sharing it is his high-powered girlfriend, Penelope Lady Cobham, whose own marriage to a wealthy West Midlands landowner had just broken up. Alas, he lost his seat in the 1997 general election. He yearns to become Lord Mellor.

Mendes, Sam, 1st August 1965, West End *wunderkind*. As artistic director he has given the Donmar Warehouse that special buzz of innovation and excitement once uniquely enjoyed by the Royal Court. With his charm, intelligence and flair he has turned revivals of musicals like *Company* and *Cabaret* into award-winning successes. "Directing combines amateur psychology, sports coaching and visual art. You become an intellectual and visual magpie." First nights, he says, have "the emotional impact of a car crash. Even I, sitting in the bar nursing my drink, am paralysed with fear!" Directing his first commercial production, *Oliver!*, at the London Palladium enabled him to make "absurd sums of money!"

Cricket-loving Mendes's family were originally Portuguese who settled in Trinidad. Sam's parents – his father was a university lec-

turer – split up when he was five. He first discovered the stage as a
14-year-old pupil of Magdalen College School, Oxford, when his
mother took him to see *The Merchant of Venice* at Stratford-upon-
Avon. "The theatre became a stabilising influence in a rather unsta-
ble childhood." At Cambridge he put on college productions. After
graduating with a First in English he took a £50-a-week job sweeping the stage at the Chichester Theatre. Director John Gale allowed
him to direct three Chekhov one-act plays – *Swansong, The Bear*
and *The Marriage Proposal* – for one night only. Rave reviews followed and at 23 he became artistic director of the newly-built
Minerva Theatre. Hailed as the "new Peter Hall" he directed Paul
Eddington in *London Assurance* and Judi Dench in *The Cherry
Orchard* and, for the RSC, *Kean* with Derek Jacobi and *Troilus and
Cressida* with Ralph Fiennes.

Theatre's most eligible bachelor lives in a converted almshouse
near Oxford. He enjoyed a three-year relationship with *Absolutely
Fabulous* actress Jane Horrocks, who starred in his productions of
Cabaret and *The Rise and Fall of Little Voice*. The fact she was less
obviously intellectual than him may have contributed to their split.
In 1996 he declined an invitation to apply to be the National
Theatre's director. "I'd love to run a big theatre some time. But I've
too many things to do first – films, musicals, opera…"

Merton, Paul, 17th January 1957, clever clogs without an autocue.
With his beer belly and greasy hair, he is the tall, slobby member of
that satirical band that grew up in the late Eighties, Messrs
Deayton, Slattery, Enfield and Elton. But his quick wit, sly charm,
zigzag mind and good heartedness makes up for it. Amidst the
bitchy camaraderie of *Have I Got News For You* he is the token
working-class lad.

Son of a Tube driver and a nurse, he grew up in 'Sarf' London.
After watching the clowns at Bertram Mills Circus aged three he
knew he wanted to be a comedian. He failed his 11-plus and went to
Wimbledon College, a Catholic comprehensive, where he made
friends by making pupils laugh. He then spent three years working
as a clerk at Tooting Employment Exchange. He quit in 1980 to start
working the comedy club circuit. He lied about his experience and
got a five-minute late-night spot at the Comedy Store. "I used to be
bitter about this Oxbridge mafia of alternative comedians who
seemed to walk into TV deals." But hard work and talent made up
for any lack of contacts. Shows like *Paul Merton's Life of Comedy*
display his surreal brand of humour. He models his dead-pan delivery – never smiling at his own or other people's jokes – on his idol,
Buster Keaton. He made his straight acting debut in *An Evening*

with Gary Lineker and dreams of becoming another Peter Sellers.

Merton believes comedians have a black sense of humour. "If you show a film of an old lady careering downhill in a wheelchair the audience will laugh only if they know it isn't real. The comedian will only laugh if it is!" Before marrying *Men Behaving Badly* star Caroline Quentin, he claims to have been shy of women. He met her in 1990 on the Euston to Glasgow train en route to an arts festival. She complained that the book he was reading was "rubbish" and so he opened the window and threw it out. Three months later he proposed to her on bended knee beside the statue of Eros in Piccadilly Circus. She looked so taken aback that a policeman intervened and asked: "Is this man bothering you, madam?" They split up in 1996 and he began dating his ex-understudy Sarah Parkinson.

Michael, George, 25th June 1963, rock's Greta Garbo. He was the archetypal teenage idol who was unable to handle the pressures of stardom. For four glorious years he and his partner Andrew Ridgeley were the hottest band since the Beatles. Wham! sold 20 million albums and 12 million singles, including *Bad Boys, Club Tropicana* and *Wake Me Up Before You Go Go*. When they broke up in 1986 Michael became a designer-stubbled Cliff Richard, with hits like *A Different Corner* and *I Want Your Sex* (banned by the BBC). His album *Faith* sold 15 million copies worldwide. But prolonged legal action with his record company, Sony, kept him out of the charts for five years.

This Greek-Cypriot superstar was born Georgios Kyriakos Panayiotou – his family still call him Yog – and brought up in suburban Hertfordshire. At Bushey Meads Comprehensive he was a tubby, bespectacled, frizzy-haired swot who played the violin and composed weird pop songs. He teamed up with Ridgeley, a handsome, would-be playboy with little musical talent but oodles of style and chutzpah. They would skip classes and busk outside Green Park tube station. But Yog's father, a Shaftesbury Avenue kebab house owner, was determined his clever son should go to university. He even tried to bribe him with "a sports car or a flat in town" if he delayed his musical ambitions. But Yog continued to record his songs with Ridgeley, who was branded "a bad influence" by English-born Mrs Panayiotou. Finally in 1982 a £20 demo of *Wham Rap*, about life on the dole, landed them a recording contact and their first hit *Young Guns Go For It*. Meanwhile diet, beauty treatments and contact lenses had transformed Yog into a blond, suntanned Adonis.

Now worth an estimated £50 million this moody, enigmatic, Versace-clad bachelor lives in Hampstead splendour with his labrador Hippy. There are occasional sightings on Hampstead Heath and at West End clubs. Gossip columnists vainly try to discover whether he has a lover. He admits that there is "a big neon question-mark" hanging over his sex life.

Miles, Roy, 9th February 1935, Lord Duveen with a punch. This bombastic art salesman has clients like Princess Michael of Kent, the Duke of Devonshire, Elton John, the Pet Shop Boys and Ivana Trump. His gallery, the West End's largest, makes a perfect setting for his splashy private views. A red carpet welcomes Café Society's leading denizens, handsome waiters mince past with trays of champagne and designer canâpés, flashbulbs keep popping.

The flamboyant, publicity-loving Miles was born Roy Marsh in the Wirral. He barely knew his father, who served in the Royal Navy, but adores his formidable mother Elsa who ran a chain of dress-shops and hairdressers. She remarried and Roy changed his surname to his stepfather's. At 19 he was already running an import-export business. He opened a hairdressing salon in Wigmore Street before buying the Mayfair salon Antoine ("but I've never cut hair"). He took a year off to study art at the Sorbonne, sold his businesses and opened his first gallery in Belgravia. Millionaire clients like Paul Mellon paid record prices for British sporting pictures.

In 1975 Miles moved to Duke Street, St James's. It was more convenient for Christie's and Sotheby's, where he spent £10 million on Victorian art over 12 years. But his arrival horrified old-established dealers like Sir Geoffrey Agnew, Sir Hugh Leggatt and Richard Green who resented his brash salesmanship. During the Arab oil boom he held the first exhibition of British art in Kuwait. Showing round a sheikh he gave his usual colourful spiel: "this is a Gainsborough from the blue period, this is a Stubbs, a very valuable picture", and so on. Afterwards the sheikh thanked him profusely and added: "tell me, Mr Miles, how do you find the time to paint so many beautiful pictures?"

In 1970 the Bach-loving dealer married Christine Rhodes, a Yorkshire heiress who breeds Cavalier King Charles spaniels. But they have lived separate lives for over 20 years. Also gone are his Knightsbridge mansion, Cannes apartment, chauffeur-driven Rolls Royce, yacht and other toys. "This decade has been about survival, so many of the big Mayfair dealers have gone to the wall".

Mirren, Helen, 26th July 1946, the lady who put sex into Shakespeare. Her blonde beauty, saucy smile and wry intelligence are a devastating combination. It has stood her well ever since she fled her Leigh-on-Sea home aged 18.

This rebel Essex girl was christened Ilynea Lydia Mironoff. Her grandfather was a Tsarist Russian grandee who fled here in 1917, but her father was a driving examiner. She upset the nuns at St Bernard's convent school by running a darts stall at Southend fairground. While attending teacher training college she enrolled with the National Youth Theatre. In 1968 she appeared in two RSC productions. Leading rôles in *Macbeth* and *Measure for Measure* followed before films lured her away.

The trashy *Caligula* and *The Fiendish Plots of Fu Manchu* were followed by *The Long Good Friday, Excalibur* and *Cal*. She stripped off in Ken Russell's *Savage Messiah*. But, despairing of finding suitable rôles here, she moved to Hollywood in 1984. Taylor Hackford, director of her film, *White Nights*, became her long-time boyfriend.

Helen has two interlocking Vs tattooed on her left hand, meaning "love thy neighbour", the result of a drunken night on a Minnesota Indian reservation. Among her more arty films are *The Mosquito Coast* and *Pascali's Island* and *The Cook, The Thief, His Wife and Her Lover*. She won excellent notices for *The Madness of King George* and was much criticised for the pro-IRA movie *Some Mother's Son*. But she will always be best-known as formidable DCI Jane Tennison in ITV's award-winning series *Prime Suspect*.

In fact, this petite, left-wing actress "dislikes" the police and would like to see the monarchy abolished. She belongs to the Scruffy Tendency, never dressing up when she can slop around at home in Los Angeles or Battersea in jeans. She hates interviews and is wont to take her acting a mite too seriously. She boasts that, since 18, she has always lived with men – they include photographer James Wedge, White Russian prince George Galitzine and Liam Neeson. She claims to have no maternal instinct.

Monckton, Rosa, 26th October 1953, Queen of Tiffany's. As a Catholic Sloane the willowy, Mediterranean-looking Rosa was genetically programmed to marry well and have children. There was nothing in her blue-blooded DNA that suggested she might one day sully her hands with trade. But she was determined to become a jeweller. She studied silver- and goldsmithing, worked for Cartier and Asprey's and spent a year flogging baubles to Arabs in Monte Carlo. In 1986 New York jewellers Tiffany's appointed her managing director of their new London branch. To drum up business she organised a series of "Breakfasts at Tiffany's".

The convent-educated super-*vendeuse* was brought up near Maidstone. Her father, Viscount Monckton of Brenchley, is a retired major-general and her grandfather, Sir Walter Monckton, the first viscount, was Edward VIII's legal adviser during the 1936 abdication crisis. Intriguingly, she has managed to combine her demanding job selling trinkets to film stars, millionaires and ladies-who-lunch with fulfilling her original destiny. In 1991 she married *Spectator* editor Dominic Lawson, son of the former Chancellor of the Exchequer. They met at a summer party given by *Harpers & Queen's* then editor, Sally O'Sullivan. "It was a real *coup de foudre*! Within days he'd moved into her Pimlico flat", recalls a friend.

Now based in Bayswater they have two daughters, Savannah and Domenica. Her close friend Princess Diana was godmother to Domenica, who suffers from Down's Syndrome. After the birth Rosa ruefully recalled John Lennon's line: "Life is what happens to you when you're making other plans". Now *Sunday Telegraph* editor, Lawson has written about his "intense, almost physically painful love" for the baby.

Monkhouse, Bob, 1st June 1928, Squire Smarm. He is currently undergoing a renaissance, fronting the *National Lottery Live*, *Celebrity Squares* and *On the Spot*. Like Nicholas Parsons and Bruce Forsyth it is fashionable to sneer at him. But he has the sharpest, most entertaining cabaret act in Britain and is constantly busy compering corporate shows. There is nothing stale about his joke books, memorably once stolen from the BBC Television Centre. He has occupied our screens since 1953 in such incarnations as *My Pal Bob*, *Bob's Full House* and *The Bob Monkhouse Show*. His trademarks are his urchin smile, infectious giggle and precise enunciation. He partly owes his longevity to being the first comic to spot the potential of TV quizzes and game shows. He has fronted *The Golden Shot*, *Family Fortunes* and *Opportunity Knocks*.

The Beckenham-born comedy legend could have entered the family business, Monkhouse Glasscock Ltd, "custard powder and jelly manufacturers to royalty". But even as a precocious three-year-old he was reciting Stanley Holloway monologues. He sold his first jokes to comedian Max Miller for five shillings aged 16. While still at Dulwich College he secretly entered a Carroll Levis talent show. "I was unbelievably awful and the whole thing was a disaster." His first job was as a trainee cartoon-animator. He began broadcasting unofficially for the BBC during his RAF national service. An officer told him: "I don't care what you do, as long as you give me the money you get for doing it!" His early career as a radio comic was in partnership with an old school chum, Denis Goodwin. They wrote gags too for Arthur Askey, Jack Benny and Bob Hope. An appearance on ITV's top variety show, *Sunday Night at the London Palladium*, launched his solo career.

In his autobiography Monkhouse revealed he once had a fling with Fifties starlet Diana Dors. He has two children, Simon and Abigail, from his first wife Elizabeth. In 1973 he married his secretary Jackie and they live in a converted Bedfordshire farmhouse, with a red public telephone box in the garden. He maintains a year-round tan with visits to his Barbados villa.

Montagu of Beaulieu, Lord, 20th October 1926, indefatigable showman. Edward Douglas-Scott-Montagu was only three when he inherited the title from his father. With it went an 8,000-acre Hampshire estate, including historic Bucklers Hard and the Beaulieu River, that had been in the family for 16 generations. His home, Palace House, is part of a 14th century Cistercian abbey.

Exotic, mischievously amusing Montagu – Eton, Oxford and the Grenadier Guards – was one of the first aristos to open his home to the public. In 1952 he turned his passion for vintage cars into the National Motor Museum. He scoured the world, particularly maharajahs' estates in India, for unusual examples of Rolls-Royces, Bentleys and other rarities. The museum ranks consistently among Britain's top tourist attractions and can be viewed by monorail. He continues to be a regular in the London to Brighton old crocks race.

Bald, jazz-loving Montagu has never been a womaniser. From his brief first marriage to Lord Somerleyton's cousin, Belinda Crossley, he has a son Ralph and daughter Mary. In 1974 he married former TV executive Fiona Herbert and they have a son Jonathan. She has been the family linchpin while his lordship concentrated on his chairmanship of the Historic Buildings and Monuments Commission and spent long periods away entertaining at his beach house overlooking the Solent. He retains a wry sense of humour.

Every decade Edward holds a mammoth fancy dress birthday party attended by royalty, showbiz and Café Society. For his 50th birthday in 1976 the theme was the "Dunkirk Spirit". Guests found searchlights raking the sky, khaki-clad marquees set up as field kitchens and Dame Vera Lynn as the cabaret. Was it a joke that made him suggest that "to reflect wartime austerity" every couple should bring a bottle of champagne?

Moore, Dudley, 19th April 1935, Woody Allen *manqué*. This 5ft 2ins, fuzzy-haired screwball was first known as the musical genius behind *Beyond The Fringe*. With three former Cambridge undergraduates, Jonathan Miller, Alan Bennett and Peter Cook, he inspired the Sixties satire boom with this mould-breaking West End and Broadway revue. His Dudley Moore Trio, featuring his jazz-influenced piano, also became a fixture at trendy joints like Soho's Establishment Club. But his career soon lagged behind the others.

This merry musical jester was the brilliant Cook's comic feed in *Not Only ...But Also*, whose signature tune, *Goodbye-ee*, became a Top 20 hit. Together they created the "Dud and Pete" TV dialogues and salacious "Derek and Clive" records. But films like *30 Is a Dangerous Age Cynthia*, *Bedazzled* and *Monte Carlo or Bust* did little for his reputation. His luck changed in 1979 when he moved to Hollywood. He starred as a lecherous British composer opposite Julie Andrews and Bo Derek in *10* and as Liza Minnelli's drunken playboy lover in *Arthur*. Gossip columnists dubbed him "the Sex Thimble". He took to the Californian lifestyle with gusto, particularly the easy availability of women – always his weakness.

Moore, a railway engineer's son, was brought up in industrial Dagenham, Essex. He suffered taunts at the local County High School because of his club-foot. A musical prodigy, he studied at the Guildhall School of Music and won an organ scholarship to Oxford. His mother's coldness towards him meant he has spent his life searching for a mummy figure. "I've always found it hard to accept that anyone would love me." At 23 he married starlet Suzy Kendall, who remains his closest friend. From his second wife, American actress Tuesday Weld, he has a son Patrick. He then had a fling with former Miss America Susan Anton, who towered nearly a foot over him. In 1988 he was briefly married to little-known American actress Brogan Lane. His fourth wife Nicole Rothschild (no rich relations!) had been a longstanding girlfriend. During their stormy marriage she had a son, Nicholas.

Malibu-based Moore's career suffered during these recent marital mishaps. Two American TV comedy series were cancelled and Barbara Streisand fired him from *The Mirror Has Two Faces* because he kept forgetting his lines. It seems a long time since he appeared in that £1 million series of Tesco ads chasing chickens round France!

Moore, Patrick, 4th March 1923, telly stargazer and Great British Eccentric. His swirling arms, ill-fitting suits, monocle and sten gun delivery have brightened BBC1's *The Sky at Night* since its 1957 debut. This world record-breaking run shows no sign of abating as his commentaries and mischievous asides remain as lively as ever. He watches the firmament from a private observatory beside his thatched Selsey, Sussex house. A prolific author, he refuses to cash in on his fame by appearing in TV commercials. "I'd rather be dead in a ditch", he told one pushy telescope manufacturer.

Now seen as a greater authority than even the Astronomer Royal, he was born Patrick Caldwell-Moore and educated at home due to illness. His fascination with the moon and the planets began at 11 when he joined the British Astronomical Association. After serving in the RAF as a Bomber Command navigator he began his prolific writing career and set up his own observatory. *The Sky at Night* made him nationally known as a tame boffin able to communicate his enthusiasm to the masses. He masterminded the BBC coverage of the early space missions. Indeed, US astronauts Neil Armstrong and Buzz Aldrin used his maps of the lunar surface for their historic 1969 moon landing. His gruff-but-nice comic potential was recognised on *The Morecambe and Wise Show*, *It's a Celebrity Knockout*, *Blankety Blank* and other light entertainment series. Such appearances rather devalue his other work.

But this quirky sky-watcher has no time for killjoys. In his local amateur dramatic society he specialises in playing pantomime demons and the xylophone. Tall, bulky and quite fierce-looking he is surprisingly patient with children who turn up demanding to see his five telescopes. His fiancée was killed in the Second World War. "Never any question of marrying anyone else. Missed out on family life and I regret that. Don't like living alone, but there it is." Touchingly this archetypal mad professor refers to himself as an "amateur" because he is self-taught and never took up his Cambridge place. He deserves a knighthood.

Moore, Roger, 14th October 1927, retired James Bond, once known in the trade as "the Big Knit". The white tuxedo and glass of "shaken not stirred" Martini fits his personality perfectly. Yet this policeman's son was brought up in a bleak Battersea terrace during the war and went to grammar school. At RADA he began to perfect that debonair manner and mid-Atlantic accent, paying his fees by modelling for knitting patterns. Even today he describes his acting range as "left eyebrow raised, right eyebrow raised".

Aged 19, Moore married fellow drama student Doorn van Steyn. He made his stage debut in *Androcles and the Lion* but the hard, unremunerative slog of the theatre did not suit him. Helped by his second wife, singer Dorothy Squires, he landed leading rôles in the TV series *Ivanhoe*, *The Alaskans* and *Maverick*. But it was *The Saint*, in 1962, which established his reputation as an all-action hero.

Moore's move to Hollywood began with trashy movies like *The Rape of the Sabine Women* and *The King's Thief*. In 1973, he became James Bond in *Live and Let Die*, bringing a lighter touch to the rôle, even if every time a gun went off he blinked. He made six further

007 films, notably *The Man with the Golden Gun, Moonraker* and *Octopussy*. Afraid of typecasting, he continued to accept other rôles, including two South African-made thrillers *Gold* and *Shout at the Devil*. But his attempts at light comedy in films like *Bullseye!* have generally been embarrassing.

Today Moore has recovered from prostate cancer and acts as a roving UNICEF ambassador. He is devoted to his three children, Deborah, Geoffrey and Christian from his 1969 marriage to Italian starlet Luisa Mattioli. He badly needs a box-office hit but characteristically says: "If I ever feel down, I just go to the bank and climb over all the gold bars". In 1996 fiery Luisa demanded a £7 million divorce settlement after he ran off with twice-married Danish socialite Kiki Tholstrup with whom he now lives in Monte Carlo.

Moran, Christopher (pronounced More-ranne), 16th January 1948, social-climbing Midas. He is the real-life personification of *To The Manor Born*'s Richard de Vere. A cocky, self-made businessman, he has spent nearly a decade and some £15 million turning Crosby Hall into his personal monument. Once owned by Henry VIII's lord chancellor Sir Thomas More, this magnificent 18-bedroomed Tudor mansion overlooks Chelsea Embankment.

Moran worked hard to escape from his underprivileged London background. He won a scholarship to Dame Alice Owen's Grammar School and read the *Financial Times* when his contemporaries were still into the *Eagle*. He would buy cigarettes in packets, and flog them individually at three times what they cost. At 16 he joined Lloyd's and by 29 was running his own brokerage firm. But in 1982 he was expelled after being found guilty of "acts and defaults discreditable to him in connection with the business of insurance". He blamed an Establishment plot. "It just means I'm no longer a member of the Brownie Club." He has since built a £150 million property empire ("I suspect it's well over that...it's astronomical").

Moran's greatest ally is his down-to-earth wife Helen, a former Miss Thames TV. They met when she was an 18-year-old model and married in 1981. They have twin sons, Charles and Jamie, whom he is determined not to spoil. "I want them to make it on their own." Opera buff Moran traditionally celebrates his birthday with a lavish dinner party for influential friends. He also holds very grand house parties at Glenfiddich, his 47,000-acre estate near Balmoral. "It's amazing the politicians and famous faces you meet *chez* Christopher", says an insider. He is as keenly competitive in his private life as Jeffrey Archer. He once lost at table tennis to a house guest. He then hired the English national coach and practised four nights a week until he was able to beat his friend.

Mortimer, John, 21st April 1923, Henley-on-Thames's answer to Charles Dickens. He is an iconoclast who relishes his double life, tilting at the Establishment while enjoying all its benefits. As a barrister for nearly 50 years he has fought valiantly for artistic freedom, defending so-called pornographers against the Mrs Whitehouse tendency. He adheres to the Dickensian credo that "you should feel compassion for the less fortunate and this should be your dominant feeling". Labour's 1997 return to power has given this sometimes cantankerous old fellow a tremendous fillip. Arise Sir John? His most original creation remains the decent, claret-loving Horace Rumpole who first donned his TV wig in 1978. Even judges praised the accuracy of *Rumpole of the Bailey*.

This shambling, sardonic intellectual comes from "middle-class Socialist" parents who were able to give him a classical education at Harrow and Oxford. He based his hit play, *A Voyage Round My Father*, on his blind papa's career as a barrister. Ironically he says "I can't now separate the dialogue I made up for him from what he actually said!" He began scriptwriting while attached to the wartime Crown Film Unit. His first stage play, *The Dock Brief*, was performed in 1958. Between appearing in juicy divorce and obscenity trials he also translated Feydeau's farce, *A Flea In Her Ear*, scripted the Dustin Hoffman film *John and Mary*, adapted Robert Graves's novel, *I, Claudius*, for TV, dashed off a series of novels and wrote his autobiography, *Clinging To The Wreckage*. But the award-winning ITV series, *Brideshead Revisited* and *Summer's Lease*, his Chianti-shire exposé, probably gained him most kudos.

Mortimer is, of course, slumming it in television. But he enjoys the celebrity almost as much as he has done women, laughing them into bed with his repartee and obscure references. His 1949 marriage to novelist Penelope Mortimer, once described as "the sexiest woman in London", lasted 23 years. In 1972 he married his present wife Penny and has two children from both marriages, including rising actress Emily Mortimer. Neil Kinnock's failure to become prime minister probably cost him the Lord Chancellorship.

Mosimann, Anton, 23rd February 1947, the Nineties' Escoffier. His chic Belgravia dining club, Mosimann's, attracts the ladies-who-lunch as well as gourmets. He bought this Victorian Welsh Baptist chapel in 1988 because he needed his independence. He prefers to call himself a cook ("'chef' sounds too grand"). "Cooking is an artist's profession and the kitchen is where I can express my creativity."

This slim, balding, slightly diffident chef has always preached the message of simple, healthy eating, eschewing fattening sauces and other culinary no-nos. He became Britain's first celebrity chef after the legendary Robert Carrier. He commercialised himself, writing more than a dozen cookbooks, lecturing in America and the Far East and constantly popping up on radio and television.

"Mozzie" was an only child who grew up outside Berne in Switzerland. Aged 12 he was already helping his Swiss-German parents cook traditional food at their country restaurant in Nidau. He became a hotel apprentice in Switzerland, then trained in *nouvelle cuisine* kitchens in France, worked in Italy, Canada and, significantly, Japan. At 28 he became the youngest ever *maître chef des cuisines* at the Dorchester. He stayed there 12 years, winning two Michelin stars, rare for an hotel.

The twinkly, Anglophile superchef jogs round Holland Park near his Kensington home. He has two sons from his long-suffering wife Kathrin; both went to Prince Charles' prep school, Hill House, and then Harrow. When he eats out he usually chooses Japanese, Thai or Chinese restaurants.

Moss, Kate, 16th January 1974, the new Twiggy. From the unlikely concrete canyons of Croydon she has become Queen of the catwalk in London, Paris, Milan and New York. She travels by Concorde and can command fees of up to £50,000 a day. But the bulk of her £3 million-a-year comes from her modelling contract with Calvin Klein. She featured in the controversial advertisements for his designer underwear and the fragrance Obsession.

Few of the boys fancied her when she was at Riddlesdown High School, Croydon. She was too thin and gawky. But it was her classic bone structure which first attracted Sarah Doukas, founder of the London model agency Storm, who spotted the 14-year-old schoolgirl as she passed through JF Kennedy Airport. Her first modelling jobs were for teen magazines and *The Face*.

Chain-smoking Kate was propelled on to the front covers of *Vogue* and *Elle* because she was right for the time. The grunge and the waifishness, the scraped-back hair, the scrubbed, innocent face was what was needed. For this 5ft 7ins ordinary-looking Bambi was the antithesis of the glamour-pusses Cindy Crawford, Linda Evangelista and Christy Turlington who had dominated the Eighties. Ironically, parents blamed her when their Kate Moss wannabe daughters started copying her trendy anorexic "look". She was once persuaded to counsel a girl who was 5ft, weighed five stone and ate only an apple a day. "I'm naturally like this", Kate told her, "I don't diet".

Kate's family broke up when she was 14. She remained with her mother while her younger brother, Nick, went to live with their travel agent father. It was while on that "JFK holiday" with him in the Bahamas that she lost her virginity to an American on the beach ("I didn't want to lose it to some nasty bloke in Croydon!") Her first "big passion" was Mario Sorrenti, the Levi ads model turned photographer. She was 20 when she started dating tempestuous Hollywood actor Johnny Depp. They went on a date in New York and got snowed into her hotel. After a spell as the most glamorous Big Apple and Shepherd's Bush couple they split up in 1997.

Mowatt, Marina, 31st July 1966, royal 'wild child'. Princess Diana and the Duchess of York heaved sighs of relief when this little-known relation briefly swept them off the front pages. She was even naughtier than they were! In 1989 she became the first unmarried royal to announce that she was pregnant and to sell exclusive photographic rights to the Press. She claimed her mother Princess Alexandra had ordered her "either to get it aborted in Harley Street or get married". Matters were not helped by her boyfriend, commercial photographer Paul Mowatt, looking like a car salesman and coming from the wrong side of the tracks. They finally married three months before Zenouska's birth. But the royal family, except for her mother and father, Sir Angus Ogilvy, boycotted the ceremony.

For the first two decades of her life Marina – or "Mo", as she preferred to be called – seemed to be a model member of the royal Second XI. Brought up at Thatched House Lodge, an elegant grace-and-favour property inside Richmond Park, she went to St Mary's, Wantage. A talented pianist and London Marathon runner, she never traded on her background. She worked for Operation Raleigh in Central America and helped disadvantaged children on outward-bound courses. Perhaps she had come to resent her comfortable background?

The impecunious Mowatts began married life in a Teddington semi. The increasingly wilful Marina then posed for a set of pictures in thigh-length kinky boots, wearing a "crown" and brandishing a fake pistol, with corgis playing at her feet. She won a 'Rear of the Year' award, wrote a weekly newspaper column and had a second child, Christian. In 1996 the couple parted, but were reconciled after he promised to give up drinking and abusing her. Prince Charles once sent her a signed copy of his book, *The Old Man of Lochnagar*, inscribed "from your disappointed godfather".

Munro-Wilson, Broderick, 18th June 1945, languid Lothario. This caddish merchant banker is the archetypal equal opportunities playboy. No colour, creed or age is excluded. His conquests range from model Samantha Bleby, his girlfriend for seven years, to journalist Cherri Gilham, "just a summer frolic". "The cardinal rule is never to use the dreaded four-letter word – love. Cads don't make commitments. They always make the running and keep everyone guessing." He insists all his lovers display a "thrusting cleavage".

After Lancing and Cambridge, Harley Street surgeon's son Munro-Wilson became a City high-flier, masterminding the flotation of Body Shop in 1984. His tertiary bank Munro Corporate was once valued at £20 million. This rapidly growing wealth enabled him to form his own polo team Rocking Horse, with Prince Charles among the players. HRH particularly enjoyed his dirty jokes.

This former debs' delight is an unreconstructed chauvinist with a Hooray Henry jolliness that some people find infuriating. He has turned his louche reputation as the "rogue in brogues" and "bounder of the boudoir" into a part-time career. He appears on ITV's *This Morning* as the token playboy/English gent, usually outraging the studio with his comments. He condemned kiss 'n' tell royal lover James Hewitt for "bringing the good name of caddery into disrepute". Another time he said he was glad he had no permanent woman in his life, because he could now "play to Polo Association Rules and change horses every seven minutes".

"BMW" is a former champion amateur jockey. He competed in the Grand National and won the *Horse and Hound* Grand Military Cup at Sandown Park three times. Nowadays he prefers more sedate pursuits, usually with a pair of Purdeys in hand. He has a son, Rodrigo, from his first marriage to a South American sugar heiress, and two daughters, Charlotte and Emma, from his second wife Carolyn. He lives alone in his Little Venice mews house.

Murray, Lady Georgina, 10th March 1967, Society beauty. She may have a butterfly tattooed on her shoulder but a century ago she would probably have married Prince Andrew or Prince Edward. She topped the eligible spinsters list for over a decade. Not just because of her up-market provenance – her father the Earl of Mansfield is one of Scotland's most distinguished landowners – but because of her vivacity and originality. She was brought up at Scone Palace, the pink-stone, castellated mansion where the Kings of Scotland were traditionally crowned. Instead of becoming an It Girl after doing the Season, she trained as a psychotherapist. She works in run-down Vauxhall, specialising in children with learning difficulties, and does voluntary work in Maidenhead. But she drives a black convertible Saab and at highland balls still looks as if she has just walked out of a *Vogue* fashion shoot. "Gina is neither a vacuous flibbertigibbet nor a Lady Bountiful calling on the poor. She does what she does, not for acclaim, but because she completely believes in it", explains a friend.

At Wycombe Abbey, Gina was "one of those fortunate people", according to her mother, "who, if she swam, found herself in the swimming team, if she dived, found herself in the diving team". She won the inter-school prize for declamations, with Lewis Carroll's *Hunting of the Snark*. Uncharacteristically failing her Oxford entrance exams she did a bilingual banking and business studies course at Poitiers University. She insisted on supporting herself by working as a motorcycle courier. "From the age of 16 she has had the ability to make every man look at her as soon as she steps into a room", explains an insider. But recently she has played down her glamour to create a more serious working image. While eligible Hooray Henries swooned over her she preferred unconventional, less snobby types. "A lean, cool, figure on a Harley-Davidson, maybe even with dyed hair", has always been her ideal, according to a friend. In spring 1997 she announced her engagement to rugged import-exporter John Bullough, a former Scots Guards subaltern.

N

Nail, Jimmy, 15th March 1954, Northern sex symbol. His gangling body, mournful expression and Mr Punch nose make him instantly recognisable. He has a granite edge to his lugubriousness that suits his most famous TV rôle, the eponymous Geordie hero, *Spender*.

The former welder was born James Bradford, son of a factory-worker. His adopted surname mirrored his local image. He was expelled from school and became a tearaway. During the punk era he cavorted on stage in a ballet dress, macintosh and pit boots, with a group called the King Crabs. He also served four months in Strangeways jail following a fight at a football match. In 1975 he moved with his wife Miriam to London. "I made an outrageous fortune renovating old properties and selling them on."

Miriam, a TV producer's daughter, "press-ganged" Nail to audition for a new ITV series called *Auf Wiedersehen, Pet*. To his surprise he was cast as Oz, the hulking, bigoted, slobby navvy. He was four stone heavier then, which he lost by giving up alcohol in 1985. He formed a production company and began writing his own scripts. His first success, in 1991, was as the maverick undercover cop in BBC1's *Spender*, with its unfamiliar Newcastle locations and hard rock soundtrack. Music was again central to BBC1's *Crocodile Shoes*, in which he played a Geordie singer-songwriter who came to London to make good. "Names were changed to protect the guilty. All the characters I've used are a potpourri of people I've known in the pop industry." Its popularity revived his singing career, with a best-selling CD and sell-out concert tour, in which he drew Tom Jones-style screams. "It's useful to have a second string. TV gobbles you up and you've got only so many tricks in your bag before it spits you out."

Nail maintains a love-hate relationship with Tyneside. Separated from Miriam in 1994, he spent most of his married life living in Wales and north London. They have two sons, Freddie and Tommy. His cameo rôle opposite Madonna in *Evita* could presage a new Hollywood career.

Naughtie, James, (pronounced Knock-te), 9th August 1951, the Bonnie Prince Charlie of the Airwaves. With his sweaty brow and rotund physique (thanks to BBC breakfasts), he has the perfect "radio face". His gentle, articulate Scottish brogue represents a ritual wake-up call for 2.2 million devotees of R4's *Today* programme. No presenter can boast of a more influential audience or guest list. Cabinet ministers, captains of industry and other opinion-formers jump at the opportunity to defend themselves. "We try to set the day's news agenda", a Naughtie acolyte says. He is less abrasive than his colleague John Humphrys. He hates to upset politicians, with whom he is often on first-name terms.

Opera buff Naughtie went to Keith Grammar School, Aberdeen University and Syracuse University, New York. He worked for *The Scotsman* before becoming *The Guardian*'s chief political correspondent in 1985. He spent six years sharpening his radio skills as a presenter of R4's flagship news programme, *The World at One*. Neil Kinnock once shouted: "I'm not going to be bloody kebabed by you" during a recorded interview. Much to the interviewee's embarrassment a pirate tape of this exchange found its way to the media.

Married, with three children, the merry, clubbable Naughtie enjoys a gossipy lunch, usually with a senior parliamentary "source", at a decent restaurant. He catnaps in the afternoon and then spends the early evening networking at political gatherings. If ever the strain gets to him he has a powerful second string as a R3 music presenter and has taken over from Richard Baker as the man who introduces BBC1's *Last Night of the Proms*. Journalism will soon reclaim him.

Neeson, Liam, 7th June 1952, Hollywood heart-throb. His portrayal of the humanitarian German businessman, Oskar Schindler, in *Schindler's List* brought him an Oscar nomination and turned him into a superstar. He followed it with another glamorous, anti-Establishment figure, *Rob Roy*. Yet he remains as Irish in spirit as the Liffey, enjoying the "craich" with his mates and keenly following the Turf. His physical presence belies his gentleness and sensitivity.

This school caretaker's son from Co Antrim was educated at St Patrick's High School, Ballymeena, and Queen's University, Belfast. He owes his skew-whiff nose to an early boxing injury. He originally wanted to be a schoolteacher and did a teacher training course in Newcastle. He then worked as a forklift operator and architect's assistant, before making his acting debut at the Lyric Players' Theatre, Belfast. He appeared in *Of Mice and Men* and *The Informer* in Dublin. He then starred in *Translations* at the National Theatre and landed film rôles in *Excalibur*, *The Bounty* and *The Mission*.

Neeson was a roistering bachelor for over 20 years. His idea of heaven was an evening in the pub with his drinking cronies and then back to the little woman at home. His male chauvinism and failure to make a commitment killed relationships with such high-profile ladies as Brooke Shields, Barbara Streisand and Sinead O'Connor. During the early Eighties he lived with Helen Mirren and later spent two years with actress Julia Roberts. Feisty actress Natasha Richardson finally claimed him after they starred together on Broadway in *Anna Christie*. They married in 1994 and live in upstate New York with their son Michael. "We're very different people, but we're soul mates", she says.

Neil, Andrew, 21st May 1949, multi-media polemicist. As *Sunday Times* editor from 1983 to 1994 he was a cheerleader for the new go-for-it Britain. Like his boss Rupert Murdoch, he supported Mrs Thatcher and big business and attacked the royals and the BBC. He railed against the Establishment, particularly "the chattering classes" who lived in Hampstead and wore Garrick Club ties.

Yet his own strict Presbyterian background – Army officer's son, Paisley Grammar School, Glasgow University – was not exactly underprivileged. He never had to wash cars or walk barefoot to school. As a politics and economics graduate his first job was at the Tory Research Department where he helped to write speeches for Ted Heath. Aged 24 he joined *The Economist*, becoming successively parliamentary, labour and American correspondent before landing the editorship in 1982.

This stern-looking Glaswegian has chilled out since falling foul of Murdoch. His skean-dhu wit and toughness is now accompanied by a broad smile. His new TV career was most responsible for this unaccustomed user-friendliness. Although a much-hyped US chat show never happened, he began presenting low-budget shows here like *The Midnight Hour*, *Westminster On-Line* and *Is This Your Life?*

Neil was little-known outside Wapping until he became front-page news himself in the *News of the World*. It exposed Pamella Bordes, his exotic nightclub companion of the previous five months, as a £500-a-night hooker. It led to the celebrated Battle of the Editors when he sued Sir Peregrine Worsthorne, former *Sunday Telegraph* editor, for making snide comments about him bringing the *ST* into disrepute. The jury awarded Neil £1,000 damages, considering that what he did in his spare time was his own affair. More damaging was Bordes's revelation about his hair-dye staining the pillowcases at his stylish South Kensington penthouse.

Neil's autobiography *Full Disclosure* settled many old scores. Now running the Barclay Brothers' newspaper empire, including *The Scotsman* and *The European*, he continues his bachelor ways. He is constantly out on the town enjoying Café Society parties or dancing at Tramp with his latest belle. Invariably they are some 20 years younger and hail from an exotic clime.

Nicholas, Paul, 3rd December 1945, actor-impresario. This tousle-haired extrovert is a wrinkly who looks ten years younger than his half-century. It must be in his genes because his father, showbiz lawyer Oscar Beuselinck, was still working at nearly 80. Paul will always be remembered as that half-spiv, half-cherub Vince Power in BBC1's sitcom, *Just Good Friends*. But he has been hitting the win button ever since he starred in the Sixties stage musical *Hair*, followed by *Jesus Christ Superstar* and *Grease* in the early Seventies. Yet somehow he never quite developed into Britain's John Travolta. "My career has been a marathon, not a sprint."

Brought up in North London, Beuselinck – the name comes from his Dutch ancestry – felt neglected in his early years. "I was an only child and lonely. My parents were not compatible and that infected everything, including me." They finally divorced when he was 15. The following year he left school to join Screaming Lord Sutch's band, The Raving Savages. He enjoyed the dressing up and comedy elements of performing so much that he turned to acting. He chose the less tongue-twisting name "Nicholas" because it was Christmas. It must have been a good omen because his stage career took off immediately. Later he enjoyed two Top 10 hits, *Dancing With The Captain* and *Grandma's Party*.

Nicholas inherited his father's business astuteness, recently becoming a leading West End impresario. With partners Robert Stigwood and David Ian his company made £45 million from musicals like *Grease, Cats, Barnum, Singin' In The Rain* and *The Pirates of Penzance*. He lives in a Georgian house in Highgate with his second wife, former dancer Linzi Jennings, and his youngest children, Alexander and Carmen. After his ex-wife, former hairdresser Susan, died in a car accident, Linzi helped to raise Susan's two children, Natasha and Oscar. "If I hadn't found such a wonderful person my life might have been very different. I could see straight away that she was very kind, implicitly good and trustworthy."

Nicholson, Vanessa-Mae, 27th October 1978, violin virtuoso. This almond-eyed Madam Precious Stream has made classical music sexy with her "techno-acoustic fusion" of pop and classics. Purists tut-tut at her blatant commercialisation of Bach, Beethoven, Brahms and Bruch. But audiences, particularly men, drool over her slim figure, sheathed in shimmering satin, as she performs on her electric violin accompanied by a full orchestra.

Vanessa-Mae has become the female version of cross-over artistes like John Williams and James Galway. She recreates famous classical pieces and mixes them with melodies from Paul McCartney, Donna Summer and Elton John. Before performing she reverentially cleans her violin with a "lucky" yellow duster and caresses the strings once a week with pure alcohol.

This delicate child prodigy was touring the world by 12. She admired Whitney Houston as much as Yehudi Menuhin. She became the youngest ever artiste to record the Beethoven and Tchaikovsky concertos and by 15 had left school and turned professional. Early posters showed her playing her violin in the sea, her white dress made transparent by the water. But she refuses to believe that her record company was exploiting her innocence. Nonetheless her first album, *The Violin Player*, sold over two million copies. In 1997 she made her singing debut on *Classical Album I*.

Vanessa-Mae's Singaporean parents separated when she was four. Her mother then married an English lawyer. The family share their London home with four Lhasa Apso dogs, but this dedicated musician spends much of the year travelling. During her 1996 Red Hot world tour she held concerts in 35 countries. She claims to be too busy recording and rehearsing to have a boyfriend.

Norfolk, Duke of, 21st July 1915, the Harvey Goldsmith of State ceremonials. This trim, moustachioed, military figure holds Britain's grandest title, which goes back over 500 years. Yet he is approachable, friendly and distinctly unpompous. As hereditary Earl Marshal of England he is paid £20 a year, fixed by Richard III in 1483, to organise coronations, royal funerals and the State opening of Parliament. He is also the final arbiter at the College of Arms over all matters concerning titles and coats-of-arms. Yet characteristically he claims: "I'm much prouder of having been a general".

Miles became 17th duke on the death of his distant cousin Bernard in 1975. He had already inherited a barony through his mother together with a Humberside stately home, Carlton Towers, which had belonged to her family since 1301. He was also Lord Howard of Glossop through his father. Alas, the Norfolk estates, which once covered most of Arundel, Littlehampton and an area near London's Temple are now much depleted. The family does still have an apartment in Arundel Castle but His Grace spends most of the year living without butlers or flunkies in a manor house near Henley-on-Thames.

Britain's premier Duke and Earl is also our leading Catholic layman. After Ampleforth and Oxford he spent nearly 30 years in the Grenadier Guards, winning the MC during World War II. Until his retirement in 1967, he was director of Service Intelligence. A devoted family man he will celebrate his golden wedding anniversary in

1998 to the former Anne Constable Maxwell, who was awarded a CBE for her work as founder of Help the Hospices. They have five children, including the Earl of Arundel, a former racing-driver, actress Marsha Fitzalan and Lady Carina who is married to Sir David Frost.

Northampton, Marquess of, 2nd April 1946, multi-millionaire landowner, known as the "Mystic Marquess". His close interest in spiritualism has involved this tall, languid Old Etonian in a gallimaufry of seances, levitations, ghosts, poltergeists and healings. Having had five marriages before he was 45 he ranks as the peerage's leading serial monogamist. Gentle-mannered, intuitive and kind he is not the sort to bellow at the butler. But his attention-span is rather short.

In 1967 "Spenny" Northampton married his first wife, willowy Dutch heiress Baroness Henriette Bentinck, who supplied his heir Earl Compton and eldest daughter Lady Lara. He was then briefly married to businessman's daughter Annette Smallwood, known as Scruff. His third wife was horsey Rosie Dawson-Damer, by whom he has a daughter, Lady Emily. He has another daughter, Lady Louisa, from his fourth wife, former German model Fritzi Erhardt. In 1990 he married his present wife, holistic healer Pamela Kyprios, who shares his spiritualist beliefs. He has not really lived up to his family motto, "I Seek But One".

Northampton owns 30,000 acres in Warwickshire, Northamptonshire and Surrey, plus the remnants of the family estate in Islington. He lives between his Belgravia home and Compton Wynyates, a battlemented and moated stately home in Warwickshire. He turned his original family seat, Castle Ashby, Northamptonshire into a conference centre. To pay for their upkeep – and his alimony – he regularly depletes his Renaissance art collection. He received £8.1 million at auction for Mantegna's *Adoration of the Magi*. In 1994 he won a long legal battle in New York for the ownership of the £40 million Sevso treasure. He had acquired these silver dishes, bowls and other Roman artefacts in the Eighties for £9 million, but was unable to sell them because of claims by the Croatian and Hungarian governments.

Nunn, Trevor, 14th January 1940, Renaissance Man. This youthful theatre director has amassed an estimated £40 million fortune from his percentage of hit shows like *Sunset Boulevard*. He could, therefore, afford to become the Royal National Theatre's new artistic director in 1997: a low-paid post that offers prestige and a near-guaranteed knighthood.

With his stocky build, inscrutable face and goatee-beard, Suffolk-born Nunn resembles a Norman archer. He went to Northgate Grammar School, Ipswich, and then Cambridge where he appeared opposite Ian McKellen and Margaret Drabble in the Footlights production of *Twelfth Night*. He joined the Belgrade Theatre, Coventry, and, at 28, replaced Sir Peter Hall as the RSC's artistic director. He directed over 30 plays, including *Macbeth*, *Juno and the Paycock*, *Othello* and *Measure for Measure*. His productions of *Nicholas Nickleby* and *Les Miserables* won a total of 13 top awards. "Trevor's hallmark is to show an intense attention to detail and text", explains one critic "and a naturalistic direction which makes what the characters think and do believable in any context".

Taking full advantage of his RSC contract allowing him three months unpaid leave a year, Nunn began earning serious money as a freelance director. He directed Andrew Lloyd Webber's *Cats*, *Starlight Express* and *Aspects of Love* and Tim Rice's *Chess*. He also made his Glyndebourne debut in 1982, directing *Idomeneo* and *Porgy and Bess*. Replete with commercial acclaim he stepped down as RSC artistic director in 1986. He has successfully filmed TV productions of shows like *Nicholas Nickleby*. Films, such as *Lady Jane* and *Twelfth Night*, have never quite shown the same sure touch as those of his fellow luvvies Kenneth Branagh and Nicholas Hytner. Whoops! He hates that word, "luvvie".

Nunn's marital upsets coincided with his commercial awakening. His 1969 marriage to classical actress Janet Suzman came to an end in 1986 when he fell in love with his former *Cats* leading lady Sharon Lee Hill. His marriage to Sharon ended five years and two daughters later when he met actress Imogen Stubbs. They married in 1994 and have two children, Ellie and Jesse.

O

O'Connor, Sinead, 8th December 1966, reformed firebrand. Her pure, clear voice is like a nightingale, her presentation like a crow. The delicate appearance – large doe eyes, angular cheekbones, slender physique – makes her seem fragile. But her tantrums belie this. She has much to be angry about: childhood abuse from her mother, an abortion, a miscarriage and a failed suicide attempt. "I really wasn't well emotionally. I needed to learn how to live." The shaved head, nose stud and grunge underlined her angst.

This flakey, Dublin-born colleen suffered when her barrister father split up from her mother when she was eight. She became an overnight star in 1989 with her magnificent version of Prince's song, *Nothing Compares 2 U*. It topped the charts in 17 countries and made her an estimated £5 million. She then split up from her drummer husband John Reynolds and moved to California, where her wacky ways soon made headlines. In 1992 she spontaneously responded to a TV appeal for African famine relief by donating her $500,000 house to the Red Cross. In 1993 she tore up a picture of the Pope on live American TV. She claimed that it was to highlight the Church's rôle in concealing child abuse by priests and to destroy her image as a neatly-packaged, middle-of-the-road pop star. "I didn't want to be Whitney Houston. I wanted to declare war through my music." She now regrets the damage her outburst caused her family. "There are things that, if I could go back, I'd do a little more... serenely!" Her return to Britain and prolonged therapy have helped her to escape from this "self-destructive" phase.

The new, more positive Sinead has begun composing lullabies. "Before, my songs were all about me growing up. Now I just want to write love songs. I don't want people to think: 'Oh, there she goes, talking about her childhood again!'" She lives in West London with her son Jake from her ex-husband and daughter Roisin from Dublin journalist John Waters. Meanwhile she studies Irish and Caribbean history at college. "Men are intimidated by me."

O'Grady, Paul (aka **Lily Savage**), 14th June 1955, drag queen with attitude. You can hardly get more alternative than this bitchy, loud, crude grotesquerie. La Savage has stormed the forbidden battlements where Danny La Rue and Barry Humphries once ruled.

Her little-known creator was born in Birkenhead, the son of an Irish-Catholic oil rig worker and a factory cleaner whose maiden-name was Savage. Paul became a social worker in Islington, caring for children whose mothers were in hospital or in prison. He began compering a pub's gay talent night. Disguised in spangly ballgowns split to the thigh and wearing a blonde walnut whip wig he would swap insults with the audience, leer at the contestants and bring the house down with his filthy quips. He graduated to more up-market venues and guest appearances on TV chat shows.

Lily spent a year strutting her stuff on C4's *The Big Breakfast*, released a video, *Lily Savage Live at the Garrick* and starred in the West End show, *Prisoner: Cell Block H – The Musical*. "Lily is my licence to misbehave and say things you couldn't come out with in real-life without someone smacking you in the gob!" *The Sun* joked that her next rôle should be *Poof in Boots*. After her one-woman TV show, *An Evening with Lily Savage*, Polly Peck hired her to advertise their tights. "Lily has got one of the best pairs of legs in showbiz – much better than Danny La Rue or John Inman."

Without his alter ego's high heels O'Grady is a gangly chain-smoking bachelor with left-wing leanings. He lives near Tower Bridge, with his dog Buster and two cats. As a result of a fling when he was 17 he has a grown-up daughter, Sharyn. "I lived with her mother for about a week. It was like *The Waltons* gone badly wrong. But I really like having a daughter."

His favourite fantasy would be to spend New Year's Eve eating oysters on Mont St Michel with former Avengers star Linda Thorson ("I'm mad about her") and Jean-Claude Van Damme "waiting for me upstairs".

O'Neill, Terry, 30th July 1938, celebrity snapper. This small, wiry Essex Lad has the best contacts book in Britain, at least where desirable women are concerned. He has photographed nearly every famous actress, supermodel and Society gel for the world's top glossy magazines. His all-time favourites are the late Diana Princess of Wales, Kate Moss, Joanna Lumley, Yasmin Le Bon and Jemima Goldsmith. "British women have always been the most classically beautiful of any nation. They have a coolness and elegance, combined with a deep-rooted sensuality which makes them irresistible."

O'Neill has sampled the best. His first wife was Fifties actress Vera Day, mother of his two children Sarah and Keegan. He suffered much Catholic guilt over their divorce. In 1981 he married Oscar-winning actress Faye Dunaway, a bad move as she was too neurotic and forceful. He neglected his photography and dabbled as a Hollywood producer. But he is devoted to their adopted son Liam.

"My problem is that I get the 13-year itch." After their divorce he briefly lived with former model agent Laraine Ashton.

O'Neill, son of a Ford factory worker from Cork, went to Gunnersbury Grammar School. During his national service he was an Army PT instructor and played drums in a jazz band. He became an early paparazzo, snapping film stars arriving and leaving London Airport. During the Swinging Sixties only David Bailey and Terence Donovan could rival him. He was the first photographer to take studio portraits of The Beatles and Rolling Stones. His wry sense of humour and cheek have endeared him to sitters from Brigitte Bardot and Raquel Welch to Greta Scacchi and Elizabeth Hurley. But his greatest honour was taking the Queen's official portrait to mark her 40th anniversary on the throne.

O'Neill dines out most nights, always dressed in dark casual clothes, with models and trust-fund babes. Every Christmas he spends a month in Barbados to "recharge my batteries".

O'Reilly, Dr Tony, 7th May 1936, leader of Ireland's meritoPats. This charismatic baked beans magnate has been his country's favourite son for nearly 40 years. Worldwide head of US conglomerate HJ Heinz, he has seen its market value rise from $1 billion in 1979 to around $10 billion today. In 1994 his pay package, including share options, was over $41 million and his personal shareholding was estimated to be worth $165 million. Yet, perversely, he remains more famous as a former Irish international rugby player. He won the first of 29 caps playing for Ireland aged 19, as well as winning a total of ten caps with the British Lions.

This ebullient, customs officer's son went to Belvedere College and then read law at University College, Dublin. He qualified as a solicitor but decided to make his fortune in commerce. As CEO of the Irish Dairy Board he did a brilliant launch for Kerrygold butter and was headhunted by the Irish Sugar Board. He moved to Heinz in 1969, using his extraordinary energy and marketing flair, first to become UK managing director, then international CEO and, finally, chairman. He has also made canny private investments in companies like Waterford glass, Wedgwood china and Independent Newspapers, which owns titles in Ireland, South Africa, Australia and New Zealand. With Mirror Group Newspapers he also controls the *Independent* and *Independent on Sunday*. After recent ill-health he has handed over more power at Heinz to his heir-apparent Bill Johnson.

Beefy, pinstriped O'Reilly married Australian musician Susan Cameron in 1962 and has three sons and three daughters, including triplets. The brightest of these, Gavin, is married to Irish actress

Alison Doody. After divorcing in 1990 Tony married Chryss Goulandris, a Greek shipping heiress worth an estimated £300 million. One report described them as "an unbeatable team whose union – before God, Wall Street and the City of London – is indivisible." They live in possibly Ireland's most beautiful house, Castlemartin, Co Kildare, where they run a stud farm and entertain lavishly.

Oldman, Gary, 21st March 1958, flawed heart-throb. This crew-cut, blue-eyed, welder's son specialises in nasty rôles. He played the tragic punk rocker Sid Vicious in *Sid and Nancy* and a corrupt detective in *Leon*. His character was formed on a tough Bermondsey council estate. His award-winning 1997 debut as a director, *Nil By Mouth*, told the autobiographical story of a South London family whose life revolves round drunkenness and domestic violence. "There's a lot of me in all the characters. But some of what happened was so horrendous I couldn't put it into the film. My father used to sit in his chair drinking at 9.30am and then the abuse would start." He is a recovering alcoholic himself. In 1994 a Los Angeles court electronically tagged him after a drink-driving conviction

Cool cat Oldman became a superstar after his riveting performance as the Count in *Bram Stoker's Dracula*, in which he copied the original star Bela Lugosi's creepy accent. As a Hollywood lover he scores ten out of ten for his impeccable selection of beautiful women. But they seldom linger – and nor does he. He was first married to actress Lesley Manville. He moved on to *Pulp Fiction* star Uma Thurman, but their marriage finished after only ten months. He was then engaged to Ingrid Bergman's actress daughter Isabella Rossellini, once known as "the face of Lancôme". They met on the set of *Immortal Beloved*, in which he played Beethoven. The wedding was postponed when she found she could not cope with his wild drinking and drug-taking. In 1996 she tried the "tough love" approach, giving him an ultimatum: "Give up drink and drugs or we're finished." He joined a Los Angeles self-help group called Cocaine Anonymous, where he fell in love with Texan model Donya Fiorentino, pop star Andrew Ridgeley's former fiancée. Next minute, they were married.

PQ

Packer, Kerry, 17th December 1937, the Wizard of Oz. Australia's richest man maintains a high profile in Britain because of his polo. Since taking it up in 1986, he has spent an estimated £50 million on the sport, including building a state-of-the-art polo ground on his £8 million West Sussex estate at Fyning Hill. A full medical team is in attendance whenever he plays. He suffered a massive heart attack in 1990 during a chukka and was clinically dead for ten minutes. "I didn't die for long, but it was enough for me. I've been to the other side. Let me tell you, there's nothing there!"

The exuberant 16-stone tycoon inherited a media fortune from his yachtsman father Sir Frank Packer. Now his company Consolidated Press rivals Rupert Murdoch's News Corporation with its wide ownership of Australian newspapers, magazines, radio and TV stations. He thrives on controversy. *Telegraph* proprietor Conrad Black describes him as "an unapologetic and atavistic philistine". In 1978 he upset the MCC by forming his World Series cricket circus, managed by former England captain Tony Greig, after his Channel 9 TV station failed to win the TV rights to the Test match. In 1989 he shook the City with his £13.5 billion bid for the tobacco giant BAT Industries, made in conjunction with Lord Rothschild and Sir James Goldsmith. It was one of his rare failures.

Packer is now worth an estimated £1.5 billion. He hated pukka Geelong Grammar School, where his dyslexia was mistaken for stupidity and he was branded "weedy" because of his childhood polio. Almost uniquely among media barons he remains happily married to his first wife, Roslyn. They married in 1963 and have two children, Jamie and Gretel. His other passion is gambling. In 1995 he is said to have won $26 million in seven blinding hands of blackjack at the MGM Grand Casino, Las Vegas. He has now bought his own gambling joint, the Sydney Harbour Casino.

Paige, Elaine, 5th March 1952, Judy Garland wannabe. No West End songstress can quite match her musical achievements. She created the rôle of Eva Peron in *Evita*, was Grizabella in *Cats*, Florence in *Chess*, Reno Sweeney in *Anything Goes*, Edith Piaf in *Piaf* and Norma Desmond in *Sunset Boulevard*. While her voice is probably too metallic to rival that of Barbara Streisand, critics can no longer

ABOVE Nicky and Lesley Clarke
BELOW LEFT Harold Pinter and his wife Lady Antonia Fraser
BELOW RIGHT Joanna Lumley

ABOVE Ian Hislop
BELOW LEFT Yasmin Le Bon
BELOW RIGHT Sir Terence Conran and his girlfriend Victoria Davis
OPPOSITE Elton John and his mother Sheila

ABOVE Paul Gascoigne, his wife Sheryl, and her chidren Bianca and Mason
BELOW LEFT Ulrika Jonsson
BELOW RIGHT Alan Rickman and Sir Ian McKellen

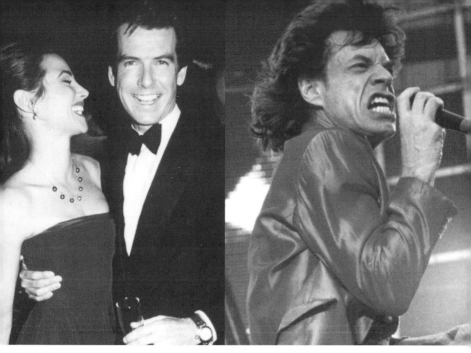

ABOVE LEFT Pierce Brosnan and his girlfriend Keely Shaye-Smith
ABOVE RIGHT Mick Jagger
BELOW Liz Brewer, Baudoin Mills, Shirley Bassey, Ivana Trump, Riccardo Mazzucchelli

ABOVE Jo-Jo Laine with the Marquess of Bath and friend
BELOW LEFT Gary Barlow
BELOW RIGHT Tania Bryer and husband Tim Moufarrige
OPPOSITE Hugh Grant and Elizabeth Hurley

ABOVE LEFT Robert Hanson
ABOVE RIGHT Tiggy Legge-Bourke
BELOW Kristin Scott Thomas, Ralph Fiennes, Juliette Binoche

sneer that she owes her career to former lover Sir Tim Rice. She now stands on her own tiny feet, as a brilliant leading lady – with an OBE!

Born Elaine Bickerstaff in Barnet, she attended the Aida Foster Stage School. Her father was a drum-playing Bognor Regis estate agent and her mother a milliner who sang with local bands. "My father used to quote *I Ching* to me: 'perseverance furthers'." Her first agent insisted that she found a more melodious surname and she chose Paige from the London telephone directory.

As a struggling chorus girl, Elaine lived in a hippy commune near Hampstead Heath with other members of the rock musical *Hair*. Her big break was as Michael Crawford's bit of rough in the hit musical *Billy*. In the mid-Seventies she nearly quit showbiz to become a nursery school teacher. But in 1978 she won *Evita* and stopped the show with her rendition of *Don't Cry For Me Argentina*. In 1981 she was the last-minute replacement for Judi Dench in Andrew Lloyd Webber's *Cats*. Its haunting song *Memory* produced her first No 1 hit and was followed five years later with *I Know Him So Well* from Rice's *Chess*. She was bitterly disappointed when American Equity refused to allow her to play Evita on Broadway and when Madonna won the film rôle.

Elegant and trim Elaine – "EP" to her friends – was an embarrassed winner of the 1984 'Rear of the Year' award. For she takes herself ever so seriously as an actress. It was her sense of humour deficit that kiboshed her chance of marrying Rice. For ten years they had an on-off relationship, during which he refused to divorce his wife Jane. They made an odd-looking couple, with him 16ins taller. But together they co-produced West End shows, recorded albums and even tried to compose a musical together. Now she misses not having had a family. For, despite being a millionairess living in a £750,000 Chelsea house stuffed with antiques and driving a top-of-the-range sports car, she remains single.

Palin, Michael, 5th May 1943, Nicest Living Englishman. He resembles a public school Outward Bound instructor. But this "frightfully good chap" image prevents producers offering him the meaty rôles he craves. He can blame those two documentary travelogue series: *Around The World in 80 Days*, in which he retraced Phileas Fogg's journey and his freezing journey *Pole to Pole*.

Palin's father was export manager for a Sheffield steelworks. He scrimped to send his son to Shrewsbury and then Oxford where Michael first met Terry Jones. They began writing sketches for *The Frost Report* until BBC2's *Monty Python's Flying Circus* brought them together with John Cleese, Graham Chapman, Terry Gilliam and Eric Idle. It became the seminal Seventies satire series. It was while filming *Monty Python and the Holy Grail* that the only recorded example of Palin losing his temper occurred. The director had asked him to crawl through the mud for the seventh time. Afterwards the other Pythons all stood up and clapped. He was upset when his rôle as a stuttering, animal-loving, dog-murderer in *A Fish Called Wanda* was criticised for making fun of the afflicted. For he had modelled it on his late father, but "it was really all a storm in a t...t....teacup!" He has since set up a Michael Palin Centre for Stammering Children in North London.

Palin married his independent-minded wife Helen in 1966. "She's very cool. I'll ring up from some far corner of the world and be saying: 'Look, I'm at the bottom of Victoria Falls' and she'll interrupt saying: 'Sorry, can't talk now, I'm just off to play badminton'." They live opposite a council estate in three knocked-together railwaymen's cottages in Gospel Oak. Their children, Thomas, William and Rachel, attended local comprehensives because Palin hates the "them and us" mentality of private education. He has two other bugbears: "I won't do cameo parts in other people's films as it smacks of being a 'celebrity' and I won't do any advertising as it's a sure way to make anyone irritable."

Palmer, Iris, 10th July 1977, aristo mannequin. She arrived like a ravishing breath of fresh air on the international catwalk. Her idiosyncratic gait differs from the gentle hip-swaying and sensual glide practised by models from Jean Shrimpton to Elle MacPherson. According to one fashion editor, her body weaves all over the stage resembling "a doped-up flapper". Her dark bob, vaguely old-fashioned figure, translucent skin and dramatic eyeshadow give her unique style. Although she first started modelling at 15 her career only took off when she was discovered by British stylist Izzy Blow. She in turn introduced her to model agent Sarah Doukas who saw in her the perfect antidote to Amazonian supermodels like Carla Bruni and superwaifs like Kate Moss. Award-winning milliner Philip Treacy then cast her in his 1996 show.

This intelligent, articulate and sensible rebel hated Bedales and St Mary's Wantage, although she did sit her A-levels. "Bedales was awful – fake liberal, full of rock stars' children. St Mary's wanted to expel me but didn't get the chance because I didn't drink or do drugs." She belongs to an eccentric family. Her father, former hippy baronet Sir Mark Palmer, spent the Eighties touring the West Country in a brightly-painted gypsy caravan. Her astrologer mother Catherine is the sister of Princess Margaret's flamboyant friend Lord Glenconner.

Grungily-dressed Iris has more than lived up to the family motto, *May The Success Be Equal To The Labour.* She plans to stop modelling when she has saved enough money "to buy a big house". Perhaps then she will turn her genius for mimicry to professional use. Her impressions of camp Hollywood goddesses, school matrons and West Country farmers' wives leave friends in stitches.

Palmer-Tomkinson, Tara, 23rd December 1971, Queen of the It Girls. This quintessential good-time girl has stretched a tiny talent a long way. She sometimes goes to three cocktail parties and functions a night, but her presence invariably galvanizes the paparazzi. She was the on-off girlfriend of restaurateur Mogens Tholstrup for 18 months. She had flings with club owners Joel Cadbury and Piers Adam and tycoon Robert Hanson. "Men may come and go but your faithful Levis are always there", is her philosophy.

This whippet-thin temptress is the daughter of Hampshire landowner Charlie Palmer-Tomkinson who taught Prince Charles to ski. Her mother, Patti, nearly died in the 1988 avalanche which killed royal aide Major Hugh Lindsay. Tara has accompanied Prince William and Prince Harry on holidays to Klosters, Balmoral and Sandringham. They treat her like a big sister.

Tara grew up on the family's 1,200-acre farm near Basingstoke. After Sherborne and stage school she pursued a brief City career, working for Rothschild's. She then moved into frivolous mode, as a fashion stylist and model. Royal patience was stretched when she modelled underwear for *The Sun* because she was "broke" and appeared in a glossy magazine with three friends, naked except for a handbag covering their behinds. She revels in her *fausse naïveté*. At dinner before speaking in a feminist debate at the Cambridge Union she observed after the Latin grace: "Oh I do love to hear people speaking Italian!"

Nominated for Best-Dressed Woman of 1996, Tara was able to turn the tables on journalists who had branded her "an airhead yum-yum" and "bimbolette". She began a *Sunday Times* diary chronicling her party-going, romances and *pensées*. "I was at Silverstone as a guest of Gianni Agnelli, which for me was as exciting as winning the Lottery." But the 'plugs' for Prada, Chanel and Versace grow tiresome.

Palumbo, Jamie, 6th June 1964, nocturnal entrepreneur. This enigmatic, Richard Branson-in-a-suit appears to be the ultimate trust-fund babe. He pockets some £1,000 a week from the family coffers. But, through his own brilliance, he was a millionaire by 30. Cool, aloof and steely he is the least likely person to own the Ministry of Sound, London's largest and most successful disco. It has spawned a record label and mail-order business. His Covent Garden shop sells Ministry tee-shirts, jumpers, rucksacks, lighters and other merchandise. Yet he is said to inspire a mixture of "fear, loathing, admiration and love". He has successfully beaten drug dealers and protection racketeers who tried to invade his Elephant & Castle patch. With sister Annabella he even sued his tycoon father, Lord Palumbo, in 1994 claiming that he was not a "fit and proper person" to run their estimated £70 million family trust. The case was settled out of court.

The Palumbo fortune derives from Jamie's grandfather Rudolph. An impoverished immigrant from Amalfi he started with a City café and built a post-war property empire. Jamie idolised his grandfather but has always had a difficult relationship with his father Peter, whom Mrs Thatcher ennobled in her resignation honours list. Sent to Eton he was teased for his *nouveau riche* origins. At 16 he became the youngest ever house captain but was forced to step down after the appointment almost caused a riot. During his gap-year he lived in California where he started a butler service. At Oxford he became a louche socialite ("a man-about-spires"). He then gained experience as a merchant banker before founding the Ministry in 1991.

Pursued by eligible and beautiful totties this darkly handsome bachelor shows a reluctance to settle down, "Getting married has never occurred to me." His most significant relationship was with Iranian-born Atoosa Hariri, by whom he had a son, Alessandro, in 1991. A political career is his next step.

Parker Bowles, Camilla, 17th July 1947, royal *maîtresse en titre*. This remarkably loyal and discreet woman is the only person who really understands Prince Charles. She provides a sympathetic, almost motherly, ear and shares his love of hunting and Goonish sense of humour. No wonder he refuses all entreaties from the Queen, churchmen and politicians to ditch her. He even paid some of her Lloyd's losses (a tradition observed by his forebear Edward VII who 'kept' Camilla's great-grandmother Mrs Alice Keppel).

Apart from a short gap after he married Lady Diana Spencer in 1981, their relationship has endured for over 25 years. Even on his honeymoon, Camilla caused a row when Diana discovered that she had just given him a pair of gold cufflinks engraved with entwined 'C's. They resumed their affair after the birth of Prince William, provoking Diana's subsequent *Panorama* outburst that three people in a marriage was "a bit crowded". Publication of a bugged telephone conversation revealing the full extent of Charles and Camilla's intimacy finally led to the "Royal Marriage is Over" announcement.

Camilla first dated Charles when she was a gadabout 24 and he a callow 23-year-old naval officer. In 1973 she married Andrew Parker Bowles, a handsome Guards officer ten years her senior. He had a large private income through his mother Dame Ann Parker Bowles, whose father was the multi-millionaire racehorse-owner Sir Humphrey de Trafford. They were therefore able to enjoy an extravagant lifestyle in Wiltshire with their children Tom and Laura. But much of their 22 year marriage was a sham.

Camilla's father Major Bruce Shand spent 16 years in the royal household as Clerk of the Cheque and Adjutant of the Yeomen of the Guard. Her mother Rosalind belonged to the wealthy Cubitt family who built Belgravia and Pimlico. Unlike the *naïve*, blushing gels who were Camilla's fellow debutantes in 1965, she was already an habitué of nightclubs like the Garrison and the Saddle Room. Her first boyfriend was aviation heir Kevin Bourke.

Camilla's Regency home, Ray Mill House in Wiltshire, lies only 16 miles from Charles's Highgrove, where she is often in residence as his unofficial hostess. She has finally listened to PR advice and glammed herself up. Her hair is expensively tinted and she no longer scowls at photographers. It remains sad that two divorced middle-aged people need to lead such furtive lives.

Patterson, Jennifer, 3rd April 1928, culinary grandma. This late-flowering talent became 1996's great TV discovery, following such eccentric upper-middle-class characters as Sister Wendy Beckett and Lady Lucinda Lambton. With co-star Clarissa Dickson-Wright she fronted BBC2's cookery series, *The Two Fat Ladies*. Their quirky gastronomic journey around Britain, with Jennifer astride her 900cc Triumph Thunderbird and Clarissa squashed into the sidecar, attracted 3.5 million viewers.

A staunch Roman Catholic spinster, Jennifer describes herself as a "sweet virgin of this parish". But she enthuses about food like a nymphomaniac enjoying an orgasm, drooling over roast pheasant with bread sauce and fine vintage claret. She abhors political correctness, cooking with lashings of butter, cream and booze. Her weakness is chocolate ice-cream and coffee pudding.

The gutsy, irrepressibly jolly, 14 stone Jennifer was brought up in pre-Communist China with an array of servants. She has never had cookery lessons but learnt while lodging with her bachelor uncle, an Army officer stationed in Benghazi. During the early Sixties she settled in London and has derived a steady, if meagre, income from food ever since. For 11 years she cooked lunches for *The Spectator* maga zine, with VIP guests like Mrs Thatcher and the Russian ambassador congratulating her. But after hacks left her kitchen in a mess she quit, throwing her saucepans out of the window. Editor Charles Moore announced she could "write for *The Spectator* but never cook here again." And so she started her gossippy food column.

Oil executive's daughter Jennifer has ridden motorcycles for over 30 years and wears a diamond-studded crash-helmet designed by Jonathan Routh. She loves truffling round delicatessens but finds clothes-shopping a bore. "I just cover myself with a tent and only expose my wrists and ankles which are exquisite!" "One advantage of being fat", she says, "is that you are less likely to get mugged. Muggers are cowards and go for the littlies!"

Paxman, Jeremy, 11th May 1950, *Newsnight* hatchet-man. This Yorkshire-born TV presenter has riled more Cabinet ministers than any other journalist, bar perhaps *Today's* John Humphrys. Terrier-like, he refuses to let them dodge his questions and is neither flattered nor deflected by their "now come on, Jeremy" matiness. Arrogant and smug, he sees himself as the natural heir to David Dimbleby as the BBC anchorman at General Elections. Failing that, a Frost-style *Jeremy Paxman Show* would do nicely.

The Great Sneer blames his aggression on being bullied as a pupil at Malvern. ("I suppose there might be the occasional happy memory buried away among all the unhappy ones.") After Cambridge he joined BBC Radio Brighton but cut his journalistic teeth as a BBC news reporter in Northern Ireland. He then worked on BBC1's *Tonight* and *Panorama* programmes. He briefly presented BBC1's *Breakfast Time*, but found it hard to quiz bleary-eyed pop stars and other publicity-seekers.

In 1989 Paxman joined *Newsnight*, alternating as presenter with Peter Snow, Penny Wark and other journalists. At the height of the miners' dispute he temporarily fazed Cabinet minster Michael Heseltine with the comment: "it's quite an achievement, isn't it, to make a hero out of Arthur Scargill?"

Spitting Image's puppet exactly mirrored Paxman's characteristic reaction to "lying" government ministers: pursed lips, arched eyebrows, eyes widening, nostrils flaring with incredulity. One sketch had him popping round to see his neighbours: "So you locked your keys in the car. Ye-e-e-es... now that was a bit stupid, wasn't it?" Ever-ambitious, he tried to become chairman of *Question Time* but was beaten by David Dimbleby in a bizarre High Noon-style audition. His consolation prize, presenter of *University Challenge*, began disastrously with his hectoring manner comparing badly with his urbane predecessor, Bamber Gascoigne.

Outside politics, "Paxo" has one other passion – fishing, about which he has written several worthy books. He describes himself as a melancholy character. But his spirits rose when TV producer Elizabeth Clough, mother of his daughter Jessica, gave birth to twins in 1997. They live in unmarried bliss at their farmhouse outside Henley-on-Thames and in Notting Hill.

Pearson, Neil, 3rd May 1959, left-wing heart-throb. He was just another handsome telly face until a cult C4 series, *Drop The Dead Donkey*, turned him into a star. As Globelink News's office Romeo, Dave Charnley, he attracted a devoted female following. Perhaps it was the gentle smile, ice-cool blue eyes and dark Hugh Grant hair flopping over his forehead that prompted one reviewer to describe him as "the man responsible for more adulterous fantasies than Julio Iglesias!" In 1992 he landed his own series, *Between The Lines*, playing maverick detective Tony Clark. "We're actually very similar characters, both of us are inclined to refuse to accept things at face value. I'm the bloke who will stand at the back of a meeting and ask: 'Why?'" His rôle of South African statesman Dr Jameson in BBC1's much-slated series, *Rhodes*, showed him in a more heavyweight context. "But I've never treated acting as a vocation. It's what I do when I'm not doing the rest of my life."

Pearson comes from a single-parent, working-class Battersea family. His panel-beater father left home when he and his two siblings were still under five. After reading Anthony Buckeridge's Jennings books about life in an English public school he persuaded his mother to educate him privately. He won a grant to attend Woolverstone Hall, a state-run boarding school in Sussex. "I had this vision of jolly japes and midnight feasts, but it turned out not a bit like that. I still benefited from it hugely." Afterwards he studied at the Central School of Speech and Drama.

This easy-going, eligible bachelor lives alone in south London. He is very guarded about his personal life, only admitting "I don't live like a monk". He has dated a string of actresses including Siobhan Redmond and Susannah Doyle. "The fact that I was left pretty much fatherless has made me determined not to do that to any children I might have." Meanwhile he keeps himself fanciable with weightlifting. "I don't want to be a fat slob at 40."

Philip, Prince, 10th June 1921, royal controversialist. He must bear much responsibility for his sons' dysfunctional lives. Arrogant, bullying and selfish, he would reduce the young Prince Charles,

Prince Andrew and Prince Edward to tears. Only Princess Anne dared stand up to him. Courtiers were afraid to tell him he was taking liberties with the use of the royal yacht Britannia: he would turn official engagements for the World Wildlife Fund into jolly cruises with his friends.

The Prince's character was formed by an impoverished and neglected childhood. Allegedly born on the kitchen table at Mon Repos palace in Corfu, his father was Prince Andrew of Greece and his mother Princess Alice of Battenberg. When he was 18 months old, political unrest forced the family into exile in England. His parents drifted apart, with Mama founding an Order of nuns and globe-trotting Papa eventually dying penniless in Monte Carlo. Philip was educated at Cheam, Gordonstoun and Dartmouth Royal Naval College. Much to his chagrin he only briefly saw wartime service during the 1944 allied invasion of Crete.

The royal marriage, masterminded by his uncle Earl Mountbatten of Burma, depended on dynastic as much as romantic considerations. To the future Elizabeth II Philip not only resembled a Viking warrior but was royal, Protestant (well, Greek Orthodox) and the right age – 26. But his previous love-life had been as busy as Fergie's. Half a century later the marriage can be judged a success in that they are still together and have had four children. But during the Fifties the Queen was often upset by his long absences abroad. There were also constant rumours of affairs, many with girls introduced to him by his late private secretary Commander Mike Parker.

Today Philip is as tactless, uncompromising and authoritarian as ever. He retains his bluff sailor's sense of humour. When told that a footman had been fired for being found in bed with a housemaid he expressed delight that at last there was one who was heterosexual. At other occasions he can be disconcertingly curt. A nervous official once greeted him on his arrival in Scotland by asking, "How was your flight, Sir?". The Prince replied: "Have you ever been on an aeroplane?". "Yes, Sir," said the trembling official. "Well", said Philip, "it was like that."

This sprightly old codger has one major regret: that the Queen has never named him "Prince Consort", a title bestowed on Prince Albert.

Phillips, Captain Mark, 22nd September 1948, royal reject. He was the first commoner to marry into the royal family since Antony Armstrong-Jones. He would have been a poor social catch, even for a farmer's daughter, let alone Princess Anne. His father was a director of Walls sausages and had no Debrett's connections. But Mark was a glamorous subaltern in the Queen's Dragoon Guards and a champion rider. "Horses rarely stop with Mark, and if they do, they wish they hadn't", Anne observed. She may not have admired his intellect, but was mightily impressed by his gold medal in the 1972 Munich Olympics and his 1971/2 victories in the Badminton Three-Day Event.

This shy Old Marlburian was "tickled pink" as he marched down the aisle at Westminster Abbey in 1973. But within four months, he learnt the drawbacks of his new exalted position when a deranged gunman ambushed their official limo in the Mall, wounding four people. Soon he began to suffer from the famous "Anne Lip" – being bellowed at and sworn at in public.

Phillips's comment when they moved into their new 1,400-acre Gatcombe Park estate did not help his image: "We're just like any other couple with a mortgage." His brothers-in-law dubbed him "Fog", because he was "thick and wet". Such was his complex that when their first baby Peter was born in 1977 he observed ruefully: "Well, at least I've done something right!" He has proved a model father to Peter and daughter Zara, and ensured that they learnt the essential royal skills of riding, shooting and fishing.

During the Eighties the couple spent long periods apart: she on official visits and he holding riding clinics in Canada, Australia, New Zealand and at his own equestrian centre beside Gleneagles Hotel, Perthshire. Tabloid gossip began over his close friendship with his Canadian publicist Kathy Birks. Then a former pupil, New Zealander Heather Tonkin, filed a paternity suit against him. This scandal, plus Anne's desire to marry former royal equerry Tim Laurence, hastened their divorce in 1992. Five years later he married American heiress and horsewoman Sandy Pflueger, owner of a swanky £2 million stud near Hungerford.

Phillips, Peter, 15th November 1977, demi-royal Action Man. This beefy chap has inherited the best characteristics of his often difficult parents, Princess Anne and Captain Mark Phillips. Tough, loyal and conscientious he has an easy, unpompous manner reminiscent of a youthful Will Carling. He left a greater impression at Gordonstoun than his uncles, Charles, Andrew and Edward. He made friends easily, became head boy and starred in the rugby XV. He also became a Scottish Schools rugby international.

Peter was the Queen's first grandchild. His nanny was Mabel Anderson, who had looked after the Princess and her brothers. He had a country upbringing at Gatcombe Park in Gloucestershire, learning to ride at six, being blooded by the local hunt at 12 and becoming a crack pheasant shot. He was sent away to Port Regis prep school.

Peter dethroned his cousin Prince William as top royal heart-throb in a recent magazine poll. But he is still too young to have sampled the fleshpots of London. His first girlfriend was fellow Gordonstoun pupil Penny Taylor, who joined him on an unchaperoned Jamaican holiday in 1995.

During his gap-year Peter worked for former world motor-racing champion Jackie Stewart and sports promoter Mark McCormack. He may lack sophistication, but his rugby ambitions should prosper at Exeter University where he is studying sports science. Exeter has so far produced 42 rugby internationals. Meanwhile he hopes to join the Royal Marines. The Queen Mother has set up a trust-fund for him and the Queen will eventually provide a property on the Balmoral estate. He is going to be very eligible.

Piggott, Lester, 5th November 1935, racing legend. He is the world's greatest jockey, a miracle-man whose racing feats will probably never be surpassed. Frankie Dettori will have to grow wings to beat his record, which includes nine Derby wins and 11 champion jockeyships. But by today's soundbite standards, he was always an unlikely hero – notoriously taciturn, rarely smiling and supposedly tight-fisted. Yet the public loved him, with housewives always "having a flutter on our Lester". He retired in 1985 to become a trainer with his wife Susan, whose father and brother were also Newmarket trainers. But that ambition ended two years later when he received a three-year jail sentence for defrauding the Inland Revenue of £2.8 million. This almost certainly cost him his expected knighthood, and the Queen even stripped him of his OBE.

Dubbed the "Long Fellow" because he is 5ft 8 1/2 ins tall, Piggott came from a well-known steeplechasing family. He rode his first winner at 12 and went on to ride more than 5,000 winners on horses like Crepello, Nijinsky and The Minstrel. As a 55-year-old grandfather he briefly made a comeback and won his 29th British Classic on Robert Sangster's Rodrigo de Triano in the 2,000 Guineas at Newmarket.

Piggott lives in a £1.5 million house outside Newmarket with his long-suffering wife Susan, a former bloodstock agent. They married when he was 25 and had two daughters, Maureen and Tracey. Life became complicated in 1993 when local horsewoman Anna Ludlow gave birth to his son, Jamie. "Some men might have chosen to divorce and abandon their first family, but I had no desire to do that. I chose to become head of two households instead." As an older father, he believes, that he can spend more time with his son than he did when his daughters were growing up. Blonde Anna, a reflexologist over 20 years his junior, became his mistress in 1981 when she was working for Susan. She now lives in a £250,000 bungalow, just a five-minute drive away in his black Mercedes. "Nothing would make me happier than to watch my son win the Derby one day", Piggott says.

Pinter, Harold, 10th October 1930, master of the pregnant pause. Despite many blips in his long career this chippy East Ender remains our greatest living dramatist. Other contenders are either, like Sir Alan Ayckbourn, too commercial and superficial or, like David Hare and Simon Gray, lack his artistic longevity. He remains excessively political and feisty. Such is his hyper-sensitivity that he once described coughing in the theatre as "an act of aggression" against his work. When directing another of his plays he drew attention to the length of a pause. "You're playing two dots when the text says three", he told the startled actor.

This pedantic Genghis Khan went to Hackney Downs Grammar School where he first experienced anti-Semitism. Using the stage-name David Barron he then became an undistinguished repertory actor. Inspired by Irish playwright Samuel Beckett he had his first three plays staged in 1957: *The Room*, *The Birthday Party* and *The Dumb Waiter*. A score of new productions followed, with *The Caretaker* and *The Homecoming* proving major West End and Broadway successes. At the same time he began scripting major British films like *The Servant*, *Accident* and *The Go-Between*.

Pinter married his first wife, actress Vivien Merchant, in 1956. When they split up 24 years later she famously said of his then mistress, Lady Antonia Fraser: "She's got big feet, you know!" He married this brilliant hostess, historian and novelist in 1980, thus joining the staunchly Catholic and literary Pakenham family. But his sharp wit and intellect have been well able to cope. They were less amused by his so-called 20th June Group, a "think-tank of the Left". This proved to be just another excuse for fellow Bollinger socialists like Melvyn Bragg and John Mortimer to enjoy a *soirée* at Lady Antonia's magnificent Campden Hill house. Pinter's study in the mews behind contains mementoes of his Sixties protests against the Americans in Vietnam and other causes. He has long prided himself, like his friend Peruvian writer Mario Vargas Llosa, as an activist campaigning against totalitarian regimes. His complete set of *Wisden* cricket annuals testifies to his other abiding interest.

Polizzi, Olga, 21st February 1947, Society hostess and interior decorator. She is the Princess Anne of the Forte clan. Strong, forthright and independent, she has inherited the best qualities of her father Charles Forte who founded the eponymous catering empire. But she has no truck with his snobbish ways. In 1996 she used her high-powered contacts to try to defeat Granada's victorious £3.8 billion takeover bid. As director in charge of design she had latterly been responsible for choosing every mirror, picture and bathroom suite. Her consolation prize was a share in the estimated £325 million price paid for the family's 8.5 per cent stake. She has recently bought a Cornish hotel.

Dark-eyed Olga was educated at St Mary's Ascot and, in retrospect, wishes she had gone on to study architecture at university. Instead she married at 19. Much to her father's pleasure she chose a dashing Italian grandee, Marchese Alessandro Polizzi di Sorrentino. "I married him primarily because he had a beautiful nose and I didn't want my children to inherit the Forte nose!" They lived in Rome where she went to art school and in Amsterdam where she learnt to paint in oils. They separated when their two daughters, Alexandra and Charlotte, were young, and he died in a car accident in 1980. The same year she joined Forte's then small design department. Her only previous foray into commerce was running a silver stall at South London's Bermondsey flea-market.

This warm, dynamic socialite spent five years as a Westminster City councillor. She enjoyed a long relationship with West End art dealer Richard Connolly. Another admirer was former Tory chancellor Norman Lamont, who once provoked a fracas when leaving her Bayswater mews house following a late-night drink. Connolly, misunderstanding his intentions, blacked his eye. In 1993 Olga became the third wife of journalist William Shawcross, eldest son of Nuremberg War Trials prosecutor Lord Shawcross. With more spare time now she can relish a scribbled note that she framed from her daughter, then aged nine: "Dear Mummy, thank you for not going out to dinner as often as you normally do, love Charlie."

Powell, Lady (pronounced Pole), 1st January 1943, the Sophia Loren of political hostesses. She is gushing, feminine and utterly beguiling. She seized the moment when her diplomat husband Charles Powell joined Mrs Thatcher as private secretary for foreign affairs in 1984. She became the PM's confidante and unofficial Lady of the Bedchamber. Once he arrived home to find his wife gassing, as usual excitedly, on the 'phone about hairdressers and dressmakers. "Please get off the line, Carla," he eventually implored, "there's a lot going on and the prime minister may want to speak to me". "But darling, it is the prime minister!" Their reward: his 1990 knighthood.

With her flashing eyes and dark skin the former Carla Bonardi resembles a Sicilian contessa from *The Godfather*. In fact she hails from Val Vigezzo on the Swiss-Italian border. She came to Oxford aged 18 to study at St Clare's finishing school. Her only contact was a local vicar who asked his shy, undergraduate nephew, Charles Powell, to show her the university. "Charles was expecting a little schoolgirl in a plain frock. But there was me, in my skimpiest outfit, with my big boobs. He didn't know where to look!" Three years later these diametric opposites married. He, the punctilious, stiff-upper-lipped, cerebral English gentleman and she, the passionate, volatile *ragazza* (nicknamed "Monte Carla", after Italy's most active volcano). She became a supportive but never submissive Foreign Office wife as he climbed from second secretary in Helsinki to first secretary in Bonn and Washington. Her one complaint was that he never made enough money. She therefore developed formidable talents for haggling, whether for oranges, antiques or designer gowns.

Mrs Thatcher's 1990 fall from power created turmoil in the Powell household. But Carla encouraged him to ditch the FO and begin a lucrative new City career, becoming a director of blue-chip firms like Jardine Matheson, NatWest bank and Christian Dior. Meanwhile she began to show non-Tory leanings: campaigning for Sir James Goldsmith's Referendum Party in the 1997 general election and giving Labour guru Peter Mandelson a bed in their Bayswater house while his nearby home was refurbished. She even complained that Mrs T "ruined our lives" by not giving Charles a peerage. She has two sons, Hugh and Nicholas.

Prescott, John, 31st May 1938, Hull's greatest statesman, nicknamed "Thumper". He may resemble a bulldog which has swallowed a wasp, but he has the last laugh. Not only is he deputy prime minister but his wife Pauline looks like an ex-Miss Blackpool. They married in 1961 and have two sons. As a steward on luxury Cunard cruise-liners he acquired the class resentment that came to dominate his political philosophy. Tory MP Nicholas Soames used to rub it in with his cries of "Another gin and tonic please, Giovanni". QE2 waiters roared with laughter when they saw pictures of him outside 10 Downing Street after the 1997 general election. "Just think", mused a former *SS Britannic* shipmate, "if John had stayed he might be a restaurant manager by now!"

Described as having a chip on both shoulders this plain-speaking, railwayman's son was an 11-plus failure at Ellesmere Port Secondary Modern School. But he later caught up: A-levels by correspondence course, an economics and politics diploma at Ruskin College, Oxford and an economics degree at Hull University. For two years he was a full-time trade union official, representing the militant National Union of Seamen during the Seamen's Strike. He entered Parliament in 1970 and is one of the few ministers to have had some previous government experience.

Workaholic, fiery-tempered Prescott was shadow spokesman on transport, energy and employment. As deputy PM he remains "the conscience of Old Labour" and tries hard to curb his salty, knock-about humour. During the 1997 general election he observed: "John Major likes going to the Happy Eater – it's the only place where they'll take his orders!" His working-class beliefs have never prevented him from enjoying the better things in life. His Hull home is an eight-bedroomed turretted Edwardian folly, and his car an old Jaguar Sovereign. He unwinds by taking his wife jiving at the local country club on Saturday nights.

Puttnam, Lord, 25th February 1941, Sixties icon. This cynical, North London spieler was responsible for producing a trio of award-garlanded Hollywood hits: *Chariots of Fire*, *The Killing Fields* and *The Mission*. He describes his taste as belonging to the "quintessential middle-class person, neither damaged by intellectual leftism nor the *Sun* readership". But he has sometimes found difficulty living up to his de Millian reputation. Meanwhile he has diversified. As a member of the "great and the good", he ran the National Film and TV School and the Council For Protection of Rural England. His reward: a 1997 life peerage.

This cocky son of a Fleet Street photographer left Minchenden Grammar School at 16 and worked for the publishers Hutchinson, humping books around. At 20 he joined go-go advertising agency Collett Dickenson Pearce, where his team included Alan Parker, Hugh Hudson and Ridley Scott. In 1966 he got bored and opened his own photographers' agency, representing David Bailey and Richard Avedon. Using his many trendy contacts he founded a film company, Enigma Productions, two years later. His early successes were with pop-orientated flim-flam: *That'll Be The Day* and *Stardust*. His taste improved with Parker's *Bugsy Malone*, Ridley's *The Duellists* and Parker's Oscar-winning *Midnight Express*. He spent 18 unhappy months trying to become a Hollywood film mogul, running Columbia Pictures. It resulted in his first failure, *Foxes*. One critic described him as being "a bit out of his depth in the American shallows".

Puckish Puttnam has never operated the casting couch. But his 1961 marriage to childhood chum Patsy survived the disclosure that he was a member of a notorious massage parlour, the Wigmore Club. Although clients like Fergie's father Major Ron Ferguson frequented it for sexual purposes, he insisted he only went to relieve painful back pains. He has two children, Sacha and Debbie, the latter married to *Masterchef* host Loyd Grossman. When CPRE chairman he once created a stir by trying to divert a public footpath running in front of his former £3 million Wiltshire millhouse.

Queen, The, 21st April 1926, royal paragon, nicknamed Brenda and Miss Piggy. Having ascended the throne in 1952 she is Europe's longest reigning monarch after Prince Rainier of Monaco. Conscientious, hard-working and professional, she conveys the majesty of her forebear Queen Victoria, whose 63-year reign she hopes to outlive. Some aristos, particularly Scots still loyal to the Stuarts, refer to our royals as "the Germans" because of their Hanoverian ancestry. But HM also claims descent from the 9th century Saxon king Egbert.

A virtual teetotaller, the Queen will toy with her glass of hock or Moselle at state banquets. She surprised the Queen Mother at Clarence House once by accepting a second glass with her lunch. "Do you think it's wise, darling? You know you've got to rule this afternoon!" She has a natural authority and can deflate the most uppity subject. Attired in head scarf and tweed skirt she once visited a supermarket near Sandringham to buy some chocolate. "My goodness", exclaimed a fellow shopper, "you look just like the Queen". "How reassuring", was the regal reply.

The Queen is often dubbed the "world's richest woman", worth anything up to £5 billion, although the *Sunday Times* lists her at only £400 million. It depends whether you exclude the royal art collection from her personal fortune and how you value her Balmoral and Sandringham estates. Her wealth includes the Duchy of Lancaster: 52,000 acres across Britain ranging from farms, grousemoors and city centres, to property in the Strand (including the Savoy Hotel). She is also said to own land in New York, France and Germany as well as a substantial share portfolio. Yet she remains personally frugal, switching off lights and seldom buying new clothes except for State occasions. No wonder she moaned about the extravagances of her ex-daughter-in-laws!

The Queen's favourite pastime is riding and she is also proud of her success at breeding racehorses and polo ponies. At a Buckingham Palace banquet a Central American ambassador once attempted to show off his racing knowledge to her. He reeled off the results of certain classic races by naming the first three horses. In each case she quietly added the names of the fourth and fifth. Former prime minister Mrs Thatcher had nothing in common with her and found their weekly meetings "a trial"!

As a firm believer in her Coronation vows the Queen would never

contemplate abdication. Alas for Prince Charles, her female forebears have proved remarkably long-lived: Queen Victoria died aged
81, Queen Alexandra 80, Queen Mary 85 while the Queen Mother is
97! She just prays for no more *anni horribili*.

Queen Mother, The, 4th August 1900, royal supertreasure. Her
sprightliness and serenity could charm even the most stony-hearted
republican. She has a gift for lifelong friendship, a flair for backing
racehorses and the constitution of a Highland grouse. Having outlived Queen Victoria she is determined to receive her centenary
telegram from the Queen. Paradoxically, she has always seemed
slightly vulgar, a sort of Windsor Pearly Queen. Indeed the Duchess
of Windsor nicknamed her "Cookie" while *Spitting Image* portrayed
her as a school dinner lady.

The Queen Mother was born Elizabeth Bowes-Lyon and raised at
Glamis Castle on Tayside, St Paul's Waldenbury in Hertfordshire
and a Mayfair townhouse. She was the Earl of Strathmore's ninth
child and her mother was a vicar's daughter related to the Dukes of
Portland. The sparky and vivacious Elizabeth had many admirers,
including the dashing World War I hero, James Stuart. She was
reluctant to marry the decent but weedy Bertie, George V's second
son, whom she had known since childhood. When she did marry him
in 1923 at Westminster Abbey and became Duchess of York, she had
no reason to believe that she would ever become Queen. The marriage helped to save the royal blood-line which had become weak-
ened by two centuries of intermarriage with decadent German
princedoms. Although disappointed she never had a son, she had two
beautiful princesses, Elizabeth and Margaret. The idyll ended in
1936 with Edward VIII's abdication and Bertie becoming George VI.

The new Queen proved an inspiration during World War II, not
only comforting Blitz-battered Londoners but boosting her husband's
morale. She never forgave her brother-in-law for putting love for
Wallis Simpson before country, thereby exposing the shy, stammering Bertie to the stresses of kingship. After he died of cancer in 1952
she assumed the unique courtesy title of Queen Mother to avoid confusion with the new Queen Elizabeth. She has thrived in widowhood
– fishing, partying and entertaining her grandchildren and great-
grandchildren. But she is "black-affronted" by recent royal scandals.

Quentin, Caroline, 11th July 1959, bouncy comedienne. She
became a household name as Martin Clunes's outspoken girlfriend
in the award-winning *Men Behaving Badly*. Its success enabled her

finally to emerge from being best-known as Mrs Paul Merton. Among many TV and stage parts she starred in a recent comedy-drama series, *Jonathan Creek*. She landed it, much to his chagrin, after he invited producer David Renwick to dinner to discuss working together. The Mertons parted in 1996, with her moving into a West End flat, claiming that she could no longer take his juvenile behaviour. "When working on scripts with his pal John Irwin they act like 14-year-olds. They throw rubbers at each other. There would be great howls of laughter from the room, but it would all grow quiet when I opened the door."

Feisty Caroline trained to be a dancer at the Arts Educational School. A talent scout spotted her performing in a comedy revue at an Islington pub in 1979. She became a stand-up comic at the Comedy Store. The Mertons later starred together in ITV's tragi-comedy *An Evening With Gary Lineker* and in the West End play *The Live Bed Show*, playing a warring couple. "If we have a row we can get rid of all the venom by screaming at each other on stage!" In 1996 she led a revolt against the producers of *Men Behaving Badly*, threatening to quit unless she and her co-star Leslie Ash received the same pay as their male co-stars Martin Clunes and Neil Morrissey. Now all four receive £100,000 a series.

Within four days of meeting Caroline on the London-to-Glasgow train in 1990 Merton dumped his long-standing girlfriend and moved into her flat. "At that point we hadn't even kissed! But I knew he was the man for me immediately." Not best pleased was her Battersea Dogs Home mutt Ollie who found there was no longer space in her bed with an additional 6ft 4ins human there. They moved into a large house in Wimbledon and he risked the inevitable jokes by inviting his mother-in-law to live in the adjoining coach-house. Cuddly Caroline should have no trouble finding a new man.

R

Rampling, Charlotte, 5th February 1946, Sixties 'wild child'. She has the powerful gifts of an Elizabeth Taylor or Lauren Bacall. "When she's on screen it's almost impossible to look at anybody else", says former co-star Sir Dirk Bogarde. In real-life she has a mesmerising effect on men. "I know I have this power...it's very dangerous. That's why I play everything down – never wear clothes that show my body or ornaments that enhance my looks."

Daughter of a NATO colonel with strict, old-fashioned views, Charley was sent to school near Fontainebleau. He banned her taking singing lessons as "too frivolous". She believes that her manic depression is partly due to his controlling influence. At 16 she rebelled and fled to Madrid, but "my father dragged me back" to an English secretarial college. With her long chestnut hair, almond-shaped green eyes and coltish figure she became a model and then appeared in two trendy Sixties movies, *The Knack* and *Georgy Girl*. But she horrified even those permissive times by revealing that she was living in a *ménage à trois*, with her manager Bryan Southcombe and male model Randy Lawrence. "The fact is I love two men and it's difficult to narrow down my emotions to just one." In 1972 she became pregnant with her son Barnaby and wed Southcombe. Four years later she met musician Jean-Michel Jarre at a St Tropez dinner-party. "It was love at first sight" and, though both were married, they eloped to Paris. Married in 1978, they had a son David whom she has brought up with her husband's daughter Emilie.

Meanwhile Charlotte's showy rôle in Visconti's kinky Nazi epic, *The Damned*, led to a string of Hollywood films. She starred in *The Night Porter*, with Dirk Bogarde, *Farewell My Lovely* with Robert Mitchum, *Stardust Memories* with Woody Allen and *The Verdict* with Paul Newman. Critics drooled over her "brooding sensuality".

Nowadays Charley is less courted by Hollywood and mainly a Continental star. She was devastated when her husband ran off with a young Parisian civil servant, Odile Froument, in 1996. Charlotte left their homes near Versailles and St Tropez, and settled in Chelsea. She will not be alone for long.

Rattle, Sir Simon, 19th January 1955, Britain's Zubin Mehta. Casual, cool and frizzy-haired, he resembles some hip recording manager: Sir George Martin twinned with Pete Waterman? Classic FM credits him with doing more than any other conductor to demystify classical music, through his TV appearances and million-selling albums. Fronting the City of Birmingham Symphony Orchestra and the Los Angeles Philharmonic his work was described by one critic as like "phosphorescence illuminating the ocean". Unusually for a world-class conductor he remains popular with his musicians who respect the fact that he has never become big-headed.

Growing up in Liverpool when the Beatles were world-exporting the Mersey Sound this passionate prodigy was pioneering his own musical revolution. At 15 he already played percussion, piano and violin and had assembled his first orchestra. While at the Royal Academy of Music he won the International Conducting Competition in Bournemouth. He then made his professional debut at 19 with the Bournemouth Sinfonietta. He became the youngest ever conductor to perform at the Royal Albert Hall, Royal Festival Hall and Glyndebourne. Since then he has travelled the world, fronting orchestras in Boston, Chicago, Toronto, Berlin, Vienna and Stockholm, and establishing himself as Sir Malcolm Sargent's natural heir. He remains the Birmingham Symphony Orchestra's music director, where he became principal conductor in 1980. He once took a year's sabbatical to study English literature at Oxford.

Charismatic Rattle lives in Georgian splendour in Islington with his second wife, psychology consultant Candice Allen. He has two sons, Sacha and Elliott, from his 1980 marriage to American soprano Elise Ross, which ended in 1995. Knighted in 1994, he deserves to be awarded the coveted Order of Merit.

Redgrave, Vanessa, 30th January 1937, Oscar-winning zealot. Over 60 years ago, Laurence Olivier announced to an Old Vic audience that his *Hamlet* co-star, Michael Redgrave, had just become a father: "Ladies and gentlemen, tonight a great actress has been born. Laertes has a daughter!" Her upbringing was strictly upper-bourgeois: nanny, chauffeur, shopping at Harrods. At Queensgate School she even became head girl and lacrosse captain. After attending the Central School of Speech and Drama she made her West End debut at 21 in *A Touch of the Sun*. At 24 she was a RSC principal and at 25 the bride of rising film director Tony Richardson. Then things went wonky.

This tall, striking, blue-eyed blonde began picking most unladylike rôles. She was arrested after a Ban-the-Bomb demo, led anti-Vietnam War marches and publicly backed the IRA and PLO when they were at their most militant. She co-founded the Workers' Revolutionary Party, dedicated to destroying capitalism, freeing the workers from oppression and abolishing the monarchy. She even stood for Parliament – and lost her deposit! Apologists blame this radical rebirth on her parents. Behind a respectable front her father was a closet homosexual and her mother, actress Rachel Kempson, had a string of lovers. Vanessa came to despise their phoney values.

Nonetheless, Comrade Vanessa had her actress daughters Natasha and Joely Richardson, privately educated. Her marriage to Richardson only lasted five years. In 1967 she began a stormy six-year affair with her *Camelot* co-star, Italian heart-throb Franco Nero, by whom she has a son Carlo. Her other great love was actor Timothy Dalton who later became James Bond. In 1996 she became close to unknown actor David Harewood, 29 years her junior, whom she met while directing him in *Antony and Cleopatra*.

Vanessa's generosity to her 'causes' means she has little to show financially for her great success in Hollywood films like *The Charge of the Light Brigade, Mary Queen of Scots, Murder On The Orient Express* and the Oscar-winning *Julia*. Now mellower, she lives in a modest Chiswick mansion-flat. She regrets being absent so much when her children were growing up. She dreams of retiring so that she can build "sandcastle cities" with her grandchildren.

Reeves, Vic, 24th January 1959, self-styled "post-ironic, cool, celebrity game show host". This creative powerhouse is all set to rival his idol Eric Morecambe. In the early Nineties he achieved a trio of hit TV series, sell-out stage shows, concerts, bestselling records, videos and books.

This Darlington-born comic terror was christened Jim Moir. He changed it because BBC's light entertainment supremo had the same name. He romanticises his past, claiming to have been a trainee aircraft engineer, pig farmer and punk rocker. His punk band was allegedly called Hot Murder and their signature tune was Help a Little Child Across The Road of Death. He moved to London where he performed in pubs and managed a comedy club at the Goldsmith's Tavern, Deptford. There he began a double act with Bob Mortimer, a solicitor with a wicked sense of humour.

The duo toured alternative venues with their satirical revue, *Vic Reeves' Big Night Out*. They invented catchphrases like "you would-n't let it lie" and "look at the size of that sausage" and naff characters like Les and Wavy Davy and The Man with the Stick. Jonathan Ross loved their anarchic humour so much that he invited them onto C4's *The Last Resort*. In 1990 C4 turned *Big Night* into a cult Friday night success. They had a sell-out national tour and their live concert video became a bestseller. They then defected to the BBC to do *The Smell of Reeves and Mortimer* and their zany game show,

Shooting Stars.

Reeves is a laconic bloke who likes drinking in pubs and driving vintage motorbikes. Success has bought him a £600,000 farmhouse in Aldington, Kent. He has a daughter, Alice, from his marriage to Sarah Vincent. She temporarily left him in 1996, claiming that he had "a growing obsession with his *Shooting Stars* co-star Ulrika Jonsson." "I've been out on the town boozing with her", he admits. "She's a whisky girl and she'll match you glass for glass."

Rhodes, Gary, 22nd April 1960, TV Superchef and Manchester United fanatic. Lithe, spikey-haired and blokeish, he enthuses about food as if discussing last night's football match. He was discovered cooking at the Michelin-starred Greenhouse restaurant, Mayfair, by former breakfast TV chef Glynn Christian. His first BBC series, *Rhodes Around Britain*, was a rhapsody to British food, demonstrating such nostalgia-laced delicacies as stuffed pigs trotters, poachers' pie and Jaffa cake pudding. Tie-in cookbooks and a nationwide cookery tour, *The Rhodes Show*, followed. "I want to show the French, the Italians and the Americans that we've got some of the best dishes in the world." Celebrity chefs now behave like rock stars.

Raised in Kent, this garrulous gastronome originally wanted to become a police dog-handler. But he was forced to learn cooking when he looked after his younger sister while his mother was out at work. He did a three-year catering course at Thanet Tech before joining the Hilton Hotel, Amsterdam as a trainee. Just 19, he suffered serious head injuries when a van hit him while he was running for a tram. He was off work for five months and temporarily lost all sense of taste and smell. He became head chef at the Reform Club, but made his name cooking at the Greenhouse and the People's Palace, Waterloo. In 1996 caterers Gardner Merchant enticed him away to turn him into a brand name and open a series of Rhodes restaurants in city centres. How does he stay so slim? "By not eating!" He was three stone heavier before vanity forced him to diet.

This Nigel Kennedy of the *bain-marie* was engaged to his wife Jenny for ten years before they married in 1989. They live in Orpington, Kent with their sons, Samuel and George, and cats Tyson and Chloe. He splurged his earnings from TV series like *More Rhodes Around Britain* and *Open Rhodes Around Britain* on a Lotus, Mercedes and two Porsches. Gloom is certainly not his second name.

Rhys Jones, Griff, 16th November 1953, *farceur extraordinaire*. As well as his trademark jawline and fizzing *bonhomie* he has that distinctive arf! arf! laugh that is a dead ringer for Basil Brush. He enjoys playing the country squire to his comedy partner Mel Smith's London urchin. As a sideline they run Talkback, a highly successful TV commercials and production company. But, while the "fat, bald, common one with bad breath" concentrates on directing in America, Griff enjoys stretching his acting talents. On stage he was the swaggering Mr Toad in *The Wind in the Willows*, a twittish upper-crust schemer in *Plunder* and a petticoated dame in *Charley's Aunt*. He is still reeling from Prince Edward's waspish backstage comment after seeing him in *Arturo Ui*: "You seemed to be enjoying yourselves more than we were!" He has cultivated a straight acting career, starring in the TV series *Porterhouse Blue* and as the embittered ex-squaddie in *Demob*.

Despite his Welsh name, chest consultant's son Rhys Jones was raised in Essex and went to Brentwood School. At Cambridge he was a Footlights contemporary of Clive Anderson and Rory McGrath, who later collaborated on early Mel and Griff sketches. The BBC 'discovered' him at the Edinburgh Festival and hired him as a radio producer. In 1979 he joined Smith, Rowan Atkinson and Pamela Stephenson on BBC2's satirical *Not The Nine O'Clock News*. In 1982 he and Mel branched out into *Alas Smith and Jones*. Their head-to-head dialogues, trading gormless observations on life's banalities, were a *Dud and Pete* rip-off. The obsessive, neurotic Griff makes the perfect counterpoint to his calmer partner, a docile St Bernard to his yappy terrier. "Mel is one of the few people I'd trust to say about a sketch 'it's bollocks, mate'".

Bookworm presenter Rhys Jones enjoys life's trappings: a sumptuous country pad in Suffolk and a converted industrial unit in Clerkenwell. He married his wife Jo, a graphic designer, in 1982 and they have two children, Catherine and George.

Rhys-Jones, Sophie, 20th January 1965, Princess in waiting. The Queen is counting on her to redress the jinx that destroyed three of her children's marriages. Blonde, blue-eyed and blossoming she was unknown before she started dating Prince Edward in 1993. Courtiers would prefer just a smidgen of blue blood coursing through her veins. But at least her presence ended the gay rumours that swirled round him during his platonic friendships with Ulrika Jonsson and Ruthie Henshall.

This tyre executive's daughter was brought up in impoverished gentility near Tonbridge Wells and went to Kent College, a local girls' school. At 22 she joined Capital Radio's press office where she learned to massage the egos of disc jockeys. She then spent 18 months on a working holiday in Australia before joining PR-man

Brian MacLaurin where Mr Blobby was among her accounts. She now works freelance for the Duke of Edinburgh's Award Scheme, the baby charity Lifeline and other non-controversial clients.

Sophie's romantic CV is busier than the former Lady Diana Spencer but not a patch on the former Sarah Ferguson. Her first boyfriend, at 15, was David Kinder, later an actor and teacher. Other teen romances included Robert Scott-Mackie, now a City insurance broker, John Blackman who taught her skiing and Rupert Keane, who runs a car-hire business. At Capital she briefly dated production assistant Andrew Parkinson, son of TV presenter Michael Parkinson. "Sophie was fairly enamoured by titles and stuff like that. She would often go to Society balls and clearly enjoyed moving in those circles, which wasn't me at all."

Sophie's most unlikely ex was Jeremy Barkley, a burly Reading motor-trader ten years her senior who gave her a 1967 Morris Minor. Her final pre-Edwardian boyfriend was Tim King, a dentist and keen amateur pilot. She could never be accused of unworldliness, but she lived with none of these ex-beaux. That changed after she met Edward at a photocall when she stood in for former Wimbledon star Sue Barker. After 18 months of constant media attention she swapped her rented Shepherd's Bush flat for his Buckingham Palace apartment. Even royals now 'live in sin'. If and when Edward proposes, will she be the first royal daughter-in-law to last the course? A new Duchess of Kent perhaps?

Rice, Sir Tim, 10th November 1944, millionaire cricket nut, rock 'n' roller and all-round good guy. While Andrew Lloyd Webber sweats playing the Big Tycoon, his erstwhile partner takes life more easily and enjoys a more varied, if less lucrative, career. He founded Pavilion Books, runs the Heartaches cricket team of unfit middle-aged cronies and sings rock 'n' roll songs at friends' parties. His fascination with pop music even extends to compiling an annual guide to British hit singles and albums, all of which he owns in his massive private collection.

The extrovert half of Britain's Rodgers and Hammerstein was born in Amersham and educated at Lancing. His father, an aviation businessman, hoped his son would go to university and then read for the Bar. Instead, he was briefly a petrol pump attendant before becoming an EMI management trainee. He met Lloyd Webber, three years his junior, at a party in 1965 and they began writing together. They hawked their first musical, *Joseph and The Amazing Technicolor Dreamcoat*, round the publishers. Eventually, impresario David Land put them each on a £25-a-week retainer to write musicals. *Joseph's* 1968 première received encouraging notices but had nothing like the impact of *Jesus Christ Superstar* two years later. Their third musical *Evita* in 1976 was Rice's brainchild with him doing all the initial research. This Odd Couple's world-wide success ensured Rice never need write another lyric, a consideration he has sometimes taken too literally.

6ft 4ins Rice has two children, Eva and Donald, from his 1974 marriage to former publicist Jane McIntosh. Although long-separated they remain friendly. Indeed, their marriage survived his on-off relationship with Elaine Paige, who starred in *Evita* and his later musical *Chess*. For some ten years he acted as her musical Svengali, even co-producing her West End show, *Anything Goes*. But he values his independence too much to start another family. He has "lady friends" and lives between his 18th century Barnes mansion, with its menagerie of rare hens, and a remote Cornish manor house.

A new Hollywood career has begun following his three Oscars for Walt Disney's *The Lion King*, *Aladdin* and *Evita*. Rice's relationship with Lloyd Webber remains rather edgy.

Richard, Sir Cliff, 14th October 1940, early rock superstar. Cynics love to knock this joyous, tennis-playing crooner for his God-bothering, anti-drugs, anti-promiscuity image. But his career has long outlived more louche stars and he remains as popular as ever with the blue-rinse brigade. His records are no longer million-sellers but he has still had more Top 10 hits than The Beatles and Rolling Stones combined. He has reinvented himself as a stage personality, co-starring with a hologram of Lord Olivier in the West End musical *Time* and as the eponymous hero of *Heathcliff*. Critics, though, slammed his portrayal of this Emily Brontë hero as being grossly miscast and just an excuse for another pop concert.

Our first rock knight was born Harry Webb in Lucknow, India, where his father, Rodger, worked for a catering firm. On independence in 1947, the family moved to Cheshunt in Hertfordshire, almost penniless. By 17 he was working as a clerk by day and strumming his guitar by night. He was 'discovered' singing in the famous 2i's coffee bar in Soho and launched in 1958 as "Britain's Elvis Presley". His twangy first record *Move It* made No 2 in the charts but the following ballads *Living Doll* and Travellin' Light reached No 1. He became a regular on ITV's seminal pop show, *Oh Boy!* where he wore a Teddy boy drape-jacket, drainpipe trousers, grey winkle-pickers and pink socks. Fans mobbed Cliff Richard and the Shadows at every concert.

Ironically. Cliff has not always been perceived as a goodie goodie. The *New Musical Express* described his hip-wiggling, lip-curling act as "the crudest exhibitionism ever seen on British TV". In 1971 his anti-apartheid record, *Sing a Song of Freedom,* was banned in South Africa and the following year he was refused entry to Singapore because his hair was too long!

Cliff claims to have been celibate since becoming a born-again Christian in 1966. He once dated tennis star Sue Barker who complained: "the trouble with Cliff is that he sees life through stained-glass spectacles." For many years he has shared his palatial Weybridge, Surrey home with his manager and fellow evangelist Bill Latham. Cliff's increasingly ravaged face no longer quite resembles Peter Pan. The miracle is that in over 40 years of performing not one scandal has touched him.

Richard, Wendy, 20th July 1946, Albert Square's raddled doyenne. With her long, platinum-blonde hair, saucy manner and shortish skirts she could only be a Sixties girl. It irritates her when she is compared to her dowdy, down-trodden alter ego, *EastEnders'* Pauline Fowler. "People think I must be a tough cookie like Pauline. But I cry very easily and my feelings get hurt very quickly." This may have contributed to her three failed marriages: to businessman Len Black, advertising man Will Thorpe and carpet-layer Paul Giorney. "My work is my life."

Fun-loving Wendy claims to have been born in a Middlesbrough pub. Her parents moved to Shepherd Market, Mayfair, and she went to the Royal Masonic School in Rickmansworth. She earned extra pocket-money working in Fortnum & Mason's fashion department. At the Italia Conti Stage School she was knocked over by a car on her first day and needed 32 stitches on her head.

Her career began at 16 as the whiney Cockney on Mike Sarne's No 1 hit, *Come Outside.* She also appeared in a Sammy Davis Jnr TV special with Mandy Rice-Davies ("we supplied the glamour!"). She became a regular in *Dad's Army*, gingering up Captain Mainwaring's geriatric gang.

It was in 1973 that Wendy's life changed dramatically when she joined BBC1's *Are You Being Served?.* As the busty Miss Brahms her *double entendres* were usually at the expense of fellow Grace Brothers employees Mrs Slocombe (Mollie Sugden) and Mr Humphries (John Inman). The series continued for 12 years and even spawned a sequel, *Grace and Favour*, in which she helped to run a country-house hotel.

In 1996 Wendy underwent surgery after developing breast cancer." I regarded it as having a bad tooth – you take it out and you're okay. It's not in my nature to be ill." She lives alone near Marble Arch with her Cairn terrier, Shirley. For amusement she collects antique frogs, clowns and condiment sets.

Richardson, Ian, 7th April 1934, latterday Alec Guinness. The silver hair, silky voice and bleak manner is unmistakable and lends weight to any production he joins. His range is remarkable, from Sherlock Holmes and Field Marshal Viscount Montgomery to that incorrigible political twister Francis Urquhart. Yet no verbal trace of his Scottish ancestry remains. He grew up in Edinburgh, went to Glasgow University and studied at Glasgow College of Dramatic Art. He then headed south, joining Birmingham Rep and the RSC.

This tall, erect, blue-eyed perfectionist is devoted to his half-Russian wife, Maroussia, whom he married in 1961. "She has made me the sort of person and the actor that I am." They met while both were appearing in *The Merchant of Venice* at Stratford-upon-Avon and she volunteered to help him perfect his accent. The director told her: "Mr Richardson will hire a boat, take you on the river and you will teach him how to speak." She gave up acting after their sons, Miles and Jeremy, were born. "Now you need someone to come home to, not someone up there on stage in competition", she told him.

Richardson went on to play Malcolm in *Macbeth*, Cassius in *Julius Caesar,* Angelo in *Measure For Measure* and many other classical rôles. But in 1972, emboldened by a major TV offer, he left the RSC. The TV series fell through and for the first time he spent a year "resting". With two children to support, Maroussia sold her jewellery and they would scavenge in Covent Garden Market for vegetables and fruit that had dropped off the barrows. "My wife made me do a crossword puzzle every morning with my coffee. She said that the brain is a muscle and while you're not working it needs to be exercised!" He still does a daily crossword.

In 1990 Michael Dobbs' political drama *House of Cards* turned Richardson into a household name. Urquhart's line "you might very well think that, but I couldn't possibly comment" became a national catchphrase. Fearful of typecasting he only agreed to do a third series if Dobbs promised it would be the last. "By 'the last' I meant the demise of the man because evil cannot be seen to triumph!" He has rejected several Hollywood offers to play more villains, usually by telling his agent to demand $1 million!

Richardson, Joely, 9th January 1965, youngest of an acting dynasty. With her mother Vanessa Redgrave, older sister Natasha Richardson, aunt Lynn Redgrave, grandfather Sir Michael Redgrave and grandmother Rachel Kempson she has plenty to live up to. Under her apparent serenity is a seething cauldron of angst and ambition. She ascribes it to demons from her past. When she was 12 months old her father, film director Tony Richardson, ran off with French actress Jeanne Moreau. She therefore grew up barely part of a one-parent family, as her mother was constantly away filming or campaigning for revolutionary causes. She was closer to her half-brother, Carlo, than Natasha.

Athletic Joely originally planned to become a tennis pro. She spent two years at a Florida tennis academy before going to boarding school in Santa Barbara. But her thespian genes eventually prevailed. With Natasha already making a name for herself in the mid-Eighties she found establishing herself harder than expected. "A lot of producers saw me out of intrigue so that they could say that they'd just auditioned Vanessa Redgrave's daughter. But it didn't get me any work." Her career received a kick-start in 1992 when she romped naked with Sean Bean in Ken Russell's much-hyped *Lady Chatterley's Lover*, which drew the highest ratings ever for a BBC costume drama.

After "resting" for a year Joely decided to cut her long blonde locks and re-invent herself as a "serious" actress. Critics praised her performance in two low-budget movies, *Sister, My Sister* and *Hollow Reed*. In 1996 she starred as the wholesome, dog-loving adversary of Cruella de Vil in Walt Disney's *101 Dalmatians*. Co-star Jeff Daniels afterwards gave her an Oscar, inscribed with her memorable line, "She's Going To Kill the Puppies". The film enabled her to wear a wedding dress for the first time. For her last-minute New York register office wedding to *Four Weddings and A Funeral* producer Tim Bevan in 1991 she had worn a nightie. "I'd had a mad crush on Tim since I was 22." Her first love was Irish peer Lord Antrim's heir Randal McDonnell. She then had a fraught three-year relationship with millionaire Scottish landowner Archie Stirling, 25 years her senior. She was heart-broken when he eventually returned to his wife, actress Diana Rigg. In 1997 fey, swan-necked Joely broke up with ambitious Bevan. They have a daughter, Daisy.

Richardson, Natasha, 11th May 1963, classic beauty. This cerebral leading lady has inherited the tall, willowy, cool blonde looks of Vanessa Redgrave. Fortunately she shares her mother's acting ability, not her "attitude". She would never inflict political views on her co-stars or go rattling collecting-boxes. Yet she vehemently defends Vanessa's right to make protests and admits that "she has taught me so much about stagecraft and timing".

As a child growing up in Hammersmith "Tash" and her younger sister, Joely, suffered from their mother's long absences away filming and setting the world to rights in Moscow, Vietnam and Israel. Natasha went to the French Lycée, St Paul's School and the Central

School of Speech and Drama. After a season at Leeds Playhouse she won starring rôles in *A Midsummer Night's Dream, Hamlet* and *The Seagull*, in which she appeared with Vanessa. Her haughty, yet reserved, grandeur in the West End musical *High Society* led to inevitable comparisons with its original star Grace Kelly.

Natasha's early success led to her TV debut in *The Adventures of Sherlock Holmes* and starring film rôles in *Gothic, A Month In The Country* and *Patty Hearst*. By 27 she was already a bankable film star and had won three 'best stage actress' awards. She has since appeared in films like *Widow's Peak* and *Nell* and TV plays like *Suddenly Last Summer*.

In 1990 Natasha married eligible West End impresario Robert Fox and seemed blissfully happy. But three years later she ran off with Liam Neeson, her hunky Broadway co-star in *Anna Christie*. "I was very daunted by Liam's reputation as a ladies' man" she said before marrying him in 1994. They named their son Michael after her grandfather, actor Sir Michael Redgrave. They live in Millbrook, outside New York. "I've spent half my life trying to get away from being 'Vanessa Redgrave's daughter' and now I'm labelled 'Liam Neeson's wife'." Marital, parental and sibling rivalry will keep her striving to be recognised as the family superstar.

Rickman, Alan, 21st February 1946, man of many parts. As an actor he possesses the chameleon qualities of Robert de Niro, brilliant at burying himself in his rôles. He shone as Juliet Stevenson's dead lover in the romantic comedy *Truly, Madly, Deeply* and won an Oscar for the repressed, frightfully proper Colonel Brandon in *Sense and Sensibility*. His trademarks are the habitual snarl, menacing hazel eyes and sarcastic tones, plus the slight speech impediment which makes audiences hang on every word.

This imposing, boney 6ft 1ins cynic could never be described as conventionally handsome. Yet he has a huge female following. "It's the searching intensity of his gaze which is so seductive", explains an admirer. His first success was as the loathsome Obadiah Slope in BBC1's *The Barchester Chronicles* in 1982. The 1985 RSC production of *Les Liaisons Dangereuses* gave him a West End and Broadway hit. His rôle as the foppish, manipulative Vicomte de Valmont launched him on a ten-year cycle of villains. In 1988 he was the manic German terrorist Hans Gruber who nearly murdered Bruce Willis in *Die Hard*. His camp portrayal of the Sheriff of Nottingham in *Robin, Prince of Thieves*, so upstaged Kevin Costner that the latter ordered certain scenes to be cut although not the sheriff's memorable rant: "Cancel the kitchen scraps for lepers and orphans. No more merciful beheadings. Call off Christmas!"

Off-screen, Rickman plays the petulant actor, spiky about revealing details about his private life. Of Welsh-Irish stock he is a painter and decorator's son brought up on an Acton council estate. He was educated at Latymer Upper School. He worked as a graphic designer before going to RADA at the late age of 26.

This socialist activist bought a £250,000 maisonette in true-blue Kensington with the proceeds of *Die Hard*. Despite his sexual predatoriness on screen he remains faithful to his girlfriend, Labour councillor Rima Horton. They have been together since meeting at Chelsea College of Art in 1965. "Alan is quite unpromiscuous, which is very rare for actors", observes a close friend. His constant absences filming keeps their relationship fresh. He is a talented watercolourist and calligrapher.

Rigg, Dame Diana, 20th July 1938, award-winning tragedienne. She vies with Dame Maggie Smith as our greatest living actress. But despite her impressive CV of films and stage plays her name will always be synonymous with the surreal Sixties TV series, *The Avengers*. She fed a million male fantasies with her leather-clad, karate-chopping Emma Peel and further intrigued with her ambiguous screen relationship with bowler-hatted Steed (Patrick MacNee).

This tall, auburn-haired thesp joined the RSC in 1959. She appeared in productions of *A Midsummer Night's Dream, King Lear* and *Abelard and Heloise*. With the National Theatre Company from 1972 she starred in *Jumpers, 'Tis a Pity She's a Whore* and *Macbeth*. She won awards for *Phaedra Britannica, Night and Day, Mother Love* and *Medea*. She has suffered disasters too, like the American TV comedy series *Diana, A Little Night Music* and *Colette*.

Educated at Fulneck Girls School, Pudsey, Diana lost her Yorkshire accent at RADA. To pay for her studies she waitressed in a coffee bar. TV director Philip Saville was her mentor and boyfriend for ten years. Aged 35 she surprised friends by marrying a struggling Israeli artist Menahem Gueffen, but they divorced three years later. In 1982 she married millionaire Perthshire landowner, Archie Stirling, whom she persuaded to go into theatre production. She rather enjoyed being the laird's wife, living in a baronial hall surrounded by grouse moors and trout streams. They have a daughter, Rachel, whom she describes as "my best production yet". But in 1988 Stirling ran off with actress Joely Richardson. The elegant Rigg lured him back, but they divorced in 1993.

Although she was a Bond girl in *On Her Majesty's Secret Service* and won a 'best actress' award for Agatha Christie's *Evil Under The Sun* she has never quite cracked Hollywood. She enjoys writing and compiled an anthology of critical barbs called *No Turn Unstoned*.

She included the 1970 critique of her nude scene as Heloise where she was described as "built like a brick mausoleum with insufficient flying buttresses". She retains her youthful vigour, appearing in demanding stage rôles like Martha in *Who's Afraid of Virginia Woolf?* and Mrs Danvers in TV's *Rebecca*.

Robinson, Gerry, 23rd October 1948, the dynamic leprechaun. As chief executive of the Granada TV and leisure group he controls an £8 billion empire employing 67,000 people. Yet he is no dull number-cruncher but a smiling maverick who charms rather than bullies. His decision to campaign for Labour during the 1997 general election owed much to his well-developed social conscience.

For Robinson is the ninth child of an Irish carpenter from Co Donegal. He was educated at St Mary's School, Castlehead. The family moved to London "in search of a better life" when he was 14. He shared a one-bedroomed flat in Whitechapel with his parents and a brother. His sharp accountant's eye for costs and even sharper eye for the main chance earned him jobs with blue-chip companies like Lesney, Coca Cola and GrandMet. He became a multi-millionaire in 1987 when he led a management buy-out of Compass, GrandMet's contract catering division.

In 1991 this corporate Napoleon was head-hunted by Lord Bernstein to run his ailing Granada. He earned his spurs in two hostile takeover battles. His acquisition of LWT in 1994 turned him into one of Britain's most powerful media barons. In 1996 his £3.8 billion takeover of Sir Rocco Forte's catering group, provoked gibes about whether an upstart motorway-caff owner was qualified to run such an upmarket company. Ironically, this was the same insult levelled at the Fortes during their unsuccessful war to win the Savoy group in the Eighties. Robinson's response was to sell off jewels like the George V Hotel in Paris and the Hyde Park in London and to stop sponsoring the Prix de L'Arc de Triomphe, an annual excuse for lavish Forte hospitality. But he kept the executive jet.

The golf, opera, and chess-loving entrepreneur lives in a Kensington mansion with his second wife Heather. He has three children. Though unassuming he does fancy himself as Sir Gerry.

Robson, Linda, 13th March 1958, TV's archetypal Essex Girl. As *Birds of a Feather*'s Sharon and Tracey, she and her best pal Pauline Quirke have given hope to thousands of other large, ordinary-looking ladies. Their exuberant personalities show that you have no need to look like Michelle Pfeiffer to have a lark in Chigwell. She is only self-conscious about one thing: "I 'ate my legs – they're short and dumpy. I wish they were like Cindy Crawford's."

Builder's daughter Linda is as down-to-earth, funny and loveable as her TV character. "When I take the kids to school I 'ave to be careful to say "ello' to everybody or else they think you've become grand!" She comes from a large Irish family, who lived in a council house off the Essex Road. She met Pauline at primary school and both attended the Anna Scher Drama School. They became child stars, appearing in TV series like *Jackanory Playhouse*. Once, while guesting in ITV's prison drama *Within These Walls*, she caught her nightdress on the side of a bunk. "A prison riot was going on and there was I suspended in my underwear in a studio full of men!" Her first major rôle was as nubile Maggie in the Eighties' comedy series, *Shine on Harvey Moon*, with Pauline playing dopey Veronica. In a hilarious documentary series, *Jobs For The Girls*, they were filmed learning to become opera singers, journalists and dog-breeders.

Linda lives in Islington with her three children, Laura, Louis and Bobbie, and her second husband Mark. He is a window cleaner, but "'e's also got this launderette going!" They originally met when she baby-sat for his sister. Every wedding anniversary she gives him a diamond for his wedding-ring. Despite her wealth he insists on keeping separate bank accounts and sharing household bills. "It might 'ave been 'arder for us to get together if *Birds of a Feather* 'ad started and I was as well-known as I am now." They avoid film premières and showbiz socialising. "We prefer to stay at home, watch a video and eat a takeaway." For a Christmas treat she once took her eight nieces and nephews to Disneyland Paris. But she admits if she had not gone into acting: "I'd probably 'ave ended up as a secretary or working in Marks & Spencer."

Roddick, Anita, 23rd October 1942, environmental campaigner and retail wizard. This Green tycoon was born Anita Perilli in West Sussex and educated at a local secondary modern. Her Italian immigrant parents ran a seaside café in Littlehampton which boasted the first jukebox and soda fountain in town! As a teenage waitress she joined CND, and went on anti-Vietnam and hunger marches. She spent a year working on an Israeli kibbutz ("the benchmark of my life") and completed a teacher training course in Bath. While working abroad for an international relief agency she began noticing the natural products Third World women concocted. Couldn't the West start using aduki beans to cure blackheads like the Africans or stimulate their scalps with cocoa-butter like the Polynesians?

In 1976 Anita opened her first Body Shop selling cosmetics in a Brighton back street, beside an undertakers who objected strongly to the name! Her guiding principles remain the same today: only to sell products that contain pure natural ingredients and involve no cruelty to animals; to avoid wasteful packaging and use recycled paper and to sell in refillable plastic containers rather than throw-away glass jars. Unwittingly she had caught the mood of the times. She persuaded her husband Gordon, a former sheep farmer, to help her to expand. With financial assistance from a local *garagiste* they opened more shops around Littlehampton where they also owned a Fawlty Towers-style b&b. Such was the demand for marmalade body scrub, Brazil nut conditioner and other products that in 1984 they floated their company on the Stock Exchange.

Despite their estimated £105 million fortune from 1,300 shops in 46 different countries, the Roddicks' idealism remains. In 1995 they helped to smuggle the brother of Ken Saro-Wiwa, the executed environmental campaigner, out of Nigeria. But critics love trying to expose Body Shop products, claiming they have been tested on animals or contain chemicals. This bohemian couple live in Arthur Rackham's old house on the South Downs and in Scotland. They have two daughters, unmarried mum Justine and hippy Samantha

Rogers, Lord, 23rd July 1933, 20th century Hawksmoor. If this Armani-clad architect was worthy of a 1996 life peerage then surely Sir Christopher Wren deserved a dukedom? Rogers's PR ability was probably greater, a fact that has edged him ahead of the equally talented, but less media-friendly Sir Norman Foster. His success in the 1971 competition to redevelop Les Halles in Paris brought him international recognition, even if the Pompidou Centre's revolutionary design looks rather sad today. The Lloyd's Building remains the other most visible of his myriad developments round the world.

Rogers' early childhood was spent in Florence – he is half-Italian. He trained at the Architectural Association and Yale University. Ironically his first practice, Team 4, set up in the Sixties with Foster and their then respective wives, Wendy Cheesman and Sue Rogers, soon closed due to shortage of commissions. His present partnership has offices in London, Tokyo and Berlin. Easy-going and convivial he keeps erratic hours at his Hammersmith practice, a nautical looking building with aluminium masts and fan-shaped blinds. "I don't see a difference between work and leisure. I get the same lift from going to my office and designing as I do skiing down a mountain, lying on a sandy beach or looking at a Brunelleschi dome." A self-confessed "sensualist" he encouraged his second wife, Ruthie, to open a *cucina rustica* restaurant in his former office canteen. Her River Café is now as famed for its showbiz clientele and bestselling cookery books as its Tuscan bean soup and artichoke *crostini*.

The Rogers's 18th century terrace house in Chelsea conceals an extraordinary hi-tech interior dominated by giant Andy Warhol originals. It is a mecca for serious entertaining, with A-list guests like Alan Yentob, Lord Palumbo and Lord Puttnam. Rogers has a total of five sons from both his marriages. A former Tate Gallery chairman he revels in collecting modern art, tasting unusual flavours and visiting architectural wonders. A definite life-enhancer.

Roslin, Gaby, 12th July 1962, zestful presenter. She has all the tenacity of a young Esther Rantzen, but without the stridency. She is no intellectual but neither is she a bimbo. She is the unthreatening older sister, who never dresses provocatively or flirts with guests. Such is her diplomacy that she managed to work with Chris Evans for three years on C4's *The Big Breakfast* without a bust-up.

Gaby comes from a close North London Jewish family. From the age of three she wanted to be a *Blue Peter* presenter. Armed with an A-level in drama she went to stage school in Surrey. Her father Clive Roslin, a veteran BBC radio newsreader, gave her extra coaching. A month after graduating she became a presenter on the Sky Superchannel kids' show *Hippo*. It was a baptism of fire but with miniscule audiences she could make mistakes without fear of offending anyone. She then joined ITV's raucous yoof programme, *Motormouth*. In 1992 she beat other zany hopefuls to present *The Big Breakfast*. Her contribution to its fast-moving in-yer-face style helped to trounce GMTV and BBC1's *Breakfast Time*.

Gaby moved on to present C4's *The Real Holiday Show*, an often hilarious series of video diaries, showing what really happens on package tours. Her attempt to do a Michael Parkinson-style chat programme, *The Gaby Roslin Show,* in 1996 was a flop. But she bounced back with the *Jim'll Fix It* clone, *Whatever You Want*.

Gaby, never a gadabout, met her husband, musician Colin Peel, when she slipped and literally fell into his arms during a charity show. A week later he turned up on *Motormouth*. "I knew deep down I wanted to go out with him, just as I knew instantly he was an Aries." He proposed to her on Valentine's Day 1995, allegedly at the end of a rainbow at Victoria Falls, Zimbabwe. They live in Notting Hill with their spaniel Chester, a present from Chris Evans. She is a vegetarian and suffers so badly from hay fever that on *Big Breakfast* she once had a sneezing fit when interviewing a woman with a cat.

Ross, Jonathan, 17th November 1960, TV's Artful Dodger. He rose to fame as a Leytonstone lad with spivvy suits, Elvis hairstyle and damaged 'r's. His gabbled interviews on C4's *The Last Resort*, often revealed more about him than his celebrity guests. The wacky formula, borrowed from America's David Letterman, was designed to replace the reverential chat show as practised by Messrs Wogan and Harty. It worked for a while, until discerning viewers wondered: "Where's the beef?" Then that cheeky Chris Evans stole his clothes, fronting C4's even more anarchic shows, *Don't Forget Your Toothbrush* and *TFI Friday*. The R Man is now trying to re-crank his career after an early mid-life crisis. "I needed to sort out my life. I was getting lazy and cocky and my weight had gone up to 15 stone." He spent nearly two years off the Box, grew caveman hair, gave up alcohol and rediscovered his family.

Grammar school-educated Ross has a degree from London University's School of Slavonic and East European Studies ("it comes in handy when I ask tricky questions about Poland in 1660"). He became a TV researcher on game shows, weeding out contestants, scripting "ad libs" and warming up the audience. By 26 he was matily chatting to superstars like Mel Gibson, Steve Martin and Liza Minnelli on *The Last Resort*. He once asked actress Sarah Miles why she imbibed her own urine as a health drink. "She just looked at me and said: 'Why? Do you eat your own s***?'" His thrice-weekly *Tonight With Jonathan Ross* was a chat show too far. But he has tried to diversify, with *The Incredibly Strange Film Show*, *Gag Tag* and *The Big, Big Talent Show*.

Perky "Wossie" claims to have lost his virginity at 21 – "I've never played fast and loose in my life". He met his wife, ex-rock journalist Jane Goldman, at Stringfellow's when she was only 16 and he 25. They live with their three children, Betty Kitten, Harvey Kirby and Honey Kinny, in a Hampstead house overflowing with his collection of antique comics. Jane is now a bestselling author.

Roth, Tim, 14th May 1961, Hollywood cult hero. This drop-out sculptor in his trademark jeans and tee-shirt has become such a superstar that people forget he comes from West Dulwich. He made his name playing thinking thugs in small-budget films: the psychotic gangster in Stephen Frears's *The Hit*, the wounded Mr Orange in Quentin Tarantino's *Reservoir Dogs* and the hit-man in *Little Odessa*. "I never wanted to play the good guy – the more outrageous the character the better." As a contrast he enjoyed "camping it up" as an English aristo in *Rob Roy*. "I looked like a hideous drag queen in my wig and frills. I thought 'if I'm gonna do a posh-frock drama, which I usually detest, I'm gonna go for it big!'"

Roth's parents – father a journalist, mother a painter – split up when he was young. Psychologists might blame the bullying he received at Dick Sheppard Comprehensive School, Brixton, for his later film portrayals. He had no formal acting training. He dropped out of Camberwell College of Art to work with Glasgow Citizens' Theatre, the Oval House and the Royal Court Theatre. In 1983 he shaved his head and daubed a swastika on his forehead for his first major role, as a skinhead in the ITV drama, *Made In Britain*. For a screen idol he is very short (5ft 7ins), but his bony physique, chiselled face and "attitude" give him a startling presence.

This once rebellious punk moved to Los Angeles in 1989. He works hard at maintaining his street cred. After finishing *Reservoir Dogs* he went on holiday with a friend, hitching and jumping on freight-trains from Canada to California. "It's illegal, but nobody ever caught us." He claims to be addicted to putting himself "in dangerous situations or rôles" because it removes him from reality. He also loves body decoration: he has a pierced nipple and his tattoos include a lace garter on his forearm. He has calmed down since meeting his American wife Nikki, a former fashion designer. "'Cor blimey', I thought when I first saw her at the Sundance Film Festival, 'she's gorgeous, but she's way out of my league!'" They married in the Belize rainforest in 1993. He remains close to his teenage son Jack from his English former girlfriend Lori Baker.

Rothschild, Lord, 29th April 1939, financier and philanthropist. He is the latest proud scion of a banking dynasty that has flourished since Meyer Amschel Rothschild broke out of the Frankfurt ghetto in the late 18th century. He is a man of huge refinement, intelligence and discrimination. His business acumen helped to enlarge the fortunes of tycoons Sir James Goldsmith and Sir Mark Weinberg, plus myriad public companies. But his cultural achievements prevent him being just another City Midas. As chairman of the National Heritage Memorial Fund he is responsible for deciding which artistic causes benefit from the annual £300 million lottery funds. It has meant downsizing his own business commitments.

This maverick financier is the son of the third Lord Rothschild, a brilliant scientist best-known for *not* being the fifth man in the Burgess-Maclean spy scandal. His mother Barbara was a member of the Bloomsbury family, the Stracheys. He hated Eton but at Oxford was lucky to fall under the benign influence of two outstanding professors, Hugh Trevor-Roper and Isaiah Berlin. With a First in history he toyed with becoming an academic himself. Due to an absence of suitable Rothschild males, he was forced to join the family bank, NM Rothschild, then in decline. At 31 he took control and rebuilt its City reputation. But a 1980 coup, led by his cousin Evelyn de Rothschild, toppled him. He founded his own investment group,

J Rothschild Holdings, now divided into two highly profitable concerns, St James's Place Capital and RIT Capital Partners. He spent £16 million restoring Princess Diana's former family home, Spencer House, as his London headquarters.

In 1961 Jacob married Canadian shipping baronet Sir Philip Dunn's daughter Serena. They have four children, Nat, Hannah, Beth and Emily. He lives in Maida Vale, weekending at the ancestral Rothschild mansion Waddesdon in Buckinghamshire and has a wonderful 15-acre Corfu estate. His estimated £260 million fortune owes much to his cousin Dollie Rothschild who left the bulk of her £93 million fortune to him in 1988.

Roxburghe, Duke of, 18th November 1954, royal matchmaker. He is one of Britain's richest aristos, living in beautiful Floors Castle on the Scottish borders. He let Prince Andrew bring girlfriends, like photographer Koo Stark, to stay for shooting weekends. Indeed it was there that the Prince formally proposed to Sarah Ferguson, by going down on bended knees. ("If you wake up tomorrow, you can tell me it's all a huge joke!", she replied). The Duke has an estimated £75 million fortune, mainly derived from his 65,000-acre estate near Kelso, which includes grouse moors and some of Britain's most valuable fishing rights. He is such a keen fly-fisherman that he leads an annual expedition of friends to Norway's arctic region.

After Eton, dashing Guy Roxburghe followed family tradition by going into the Army. He passed out of Sandhurst with the coveted Sword of Honour and joined his regiment, the Blues and Royals. While serving in Northern Ireland he met his bride-to-be, Lady Jane Grosvenor. As the sister of the present Duke of Westminster she made the perfect dynastic wife. They married in 1977 and she dutifully ensured the succession by providing three children, the Marquess of Bowmont and Cessford, Lord Edward and Lady Rosanagh. Meanwhile he left the army, partly because the Ministry of Defence warned that his ducal handle made him a possible IRA target. He studied land economy at Cambridge. Alas, his incorrigible philandering caused his wife to leave, muttering "boys will be boys". She added: "Nobody fought harder to save a marriage than I did." In 1992 he married interior decorator Virginia Wynn-Williams and they now have two children, Lady Isabella and Lord George.

His Grace has a lucrative sideline hiring out the castle as a film location, notably for the 1984 Tarzan epic, *Greystoke*. His financial stability was guaranteed by his grandfather's 1903 marriage to New York heiress Mary Goelet. She brought a £5 million dowry, just the ticket for restoring the battered Georgian castle and furnishing it with priceless antiques.

Royal, The Princess, 15th August 1950, royal paragon. She used to be "Princess Stroppy" who told journalists to "naff off". Now she is perceived as the strongest and most effective of all the royal children. Queen Anne II would be a popular monarch! She is industrious, dignified and discreet. She carries out her royal duties and Save The Children Fund visits with none of the razzmatazz of her former in-laws. She wastes no money on couture gowns, foreign holidays or pampering herself. She is happy living at Gatcombe Park, the Georgian mansion bought for her as a wedding present by the Queen. But she can give speeches without notes or teleprompter.

The Princess went to Benenden but never had the option of going to university like her brothers. She became one of Britain's top three-day eventers. She won the 1971 European Championships at Burghley, was voted the BBC's Sports Personality of the Year two years later and in 1976 competed in the British Olympic team at Montreal.

Blunt-speaking Anne is much prettier and sexier in real-life than in photographs. Before her 1973 marriage to Captain Mark Phillips she was entranced by Olympic rider Richard Meade. But he never considered marriage because it would have meant losing his privacy. She then dated handsome polo player Sandy Harper, who lacked the strength of personality to cope with her. Then along came Phillips, a dashing Olympic gold medal winner. Their marriage failed partly because he was a "kept man", farming her Gloucestershire estate. His attempts to be independent, running the Gleneagles equestrian centre and giving horsey seminars round the world, merely enabled him to be unfaithful. A New Zealand pupil claimed he had fathered her daughter after a one-night stand in 1986. Rumours that Anne too had had affairs, with actor Anthony Andrews and a police bodyguard, remain unproven.

In 1992 Anne swapped this Walls sausage-maker's son for her second husband Tim Laurence, a glamorous naval captain whose family had changed its name from Levy to avoid anti-Semitism. He has proved a steadying influence and a caring stepfather to her two children, Peter and Zara Phillips. She could end up an Admiral's wife. Constitutional experts predict that if Prince Charles never remarries, Anne will become his consort on State occasions.

Rushdie, Salman, 19th June 1947, fugitive literary figure. This lifelong Spurs supporter was born into a wealthy Indian family. He went to the Cathedral School, Bombay and then Rugby. He found his literary muse at Cambridge, as well as his left-wing leanings. In

1981 his second novel, *Midnight's Children,* won the Booker Prize. But it was his fifth book, *The Satanic Verses,* winner of the 1988 Whitbread Novel Award, which provoked the Ayatollah Khomeini's *fatwa* that has blighted his life.

With a £1.5 million price on his balding head, Rushdie accepts he can never venture outside without his Special Branch bodyguards. He lives between "safe" houses, occasionally visiting restaurants, theatres, cinemas, concert halls, museums and galleries. This Anne Frank-like existence has allowed him plenty of time to write. Surprisingly, the shortcomings of a life denied normal social contact doesn't seem to have blunted his creative juices. His increased output includes *Imaginary Homelands* and *East, West.* In 1995 he just failed to win the Booker Prize with *The Moor's Last Sigh.* With police protection 24 hours a day he has, ironically, had to revise his poor opinion of them, particularly as they have already foiled two murder attempts.

Rushdie has a son, Zafar, from his first marriage to heiress Clarissa Cunard. He originally shared his "imprisonment" with his second wife, American author Marianne Wiggins. But they divorced in 1993 and she subsequently revealed how she had had to dress up in clothes from a Soho sex shop to whet his appetite. He now "escapes" more often to literary events but his romantic wanderings have ceased with the birth of his son Milan by his girlfriend, a London publisher. Puckishly he once told a TV interviewer who asked him what he did for sex: "To tell the truth I'm quite grateful for the rest." How much longer can he remain the world's most wanted man, a prisoner of his own principles?

Ryan, Ned, 8th February 1933, royal favourite, dubbed the "Court Jester". This rumbustious son of a Co Tipperary farmer drove a No 19 bus and sold carpets in the Army and Navy Stores when he first arrived in London in the Fifties. He then opened a Portobello Road silver stall and began investing in residential property. Through shrewd dealing and Irish luck he built up a valuable portfolio, including office blocks, shops and warehouses. His success owes much to his business partner, former playboy Charles Delevingne, whose wide contacts enabled him to move in more rarefied circles. Hotelier Anouska Hempel is another close ally, as her late husband Constantine was an old business crony.

The constantly dieting *bon viveur* is a leading member of the Princess Margaret Set. He has taken her to Rolling Stones concerts and Covent Garden, served her Irish stew in his Knightsbridge kitchen and escorted her at dawn around Portobello with breakfast afterwards in a greasy spoon caff. She values his high spirits, folksy

wisdom and human qualities. He is one of the few intimates allowed
to tease her and can lift her from the blackest moods. She will telephone him late at night knowing he will help. "Life's always a party
when Neddy's around", explains a friend. Another adds: "He does
laugh at one's jokes. In fact he laughs when one
hasn't made a joke!"

Briefly married at 20, property developer Ryan is wedded to society. He once had a penchant for squiring pretty, often titled, young
ladies, usually after they had suffered some emotional upset. Lady
Carina Fitzalan-Howard (now married to Sir David Frost), Kate
Lady Vestey and baronet Sir Nicholas Nuttall's former wife Miranda
have all cried on his burly shoulder. Lacking his own family he collects godchildren and holds an annual party for all 21 at his South
Kensington office. Social-climber? No, a social enhancer.

S

Saatchi, Charles, 9th June 1943, advertising legend. There is little in his Sephardic Jewish bloodlines that would suggest a dazzling media career. He was born in Baghdad where his father Nathan was a prosperous businessman. The family moved to London in 1947 to escape persecution and settled in North London. He went to Christ's College, Finchley, and then became a copywriter for Benton and Bowles before being made an associate director of Collett Dickenson Pearce. In 1970 he and his younger brother Maurice founded Saatchi & Saatchi. An early winner was their Health Education Council poster of a pregnant man with the caption: "Would you be more careful if it was you that got pregnant?"

This tall, athletic Elliott Gould lookalike helped the Tories to win four general elections. With their honorary brother Tim Bell they invented the slogan "Labour Isn't Working" beside a picture of a long dole queue. For a 'meejah' honcho he has one peculiar characteristic: he never gives interviews and avoids being photographed. By 1986 he had achieved his ambition of making S&S the world's largest agency, with profits nudging £90 million. But a boardroom coup resulted in both brothers being ousted and their formation of a new agency, M&C Saatchi, in 1995.

Apart from politics the secretive, tennis-playing Charles's overwhelming interest is contemporary art, particularly encouraging young, unknown artists. Among his protégés have been Cy Twombly, Anselm Kiefer and Julian Schnabel. He founded a private gallery in St John's Wood in 1984. He resigned as a patron of the Tate Gallery after critics accused him of being both a collector and a dealer. A major influence on forming his taste was former American copywriter Doris Lockhart, who became his wife in 1973. After their 1990 divorce he married modern art dealer Kay Hartenstein, another striking blonde. They live in Chelsea.

Said, Wafic, 23rd December 1938, Anglophile Sheikh Fixit. This courteous, pinstriped charmer has replaced Adnan Khashoggi and Madhi al-Tajir as the Middle Eastern Midas who really counts in Britain. He first became famous as "the man who made Mark Thatcher rich". He gave him useful Saudi business contacts. He still idolises Lady Thatcher, lavishly entertaining her and Denis at his £9 million Mayfair house and 3,000-acre Tusmore House estate near Banbury. He also has homes in Monte Carlo, Marbella, Monaco and Paris, plus a Boeing 737 to commute to them. The Syrian-born, eye surgeon's son attended a local Jesuit school. He moved to Britain in 1960 and spent a year at Cambridge University studying economics. He left to join the Syrian foreign office but fled after a military coup. He helped his brother run the Caravanserai, one of London's first Lebanese restaurants, before switching to banking. The business opportunities presented by the early-Seventies oil boom in Saudi Arabia enabled Wafic to build a fortune now estimated at £300 million. He vigorously denies he has ever been an arms dealer: "I've never sold so much as a penknife." Nonetheless, in 1987 his influence in Saudi Arabia was crucial in enabling Britain to beat the French and Americans to land the massive £20 billion Al-Yamamah defence contract. Not every project is so remunerative. He invested in his friend Frederick Forsyth's ill-fated film *The Fourth Protocol* and also the shortlived *Sunday Correspondent*.

Philanthropic, racehorse-owning Said married Bradford bank manager's daughter Rosemary Buchanan in 1969. Educated at Cheltenham Ladies College, she has been a great social asset. In 1981 their ten-year-old son Karim died in a swimming pool accident at the home of Saudi Defence Minister Prince Sultan. Under Islamic custom the loss is said to have created a special bond between Wafic and the Saudi royal house. Their second son Khalid went to Eton and Balliol College, Oxford, and they have a daughter Rasha. In 1997 Said was shocked when Oxford dons initially turned down his £20 million gift to found a new business school. He is better off captaining his Oxfordshire cricket team.

Sangster, Robert, 23rd May 1936, man-about-Turf. Despite competition from the Aga Khan and sundry Arab sheikhs he is still Britain's greatest racehorse owner. He invested £17 million into turning his 2,000-acre spread at Manton, Wiltshire into one of the world's finest racing stables. To further his ambitions he has always employed the very best: trainers like Vincent O'Brien and Peter Chapple-Hyam and jockeys like Pat Eddery and Lester Piggott.

This stubby, reserved *bon viveur* was brought up in flashy Cheshire luxury. But his father Vernon Sangster, founder of Vernons Pools, insisted that during school holidays he sifted pool coupons. On leaving Repton he joined the firm but soon found the lure of the racetrack too strong. He began investing his £8 million inheritance in bloodstock. But it was not until 1977 when The Minstrel won the Derby and Alleged won the Prix de l'Arc de Triomphe that he began to see the results. He has subsequently owned some 700 Stakes winners, with victories in the Irish Derby, Melbourne Cup, French Derby and 2,000 Guineas.

Sangster's other main interest has been women. His 1960 marriage to Christine produced four children Guy, Ben, Adam and Kate. He then eloped with Susan, a frisky Australian socialite formerly married to Melbourne politician Andrew Peacock. Known as "the Sheila" she would celebrate his wins by screaming *Waltzing Matilda* on table tops. But he eventually tired of her and cantered off, first with supermodel Jerry Hall during one of her spats with Mick Jagger and then with shoe-shop heir Peter Lilley's wife Sue. In 1985 he married Sue, 20 years his junior, and friends reckon this third marriage is for keeps. They have two sons, Sam and Max.

They live in the Nunnery, Isle of Man, famed venue for Sangster's parties for over 20 years, palatial villas in Barbados and the South of France and a London pad. Robert's biggest winning streak came in 1988 when he sold Vernons Pools for £90 million, shortly before the National Lottery would have decimated profits.

Saunders, Jennifer, 12 July 1958, Britain's answer to Whoopi Goldberg. Left to her own devices she might have ended up on the dole because she is terminally lazy, or so she claims. Luckily talent will out, particularly if prised apart by the go-getting Dawn French. Their partnership was the making of them both.

This Lincolnshire-born, RAF officer's daughter will forever be linked with *Absolutely Fabulous* and its brilliant satire of the crazy worlds of glossy magazines, fashion and PR. It grew from a sketch in their long-running BBC2 series, *French and Saunders*. The media hag Edina is as much a stereotype of her own excesses as former fashion PR Lynne Franks.

Jennifer originally wanted to teach, like her mother. She trained as a drama teacher at the Central School of Speech and Drama. There she teamed up with Dawn. "Initially we didn't hit it off. I found her too bossy and she found me too aloof." Nonetheless they began touring in cabaret as the Menopause Sisters and appearing at the Comedy Store.

In 1982 the pair joined C4's *The Comic Strip Presents,* the spoof and satire series which launched a generation of new comedians, including Robbie Coltrane, Rik Mayall and Alexei Sayle. One skit explored the Miners Strike through the eyes of Hollywood, with Peter Richardson as Robert de Niro playing Arthur Scargill and Jennifer as Meryl Streep playing Mrs Scargill. She also played various members of the Fuddle family in Ben Elton's BBC1 sitcom, *Happy Families* and slow-witted Jennifer in ITV's sitcom *Girls on Top*, co-written with French and Ruby Wax.

It was Dawn the Matchmaker who forced Saunders to date her future husband, fellow Comic Stripper Ade Edmondson. While she is the main breadwinner he plays the house-husband, cooking, washing and looking after their three daughters, Beattie, Ella and Freya. Offscreen, their idyllic Enid Blyton lifestyle includes frequent bucket-and-spade holidays and parties at their homes in Richmond and Devon. She is "sick" of drinking 'Bolly', and can be quite sullen with strangers.

Scacchi (pronounced Scar-Key), **Greta**, 15th February 1960, Britain's Demi Moore. She has always shone as a class act. Her precocious 1983 debut in Merchant-Ivory's *Heat and Dust* drew tempting Hollywood offers which she resisted to concentrate on rather earnest TV work. She starred opposite Lord Olivier in *The Ebony Tower* and in Graham Greene's *Dr Fischer of Geneva*. She now regrets weakening to do the meretricious comedy, *The Coca Cola Kid*: "I loathed every ghastly minute of it".

Greta seems more Continental in manner than British. She was christened by her Italian painter father after his childhood idol Greta Garbo. Her parents split up soon afterwards and she was raised by her English mother, a former Bluebell dancer, in the wilds of Sussex and Perth, Australia. She made her acting debut aged eight playing Water Rat in a school production of *Toad of Toad Hall*.

Ambitious, gorgeous Greta tried modelling and then became a drama student at the Bristol Old Vic. Later she received not one reply when she wrote to repertory companies asking for a place as an assistant stage manager. A mobile theatre group observing her slight build sneered that she "didn't look the sort of girl who could load and unload trucks". A small part in BBC1's *Bergerac* led to *Heat and Dust*. She then tantalised filmgoers by appearing nude in *White Mischief* opposite Charles Dance and *Presumed Innocent* opposite Harrison Ford. Her films *The Player*, *The Browning Version* and *Jefferson in Paris* were quality productions.

Greta's fluency in French, German and Italian makes her popular with foreign movie producers. But she can be moody and capricious in her private life. She dresses in grunge, wears no make-up and hates giving interviews.

Determined to be considered a "serious actress", she turned down a £1 million cosmetic contract in 1990. For four years she shared her South London house with little-known rock musician Tim Finn, although she was usually away filming. In 1992 she had a baby, Leila, by rising Hollywood star Vincent D'Onofrio, but their relationship ended shortly afterwards. For a screen siren she has one endearing habit: she bites her nails.

Scott Thomas, Kristin, 24th May 1960, toppa the lust league. This classic English Rose has never looked back since Hugh Grant dumped "Fiona" in *Four Weddings And A Funeral*. She starred opposite Tom Cruise in *Mission: Impossible,* won an Oscar nomination for *The English Patient* and beat Meryl Streep to play in *The Horse Whisperer*. She brings inner calmness and complexity to every role.

Kristin and her younger sister, actress Serena Scott Thomas, were brought up in deepest Dorset. She found *The English Patient* uncannily mirrored her own family tragedies. She played a woman who loses both her husband (Colin Firth) and lover (Ralph Fiennes) after plane crashes. In real-life her father, a Fleet Air Arm pilot, was killed in a flying accident when she was five and her stepfather, another pilot, died in a similar crash six years later. Her mother taught herself silversmithing to pay Kristin's fees at a local convent school and Cheltenham Ladies College. She then came to London and found a job in a West End department store, living above a fish 'n' chip shop in Hampstead. She enrolled at the Central School of Speech and Drama but left after a teacher warned her that she would never make the grade as an actress.

The disillusioned 18-year-old fled to Paris where she worked as an *au pair*. It financed her studies at the Ecole National des Arts et Technique de Théâtre. In 1986 she made her film debut in *Under The Cherry Moon*, opposite Prince and two years later won a 'best newcomer' award for her portrayal of an upper-class gel in *A Handful of Dust*. She played Hugh Grant's frigid wife in Roman Polanski's black comedy, *Bitter Moon* and the tortured Sister Gabriel in the ITV series *Body and Soul*. Her only dud was a comedy opposite Jeff Goldblum called *Framed*.

Kristin lives a very un-Hollywood life on Paris's Rive Gauche with gynaecologist Francois Oliviennes, whom she married in 1987. "I do like dressing up on special occasions, but I don't do it very often." Despite further success in the wacky Thirties' version of *Richard III* and the Victorian sexual melodrama *Angels and Insects*, she always feels guilty leaving her children, Hannah and Joseph.

Scott, Selina, 13th May 1951, the Greta Garbo of the autocue. This ambitious daughter of a police sergeant was brought up near Scarborough, where her mother sold antique bed linen, nighties and underwear. After attending local state schools she studied English at the University of East Anglia. She became a cub reporter on the *Darlington and Stockton Times*. A skiing accident made her apply for a less stressful job as the Isle of Mull's press officer. Grampian

TV enticed her away in 1978 to become a newsreader and presenter. There she met programme director Ted Brocklebank who became her mentor.

The late *Sunday Express* editor Sir John Junor 'discovered' Selina. After being interviewed by her he drooled in his column about "this beautiful lassie with blue eyes" who made Anna Ford and Angela Rippon look like "sock-knitting crones". Shortly afterwards she became Ford's replacement on *News At Ten* and fuelled a million male fantasies with her Shy Di expressions and enigmatic smile. In 1983 BBC1 poached her to present its new *Breakfast Time* show with Frank Bough. Critics subjected her to an Anthea Turner frenzy of insults, complaining about her bird-brained waffling, fluffed links and inability to ask serious questions or listen to the answers. While presenting the BBC's live coverage of the Booker Prizegiving she memorably asked Angela Carter, one of the judges, whether she "had read any of the books?"

But public ridicule bounces off Selina like footballs off a wall. No sooner had she tired of the 3am reveille for breakfast TV than she was anchoring BBC1's *The Clothes Show* and had become Sky TV's first major signing. She has since worked in America for CBS's *West 57th* show and as anchor of NBC's European talk series, *The Selina Scott Show*. But her best works are her documentary profiles of King Juan Carlos of Spain and Donald Trump. She ribbed the latter mercilessly and he later described her as "totally uptight and insecure".

Selina's private life is just that: paparazzi rarely catch her at parties or out on the town. She enjoys being single, living between a Kensington flat and a converted *finca* in Majorca. Maybe she should marry her frequent holiday companion Ted Brocklebank, if only to quell false rumours that she is gay!

Seagrove, Jenny, 4th July 1958, grown-up starlet. This ethereal, fragile-looking English Rose has rarely enjoyed the happiness she deserves. Born in Malaysia she was still a toddler when her mother suffered a stroke. Her businessman father took charge of caring for Jenny and his first act was to stop giving her a bottle. She believes these two events had a lasting effect on her psyche, causing a continuing loss of self-esteem. At nine she was incarcerated in an English boarding school. "I always felt left out at sports days and prize-givings because my parents could never be there." She trained at the Bristol Old Vic and soon afterwards won leading TV rôles in Wilkie Collins's *The Woman In White* and RF Delderfield's *Diana*.

Jenny made her name in the 1985 Barbara Taylor Bradford miniseries, *A Woman of Substance*. She has appeared in films like *Local Hero*, *Moonlighting* and *The Guardian*, but is better-known as a stage actress. One critic, reviewing her in *The Miracle Worker*, wrote: "The presence of Jenny Seagrove on the London stage is becoming more and more a cause for celebration."

The three men in this complex beauty's life have all been wrinklies. Her ex-husband, Indian actor Madhav Sharma, was 15 years her senior, film director Michael Winner 23 years, and her present beau, West End impresario Bill Kenwright, 13 years. But she firmly rejects the "father-figure" explanation. "Some of the older men I've been with have been just boys inside." Her marriage ended in a £10,000 court battle for custody of their pet spaniel, Tasha, which she won. "I was weak and easily led in those days." Her six-year relationship with Winner began after she starred in his 1988 comedy, *A Chorus of Disapproval*. This lovely creature would arrive at film premières wearing the flimsiest mini-skirt and cheesiest of smiles, her dumpy lover incongruously beside her. But she always kept her own flat, conveniently close to his Holland Park mansion.

Since 1993 retired ladies' man Kenwright has proved a stabilising influence. She shares his Maida Vale house and appears in his shows. Psychotherapy has taught her to be less submissive.

Sewell, Rufus, 29th October 1967, telly's Mr Lustbox. This curly-haired pretty-boy catapulted to fame as TV's most romantic leading man in 1995. He was the tenderly heroic Ladislaw in *Middlemarch* and the brainy Septimus in *Arcadia*. Critics, mainly male, labelled him Mr Pouty and Mr Broody. But the sight of him in frock-coat and tight breeches excites Byronic fervour from female fans. Madonna wanted to meet him so badly she invited him to dinner at Le Caprice. Ungallantly he darted off before the pudding.

Sewell had an unconventional London upbringing. His father was a boozy Australian animator, responsible for the Beatles' *Yellow Submarine* and *Lucy In The Sky With Diamonds*. He deserted his young family to live in Soho and died when his son was ten. To compensate his mother gave Rufus and his brother Casper almost total freedom. She even allowed him to wander around the house naked until he was eight "to prevent him growing up repressed!" "If my life had been more regimented then I'd be more self-disciplined now." Curiously he was always rather a plump, unattractive child.

Sewell was so poor at drama school that he used to go shoplifting for food. He made an acclaimed West End debut as Jane Asher's manipulative bisexual lover in *Making It Better*. He then played Patsy Kensit's junkie boyfriend in *Twenty-One* and Lia Williams' perverted neighbour in *Dirty Weekend*. But not all his rôles have been so overtly sexual. He was a vicious IRA terrorist in the West End play, *Rat In The Skull* and a Shakespearian grandee in BBC2's adaptation of *Henry IV*. A typically scruffy actor, he uncharacteristically decided to splash out on an Armani suit with some of his earnings from *Middlemarch*. "I then didn't have enough money to get the train home from Brighton, so I bunked the train, but left the suit on it. What karma!"

Happily single, he split from long-standing girlfriend, actress Helen McCrory in 1995. "I'm not the sort of man who needs the security of a relationship." He then enjoyed a three-month fling with his *Hamlet* co-star Kate Winslet.

Shand Kydd, Frances, 10th January 1936, royal granny. The late Diana Princess of Wales inherited her mother's fine bone structure, slim figure and steely determination. She has poise, sex appeal and elegance. Although she professes to shun publicity her outspokenness about her daughter kept her in the news. "Who on earth wants a wishy-washy mother? I don't know any family that doesn't have arguments." In 1996 she was banned from driving for a year after being convicted of drink-driving. She took to riding a mountain bike.

The feisty *grande dame* was born Frances Roche, daughter of the fourth Lord Fermoy, former MP for King's Lynn. Her music-loving mother Ruth was a lifelong friend of the Queen Mother and was her lady-in-waiting for nearly 40 years. Frances was only 18 when she married the eligible future Earl Spencer, then 30, and went to live on the Sandringham estate. She quickly did her dynastic duty, providing an heir, the present Lord Spencer, and three daughters, Lady Sarah, Lady Jane and Lady Diana. But in 1967 she "bolted", having fallen in love with the handsome wallpaper heir Peter Shand Kydd. Her husband won a bitter High Court custody battle over the children, with Ruth testifying against her daughter.

Frances married Shand Kydd and went to live on his New South Wales sheep station and on the Isle of Seil in Argyllshire. As a hobby she opened a gift-shop in nearby Oban. She was once serving a customer who started eulogising to their husband about Diana. "What do you think?", she asked Frances. "It's a bit difficult for me to say", she replied diplomatically. "Quite right, my dear, as a shop assistant you shouldn't give an opinion!"

In 1988 Frances was "devastated" when Shand Kydd left her for another woman. She moved into a bungalow on Seil and converted to Catholicism. She is a local Lady Bountiful and is particularly proud of having raised the money to build the first Catholic chapel on the nearby island of Iona for 400 years. "I'm now addicted to the 'Home Alone' club and would never marry again. I like my freedom to do what I want, when I want!" The death of her youngest daughter can only make her even more reclusive.

Skinner, Frank, 28th January 1957, Britain's oldest teenager. This cheeky rascal with the tousled brown hair and *Just William* smile was a late starter in showbiz. He worked in a West Midlands factory "hitting lumps of hot metal", spent periods on the dole and, after being a mature student at Warwick University, became a college lecturer. While running evening classes in comedy he performed as a lewd and loud stand-up comic. He perfected his routines in local clubs and won the Edinburgh Festival's prestigious Perrier Award for live comedy in 1992. He then appeared in Bob Monkhouse's BBC1 quiz *Gagtag*, out-smarted Paul Merton on *Have I Got News For You* and scripted his own C4 sitcom, *Blue Heaven*.

But Skinner is best-known for BBC2's laddish *Fantasy Football League*. Lolling on a sofa he manages to make the most banal aside sound witty to its post-pub Friday night audience. For three years he shared a North London flat with his co-presenter David Baddiel. Their soccer song, *Three Lions*, co-written with the Lightning Seeds, went to No 1 and became the unofficial Euro '96 anthem. He has enjoyed his share of what he calls "cult comedian sex-god status". He has a preference for blondes ("I once went out with seven on the trot") and confesses to having had a ten-month marriage to a student called Lisa in 1990. A "cradle Catholic" he still "goes to church every Sunday wherever I am in the world".

This fanatical West Bromwich Albion supporter was born Chris Collins and borrowed his stage-name from a member of the local dominoes team. His father was a factory worker and their Oldbury council home had an outside loo with newspaper on the nail. His very first joke came when he was watching *Robinson Crusoe* on TV aged seven. "My dad told me it was the Russian version and I replied: 'no, it can't be, as it would be called Robinson Khrushchev!'"

Slade, Sir Benjamin, 22nd May 1946, Turf-loving extrovert. This pug-faced baronet, with his thatch of white hair, is a popular man-about-town. He is on the A-list of many party organisers and enjoys trawling private views and cocktails for suitable, increasingly young, ladies. Despite his penchant for social chitchat and naughty-boy jokes he is a self-made tycoon with an estimated £20 million fortune. His motto "Faithful and Bold" is singularly apt. He was one of the first Brits to spot the potential in cargo ship containers, founding Shirlstar in 1973. During the 1995 Tory leadership battle he funded right-winger John Redwood's brave but unsuccessful campaign against John Major.

Slade is the latest in a long line of distinguished empire-builders.

The first baronet was a Peninsula War general, the second an eminent QC and the third a Crimean War hero and Inland Revenue supremo. "Benjy" went to Millfield and was a busy debs' delight. In 1977 he married South African heiress Pauline Myburgh. She shared his battered, pet-infested stately home near Bridgwater, Somerset for nearly 15 years, but they divorced in 1991.

This fizzy baronet and entrepreneur has one unfulfilled ambition: to sire an heir. Otherwise his baronetcy, founded in 1831, dies with him. Recent girlfriends have included businesswoman Fiona Aitken and actress Kirsten Hughes. "As a Gemini I take things day by day."

Slattery, Tony, 11th November 1959, television's Mr Sarky. Some clever dick once described him as "looking as though he'd got up in a hurry and pulled on the wrong body by mistake." On C4's cult programme *Whose Line Is It Anyway?* he was the well-fed one with the cheeky manner and wicked choirboy smile. Yet he can be quite chippy and grow irritated with less gifted contestants. His C5 medical quiz show, *Tibs and Fibs*, introduced him to a more populist audience.

"Slatters" comes from a working-class Irish Catholic family in North London. As a teenager he commuted across town to Gunnersbury Grammar School where he achieved three As at A-level. He was at Cambridge with Stephen Fry, Imelda Staunton, Emma Thompson and Hugh Laurie. But he revealed swot-like tendencies until Fry sidled up to him one day and said: "Tony dear boy, you simply must audition for the Footlights." He began appearing in university revues.

Today, he regrets not having quite reached the dizzy heights achieved by his go-getting contemporaries. "The trouble with Tony is that he is a telly tart – he can't say 'no'", explains a friend. One moment he is hosting a TV quiz, the next appearing in a West End comedy like *Neville's Island* and then doing *Whose Line* improvisations. He once shocked the nation in his TV sitcom, *That's Love,* by baring his behind. He had fallen over backwards into a prickly bush and his co-stars had to remove the thorns.

In real-life this hyperactive *Coronation Street* addict is bigger and more oafish-looking than he appears on television. His size somehow mismatches his cute, soft-voiced image. Yet he claims to be a judo blackbelt and to have fought off muggers when returning to his Clapham home late at night. Periodically he suffers from bouts of depression and will take to his bed for a week. He will refuse to answer the telephone or open the door. His romantic activities remain a mystery. He claims that he was once engaged at Cambridge, but broke it off after finding his fiancée in bed with another woman. He could surprise us all.

Smith, Delia, 18th June 1941, goddess of grub. Recipes have made "Saint Delia" into our first foodie multi-millionaire. No other chef can rival her ten million-plus book sales (*Delia Smith's Winter Collection* sold 1.5 million copies in two months). Her mentioning cranberries or lemon zesters on telly unleashes a stampede of customers into the supermarkets. Dinner party guests will prod their Chicken Basque and say: "Oh, is this Delia?" But despite this fame she genuinely remains a very private person who hates inviting interviewers into her kitchens in Suffolk and Wapping.

In foodie circles Delia is treated with the disdain normally reserved for Oxo cubes. Gourmet Egon Ronay lambasted her for being "the missionary position of cooking while others hope to be the *Kama Sutra*". Another critic sneered "she has the great gift of the populariser, of being exactly one step behind."

This printer's daughter from Bexleyheath has been a hairdresser, travel agent and waitress. She then became a family cook in Harley Street. In 1969 literary agent Debbie Owen encouraged her to try writing. From 1972 to 1985 she was the *Evening Standard's* cookery writer and author of a dozen humdrum recipe books. The BBC gave her a lunchtime TV slot in 1973. It led to her 30-part series *Delia Smith's Complete Cookery Course*, which turned into her first bestseller. Simplicity is her secret, with none of the jokes and flourishes of TV chefs like Keith Floyd. "I'm not a great cook. What I can cook, anyone can cook!"

Delia is a devout Roman Catholic who attends Mass most mornings and writes religious books. She recently celebrated her silver wedding anniversary to her journalist husband Mike Wynn-Jones. They founded the *Sainsbury's Magazine*, which now attracts a phenomenal 415,000 readers. They are both directors of Norwich City FC. Her one regret is that they have never had children. So wedded is she to her culinary calling that she turned down Tony Blair's 1997 offer of a 'working' life peerage.

Smith, Dame Maggie, 28th December 1934, *grande dame* of British theatre. No actress of her generation quite matches her wit, technique and presence. In 1962 she won the *Evening Standard's* 'best actress' award for *The Private Ear and The Public Eye* and in 1963 became the Variety Club's 'actress of the year' for *Mary, Mary*. She has been winning prizes ever since, including Oscars for *California Suite* and *The Prime of Miss Jean Brodie*. Curiously some critics still complain her performances are too mannered (ie too Maggie Smith).

This bright, lab technician's daughter grew up in working-class Cowley, but nearby Oxford university was always her spiritual home. Even as a six-year-old shopping with her mother she knew how to attract an audience. "She was wearing a ballet frock once and just started dancing and singing on the pavement. A crowd gathered and kept clapping her on", recalled her father Nathaniel Smith.

At Oxford High School for Girls, Maggie was taught for her English A-level by a Scottish mistress who later became the model for Miss Brodie. When her grandmother heard that at 16 she wanted to act she cracked: "Oh, you can't dear – not with that face!" But Maggie joined the Oxford Playhouse School and made her debut in 1952 as Viola in *Twelfth Night* with the Oxford University Dramatic Society. By 1963 she was a member of the National Theatre, playing Desdemona opposite Sir Laurence Olivier in *Othello* at the Old Vic. Films like *Oh! What a Lovely War, A Private Function* and *A Room With A View* garnered reviews as glowing as her theatre work.

The Dame has two sons, Christopher and Toby, from her first marriage to the libidinous actor Sir Robert Stephens. They divorced in 1975 following his relationship with author Lady Antonia Fraser. The same year Maggie married her old Oxford flame, playwright Beverley Cross, whom she had dumped to marry Stephens. "Bev is my rock", she reflects.

Smith, Mandy, 17th July 1970, superannuated bimbette. Her life was irrevocably changed at 13 when she met Rolling Stone Bill Wyman, 34 years her senior. Although an habitué of North London discos, she was more interested in playing with make-up than playing with boys. But he represented paternal stability: her father, a snooker hall manager, had left home when she was five. Wyman seduced her one weekend at his Suffolk mansion, Gedding Hall. While fellow pupils revised for their O-levels he would take her to Tramp and Stringfellow's. Her mother Patsy condoned these activities because she never wanted Mandy "to end up marrying a local mechanic". The 1989 marriage lasted two turbulent years. But, despite sharing her most formative years with him, her £580,000 settlement barely dented his estimated £35 million fortune.

This damaged butterfly dedicated her autobiography, *It's All Over Now*, to "every woman and girl who has suffered abuse – sexual, emotional and psychological – at the hands of a man". She believes the Wyman experience profoundly injured her. She suffered from a wasting illness during and after her marriage, at one time weighing just five stone. Some sufferers of *anorexia nervosa* find the only way they can deal with the abuse they have suffered is by remaining as physically childlike as possible, so as not to attract male attention.

But the official explanation ascribed her emaciated physique to unspecified "food allergies".

This negation of her adult sexuality explains why sometime model Mandy continues to share with Patsy and sister Nicola her North London home, dubbed by neighbours the "House of Dolls". This set-up even continued during her brief second marriage, to Tottenham footballer Pat van den Hauwe. In another life, she might have become a secretary or nursery nurse. But, for a girl whose physical appearance has always defined her, it is sadly inevitable that she already worries about her looks fading.

Snowdon, Earl of, 7th March 1930, photographer and former royal consort. Despite early Buckingham Palace forebodings he has proved to be the least troublesome of the Queen's growing list of former in-laws. During his 18 year-marriage to Princess Margaret he was careful never to be rude, bolshy or controversial in public. He was dignified during their 1978 divorce, even shedding a tear when confirming on television that they were living apart. It is said he rejected book and newspaper deals worth nearly £500,000.

The former Antony Armstrong-Jones was the son of a QC and a Jewish stockbroking heiress, Anne Messel. He caught polio at 16 and has walked with a limp ever since. At Eton he was a DIY fanatic, building his own radio and gramophone and at Cambridge he coxed the victorious 1951 Boat Race crew. As a Society snapper he is remembered as being "small and cocky". Indeed, he was once flung into the ornamental pool outside the Savoy Hotel by some rowdy Hooray Henries at a deb ball.

It was Tony's bohemian and artistic lifestyle that attracted Margaret after she had rejected more eligible suitors. He rode a motorbike and had a studio in run-down Rotherhithe where he entertained girlfriends like actress Jacquie Chan. Tony and Margaret married in Westminster Abbey in 1960. He accepted an earldom when she was having their first child David so as to avoid the Queen having a commoner nephew. By the time Lady Sarah was born in 1964 the marriage was already in trouble, with him tired of his restricted life at Kensington Palace. "I'm not royal, I'm just married to one", he complained. As well as working for the new *Sunday Times* colour magazine he organised the Prince of Wales' investiture at Carnarvon Castle, built London Zoo's new aviary and designed a special wheelchair for the disabled.

In 1978 this moody, slightly camp charmer married Irish divorcee Lucy Lindsay-Hogg and they have a teenage daughter Lady Frances. She gallantly ignored the 1997 scandal caused by the suicide of his secret mistress, freelance writer Ann Hills.

Soames, Nicholas, 12th February 1948, Tory grandee, nicknamed "Bunter". This popular, 17-stone hedonist is to *nouvelle cuisine* what Henry VIII was to Weight Watchers. For a bet he once shed two stone, raising £100 for charity for every pound he lost. He may be arrogant but he has an ebullience that enlivens the grey Tory frontbench. He was born to rule, although some people think that he "sprang fully formed from a *Blackadder* sketch". His ambassador father Lord Soames was leader of the House of Lords. His slim and beautiful mother Mary was Sir Winston Churchill's daughter.

After Eton *foie gras*-loving Soames served in the 11th Hussars and spent two years as Prince Charles's equerry, the beginning of a lifelong friendship. After a short spell in the City he became MP for Crawley in 1983 and now finds "the adrenalin thrill of politics addictive". But his toffish background and buffoonery held back his career under Thatcher and John Major. As Minister of Food he once thundered that he had "a brace of grouse and a bottle of claret" for breakfast. As Armed Forces minister his gung-ho manner went down well with top military brass. "The British armed forces remain undefeated since 1812", he would tell them. His description of Princess Diana after her *Panorama* interview as being "in the advanced stages of paranoia" was unwise, but typical of his loyalty to Charles.

Soames's jolly bombast and powerful connections have always attracted women. Tory MP Alan Clark wrote in his bestselling *Diary*: "Soames told me about an incredibly powerful new aphrodisiac. I drove him to his flat and he brought down a phial...a herbal concoction, apparently, which needs to be kept in the fridge." In 1981 he married Scottish heiress Catherine Weatherall and had a son, Harry. But they divorced in 1990 after she had a fling with four-times married playboy Piers von Westenholz. At a matchmaking dinner, hosted by former Tory minister Paul Channon, he developed "a hot pash" for 6ft beauty Serena Smith, an ex-Tory MP's daughter. They married in 1993. With characteristic understatement, he later described their newly-born daughter Isabella as "the size of a decent salmon".

Sokolow, Countess Bienvenida, 15th February 1957, Spanish *femme fatale*, aka Bienvenida Buck. This serial Salome was a late arrival in Café Society. Launched by Max Clifford in 1994, she sold her story about being the mistress of Sir Peter Harding, Chief of the Defence Staff during the Gulf War. She revealed they discussed Nato matters under the bedclothes in London hotels and how mean he was with presents. His career was ruined. The affair also ended her brief first marriage to Sir Anthony Buck, a Tory MP over 30 years older than her.

This coquettish glamourpuss is a high-maintenance lady who shops in Bond Street and Knightsbridge, preferably with a man in tow. She models her behaviour on Marlene Dietrich. Despite her raunchy image she rarely wears low-cut gowns, see-through dresses or mini-skirts. But her store of Janet Reger undies makes up for that. In her autobiography, *Bienvenida: The Making of a Modern Mistress* she reveals there is no point dressing up in beautiful clothes if you look embittered. "A smile is the most important thing to wear."

The former Maria-Bienvenida Perez Blanco had an impoverished upbringing in Valencia, mainly brought up by her grandparents. Her father was a watch-maker. Maria moved to London aged 16 where her mother worked as a housekeeper. She was determined to infiltrate upper-class life. She took a degree in business administration at St Godric's College, Hampstead and found her first job working for an engineering firm. She used her well-groomed looks and smart intellect to seduce older, influential men, often Arabs. She claims these social contacts enabled her to earn commission fronting oil, arms and real estate deals. By her early-30s she was an independent lady with a £300,000 apartment in St John's Wood. She now mainly lives near Marbella, where she collects stray dogs. She is estranged from her long-suffering husband, Count Nicholas Sokolow.

Spencer, Earl, 20th May 1964, Diana Princess of Wales's kid brother. Few non-royals have been born to such privilege. He was raised in the ancestral home Althorp (pronounced All-thrupp), a magnificent 16th century mansion, set in 8,500 acres of Northamptonshire, with Van Dycks and Italian Renaissance masterpieces on the walls. For two years he was a Page of Honour to his godmother the Queen. The only problem was his overpowering stepmother Raine, the former Countess of Dartmouth. He and his three sisters, resented her influence over their beloved father, the eighth earl.

Charles Spencer operates well below his intellectual capacity and often appears to be naïve, but he was brainier than most of his Eton contemporaries. At Magdalen College, Oxford he moved in the wrong circles, earning a newspaper reputation as "Champagne Charlie". He was involved in brawls and was banned from a local nightclub for being "arrogant and obnoxious". He unfairly took the blame when some chums tried to de-bag DJ Tony Blackburn at a Kensington restaurant. For his 21st birthday his father threw a lavish £100,000 ball at the family's St James's mansion, Spencer House.

Spencer once boasted that he was the first member of his family ever to work for a living. He was a reporter with the American TV station NBC for six years and then spent two years making documentaries with Granada. But his father's death in 1992, death duties and the need to re-organise the estate put paid to that career.

The red-headed Earl – said to be worth £80 million – has always enjoyed a rackety romantic life and for a time was a regular at Stringfellow's. His most enduring relationship was with doctor's daughter and sculptor Katie Braine whom many friends predicted he would marry. Instead, in 1990 he wed model Victoria Lockwood, a former anorexic. Shortly afterwards an unwise liaison with cartoonist Sally Ann Lasson ended with her selling a kiss 'n' tell story. The Spencers separated in 1995 after having four children: Louis (Viscount Althorp), Lady Kitty and twins Lady Eliza and Lady Katya. Partly to escape the tabloids they moved to South Africa, occupying his 'n' hers villas in a Cape Town suburb. But local paparazzi continued to dog their movements, particularly during his relationships with dress designer Chantal Callopy and former model Josie Borain. After Diana's death he vitriolically attacked the Press for having "blood on their hands".

Spencer-Churchill, Lord Charles, 13th July 1940, man-about-town, nicknamed Nutty. This 6ft 6ins charmer manages to be at all the right parties and restaurants. Contacts are his business. As the Duke of Marlborough's younger brother he has often had to act as family spokesman when his wayward nephew, the Marquess of Blandford, has been in trouble with the police over drugs. A keen racegoer and clubman he displays a boyish enthusiasm, particularly towards women.

Charles was born in the Dorchester Hotel during the Blitz and brought up at Blenheim Palace. As a younger son he knew that he had to make his own way in life. After Eton he studied at Vanderbilt, the Tennessee university founded by his great-great-grandfather, railroad tycoon Cornelius Vanderbilt. He then worked for a City stockbrokers, Sotheby's PR department and Trusthouse Forte. Through contacts in the French Jockey Club he enabled his socially-ambitious employer Lord Forte to sponsor the Prix de L'Arc de Triomphe at Longchamp. Immaculate in his customary blue pin-stripe suit, cream shirt and understated tie he once toured America for three years publicising a "Churchill Line" in suiting. Well, his distant cousin was Sir Winston Churchill.

This Mayfair-based Bertie Wooster was cushioned by an inheritance from a Vanderbilt relation, which included a Palm Beach villa and $1 million. He was briefly married in 1965 to Texan heiress Gillian Fuller. He then married Jane Wyndham, an interior decorator. They have three sons, Rupert, Dominic and Alexander, but parted in 1988 when he ran off with Irish beauty Elaine "Legs" Lawlor. He then had a long relationship with TV researcher Susie Brooks.

Stark, Koo, 26th April 1956, Garboesque *femme fatale*. Prince Andrew was infatuated with this passionate, vulnerable woman four years his senior. He found her playful, uninhibited and sexy: very different from his Sloane girlfriends. During 18 months together they spent many discreet weekends away at friends' houses. To flummox the paparazzi chasing her she would whip out an Olympus and start photographing them.

Unfortunately her spicy background prevented her being considered as a royal bride. The Queen liked her bubbly, natural personality when they met at Balmoral. But the couple parted after his return from the Falklands War. To her credit she has rejected £250,000 offers to tell her story. But she has won an estimated £500,000 in libel actions over allegations that the romance continued during his marriage to Fergie.

This diminutive vegetarian was christened Kathleen. But her father, B-movie producer Wilbur Stark, nicknamed her Koo because she loved imitating pigeons in the garden. She was two when he split up with her mother Cathi Norris, a New York TV presenter. Koo was expensively educated at Miss Hewitt's School for Young Ladies, ironically the Manhattan *alma mater* of that other Society temptress Margaret Duchess of Argyll. Aged 16, she arrived in London, where her little-girl-lost appeal quickly found rich admirers. In 1975 she was billed as the British Emmanuelle in the soft-porn movie *Emily* directed by the Earl of Pembroke and later played a lesbian nun in *Cruel Passions*, based on a novel by the Marquis de Sade.

This hippie chick, famed for her beautiful eyes, long hair and gentle manner, lived for four years with North London businessman Robert Windsor but dumped him the day before their wedding. Later admirers included Turkish entrepreneur Touker Suleyman and Greek shipping heir Constantine Niarchos. In 1984, on the rebound from Prince Andrew, Koo married Green Shield Stamps heir Tim Jefferies, owner of a Mayfair photographers gallery.

The marriage lasted 16 months. Meanwhile, she became a portrait photographer and a Buddhist after meeting the Dalai Lama while photographing elephant polo in India. She was briefly engaged to lanky PR-man Bertie Way in 1993. Four years later she had a baby Tatiana by wealthy American investment banker Warren Walker. She also has a parrot called Bimbo. Had she become Duchess of York she would certainly have had to shed her diamond nose-stud.

Starzewski, Tomasz, 13th August 1961, frockmaker to the glitterati. Most couturiers could only dream of such a clientèle: Sarah Duchess of York, Sophie Rhys-Jones, Countess Spencer, Ivana Trump, Joan Collins and Lady Thatcher. He made his name with the sculptured cocktail dress that helps make the fuller-figured woman look slim and desirable. "My job is to bring out the beauty that every woman possesses."

Both Starzewski's parents are Polish: his father is an architect and his mother a dressmaker. Tomasz grew up in London and went to Emanuel School. He studied design at St Martin's School. In 1990 his couture collection was nominated for a British Fashion Award. The *schmutter* world dotes on this gossippy, bespectacled livewire, with his impeccable taste, style and colour sense. In 1991 his first fashion house in Pont Street drew fanfares from the glossies and one of his first customers was Princess Diana. His two Knightsbridge salons are strategically sited for the ladies-who-lunch. In 1993 royal jewellers Asprey's invested £3 million in his business.

The magnetic Pole enjoys close friendships with his clients. But even he was surprised when a gossip columnist suggested that he was about to marry Maya Flick, who had just won a £9 million divorce settlement. "This must have been his first girlfriend for 15 years", joked a male friend. "The price of my career has been solitude", reflects Starzewski mournfully. He lives in an eclectically-designed basement flat in South Kensington. "I wanted to recreate a Turkish whorehouse!" Celebrated for hosting caviar and champagne dinner-parties, he entertains in his 40-foot drawing room-cum-dining room. He has a very small bedroom which is convenient, as he claims to be celibate. Like the late Sir Norman Hartnell, he can be pernickety and occasionally throw artistic tantrums. Every year he spends ten days at Lourdes cooking for the disabled.

Stewart, Rod, 10th January 1945, rock's elder statesman. Old Gravel Voice will soon find it embarrassing to keep performing his balletic, mike-waving *"Do ya think I'm sexy?"* stage antics. But the faithful, now in their late-forties, still flock to concerts, drooling over their increasingly paunchy idol. *Maggie May*, *Sailing* and *The Ballad of Georgie* have become classic golden oldies. "I treat my body like a machine and look after it. It's like an old Austin 70." Worth an estimated £60 million, he floats between homes in Los Angeles, Epping Forest and Palm Beach. His migrations are often dictated by his beloved Scotland's football fixtures. He donated all royalties from his Scottish Euro '96 single to the Dunblane massacre fund.

Underneath the flamboyant outfits and razzmatazz, Stewart remains a tough South London Mod. "My passions are soccer, drinking, women – in that order." He really was a gravedigger once. "Without fame I'd probably have become some fat bloke living in pubs." He began as a very average guitarist with the Hoochie Coochie Men who backed legendary blues singer Long John Baldry. He became lead singer with the Faces, enjoying his first Top 10 hit, *Stay With Me*, in 1970. Stewart-mania then broke out.

At his peak the snake-hipped, spikey-haired "Tartan Terror" was spoilt, moody, capricious and God's gift to groupies. His penchant for tall, leggy blondes led to well-publicised romances with actresses Britt Ekland, Joanna Lumley and Susan George, and models Bebe Buell and Dee Harrington. "It all helped the image." For five years he was married to Hollywood actor George Hamilton's ex-wife Alana, but they divorced in 1984. They have two children, Kimberley and Sean, and he then had Ruby with American model Kelly Emberg. His 1990 marriage to New Zealand model Rachel Hunter works because she accepts no nonsense and sticks to him like Velcro. They have two children, Renee and Liam. "I've earned my money and I've got everything I want and so I'm able to give the kids a lot more attention." Maybe the hell-raiser has finally settled down?

Stigwood, Robert, 16th April 1934, legendary showbiz mogul. He began in the Sixties as the archetypal Aussie hustler: brash, pushy, enterprising, very sharp. He became Britain's most successful pop tycoon, with a Liberace-style yen for exotic companions, mock-Tudor mansions, white Bentley convertibles and other toys. While contemporaries like Larry Parnes and Brian Epstein long ago joined the great Tin Pan Alley in the Sky, he is now worth an estimated £170 million.

An electrical engineer's son, Stigwood went to Sacred Heart College, Adelaide, and then took the hippy trail to Europe. He arrived in London in 1959 with just £3 in his rucksack. His first job was as a welfare officer in an East Anglian hostel for backward boys. In 1961 he became a pop manager, launching John Leyton and Mike Sarne whose records, *Johnny Remember Me* and *Come Outside*, respectively topped the charts. He was the first manager to combine being record producer, music publisher and concert promoter. Alas, Beatlemania and personal extravagance forced his company into voluntary liquidation.

Stiggy's second coming coincided with meeting three gawky Australian singers whom he named the Bee Gees (a mnemonic for Brothers Gibb). He promoted them as teenage idols and used their music when he moved into film production. Their high-pitched wailing was heard on the soundtracks of *Saturday Night Fever*, *Grease*, *Stayin' Alive* and *Grease II*. The group is said to have earned him well over £100 million. On stage he co-produced such seminal Sixties musicals as *Hair*, *Oh, Calcutta!* and *The Dirtiest Show In Town*. He also spotted the potential of Andrew Lloyd Webber and Tim Rice, backing *Jesus Christ Superstar* and *Evita*. "I've a nose for knowing what the public want."

This flamboyant bachelor semi-retired in the late Eighties, enjoying life on his 27-acre Bermuda estate and aboard his 247-foot yacht, El Petal. "Then, like eating chocolate all the time, the novelty of leisure wears off." Leathery-faced with wispy white hair, he benevolently presides over Barton Manor, a wine-producing estate on the Isle of Wight, once owned by Queen Victoria.

Sting, 2nd October 1951, pop idol turned human rights campaigner. For three frenetic years this wiry, would-be intellectual enjoyed international success with the pop group Police. Songs like *Message In A Bottle*, *Walking On the Moon*, *Don't Stand So Close To Me* and *Every Little Thing She Does* were the melodious antithesis of contemporary punk. Bored with touring he became an actor, despite never having had drama lessons. But he made a creditable debut in *Quadrophenia* in 1979, followed by *Brimstone and Treacle* and lesser films like *Dune*, *Plenty* and *The Bride*.

Milkman's son Sting, born Gordon Sumner, grew up Newcastle. He acquired his stage-name – now something of an embarrassment – after the wasp-striped tee-shirt he wore when playing guitar at school hops. After dropping out of Warwick University he became a primary school teacher. He married Irish actress Frances Tomelty in 1976 when still a struggling rock musician. Police's chart success with *Roxanne* in 1979 led to them being hailed as the new Beatles and their album *Synchronicity* sold over seven million copies. Fans went wild when their slim, blue-eyed hero with the gold earring and tousled dyed-blonde hair cavorted on stage.

Cushioned by his estimated £70 million fortune from singing, publishing and composing, Sting and his second wife Trudie now devote much of their time to Green issues. They started the Rainforest Foundation in 1988 after seeing the destruction of the Amazon rainforest and its inhabitants' way of life. The Stings hire New York's Carnegie Hall for an annual fund-raising concert starring their pop friends. In 1996 he was criticised for advocating the legalisation of soft drugs in Britain.

This rock legend has two children, Joe and Kate, from his first marriage (which ended in 1984). He lived with actress-turned-documentary-maker Trudie Styler for ten years before marrying in 1992.

They became known for their tantric sex marathons and now have four children, Mickey, Jake, Coco and Giacomo. They swan between homes in Highgate, Wiltshire, New York and California.

Stoppard, Sir Tom, 3rd July 1937, 20th century Shakespeare. In 1997 he finally joined Andrew Lloyd Webber and Alan Ayckbourn as a theatrical knight. It had a certain extra synergy because this bouffant-haired playwright was a longstanding Labour luvvie and Amnesty International supporter. He already had enough drama awards from the *Evening Standard*, New York Drama Critics Circle and BAFTA to decorate both his up- and downstairs loos.

This Czech-born genius began life as Thomas Straussler. His father worked for the Bata shoe company but was killed during the Second World War. Tom assumed his stepfather's name on his mother's remarriage to an English army officer stationed in Darjeeling. The family came to live in Yorkshire where he attended Pocklington Grammar School. While working as a freelance journalist in Bristol he began writing plays for radio and television. His National Theatre debut with *Rosencrantz and Guildenstern are Dead* in 1967 became a box office hit in London and New York. It was followed by *The Real Inspector Hound, Jumpers, Travesties, Night and Day, On The Razzle* and *The Real Thing*. His royalties were enhanced by writing screenplays for films like *The Romantic Englishman, Empire of the Sun* and *Russia House* .

A wryly amusing dandy and weekend cricketer, Stoppard has two sons from both his former wives. His 20-year second marriage to TV personality Dr Miriam Stoppard ended in 1991 when he fell in love with longstanding leading lady Felicity Kendal. Theatricals still miss the summer garden parties the Stoppards held at their Vanbrugh-designed Buckinghamshire mansion. His Chelsea home is only minutes away from Felicity, who starred in his recent productions of *Arcadia* and *Indian Ink*. "Stoppard doesn't write for people, he writes for ideas," she says. "Your job is not to get the character right so much as to get the author right!" In 1997 there were reports he was romancing Hollywood star Mia Farrow.

Street-Porter, Janet, 27th December 1946, telly's revenge for Danny Baker. With her freaky hair, Dame Edna specs, and towering physique she is unmistakable. "A traffic-light that talks like a tannoy" was one description. She seriously irritates people. But there also seems to be an endless queue of suitors who not only hire her for her gush of opinions, but also chase her romantically. As one professional door closes she emerges from another, reinvented. She has even written a book on Britain's greatest scandals and one on her hobby, collecting teapots.

JSP's career might have been blighted had she stuck to her original surname of Bull. Instead she permanently "borrowed" that of her first husband, photographer Tim Street-Porter. It creates an interesting juxtaposition between the rough and the toff. Despite the "mockney" tones she actually comes from 'Sarf' London and attended Lady Margaret Grammar School, Fulham. After two years' architectural studies she joined *Petticoat* magazine as home editor and then the *Evening Standard* as Fleet Street's most with-it fashion writer.

Janet moved to other 'meejah', fronting LBC's breakfast show and children's programmes for LWT. She co-hosted *The Six O'Clock Show* and began yet another career as a TV producer with *20th Century Box*. Despite hating gossip columns she hosted two vicious telly versions, *Saturday Night People* and *Around Midnight*. In 1988 she became a senior BBC executive and dreamed of being BBC2's first female Controller. "But the telly establishment is too middle-class, middle-aged and male." Thwarted, she launched L!VE TV, a chaotic cable station, but left after a tiff with her boss, Kelvin Mackenzie. Her current roost is president of the Ramblers Association. Career-wise has she finally run out of paths?

Janet's second marriage, in 1976, was to *Time Out* founder Tony Elliott. In 1978 she married award-winning TV director Frank Cvitanovich but divorced ten years later. During a marital lull she dated Tony James, a musician with Sigue Sigue Sputnik who wore multi-coloured headdresses at parties, and a rap artist called Normski. She was then briefly wed to David Sorkin, a salesman 22 years her junior. She now lives alone in the hi-tech house she had built in Clerkenwell and her remote cottage in the Yorkshire Dales.

Stringfellow, Peter, 17th October 1940, self-proclaimed "world's greatest disco owner". He has the looks and charisma of Mick Jagger, the publicity flair and childishness of Richard Branson and the luck and resilience of Jeffrey Archer. The early Nineties recession caused the closure of his clubs in Miami, New York and Los Angeles. But he has bounced back with his lap-dancing *Cabaret of Angels*. Even his old foe Nigel Dempster writes about him now.

Few people outside the North had heard of this flamboyant character when he launched Stringfellow's in a derelict former Covent Garden office block in 1980. With its garish chromium décor, harsh strobe-lit dance floor and slinky waitresses in silk cami-knickers and stockings, it was brash by any standards. But Stringy's ability to attract showbiz stars like Rod Stewart, George Michael, Kevin

Costner and Jack Nicholson kept the media constantly interested. His transformation of the nearby Talk of the Town into the hi-tech Hippodrome only added to his success.

This exuberant son of a Sheffield steelworker grew up sharing a bed with his three younger brothers in a terrace house with an outside privy. He left school with no qualifications and joined the Merchant Navy at 17 where he first fell in love with New York. By 1962 he was organising village hops in church halls, playing the latest records on his granny's old Deccalian and hiring then unknown groups like The Beatles and The Hollies for £85 a night. His mother and his future wife Coral would collect the money at the door. His first proper disco was the Mojo Club in Sheffield. He then opened two upmarket clubs, Cinderellas and Rockafellas, in Leeds. He sold them to open the glitzy Millionaire Club in Manchester which, in turn, eventually funded Stringfellow's.

Stringy's private life is a cross between the Marquis de Sade and Johnny Depp. The girlfriends get younger and raunchier. He has two ex-wives: teenage sweetheart Norma, mother of his beautiful daughter Karen, and the lively Coral, mother of racing-driver Scott. To fund his second divorce, Stringy sold the Hippodrome for £7 million. He had a longstanding girlfriend with pink hair called Frizzby Fox. He thrives on adrenalin, vodka and sex, even though he is going deaf in one ear and his blonde coiffure takes longer to style. His future includes opening more girlie clubs and enjoying a Falstaffian old age surrounded by lissom lasses, grandchildren and cats.

Stubbs, Imogen, 20th February 1961, the future Judi Dench. She is one of our finest young classical actresses. But she belongs firmly among the grunge school of thespiennes led by Helena Bonham-Carter: conceal your physical assets so men will appreciate you for your mind rather than your body. This is a shame as blonde, blue-eyed, Rapunzel-haired Imogen has a trim chassis that could dazzle a Ferrari showroom. She also has an Oxford double first and so no-one is likely to mistake her for a Page 3 girl. It upset her feminist instincts when she had to wear a mini-skirt in the TV detective series *Anna Lee*.

Northumberland-born Imogen spent her childhood living on a creaky old Thames barge. Her father, a retired naval commander, sent her to St Paul's School where she was called "Midge" because of her size. After RADA she became an RSC actress in productions like *Richard II*, *Heartbreak House* and *St Joan*. Her rôle as the sweetly-bitchy Lucy in *Sense and Sensibility* won her most praise. Still she complains: "I must do something, like *Prime Suspect*, that has street credibility. I haven't yet shown I have guts as an actress."

In 1994 Imogen married multi-millionaire theatre director Trevor Nunn, 21 years her senior. They have two children, Ellie and Jesse, and live in Georgian splendour in Chiswick. Ironically, two years later, she played the frustrated wife of a much older man in Chekhov's *Uncle Vanya* at the Chichester Theatre. "Trevor threw back his head and groaned: 'Oh nooo! Everyone will say you must know how to play her because your own situation is similar! But Trevor has never come across to me as old and we've got children to disprove the other part!" He became "everything to me" following a spate of sad experiences. Both her parents died from cancer, and she had a miscarriage in 1987 during her relationship with French actor Jean-Philippe Ecoffey.

TUV

Tarrant, Chris, 10th October 1946, motormouth. This gangling, blond DJ has become an institution with his daily badinage on London's Capital Radio. He has also developed an alternative career as king of the voice-overs and owns an Italian clothes firm. After a boozy lunch he is once said to have visited the Earl's Court Boat Show and bought a £250,000 yacht!

Reading-born Tarrant – aka "Chrissy Wissy" on his breakfast show – was an only child. At the King's School, Worcester he was caned for truanting with girls from the nearby boarding-school. As a Boy Scout he nearly died when he was swept out to sea during a swimming exercise in Devon. At Birmingham University he graduated with "a bluffer's degree" in English but couldn't find a job. He was a long-distance lorry driver and a security officer before finally becoming a schoolteacher in East London. For six months he lived in a mini-van.

Brash Tarrant was a late-starter in television, joining ATV as a trainee reporter at 28. He produced and starred in the anarchic children's show *Tiswas*, chucking lemon tarts and buckets of water at co-presenters Sally James and Lenny Henry. It led to the controversial late-night series, *OTT*, again featuring girls being dunked in custard and men showing their bottoms. He has hosted numerous quiz shows, including *Lose A Million*, *The Main Event* and *Pop Quiz*. He fronted ITV's short-lived series, *Man O Man*, a male beauty contest in front of 300 shrieking women. But his natural habitat remains radio. There his matey, pubby personality can connect with an audience, without viewers having to watch his beer belly and annoying mannerisms.

This retired Lothario is said to have once made love to four girls in a single day. He has six children from two marriages and claims to be a strict father. He lives with his Norwegian second wife Ingrid in Cobham, Surrey. If life becomes too frenetic he goes fishing.

Tavistock, Marquess of, 21st January 1940, decent toff. Stately homes come no statelier than Woburn Abbey, the Russell family seat since Henry VIII's dissolution of the monasteries. Set in a deer park it contains an art collection worth an estimated £90 million, which includes works by Holbein, Rembrandt and Velazquez. His father, the Duke of Bedford, became known as the "showman Duke" after he opened it to the public and used every PR-trick to lure punters.

Robin Tavistock's mother died when he was five, and the future 14th duke was sent to the Swiss public school, Le Rosey, which at least enabled him to become an excellent skier. He then took an economics degree at Harvard University. He was a 21-year-old City stockbroker when he married former 'deb of the year' Henrietta Tiarks, a rich banker's daughter. His career as an investment manager came to a juddering halt in 1974 when the Duke announced that the new Labour government had forced him into tax exile. A reluctant Tavistock had to move his family into Woburn and run the 13,000 acre estate, which still includes some Bloomsbury properties around Bedford, Tavistock and Russell Squares. "It was extremely selfish of my father-in-law", Henrietta later said. "Robin was enjoying his life. At 34 to be made a prisoner of inheritance is very cruel."

In 1988 Tavistock – worth an estimated £175 million – suffered a near-fatal stroke. But sheer willpower and his wife's devotion has enabled him to walk and speak again. He admits that he has now become "a much easier person to get along with". He has also established the Tavistock Trust for Aphasia and donated £250,000 to two research projects. Meanwhile, Lord Howland, the eldest of his three sons, is increasingly taking over Woburn's responsibilities, leaving his parents freer to concentrate on their Newmarket stud.

Taylor, Lady Helen, 28th April 1964, royal *mater*. The pouting, former royal vamp Lady Helen Windsor has transmogrified into a typical Sloane mum. She lives in Belgravia, drives a Range Rover, wheels her baby pram round Hyde Park and meets girlfriends for giggly lunches. Any embarrassment she ever caused her cousin the Queen was tiny compared with Princess Diana and Fergie. In her single days she moved with a fast Chelsea set and her revealing dresses earned her the sobriquet "Melons". She was even caught sunbathing topless while on holiday in Corfu.

Helen – 26th in line to the throne – inherited her blonde English Rose looks from her mother, Yorkshire baronet's sister Katharine Worsley. The lack of any discernible chin is perhaps down to her overbred father, the Duke of Kent. After St Mary's Ascot she transferred to Gordonstoun for her A-levels, managing only one, in Art. She became a receptionist at the Mayor Gallery in Mayfair and worked in Christie's modern picture department.

Coquettish Lady Helen rejected every eligible suitor, preferring handsome middle-class lads with sports cars. Her first boyfriend was stockbroker's son John Benson who ran a mobile disco and took her on unchaperoned skiing holidays to Switzerland. After two years she tired of him and had a fling with another Old Etonian, man-about-town Simon Oakes. But her most enduring relationship was with David Flint Wood. Friends were puzzled what she saw in this staid advertising man who subsequently fell in love with royal model India Hicks. She replaced him with art dealer Tim Taylor, a Clark Kent lookalike and naval commander's son. In 1992 they married in a low-key St George's Chapel, Windsor ceremony. Their first child Columbus was named after her favourite restaurant.

Te Kanawa, Dame Kiri, 6th March 1944, down-to-earth diva. Not for her the tantrums and histrionics of Maria Callas. Her solid Kiwi background gave her values and beliefs she has never lost. Although she has performed in all the world's major opera houses she has never reached a larger audience than at Prince Charles's wedding in 1981. Over half a billion TV viewers listened to her Handel aria. Thanks to him she became a Dame the following year at only 38.

The award-winning soprano was born in Gisborne, North Island, of Maori parents. She was adopted ten days later by her "mother" Nell, whose husband was Maori and great-great-uncle was composer Sir Arthur Sullivan. Nell quickly recognised Kiri's remarkable gifts and persuaded the family to move to Auckland where her daughter could receive professional tuition. In 1966 Kiri won a four-year scholarship to the London Opera Centre. At 27 she made an outstanding debut in *The Marriage of Figaro* at the Royal Opera House. Three years later she won over New York opera buffs when she deputised at a few hours' notice for a televised performance of *Otello* at the Met. Rave notices followed at Paris, Sydney and Cologne opera houses, at La Scala and the Salzburg Festival. One critic described her voice as "flowing across an audience like golden cream".

Tanned, glossy-haired Kiri may be Britain's highest-paid opera singer but, compared with male rivals like Placido Domingo and Luciano Pavarotti, she lives relatively simply. She is based in London but has holiday homes near Bordeaux and on Lake Taupo, New Zealand. She met her husband, retired Australian mining engineer Desmond Park, on a blind date in 1967 and married him three months later. "Des is the mainstay of my life. Marrying him was the best contract I've ever signed!" Alas, in 1997 they divorced because of his adultery. Typically she seems more concerned about its effect on their two adopted children, Antonia and Tom.

Tennant, Stella, 17th December 1971, aristo catwalker. She was a pioneer of the English Rose-with-attitude models of the mid-

Nineties. Like her rivals Jodie Kidd and Honor Fraser, she is not conventionally beautiful. Indeed her dark eyes and pronounced eyebrows look quite freakish. But she definitely has character and wears clothes with unselfconscious nonchalance.

Stella was raised in Roxburghshire grandeur. Her father Toby Tennant is the half-brother of Lord Glenconner, better known as Princess Margaret's best friend Colin Tennant. Her mother, Lady Emma, is the daughter of the Duke of Devonshire. Stella's cousin is baronet's daughter and fellow model Iris Palmer.

This Nineties Penelope Tree was once regarded as a "kooky waif with a ring through her nose and navel". She was discovered after appearing in a "real people" shoot for *Vogue*. Her initial catwalk sorties were embarrassing. "She was gawky and hunched. I was reminded of a schoolgirl walking up to receive something from the headmistress during assembly", recalls one fashion editor.

Her career took off in 1995 after she was photographed for Italian *Vogue* by Bruce Weber draped on a chaise-longue in the drawing-room of Chatsworth, her grandfather's stately home in Derbyshire. Gone were the extraneous rings, fake tattoos and sullen expression and in their place a studied hauteur. Designers Yves St Laurent, Valentino, Christian Dior and Gianni Versace booked her for their catalogues. Photographers Mario Testino and Paulo Roversi queued to use her for fashion shoots. But her greatest coup was Karl Lagerfeld selecting her to replace Claudia Schiffer as the new Face of Chanel. Stella sees modelling as only a temporary phase. She wants to return to her first love, sculpting.

Thatcher, Baroness, 13th October 1925, the great She Elephant. With her steely determination and clear vision of what was wrong with Britain she restored her country's pride. During a record-breaking three consecutive terms as prime minister she destroyed the unions' power, revived the economy, resisted Common Market bullying and almost destroyed the Labour party. Her 1990 fall from power, though a massive Tory stab in the back, was warmly greeted by many former allies. An ironic result of Tony Blair's landslide victory in 1997 was his promise to "continue the Thatcherite revolution of our institutions, but add the kindness she left out."

Margaret Hilda Roberts's elevation from Grantham grocer's daughter to PM owed much to her marriage to millionaire businessman Denis Thatcher in 1951. Ex-Grantham High School and Oxford, she was then a research chemist and quite naïve and suburban in her attitudes. She could now afford to take time off to read for the Bar and raise a family while trying to pursue a political career. Ten years her senior, Denis proved to be the most devoted and helpful consort since Prince Albert. "C'mon Margaret, time for bed", he would say, interrupting a late-night meeting at No 10

Their twins Mark and Carol, born in 1953, have both been supportive. But, while journalist Carol, with her jolly exterior, modesty and troublesome 'r's, has never embarrassed her mother, Mark has been a constant worry. He made her cry when he was lost in the Sahara desert during the 1982 Paris-Dakar rally, mysteriously became a multi-millionaire during her premiership and later suffered marital problems. "The boy can do no wrong – she adores him come what may", explained her former press secretary Sir Bernard Ingham. But she now has to trek to South Africa to see him and her grandchildren.

A spry septuagenarian, the former PM at one time hankered for a return to power "to finish off the job". With two volumes of autobiography behind her she now prefers to be an elder stateswoman and can earn £30,000 a speech spreading her views round the world.

Tholstrup, Mogens (pronounce Moans), 16th May 1961, dreamboat restaurateur. This tall, lean, casually elegant Dane with a mop of golden-brown hair resembles a Hollywood matinée idol. Owner of Daphne's and The Collection, he has redefined chic but informal eating. His high-profile means that he collects the right people while his foodie instincts prevent *prima donna* chefs bullying him.

Tholstrup was born in Finland where his father ran a gas company. His parents had homes in Copenhagen, Switzerland and the South of France. The family fortune comes from Tholstrup cheese, a variety of Danish Blue invented by his grandfather. After taking a science degree at Copenhagen's School of Economics and Business Administration he dabbled in shipping, finance, advertising, even photography. He came to Britain in 1985 to woo a beautiful model who then dumped him. With his private means he became a playboy, studying furniture design by day and dancing at Tramp by night. As a sideline in 1991 he opened Est, a tiny Soho bistro that he designed himself with minimalist chairs and modern art. Its success led to him hiring interior decorator Emily Todhunter and Annie Foster-Firth as Miss Fix-it to re-vamp the Sixties restaurant Daphne's.

Daphne's became the San Lorenzo of the mid-Nineties, with everyone from Princess Diana to Richard Gere clamouring for tables. But the blue-eyed Dane's proximity to so many young, beautiful and available women presented him with too many temptations. He began dating It Girl Tara Palmer-Tomkinson and broke up with his wife, Paola Schlansen, a German-Italian model, whom he had married in 1991. The Tholstrups have a daughter, Christina. In 1996 he bought Katharine Hamnett's former fashion emporium at Brompton

Cross and transformed it into The Collection. Tholstrup lives in an immaculate Knightsbridge apartment. His latest squeeze, 15 years younger than him, is model Lady Victoria Hervey.

Thompson, Emma, 15th April 1959, Britain's premier actress under-40. This controlled English beauty has a touch of the Goldie Hawns and Iris Murdochs. Earthy, wacky and super-intelligent she is almost too forthright. Her career has rocketed since her marriage to Kenneth Branagh broke up. In 1996 *Sense and Sensibility* won her an Oscar for 'best screenwriter' and a nomination for 'best actress'. The Arnold Schwarzenegger film *Junior* showed that she could tackle comedy as well.

Emma's father, Eric Thompson, narrated BBC1's cult children's series, *The Magic Roundabout*, and her mother is actress Phillida Law. While studying at Cambridge she became a leading Footlights player, appearing at the Edinburgh Festival and touring Australia. In 1983 she co-starred with Ben Elton, Stephen Fry and Robbie Coltrane in ITV's comedy series *Alfresco* and then won BAFTA's 'best actress' award two years running for *Tutti Frutti* and *Fortunes of War*. Her only TV failure has been the one-woman comedy show *Thompson* in 1987. On stage she has starred in *Look Back in Anger, King Lear* and *A Midsummer's Night Dream*. She won an Oscar for *Howard's End* in 1993 and was acclaimed for *The Remains of The Day* and *In The Name of the Father*. Typically, she keeps her Oscars in the downstairs loo of her Hampstead home.

The apotheosis of the Ken 'n' Em show was their whirlwind courtship and wedding in 1989. Admirers spoke about the new Laurence Olivier and Vivien Leigh. But six years later the marriage was over. He complained: "I have to make an appointment to see Emma because she's so busy." Asked if they had ever considered having children, she replied: "Ken is so tired his sperm are on crutches." She consoled herself with Greg Wise, her *Sense and Sensibility* leading man. At the Cannes Film Festival frisky Emma once admitted she had enjoyed "a varied sex life since I was 15", and at Cambridge she was particularly noted for enjoying alfresco encounters.

Thurso, Viscount, 10th September 1953, noble fat-farmer. With his thick black hair, bushy moustache and imposing stature he would win any Lord Lucan lookalike contest. It is not a comparison he relishes because he would hate anyone to feel that he had murdered the family nanny! Sensitive, charming and courteous he is that rare Nineties species, an Old Etonian aristo who thrives in the jungle of commerce. But his first job was on an Arkansas cattle ranch. On seeing his luxuriant Flower Power locks the rancher drawled: "If you don't git a haircut right now the boys at the ranch will darn well do it for ya, only they'll use shears!"

The former John Sinclair joined the Savoy Hotel as a management trainee aged 19. He learnt every skill from working on the front desk to waiting and bartending. In 1981 he was appointed general manager of the group's Lancaster Hotel in Paris. He was then head-hunted in 1985 to launch the new Cliveden Hotel, in Viscount Astor's magnificent former stately home. He dispensed with check-in desks and hired a butler so that guests could feel they were joining a house party. His skills were recognised in 1995 when he was hired to run an ailing Hertfordshire health farm, Champneys. One of his first moves, recorded in a BBC1 documentary *Trouble at the Top*, was to lose the flab concealed by his carefully cut pinstripe suits. Within 12 months he had shed three stone and begun to turn £2 million-a-year losses into a thriving business.

The kilted Lib Dem peer lives up to his family motto, *J'aime Le Meilleur*. He enjoys the grouse moors and salmon beats surrounding Thurso East Mains, the draughty Caithness castle he inherited with his title in 1995. Thurso married his American wife Marion in 1976 and they have three children, Louisa, James and George. He hopes to emulate his parents' marital example – they were still "madly in love" after over 40 years together. Meanwhile he plans to open satellite Champneys in other European countries. Having restored the family coffers – much depleted by double estate duty – he then wants to settle down as a Highland laird.

Turner, Anthea, 25th May 1961, Ms Goody Two Shoes. A sweet, talentless, blonde bimbo? Or a manipulative, ruthless career woman? The media can never quite make up their minds. But the debate crystallised on GMTV's sofa, where co-presenter Eamonn Holmes sneered at her amateur interviewing technique and accused her of throwing tantrums to get her own way. After two-and-a-half years she finally resigned in 1996 to star in her own series, *Pet Power* and *Turner Round The World*, and to present *Wish You Were Here...?*

Pert, cheerful Anthea was raised in Stoke-on-Trent where her father runs a soft furnishings business. She moved from Holden Lane Comprehensive to a private convent school when doctors discovered that she was dyslexic. Her first job was on the switchboard of the AA's breakdown department. At 19 she was doing traffic reports on local radio stations when she met her first big love, Bruno Brookes, the star DJ on Radio Stoke. Meeker and milder in those days, she subordinated her ambitions to his. They both moved to London when he joined Radio One. At a party she overheard that Sky TV were auditioning for a video jock, turned up and got the job. Later she fronted the BBC1 children's series *Up2U* and *Going Live*.

In 1990 Anthea secretly dated Brookes's best friend, showbiz manager Peter Powell, and married him four months later. At the late age of 32 she became a *Blue Peter* presenter. During a 'live' outside broadcast from the Royal Tournament she was hit by a blazing motorbike and her face was badly burned. "I never thought I'd look the same again, but my skin healed amazingly". Ironically it was her perfect skin, clear eyes and fresh personality that landed her the GMTV job in 1994. She became TV's top-paid woman after Cilla Black when she began presenting the *National Lottery Live*. "I've learnt that how I look – clothes, make-up, hair – is probably the biggest single factor that affects my career."

Anthea models for down-market Littlewood's catalogues and has produced a health and beauty video. She invested her £500,000-a-year earnings in a Georgian-style mansion in Twickenham. She cannot decide whether her career is more important than starting a family. "I just hope the plumbing works. Pete and I will just take things as they come."

Twiggy, 19th September 1949, Face of the Sixties. She is a lone survivor among the dolly birds and starlets who once paraded the Biba, Mary Quant and Ossie Clark catwalks. She was even more famous then than Naomi Campbell and Kate Moss are today. With her streetwise Cockney manager and lover Justin de Villeneuve, she embodied the glamour and freedom of that crazy decade. Fortunately the drink, drugs and sex overkill passed her by. Her career continues because she repackaged herself as an actress.

In 1971 film director Ken Russell starred her in *The Boy Friend* opposite Glenda Jackson. Critics expressed surprise that she could play any rôle other than a dumb, Cockney superwaif. After taking acting, singing and dancing lessons in America she won the lead in the Broadway musical *My One and Only*. Again she was garlanded with praise and awards. She has since made records, TV series and films but never quite fulfilled her early Ginger Rogers potential.

Mayfair hairdresser Nigel Davies discovered this gawky 15-year-old ingénue while she was at Kilburn High School. He changed her name from Lesley Hornby to Twiggy ("cos my legs are all peculiar and thin like twigs, see?"). He himself acquired the absurdly grandiose monicker, Justin de Villeneuve. With her flat-chested figure, cropped blonde hairstyle and "bloomin' liberty" accent she became a cult, chased by fashion editors, couturiers and advertisers.

Fans bought "Forget Oxfam, Feed Twiggy" badges and wore fake freckles and tarantula-like eyelashes. She paid for her parents to move from dull Neasden to up-market Twickenham.

Having broken up with de Villeneuve, strait-laced "Twigs" surprised friends by marrying a struggling American actor, Michael Whitney. The birth of her daughter Carly had the beneficial effect of giving her a curvier, more buxom figure. But Whitney's heavy drinking drove them apart. He died in 1983. Five years later she wed TV heart-throb Leigh Lawson and settled in South Kensington. They remain devoted. She has one moan: "The older I get the sillier 'Twiggy' sounds!"

Van Randwyck, Baroness Isabelle, 1st November 1963, Barbie Doll with Bassey pretensions, known as Issy. By day she was a Sloane Ranger estate agent in straight skirt and passion-killer tights. By night she underwent a Clark Kent transformation. The vamp appeared in a bodice-ripping gown, basque, silk stockings and stilettoes. She would then sing her heart out at Madame Jo Jo's, a Soho club famed for its transvestites and fashionable clientele. She now has a cult following as a member of the *risqué* all-girl group, Fascinating Aida, with Dillie Keane and Adele Anderson.

This tall, eccentric *chanteuse*, with the peroxide hair, chiselled cheekbones, dangly earrings and perfectly formed beauty spot, belongs to an old Dutch family called Van Randwijck. She was brought up in Kent from the age of nine. At West Heath school she "acted, sang, recited, danced, entered competitions – anything to get on stage". She even sang with the Bach Choir under Sir David Willcocks in the *St Matthew Passion*. She then did a secretarial and cookery course to please her parents but failed to win a place at drama college. "I was devastated when none of them wanted me." She began singing with a rock band and in cabaret at Madame Jo Jo's. "I was the only girl among a bunch of drag queens. It was the place to be at the time, with queues up Wardour Street." In 1991 she performed with harmonica-player Larry Adler at the Edinburgh Festival and later sang on his bestselling album, *The Glory of Gershwin*.

At last producers began taking blue-eyed Issy seriously as a singer/actress. She appeared at the National Theatre in Stephen Sondheim's *A Little Night Music* and *The Taming of the Shrew*, in cabaret at Pizza on the Park and on TV in the award-winning sitcom, *Waiting For God*. In real-life she is nothing like her zany, blonde bombshell image. Warm, friendly and surprisingly vulnerable, she relaxes by doing tapestry. Her actor boyfriend, Jon Cryer, lives in Los Angeles: "We link up whenever we can!"

Venables, Terry, 6th January 1943, former England football coach. This slate-haired, ruddy-complexioned legend has always aroused strong emotions, not least because of his showmanship. If sport had not claimed him he might have become an Essex Englebert Humperdinck. Interviewers complain about his defensiveness and habit of adjusting his tackle – or "three-piece suite" as he calls it.

Ex-Barcelona manager "El Tel" may be flash but at least he has a sense of humour. He claims he was named after Terry's Chocolates. After a non-education at Dagenham High School he had to become streetwise to survive. From his early days captaining Chelsea in 1962 and winning the 1967 FA Cup Final with Tottenham Hotspur he has always striven to be more than just a footballer. He has had a men's tailoring business in Soho, written pop songs, designed a board-game called "The Manager" and launched a chain of pubs. He even marketed Thingummywigs, a hat-cum-wig designed to be worn over curlers!

Venables was once described by Bill Shankly as "the HG Wells of football". He enjoys writing – or at least chatting into a tape-recorder with a ghost-writer. He found success in the Seventies with his *Hazell* detective novels, later turned into an ITV series starring Nicholas Ball. He shared his football philosophy in *The Best Game In The World* and hopes to publish a second autobiography, called *I Lied The First Time*.

Puffing his cigar and quaffing champagne, the ebullient, docker's son revels in his image as a wheeler-dealer. A great support is his sparky second wife Yvette, known as Toots, 16 years his junior. "She's my best friend and one of the funniest people I've ever met." He had courted her for eight years. "The only quality I had which Terry's other girlfriends lacked was an inheritance." He has two daughters, Nancy and Tracey, from an earlier marriage.

W

Wales, Prince of, 14th November 1948, His Royal Selfishness. "Being Prince of Wales is not a position it's a predicament", pronounced the future George IV. With the Queen in apparent good health, Charles could wait another 20 years to succeed her. For, although he may soon play a larger ceremonial role, deputising at investitures, state visits and the opening of Parliament, he still has no constitutional power. Despite assiduously courting Tony Blair he is likely to inherit a throne with a much diminished rôle.

The spoilt, moody and confused Dauphin was the first heir for nearly 300 years to be born without the Home Secretary being present. He again broke tradition by being educated outside Buckingham Palace, at Hill House and Cheam prep schools and Gordonstoun. He hated the hearty, non-intellectual régime at this Scottish Colditz and made few friends. His happiest moments were at Trinity, Cambridge where the Master, former Tory minister Lord Butler, proved a civilising influence. He also gave this naïve, rather lost undergraduate a key to the Lodgings where he could safely entertain his Chilean girlfriend, Lucia Santa Cruz.

Thanks to Prince Philip, Charles then wasted time in the Services. He learnt to fly jets at RAF Cranwell and nearly died during a parachute jump when his feet became entangled in the harness. He went to Dartmouth Royal Naval College before serving on HMS Norfolk, Hermes and Bronington. A period in the City, Foreign Office and Whitehall would have given him a more relevant training for the monarchy.

The future Charles III made little effort to find a suitable bride. He rejected the only contender of the right age, status and religion, Princess Marie-Astrid of Luxembourg, as well as the Queen Mother's favourite, Lady Leonora Grosvenor. Instead, he frolicked with frivolous creatures like Sabrina Guinness, Susan George, Georgiana Russell and Anna Wallace. He chose Lady Diana Spencer as much because of media pressure – how could he dump this sweet, virginal 19-year-old? – as to fulfil his duty to secure the succession. She duly supplied the heir and spare, Prince William and Prince Harry, but failed in every other respect to satisfy his complex needs. Hence his cussed refusal to give up his old flame Camilla Parker Bowles.

Diana's shocking death in 1997 made him feel guilty that he had failed to treat her better. But it now gives him an opportunity to regain his reputation by devoting himself to the upbringing of these two sensitive teenagers. He could further redeem himself by renouncing the throne in favour of his son. This would spike growing republicanism and allow William to rule as a young, untainted monarch. Only then might the public accept a Princess Camilla.

Walker, Catherine, 27th June 1946, royal seamstress. Her ballgowns, cocktail dresses and suits adorn the flanks of fashion icons like Selina Scott, Shakira Caine, Darcey Bussell, the Duchess of Westminster, Joely Richardson and Queen Noor of Jordan. Yet this tall, softly-spoken, peaceful lady is unfazed by her illustrious clients. They rely on her for their seasonal wardrobes because they trust her impeccable taste. For Princess Diana she created the refined, elegant, understated look that made her the world's most famous clothes-horse. But, unlike many royal "friends", she never exploited their connection or gossiped to the media. Indeed she turned framed photographs of Diana to the wall on the rare times that journalists entered her Chelsea design studio.

Calais-born Catherine Beheux came to London in 1970 after marrying English solicitor John Walker. With a doctorate in philosophy from Lille University she was able to find work at the French Institute and the French Embassy. Four years later her husband died in a tragic accident, leaving her to support two young daughters, Naomi and Marianne. After winning a bet to stop smoking she was able to acquire an electric sewing-machine. With no formal training she set up as a dressmaker. With her natural talent she began acquiring a fashionable clientele, mainly by word of mouth. In 1976 she founded the anonymously-named Chelsea Design Company off Fulham Road. "In France you would be laughed at if you opened a shop and put your name on the door as a couturier, unless you had the obvious skill to back it up." It was not until 1994 that she shyly restyled her two boutiques and label "Catherine Walker". While other designers vanished during the recession she has survived, mainly because she is never gimmicky or over-trendy. "I like women who wear clothes for their own pleasure, regardless of fashion. While one notices their individuality you also feel they belong together."

This hard-working recluse stoically described her breast cancer surgery in 1995 as just a "hiccup". "I told my staff three things: one, I'm going to fight it; two, I'm going to beat it; and three, it's going to be business as usual."

Walters, Julie, 22nd February 1950, Birmingham's Funny Girl. Kooky, unpredictable and versatile she has all the makings of a new

Shirley Maclaine. But, despite a 1983 Oscar nomination for *Educating Rita* and acclaim for *Stepping Out* opposite Liza Minnelli, she turned her back on Hollywood stardom. Instead she built a Laurel and Hardy combo with comedienne Victoria Wood. Walters made the perfect foil for Wood's zany humour in the award-winning series, *Wood and Walters*. Julie also scored as Adrian Mole's mum in *The Secret Diary of Adrian Mole, Aged 13 3/4*, a Lancashire landlady in BBC2's *Brazen Hussies* and Robert Lindsay's pensioner mum in C4's council-rigging drama serial *GBH*. The series, *Julie Walters and Friends*, gave her a rare opportunity to be her loud, luvvie-ish self. But why did she appear in those British "comedies", *She'll Be Wearing Pink Pyjamas* and *Car Trouble*?

Julie describes her background as "upper-working-class". Her Irish father was a builder and her domineering Catholic mother a post-office clerk. After being expelled from Holly Lodge Grammar School, Smethwick for being "subversive" she became a nurse at Queen Elizabeth's Hospital, Birmingham. A boyfriend, smitten by her exhibitionist personality and brilliant impressions, persuaded her to study drama at Manchester Poly. She has since built a career playing salty, indomitable working-class women with flashes of humour.

This fizzy, neurotic actress's trademark Restoration curls are now shorn, a sign of growing maturity. She has never married, mainly because she relishes her independence. In 1985 she met her current partner, Grant Roffey, in a Sloaney Fulham wine bar when she was "tiddly". "I bet no-one here's a member of the Labour party?", she yelled. But this former AA patrolman, seven years her junior, insisted he was and then came home to mend her washing-machine. They now live on an 70-acre West Sussex farm, rearing sheep, pigs and chickens. "It's all very organic." He acts as house-husband while she "keeps the bank manager sweet". For five years she devoted herself to finding a cure for their daughter Maisie's leukaemia. "It's just heaven seeing her normal again!"

Waterstone, Tim, 30th May 1939, maverick retailer. This cheery radical revolutionised bookselling in the Eighties with his eponymous chain of shops, with their wide stock and well-read assistants. The relaxed manner, *politesse* and twinkle in his eye is very Richard Branson. 1997 marked the beginning of a new ambition: to open children's megastores round the country, called Daisy and Tom. "It should finally end the parents' nightmare of knowing what to do with their children at weekends." As a father of three sons and five daughters from three marriages, he wants to recreate the excitement he had going to Hamley's as a child.

Glasgow-born Waterstone was the son of a First World War drum-

mer who became a tea planter in India. He went to Tonbridge
School: "I don't know where the money came from, because my
father died not leaving a cent!" After reading English at Cambridge
he joined the Calcutta broking firm Carritt Moran, where he could
"follow up ancestors who were missionaries". In 1964 he returned to
live in England, with typhoid, a wife and a child. Within months of
joining the sales department at Allied Breweries his boss died. "They
said: "You look like a nice lad", and so I became marketing manager
at only 24. It was terribly grand." He moved to WH Smith in 1973 but
lost his job eight years later. "I really was very, very unhappy there."

The would-be tycoon's timing could hardly have been worse when
he sought City backing for his first bookshop in 1982. The computer
era was allegedly threatening the written word and rival booksellers
were cutting back on branches and stock. "I was also absolutely
broke, having been wiped out by yet another divorce." Instead,
Waterstone's became one of the decade's most successful venture
capital businesses, with branches opening in nearly every major city-
centre. In 1993 Smith's decided to buy out the competition. "It was
really very funny. I told them there was a nominal £1 million on the
price for being fired!" He is said to have pocketed £9 million from the
£47 million deal. Waterstone's third wife Rosie is a TV producer 25
years his junior.

Wax Ruby, 19th April 1953, Ms American Neuroses. The intrusive
star of series like *Don't Miss Wax*, *The Full Wax* and *Ruby Wax
Meets...* hates having her own private life dissected. On TV she
hams up the brash, aggressive, strident side of her character. She
also has a strong line in self-deprecating humour. It is a mix that
works hilariously on British TV but has so far failed to find favour in
America. Too close to home?

Ruby was born in Chicago, the only daughter of Austrian-Jewish
immigrants. Her father (real name Wachs) was a wealthy sausage-
skin manufacturer and her mother an accountant. "They had no psychological understanding of me. They tried to put clamps on me."
She ran away from a Swiss finishing school after two months. She
also dropped out of a psychology course at Berkeley, California,
because she wanted to act. The only drama school that would take
her was the Royal Scottish Academy of Music and Drama in
Glasgow. With her newly-perfected English accent she joined the
Crucible Theatre in Sheffield and then spent five years with the RSC
("mostly playing wenches"). Realising she was never going to headline on Broadway she turned to writing comedy scripts for *Not The
Nine O'Clock News*. In 1985 she devised her first TV series, *Girls On
Top*, starring Dawn French, Jennifer Saunders and herself.

The sharp-witted, intuitive Ruby is a one-off comedienne. No good at stand-up, but brilliant at teasing and exposing interviewees. She persuaded former Philippines first lady Imelda Marcos to croon love songs in her drawing-room, Sarah Duchess of York to reveal her kitchen secrets and Hollywood actress Sharon Stone to discuss her sex life. She always bonds better with women than men.

This 5ft 2ins chatterbox is over a foot shorter than her "terribly English" husband, TV director husband Ed Bye. They married in 1986 after meeting on the set of *Girls on Top*. "I thought he was too tall for me and too nice." She rarely discusses her brief first and second marriages. The Byes live in a swanky Holland Park house, with their three children, Max, Madeleine and Marina, and employ three servants. In real life Ruby Wax is softer, pleasanter and thinner than her TV persona.

Wellesley, Lady Jane, 6th July 1951, television's first Lady. The so-called Curse of Prince Charles has afflicted the marital chances of several ex-girlfriends. Like heiress Sabrina Guinness she has never married, but has instead fulfilled her own quite unexpected destiny – as a television producer. As the Duke of Wellington's only daughter she was expected to marry within that exclusive milieu. The Dukes of Westminster, Roxburghe or Atholl would have made splendid matches. She grew up at Stratfield Saye, the historic mansion near Basingstoke, presented to the Iron Duke after the Battle of Waterloo. Her London address when she did the Season was the family apartment at Apsley House overlooking Hyde Park Corner.

This industrious, slightly mischievous, former journalist never uses her title. She began in television on the *Radio Times* and was a researcher on Robert Kee's award-winning 1980 documentary series, *Ireland: A Television History*. She founded Warner Sisters (sic) with her business partner Lavinia Warner in 1984. Their credits include *Selling Hitler*, *Rides*, *A Village Affair* and *Dressing for Breakfast*.

Jane's friendship with Charles began with children's parties at Buckingham Palace. She was his girlfriend for two years after Camilla Shand married Andrew Parker Bowles in 1973. While out shooting with Jane on the Wellingtons' 30,000-acre estate near Granada she was observed pulling the Prince's hair and "playfully throwing melons at him". Marriage rumours grew when he invited her to Sandringham for the New Year celebrations and 10,000 people turned up to see them attend Sunday matins. "Such was their conviction", Charles later said, "that I almost felt I'd better espouse myself at once so as not to disappoint them!" The relationship fizzled out because neither was ready to settle down. Afterwards she enjoyed a long friendship with TV presenter Melvyn Bragg.

Wesley, Mary, 24th June 1912, literary institution. Spry, disciplined and energetic, this Grandma Moses of fiction can show up women nearly half her age. She published her first bestseller, *Jumping The Queue*, aged 70 and followed it with eight more, including *Harnessing Peacocks* and *Part of The Furniture*. Ageist journalists professed amazement at their raunchiness, as if they expected her to have traded her sexuality for a bus pass at 60. A more positive critic described her as "a master at peeling back the layers of relationships to reveal the passion and despair that lie below the surface". She herself describes writing as "a sort of illness, a compulsion, something extremely painful that one has to do".

This elegant colonel's daughter with her halo of thick white hair adopted the name "Mary Wesley" because her real one, Mary Siepmann, sounded uncommercial. A Roman Catholic convert she lives in an idyllic Totnes cottage in Devon. She is really rather grand, related to the Duke of Wellington through her mother. During World War II she found the air raids "absolute heaven! I'd be taken out of bed down to the servants' hall, wrapped up in eider-downs and given cocoa and ginger biscuits by the cook". While a debutante she developed her Socialist leanings, dishing out food to down-and-outs from a stall near Waterloo station. She then read international politics at the LSE.

At 25 Mary married barrister Lord Swinfen and had two children, the present peer and literary agent Toby Eady. After their 1945 divorce she married author Eric Siepmann, who encouraged her to write children's books. After his death she tried adult fiction, but *Jumping The Queue* was rejected by five publishers. The second, *The Camomile Lawn*, sold over 500,000 copies and was later turned into a TV serial, starring Tara Fitzgerald. "I hated all those nude scenes – quite out of keeping with the period, as there was no central heating in those days. We'd have frozen to death!"

Westminster, Duke of, 22nd December 1951, Britain's richest landowner, nicknamed "Himself" by his peasantry. He can trace his ancestry back to William the Conqueror's senior huntsman, Hugh Le Gros Veneur. Only the Queen can rival his real estate portfolio, worth some £3 billion. It includes: 300 acres of Mayfair and Belgravia, 13,000 acres of Cheshire, 12,000 acres of Vancouver and a 10,000-acre Australian sheep station.

Ulster-born Gerald Westminster is tougher and more together than he looks. He may only have achieved two O-levels at Harrow but such was his sporting prowess that Fulham Football Club offered him a trial. On leaving school he sweated as an "ordinary" cowboy in British Columbia and New Zealand. He came into this vast inheritance aged 21, thanks to a canny will devised by the legendary four-times-married second duke, "Bendor", who died in 1953. To save death duties, he bypassed the elderly heirs who were to become third, fourth and fifth Dukes.

His Grace has enjoyed a scandal-free existence envied by his pal Prince Charles. In 1978 he disappointed the fortune hunters by marrying "Tally" Phillips, grand-daughter of the Queen's close friend Lady Zia Wernher. After having two daughters, Lady Tamara and Lady Edwina, she finally produced an heir, Earl Grosvenor, in 1991 and a further daughter Lady Viola. The duke travels by private Cessna between London and Eaton Hall. He has recently remodelled this ugly Sixties building – which replaced the former Victorian mansion, with its 600 ft frontage – in Cheshire Tudor style.

Westminster, a Territorial officer for over 20 years, was chuffed to be promoted to Colonel in 1992. He shows less willpower trying to give up his Marlboros! Already patron of some 150 charities, he receives hundreds of begging letters a month. In 1997 he mysteriously announced that doctors had advised him to take a three-month break from his responsibilities.

Westwood, Vivienne, 8th April 1941, former punk prophet, now Queen of street-cred. She is the maverick designer who gave the world bondage trousers, razor-slashed sleeveless vests and peek-a-boo bottom flaps. Now married to Austrian toy boy Andreas Kronthaler, she has confounded the fashion industry by going legit and running a business worth £20 million. But she still keeps her old Clapham council flat where she once lived with former Sex Pistols manager Malcolm McLaren.

The rag trade originally branded Vivienne just another King's Road flash-in-the-pan, even though she designed for Boy George, Adam Ant and Bananarama. They would steal her original ideas and mass-produce them. She then surprised critics by opening a Mayfair salon and twice being voted 'designer of the year'. She still describes the fashion world as "just a big hype-machine".

Mercurial Vivienne's weird personal packaging belies her extraordinary talent and business acumen. She appears shy, scatterbrained and easy-going, yet runs a successful business in a notoriously cutthroat world. She drones on in that quiet *Coronation Street* accent, very serious and yet crazy. She once appeared on a TV chat show wearing a see-through green jumpsuit stitched with strategic figleaves. In 1992 she revealed for photographers that she was wearing no knickers when collecting her OBE from the Queen!

But the wacky designer grew up conventionally in the Derbyshire Peak District village of Tintwistle. Her shopkeeper father played in the local brass band and her mother was a mill worker. Viv studied at Harrow School of Art and became a schoolteacher. Aged 21 she married Hoover factory worker Derek Westwood, by whom she has a photographer son Ben. Meeting McLaren in 1975 changed her life.

They opened Seditionaries, a tiny Chelsea boutique with distorting mirrors, to sell rubber body suits, fake fur G-strings and other punk paraphernalia. Fashion editors soon pounced on Westwood originals, like her conical external bra which made wearers look like Martians and her medieval tunics with giant polka-dots. "Fashion is about sex." But she eventually felt unable to cope with her lover's anarchic nonsense ("it was like having ten children") and he decamped to California. Their son Joe founded a Soho lingerie boutique called Agent Provocateur.

White, Marco Pierre, 11th December 1961, reformed Brat Pack chef. Arrogance is a main ingredient in this temperamental genius's complex personality. Women find him irresistible while men find his broody Hamlet image interferes with their appreciation of his culinary talents. But no other cook of his age, let alone a Brit, has ever won three Michelin stars. His limitless ambition will perhaps one day enable us to buy Big Marco Burgers or Pierre White milkshakes in every high street.

Despite his plummy accent, the wild-haired McEnroe of the Magimix was raised on a Leeds council estate and went to the local comprehensive. His Italian mother died when he was six and he describes his father as a "wheeler-dealer". At 17 Marco became a kitchen porter at the Hotel St George, Harrogate. Instead of going to catering school – "college lecturers don't know the back end of a chicken" – he trained at Le Gavroche under Albert Roux whom he regards as his mentor. White enjoyed whirlwind success with his first restaurant Harvey's in South London, even though he admits the original decor resembled "a posh toilet". He became a teenybopper Peter Langan, lambasting customers and journalists who displeased him. "I was young, egotistical and silly", he reflects. Some critics think he still is.

The tousled superchef's flagship is the magnificent Oak Room of Piccadilly's Meridien Hotel, which he took over (together with the management of six other hotel restaurants) in 1997. He is also involved in the Criterion and Quo Vadis. But his partnership with Michael Caine in The Canteen ended acrimoniously when the superstar insisted on putting bangers and mash on the menu. He annoys other chefs by "overpaying" his staff.

Teetotal White blames the break-up of his first marriage to sur-geon's daughter Alex McArthur on his relentless pursuit of Michelin glory. They have a daughter Letticia Rose. He was then married for four months to model Lisa Butcher. His personal life has become calmer, but he will never be a home bod. He has two children, Luciano and Marco, from his Spanish girlfriend Mati. When the pressure builds up he goes fishing.

White, Michael, 16th January 1936, party-loving impresario, nick-named Chalky. He is a shrewd, tough operator who constantly gam-bles on his remarkably catholic taste and judgement. "I must be the only person in Britain to have gone to see *Götterdammerung* one night and Oasis the next." He has London's best "little black book" of eligible women. It was he who introduced Prince Charles to Sabrina Guinness and Prince Andrew to Koo Stark.

This stage-struck, Glasgow businessman's son was schooled in Switzerland because of his asthma and then studied comparative lit-erature at the Sorbonne. He briefly worked on the New York Stock Exchange before spending five years as West End producer Peter Daubeny's assistant. In 1961 he formed his own theatrical produc-tion company, initially enjoying huge success, with hit musicals such as *Oh, Calcutta!*, *The Rocky Horror Show*, *A Chorus Line*, *Annie* and *The Pirates of Penzance*. He also suffered notable failures like *Y*, *Dracula* and *Flowers for Algernon*. His success rate plunged in the Eighties, partly because of his attempts to become a Hollywood film producer. He produced comedies like *Monty Python and The Holy Grail*, *The Supergrass* and *Nuns On The Run*. His wiry, bespectacled figure can also be glimpsed as a film extra in Art Garfunkel's thriller, *Good To Go*. His recent stage hits *Crazy For You*, *She Loves Me* and *Fame* have begun to restore his batting average.

Gentle-mannered Chalky has always maintained a high social pro-file, frequenting major premières, dining in chic restaurants, bop-ping at trendy discos and hosting parties at his immaculate Knightsbridge home. He is always surrounded by beautiful models and actresses. No wonder those noted Lotharios Jack Nicholson, Mick Jagger and Michael Douglas are among his best friends. In 1985 he was teasingly said to have "won the pools without filling in a coupon" when he married Louise Moores, a hippy heiress 26 years younger. She was the grand-daughter of Littlewood Pools co-founder Cecil Moores. They had a son, Benji, but split up in 1991. He had earlier brought up the three daughters from his 1965 marriage to ex-model Sarah Hillsdon. But his most enduring relationship was with Australian TV reporter Lyndall Hobbs, now Al Pacino's girlfriend.

William, Prince, 21st June 1982, post-Millennium sovereign. On this shy Etonian's slender shoulders rests the future of the House of Windsor. Untainted by scandal he can repair the damage wrought by his parents, uncles and aunts. Alas, he is unlikely to reign until the middle of the next century unless Prince Charles bows to public opinion and allows the Crown to skip a generation. As William V he will become the 42nd monarch since William the Conqueror and the most British one since James 1. Even then, his blood is only 39 per cent English (16 per cent Scottish and six per cent Irish, with German, American, Danish and Russian corpuscles thrown in).

Charles broke tradition by being present in the Lindo wing of St Mary's Paddington when royal gynaecologist Sir George Pinker delivered William. The baby prince initially had more parental attention and love than any of his nanny-reared predecessors. Charles even learned to change nappies. As a toddler "Willie Wombat" once dangled his brother, Prince Harry, out of an upstairs window! His first public duty, aged four, was as a page at his Uncle Andrew's wedding to Fergie in Westminster Abbey. Princess Diana later chided him for pulling the bridesmaids' hair and giggling. He learnt early the travails of being a royal when a paparazzo snapped him having a pee in the school playground. By six he was turning into a spoilt brat. "Put me down at once, don't you know who I am?" he once roared at a sculptor who dared to pick him up. And to a play-mate: "When I'm King I'm going to send around my knights to kill you!"

Wills began at boarding school, Ludgrove, aged eight. Masters hid the tabloids from him but failed to stop sneaky pupils teasing him about his parents' indiscretions. He excelled on the football field and in school holidays became a keen participant in all blood sports. But his academic standards would never have won him a place at Eton had royal strings not been pulled. Already taller than his father, he will soon become Europe's most eligible bachelor. He will then face an ordeal by paparazzi, whom he will forever associate with the death of his mother.

Wilson, Richard, 9th July 1936, forever Victor Meldrew. Listen closely to this cult actor's fastidious Scots accent and he could be Ronnie Corbett. Although raised on a Strathclyde council estate he has spent most of his adult life down South. Fellow Greenock High School pupils branded his acting ambitions "cissy" while his drama teacher scoffed: "Don't be silly, boy, you can't speak properly!" Instead he became a lab technician and did his national service with the Army Medical Corps. He finally reached RADA at 27. For almost two decades he specialised in vicars, doctors and other supporting rôles. Indeed, he was almost more respected as a stage director.

In 1990 BBC1's *One Foot In The Grave* transformed his life, sometimes attracting a record 20 million viewers. The curmudgeonly Meldrew's cry "I don't beleeeve it" has entered our lexicon of historic outbursts. Interviewers find him every bit as grumpy: quick to complain about "fatuous" questions, correct any politically incorrect remark and ban them smoking. "The tight smile that acknowledges my excuse for lack of punctuality (the traffic) is about as unforgiving as an executioner's." Even he admits that "sometimes people back off a little when they meet me". He resembles a macho Jean Brodie, his precision and prissiness alternating with an unexpected dandyish and fun-loving side. He plays fiercely competitive squash twice a week, has a rigorous exercise programme and, though he adores wine, is teetotal three days a week.

Brought up a strict Presbyterian this truculent, Clydeside shipworker's son is now an atheist. "Were I to be reincarnated I'd come back exactly as I am, with hair." As a child he suffered from an inferiority complex caused by his scrawny physique. "I used to put up prayers to God that I would get fatter – now I wish I hadn't said those prayers!" A fiercely self-protective bachelor he hates outsiders visiting his Hampstead home or prying into his life. "The less people know about me the more I can fool them. Acting should be a metamorphic process." Though unattached, he is no hermit, hosting wild Hogmanay parties with a piper playing a lament in the garden.

Winner, Michael, 30th October 1935, professional Mr Moan. The once aggressive, foul-mouthed film director has mellowed a bit since *Death Wish*. In 1984 he even founded the Police Memorial Trust following the murder of WPC Yvonne Fletcher outside the Libyan Embassy in London. He then fronted the ITV series, *Michael Winner's True Crimes,* in which notorious murders and fraud cases were recreated. Independently wealthy, he travels the world with the latest of his young companions, fitness instructor Vanessa Perry. She seems to have had little effect on this increasingly corpulent, red-faced figure.

Winner, a property tycoon's son, was raised in the Holland Park mansion where he still lives. His beloved mother, Helen, spent a long widowhood in Cannes, gambling away an estimated £3 million of her son's inheritance. As a boarder at a Quaker co-ed school in Hertfordshire he was only allowed vegetarian food. During school holidays he wrote a showbiz column for his local newspaper. After Cambridge he became a trainee gossip columnist on the *Evening*

Standard. But he was sacked for inventing a frisky debutante called "Venetia Crust", the life and soul of every ball. Her father "Arnold Crust" still survives as Winner's photographic *nom de plume* in his *Sunday Times* restaurant column.

Winner prospered throughout the Sixties as a film director, producer and screenwriter, with such forgettable titles as *Play It Cool* and *I'll Never Forget What's 'is Name*. Westerns and action films followed like *Lawman*, *The Nightcomers*, *Chato's Land* and *The Stone Killer*. But his real bonanza were *Death Wish* in 1974 and its two sequels, starring Charles Bronson as a sadistic vigilante. In 1988 Winner won rare praise for *A Chorus of Disapproval*, featuring his then girlfriend Jenny Seagrove, Jeremy Irons and Anthony Hopkins. A brief fling with a young starlet in his 1993 film *Dirty Weekend* led to a kiss 'n' tell story in which she 'outed' his enormous Y-fronts.

When his Hollywood career ran out of puff, Winner re-invented himself as a crotchety restaurant critic. His flash gimmick was to arrive by helicopter or Bentley, order the most expensive claret and then start an argument. He berates *maître d*'s for giving him a 'bad' table or insisting that he wears a tie. Gruesome.

Winslet, Kate, 5th October 1975, Queen of Corsage. This superstar prodigy is on track to being a cerebral version of Sharon Stone. Blonde, fresh-faced and bee-sting lipped she is described as having "Lauren Bacall's strength and Nicola Pagett's sweetness". Add to that Emma Thompson's articulacy and wisdom. But first she must brush up her off-screen wardrobe and not slop around in Doc Marten grunge with a fag hanging from her lips.

Kate's career rocketed in 1996 when she played Emma Thompson's sister in *Sense and Sensibility*. She won a Golden Globe and Oscar 'best newcomer' nomination. Kenneth Branagh chose her to play Ophelia in his film version of *Hamlet*. While filming she enjoyed a three-month fling with hunky co-star, Rufus Sewell. It perhaps helped to mend her heart after her break-up with actor Stephen Tredre, her boyfriend since she was 15.

The 5ft 6ins Kate comes from a close theatrical family. She was a chubby child but managed to slim down to her present eight-and-a-half stone after joining Weightwatchers and briefly bordered on anorexic. The "fatty" teasing only stopped when she enrolled at Redroofs drama school in Maidenhead. "I used to be so nervous about exposing my body that I went into high anxiety overdrive. I starved myself, drank too much coffee and smoked too many cigarettes." By 20 she was a fully-fledged film star, making her debut as a homicidal teenager in *Heavenly Creatures*. In *Jude* she had her first nude scene, in which co-star Christopher Ecclestone passionately kissed her breasts. "Eek! I haven't dared watch it with my parents. It would be too embarrassing."

Kate made her Hollywood debut in the 1997 blockbuster *Titanic*. Afterwards she had to make a public apology to director James Cameron for unflattering comments she had made about him.

Wise, Greg, 15th May 1966, brooding beefcake. He smouldered his way to the top of the blouse-and-breeches brigade in *The Buccaneers*, *The Moonstone* and *Sense and Sensibility*. He was helped by his relationship with award-winning actress Emma Thompson, which began in 1994. Her heart apparently skipped a beat when he arrived on the set of *Sense and Sensibility* clad in long leather riding boots and a silk brocade waistcoat. "8.20am. Greg Wise turned up to ride, full of beans and looking gorgeous", she wrote in her diary. "Ruffled all our feathers a bit." Days later she added that "it was like having a colt in the make-up caravan".

Wise grew up in Newcastle, the son of an English father and Serbo-Croat mother, both architects. He graduated in architecture himself and maintains it is "more important to leave a beautiful building behind than a film". After studying drama in Glasgow he took a year off, travelling round the Far East. "My priorities were getting healthy and discovering a different outlook on life." His first break was playing toffish Alister in BBC1's comic drama *The Riff Raff Element*, about two families from different backgrounds sharing a Lancashire stately home. Wilkie Collins's period piece *The Moonstone* provided his first opportunity to swashbuckle.

This guitar-playing thespian infuriates male journalists with his smugness, preciousness and inscrutability, particularly over his relationship with Emma. "I give an impression of arrogance, apparently. Those who bother to get to know me soon change their minds." But female hacks drool over his "dark-eyed good looks and heart-stopping profile".

Wood, Victoria,19th May 1953, Alan Bennett in a skirt. This award-winning playwright and comedienne claims to gargle with Fairy Liquid to keep her tonsils in shape. In her trademark loose jackets and trousers she can fill the Royal Albert Hall for 15 nights running. TV showcases like *Victoria Wood Now* and *An Audience With Victoria Wood* artfully bridge the gap between comedy as a hip diversion for thirtysomethings and mass entertainment such as *The Two Ronnies*. But she denies her scripts are "cosy and domestic". "I'm quite subversive really."

The Manchester-born comic superstar used to be "fat, spotty, shy
and skint. I grew up with chip butties in the blood." After Bury
Grammar School she studied drama at Birmingham University. In
1975 she was runner-up to Marti Caine in the talent contest *New
Faces* and later wrote topical songs for BBC1's *That's Life*. Her partnership with comedienne Julie Walters led to the hilarious *Wood
and Walters* sketch shows. Most of her material comes from things
that happen to her in real life. After a night out in Soho once she
remarked to a friend outside the Groucho Club how "nice it was that
no-one recognised me". An autograph-hunter suddenly appeared,
gushing "You're my favourite, Pam. I know all your poems by heart."
Victoria dutifully signed: "Love from Pam Ayres."

This down-to-earth, self-proclaimed "fat frump" is actually an elegant nine stone who cares nought about designer clothes, status
symbols or showbiz falderols. She enjoys a quiet, if luxurious, life in
Highgate with her husband, Geoffrey Durham "who's as barmy as
me!" She married this magician (aka The Great Soprendo) in 1980
and they have two children, Grace and Henry.

Worrall Thompson, Antony, 1st May 1952, culinary controversialist with Henry VIII features. It is hard to keep up with this mercurial character. He has married three times, gone bust once and is a
Meilleur Ouvrier de Grande Bretagne (the cook's Brit award). His
rotund, bearded presence is constantly glimpsed on TV series like
Ready, Steady, Cook and *Masterchef*. Until 1997 he was in charge of
14 major London restaurants, including 190 Queensgate, the Atrium
and Zoe. He now has a North Kensington restaurant called Woz.

Worrall Thompson's parents, both actors, split up when he was
three. He was a problem child who boasts of having "thrown pots of
paint at Rolls-Royces". His grandmother, a general's widow, paid his
fees at King's School, Canterbury. "She treated me like the son she
lost in the war and wanted me to join the Army." Instead he did a
hotel management course at Westminster College. Despite his cuddly charm his manner still infuriates former employers like John
Brinkley and Dan Whitehead. Cheekily he called his first restaurant, in Knightsbridge, Ménage à Trois. "I was sleeping with someone I shouldn't have been at the time. Something like The Boss, The
Cook, His Wife and Her Lover." He introduced the filo parcel to fashionable eating, rediscovered the lentil and was one of the first chefs
to serve baked garlic as a vegetable.

The most dramatic event in Wozza's life happened when his face
was badly mangled in a school rugby scrum. He had to wait until he
was 21 to have plastic surgery and spent 12 weeks in hospital afterwards. "Until then I couldn't bear even to look at a woman because I

felt so disfigured." In 1974 he married his first wife Jill whom he met while working at an Essex hostelry called Ye Olde Logge. His second wife was an Australian backpacker called Militza. They had two sons, Blake and Simon, who now both live in Melbourne. His roving days seem to be over, with his discovery of Jacinta, a former Stringfellow's waitress. "When I first met Antony I thought he was a pumped-up *prima donna* who floated around thinking he was God." Even so, she became the third "and final" Mrs WT in 1996. They live near Henley-on-Thames with their children, Toby and Billie-Lara.

Wogan, Terry, 3rd August 1938, the Blarney Tone. His Hibernian jolliness and impish wit daily charm his R2 listeners. Subliminally he helps to balance Ireland's IRA-battered image. His mocking ad-libs and raised eyebrows have even brightened stilted BBC perennials like *Come Dancing*, *Miss World* and *The Eurovision Song Contest*. "TV suits me because I'm very lazy and don't really want to work for a living". Producers complain he rarely reads a script or briefing note in advance.

Limerick-born Wogan studied under the Jesuits and read philosophy at Belvedere College, Dublin. His father Michael was managing director of a grocery and off-licence chain. Young Tel spent five years as a Bank of Ireland cashier, becoming "probably the best soiled-note sorter in banking's history". In 1961 he began on RTE Dublin reading out the cattle market reports and was soon a station announcer. He moved to BBC Radio in 1965 and landed *The Terry Wogan Show* four years later. His "foight-the-flab" campaign and constant jests about BBC1's *Dallas* and rival DJ Jimmy Young's age soon made him a national institution. After compering BBC1's game show *Blankety Blank* he landed his thrice-weekly chat show, *Wogan*. One critic described how he gently conducted celebs, wannabees and has-beens through a well-rehearsed advertorial routine. "You're wonderful aren't you? And so am I to be sure, ha ha. Now would you like to tell us about your new film/song/play/book? Thank you, the very best of luck to you..."

While interviewing Broadway composer Marvin Hamlisch once our Tel congratulated him on his "marvelous show, *Company*". "Would you like me to impersonate Stephen Sondheim?", the nettled star replied. When Wogan was finally axed in 1992, he showed a remarkable ego-effacement when he slunk back to his old R2 slot. But BBC honchoes keep rewarding his loyalty with easy presenting jobs like *Children In Need*, *The National Lottery* and *Auntie's Sporting Bloomers*.

Away from the razzamatazz this roguish, winsome, flirtatious paddy remains a very private man, preferring his Maidenhead mansion to showbiz parties and flash restaurants. He married his wife, former model Helen, in 1965 and they have three children, journalist Alan, TV chef Mark and PR-girl Katherine. Their first-born Vanessa died of a heart condition at three weeks. Tabloids have always failed to reveal a malicious side to him. Like the good Catholic boy he is, you won't find him keeping a mistress, drinking the Liffey dry or scandalizing the neighbours with nude sunbathing. If you really want to rile him mention hair-weaves, middle-aged paunches or writing his biography.

Wyman, Bill, 24th October 1936, former Dirty Old Man of Pop. This born-again family man and Sticky Fingers restaurateur spent 20 years as the invisible Rolling Stone. He plunked his bass guitar expressionlessly while Mick Jagger and Keith Richard cavorted cen-tre-stage, and he let them to steal all the glory in interviews. Then that mini-skirted Brigitte Bardot, Mandy Smith, swept him off his feet and into the tabloids. She was 13 when they first met and he narrowly avoided prosecution for having sex with a minor. Once asked his girlfriend's age by Michael Caine, he replied with charac-teristic dry wit: "About as old as your suit, Michael." The Wyman's 1989 marriage barely lasted two years and he was miffed when his son Stephen then dated Mandy's mother Patsy.

The monosyllabic, bricklayer's son from Penge was born Bill Perks. In the early Sixties he began jamming with a quartet of long-haired Teddy-boys led by the late Brian Jones. The Stones' rough blues songs and outrageous lifestyles contrasted with the Beatles' purer sound and image. The Stones' hits like *It's All Over Now*, *Little Red Rooster* and *Satisfaction* have become pop's national anthems constantly played in discos and "golden oldie" radio shows. It explains why, even though he left the group in 1992, he is worth an estimated £50 million.

Leathery-faced Wyman's first marriage to childhood sweetheart Diane was concealed for five years to protect the Stones' image. Stephen was born and they divorced in 1969. He then spent the next two decades bonking for Britain. He once boasted he had bedded 278 women between 1963 and 1965. As the group's honorary archivist he is good with statistics. "You can't overdose on ladies", he explained. Well, eventually he did. In 1993 he married Californian fashion-designer Suzanne Accosta and vowed his Errol Flynn days were over. He is a doting daddy to their daughter Katharine. He mainly lives in his 15th century moated Suffolk mansion, Gedding Hall, where he plays with his metal detector. His proudest boast is that he has never touched drugs.

XYZ

Yates, Paula, 24th April 1960, ageing *femme fatale*. This pocket-sized Janet Street-Porter with Fergie-like pretensions thrives on being provocative. "I always spray perfume on myself where I want to be kissed," she once observed, "and that means I spray it ALL over!" Her father, Jess Yates, was the sanctimonious presenter of ITV's *Stars on Sunday* who ran off with a showgirl. Her mother, Heller Toren, is a former Bluebell Girl who writes sexy novels. Predictably, their skinny, peroxide-blonde daughter became a tearaway at St Clare's School, Oxford. For a jape she once posed naked at the Reform Club for a Penthouse centrefold. As an 18-year-old punk she developed a crush on rising pop star Bob Geldof and was nicknamed "the Limpet" because she pursued him so relentlessly. He finally succumbed in Paris and the pair spent the next 19 years together.

Cannily, Paula used her inside track to write gossip columns in the *Record Mirror* and the *News of the World*. For a photographic book, *Rock Stars in their Underpants*, she enticed friends – from Duran Duran to Spandau Ballet – to strip off. In 1982 she became co-host of C4's *The Tube*, a chaotic pop show featuring top bands from Elton John to Frankie Goes to Hollywood. On ITV's *Sex With Paula* she interviewed pop stars about their private lives, a format she repeated on C4's *The Big Breakfast* where she reclined on a king-size bed trying to stifle her yawns.

Shortly before Fifi Trixibelle was born in 1983, Paula announced that it would be "wally and wet" to marry just because she was pregnant. They did marry three years later and then had Peaches and Pixie. But their marital vows never prevented either from pursuing independent lives. In 1995 she fell for Australian rock star Michael Hutchence, had her breasts cosmetically enlarged and gave birth to another daughter, Heavenly Hiraani. After their divorce Paula, bitter at being portrayed as the scarlet lady, insisted: "Bob isn't the saint that he'd like the world to think he is."

York, Duke of, 19th February 1960, the Queen's favourite child, aka Duke of Pork. Fergie's cuckolded ex-husband regained his enthusiasm for life following his 1997 romance with BBC researcher Henriette Peace. But for how long?

Named after his grandfather Prince Andrew of Greece, the Duke was a cheerful, smiley child. But he was so mollycoddled by the Queen that royal servants called him Andy Pandy and his low profile led to rumours that he was handicapped in some way. He went to Heatherdown prep school but came into his own at Gordonstoun where he captained the cricket team, played hockey and enjoyed romances with two female pupils. Academically he was slow, but compensated by becoming a practical joker, once even placing a whoopee cushion on the Queen's favourite chair.

Sarah Ferguson thought she was marrying a glamorous war hero when she walked up the aisle at Westminster Abbey in 1986. Andrew's bravery during the Falklands War had done wonders to his lightweight "Randy Andy" image. But he proved to be the archetypal himbo, with a very narrow view of the world, and unable to control her. His previous relationships were all short-term and included baronet's daughter Vicki Hodge who kissed 'n' told about their frolics on a West Indies beach. He would have been wiser to have married the discreet Koo Stark. Unfortunately her naughty past as a soft-porn actress ruled her out. Following the break-up with his wife, he dated Lord Braybrooke's daughter Cazzy Neville and former model Catrina Skepper, but they married other people.

Today Lieut-Commdr the Duke of York faces an uncertain future. He has a desk job in Whitehall and must leave the Royal Navy in 1999 without having achieved his birthright of becoming an admiral. He could cut rather a tragic figure, with no constitutional rôle and limited job prospects. The only benefit from his scandal-ridden decade with Fergie are his delightful daughters Princess Beatrice and Princess Eugenie. His abiding ambition is to raise his golf handicap of eight.

York, Sarah Duchess of, 15th October 1959, royal albatross. It was a tragedy for the House of Windsor when Sarah Ferguson joined them in 1986. Her vulgarity, spend-spend philosophy and infidelities with Steve Wyatt and John Bryan knocked platinum nails into the royal family's coffin. Yet it all began with her being welcomed as a youthful and lively addition. Even her background apparently boded well. Her father, Major Ronald Ferguson had served in the Life Guards and commanded the Sovereign's escort. He played polo with Prince Philip and Prince Charles and became the latter's polo manager. Her mother Susan was Viscount Powerscourt's niece and a noted Society beauty. Alas, this chummy redhead turned out to have inherited the worst of her parents' character traits.

Fergie had a traditional horsey childhood living on an 800-acre Hampshire farm. The break-up of her parents' 18-year marriage in

1974 was probably most responsible for her emotional instability. At Hurst Lodge School she was head girl and obtained six O-levels ("A-levels? You must be joking!") Afterwards she took the familiar Sloane route: Queen's Secretarial College in South Kensington, cookery lessons and a laid-back first job with Knightsbridge PR-man Neil Durden-Smith. For two years she romanced Kim Smith-Bingham, a rangy Old Etonian who ran a ski equipment firm in Switzerland. Aged 22 she took off on a year's South American odyssey, dropping in on the remote Argentinian *estancia* of her polo-playing stepfather Hector Barrantes.

Freckly Fergie then worked for a flat letting agency and for Covent Garden gallery owner William Drummond. Her new love was Paddy McNally, a rich widower 22 years her senior. She would spend the winter skiing and running his palatial chalet in Verbier. She married Prince Andrew on the rebound, only 12 months after McNally had rejected her "marry me or I'm leaving" ultimatum. The Yorks' marriage quickly deteriorated, with Fergie wanting to party and her husband happy slouched in front of the telly watching *Rambo* videos. His long periods at sea on naval manoeuvres added to the strain. It led to her seeking comfort with American playboy Steve Wyatt in 1990 and then her "financial adviser" John Bryan. But, despite her sexual peccadilloes and gallivanting round the world to clear her £4 million debts, she has been a good mother to Princess Beatrice and Princess Eugenie.

York, Peter, 10th November 1946, the man who invented the Sloane Ranger, aka Peter Wallis. This black-bouffanted social anthropologist spent a busy ten years as style editor of *Harpers & Queen*, mainly dividing its readers into tribal identities. His *Sloane Ranger Handbook*, compiled with his mentor Ann Barr, taught "noovs" how to behave properly, what to wear, where to shop and how to pronounce Cholmondeley.

This buzzy style *aficionado* comes from a left-wing Hampstead background. His civil engineer father designed bridges and sent him to a "progressive" day school, King Alfred's in Hampstead. He only started in journalism at 26 and never learned to type. Until his early-40s he wore a distinctive Fifties Teddy boy look: greased Presley quiff, dark zoot suits and winkle picker shoes. A wealthy, self-made bachelor he used to escort fashion journalist Lendal Scott-Ellis and eccentric oil heiress Olga Deterding. A wit once described his dancing style as "stiff in all the wrong places". Today his elegant, Regency house near Marble Arch is a shrine not only to his earning power but to his good taste. His collection of modern art includes Augustus Johns, Laura Knights and Osbert Lancasters.

The debonair, lateral-minded Peter Wallis adopted the macho "York" as his *nom de plume* to prevent confusion with his main business as a management consultant. His company, SRU, began by advising clients like Bergasol, the Milk Marketing Board and Levi Jeans. Labour spin doctor Peter Mandelson was among SRU's employees and remains a close friend of York. Nowadays he advises the EMI group, Kingfisher and WH Smith. "As a journalist I wrote essentially frivolous stuff which perhaps lacked the intellectual gravitas that my clients expected." York/Wallis is also a peripheral member of 'the great and the good', chairing a high-powered DTI committee on leisure and the media.

Young, Richard, 17th September 1947, the "Beigel Snapper". This leather-jacketed highwayman with a Leica has joined the ranks of David Bailey, Lord Snowdon and Barry Lategan with his classic images of Café Society. The outsider has become the insider. He still tears round London on his Harley-Davidson to loiter by Tramp, Daphne's and Annabel's. But, thanks to friendly PRs and Society contacts, he is now often the only photographer who is allowed into the party.

A bleeped tip-off from one of his "deep throats" can change the course of social history, revealing a pop star's new romance, a playboy's infidelity or a supermodel's pregnancy. He has caroused with Jack Nicholson and had his camera smashed by Roman Polanski. Hours later Rex Features will be syndicating his 'hot' pictures round the world. "Richard is the only man in London who can grease his way through a door without opening it," said the late Mayfair restaurateur Peter Langan.

This Rasputin-bearded charmer left his Hackney secondary school at 15, without O' or A-levels. He developed his 'people skills' flogging shirts and ties on his father's Soho barrow. He then hung out in Chelsea, selling menswear in King's Road boutiques and developing his musical talents. He spent four years in New York, working as a window dresser and recording engineer.

Young began his career as a photographer in 1974. Thanks to a journalist friend he took the first photograph of tycoon J Paul Getty's grandson after kidnappers had released him, minus an ear. He also obtained exclusive snaps of the 50th birthday party Liz Taylor threw for Richard Burton in 1975, by sneaking into the Dorchester as part of the band!

Young goes jogging, and rarely touches alcohol. His anchor is his jewellery designer wife Susan, whom he married in 1985 after his first wife, Finnish former *au pair* Riitta, died of cancer. Susan, mother of his daughter Hannah, has been a brilliant stepmother to his sons Danny and Sammy. Their North Kensington house is a shrine to Young's two hobbies: rock music and Harley-Davidsons.

Zeta Jones, Catherine, 25th September 1969, Welsh stunna. She leapt to fame as Mariette in ITV's *The Darling Buds of May* and was dubbed the new Greta Scacchi. Unfortunately she believed the publicity and turned down TV parts to try her luck in Hollywood. She chose three duds, *Splitting Heirs*, with Eric Idle, the surfing movie *Blue Juice* and *Catherine the Great*. Her attempts to make a hit single also failed. Now, despite earning better notices as a leather-clad villain in *The Phantom*, her career needs hauling back on the rails. Otherwise she may fall victim to Diana Dors Syndrome, and be better known for her cleavage and men than her acting.

Raised near Swansea, Catherine remains close to her parents. She won a Butlin's talent show aged ten and began her professional career in 1980 in the musical *Annie*. She became a dancer, touring the country in shows like *The Pyjama Game*. She was in the West End musical *42nd Street* when she unexpectedly won the part of the innocent Mariette in 1991. Ironically, she had just stripped off to play a slave girl in the French film *Scheherazade* and appeared topless in a BBC play, *Out of the Blue*.

This voluptuous heart-breaker has enjoyed a busy social life. Her first love was film producer Nick Hamm, but his age and grey ponytail were said to have upset her parents. She became briefly engaged to former *Blue Peter* presenter John Leslie, but they split up in 1993. She then nearly married *Soldier, Soldier* star Angus MacFadyen but dumped him for actor Paul McGann, her *Catherine the Great* co-star, who eventually returned to his wife. In 1996 she moved to Hollywood, where film mogul Jon Peters helped to open doors. Will film director Michael Winner be proved wrong? He dismisses her as "just a former dancer. They're almost always rather nice, jolly people who go through life having a ball. But you never seem to hear much about them when they get older."

Compton Miller's Social Register

1
General

Living Legends
Lord Menuhin
Stephen Hawking
Lord Denning
Sir Magdi Yacoub
Earl of Longford
Sir Edward Heath
Monsignor Alfred
  Gilbey
Lord Mishcon
Bernard Levin
Lord Tonypandy
Dr AL Rowse
Sir Isiah Berlin
Lord Cudlipp
Peter Carter-Ruck
Sir Michael Tippett
Enoch Powell
Lord Soper
Trevor Huddleston
Sir Peter Saunders
Lord Wyatt

Dame Barbara
  Cartland
Mary Wesley
Baroness Thatcher
Dame Alicia
  Markova
Dame Joan
  Sutherland
Miriam Rothschild
Dame Ninette de
  Valois
Fanny Waterman
Elena Salvoni
Lady Ryder
Dame Veronica
  Wedgwood
Nuala Allason

Winning Siblings
David and Frederick
  Barclay
John and Peter
  Beckwith
Sir Charles,
  Jonathan and
  Chris Powell
John Gummer and
  Lord Chadlington
Tony and Ridley
  Scott
Sri and Gopi
  Hinduja
Joely and Natasha
  Richardson
Vanessa, Corin and
  Lynn Redgrave
Dai and Roddy
  Llewellyn
Paul, Joe and
  Mark McGann
James, Edward and
  Robert Fox
Sinead, Sorcha
  and Niamh Cusack
Maurice, Barry and
  Robin Gibb
Hayley and
  Juliet Mills
Jonathan and
  Paul Ross
Anthea and
  Wendy Turner
Matt and Luke
  Goss

Enduring Loves
John McCallum and
  Googie Withers
Duke and Duchess
  of Kent
Sir John Mills and
  Mary Hayley Bell

Michael Denison
  and Dulcie Gray
Bryan Forbes and
  Nanette Newman
Johnny Dankworth
  and Dame Cleo
  Laine
Milton Shulman
  and Drusilla
  Beyfus
Sir Ludovic
  Kennedy and
  Moira Shearer
Sir Angus Ogilvy
  and Princess
  Alexandra
Sir Leslie and Dame
  Shirley Porter
Johnny and Jan
  Gold
Lord and Lady
  Puttnam
Anthony and Dr
  Rose-Maria Letts
Bob and Mary
  Holness
Lorenzo and
  Mara Berni
William and Shan
  Legge-Bourke
John and Norma
  Major
Laurence and Anne-
  Marie Graff
Allan and Tanya
  Wheway
Michael and
  Amanda Dobbs
Desmond Wilcox
  and Esther
  Rantzen
Charles and Patti
  Palmer-Tomkinson
Nick Lander and
  Jancis Robinson

Surprise Couples

Harold Pinter and Lady Antonia Fraser
Paul Mowatt and Marina Ogilvy
Darius and Patricia Guppy
John Cleese and Alice Faye Eichelberger
Shura and Joan Shihwarg
Sir Charles and Lady Powell
Ken Foreman and Mandy Rice-Davies
Sir Peregrine Worsthorne and Lady Lucinda Lambton
Carl Davis and Jean Boht
Kevin and Pandora Maxwell
Kit Hesketh-Harvey and Katie Rabett
Sir David and Lady Carina Frost
Bryan Ferry and Lucy Helmore
John and Lady Sally Aspinall
Richard Dawkins and Lalla Ward
Sir Nicholas Lloyd and Eve Pollard

Power Couples

Tony Blair and Cherie Booth
Lord Rogers and Ruthie Rogers

Sir Mark Weinberg and Anouska Hempel
Lord Jenkins and Dame Jennifer Jenkins
Michael Holroyd and Margaret Drabble
Neil and Glenys Kinnock
Rupert and Anna Murdoch
Lord Owen and Debbie Owen
Philip Gould and Gail Rebuck
Jonathan Dimbleby and Bel Mooney
Dominic Lawson and Rosa Monckton
Ken and Barbara Follett
Peter and Gail Lilley
Phil and Frances Edmonds
William and Susan Boyd
Michael and Sandra Howard
Clive and Dr Jane Anderson
David Spanier and Suzy Menkes
Julian Barnes and Pat Kavanagh

National Treasures

Sir Hardy Amies
Lord Grade
Sir John Mills

Egon Ronay
Murray Walker
Sir John Gielgud
Patrick O'Brian
Stirling Moss
Dickie Bird
Alistair Cooke
Sir Harry Secombe
Quentin Crewe
Sir Denis Thatcher
Peter Coke
Jimmy Young
Milton Shulman
Lord Attenborough
Henry Cooper
Spike Milligan
Godfrey Smith
Peter Herbert
Max Bygraves
Larry Adler
Sir Freddie Laker
Winston Graham

The Queen Mother
Dame Vera Lynn
Baroness Castle
Dame Cicely Saunders
Mary Whitehouse
Betty Kenward
Penelope Hobhouse
MM Kaye

Gurus

Peter Mandelson
Beechey Colclough
Robert deWynter
Raymond Tooth
DG Hessayon
Hugh Johnson
Keith Butt
Stephen Bayley
Matthew Manning
Peter York

Stefan Buczacki
Sir Tim Bell
Ravi Shankar
Dr Anthony Clare
Philip Mould
Bob Worcester
Roger Phillips
Josh Saltzman
Maxwell
  Hutchinson

Lotte Berk
Mary Spillane
Claire Rayner
Barbara Follett
Lesley Kenton
Zelda West Meads
Susie Orbach
Rosemary Conley
Mary Portas
Serena Sutcliffe
Shelley von
  Strunckel
Barbara Eyton

National Irritants
Chris Evans
Des O'Connor
Michael Winner
Rev Ian Paisley
Alan Duncan
Eric Morley
Danny Baker
Terry Christian
Yuri Geller
Peter Hain
Peter Tatchell
Jonathan King
Gyles Brandreth

Princess Michael
  of Kent
Julie Goodyear
Ruby Wax

Sandi Toksvig
Pam Ayres
Katie Puckrik
Julie Burchill
Mandi Allwood
Anne Atkins
Magenta de Vine

Power Brokers
Lord Irvine
Betty Boothroyd
Eddie George
Dame Barbara Mills
Sir Robin Butler
Pauline Clare
Sir Robert Fellowes
Baroness Scotland
Sir Christopher
  Bland
Marjorie Wallace
Lord Bingham
Tessa Keswick
Duke of Norfolk
Helen Wilkinson
Lord Woolf
Sue Slipman
John Kemp-Welch
Anna Coote
George Carey
Michael Peat
Marquess of
  Hartington
Lord Alexander
  of Weedon
Sir Jocelyn Stevens
Earl of Gowrie
Sir George Russell
Lord Wakeham
Earl of Airlie
Nicholas Snowman
Nicholas Serota
Sir Shane Blewitt
Tom Shebbeare
Howard Davies

Bovver Bandits
Lord Tebbit
Ken Livingstone
Bernard Manning
Paul Johnson
Damien Hirst
Sir Bernard Ingham
David Hart
Jimmy Knapp
Dennis Skinner
Brian Hitchen
David Austin
Professor Richard
  Lacey
Sir Ian McKellen
Dr David Starkie
Bill Cash
James Pickles
Lord Janner
Tony Marlow
Sir Jonathan Porritt
John Carlisle
George Monbiot

Bovver Bandettes
Esther Rantzen
Victoria Gillick
Lady Fretwell
Diana Lamplugh
Jayne Zito
Teresa Gorman
Marchioness of
  Worcester
Baroness Jay
Edwina Currie

**Establishment
Gadflies**
Ian Hislop
Sir Ludovic
  Kennedy
Peter McKay
David Irving

Duncan Campbell
Paul Foot
Nigel West
Tariq Ali
John Pilger
Count Nikolai
  Tolstoy
Malcolm McLaren
Michael Cashman
Salman Rushdie
Bruce Kent
John O'Sullivan
Christopher Booker
Roger Scruton
Michael Thornton

Heroes
John McCarthy
Sir Ranulph
  Fiennes
John Hume
Tony Bullimore
Richard Branson
Robin Hanbury-
  Tenison
Terry Waite
Simon Weston
Chay Blyth
John Blashford-
  Snell
Chris Bonington
Sir Robin Knox-
  Johnston
Dr Michael Stroud
Sir Rex Hunt
Doug Scott
Don McCullin
Bob Champion

Heroines
Rebecca Stephens
Tracy Edwards
Ffyona Campbell

Sarah Ford
Christina Dodwell
Clare Francis
Judy Leden
Lisa Clayton
Rosie Clayton
Kate Adie
Rosie Swale

Sixties Icons
Twiggy
Lord Puttnam
Sir Paul McCartney
Dame Diana Rigg
Enzo Apicella
Vidal Sassoon
Harry Hyams
Dr Germaine Greer
Michael Caine
David Hockney
Marianne Faithfull
Julie Christie
David Bailey
John Barry
Leonard Lewis
Earl of Snowdon
Jane Birkin
Chris Blackwell
Robert Carrier
Richard Ingrams
Barry Lategan
John Peel
John Kasmin
Sarah Miles
Michael Chow
José Fonseca

**Sixties Models
(that never fade)**
Jean Shrimpton
Sandra Paul
Edina Ronay
Tania Mallett

Patti Boyd
Kari-Ann Moller
Celia Hammond
Jill Kennington
Penelope Tree
Grace Coddington
Maudie James
Annegret
  Easterman
Paulene Stone
Lady Tuck
Ellie Summerill
Dorothy Bond
Penny Patrick
Jan Ward
Hazel Collins
Barbara Ray
Greta Morrison
Immy Bickford-
  Smith

2 High Society

The Queen's BFs (Best Friends)
Earl and Countess
of Carnarvon
Lord Charteris
Jane Countess of
Westmorland
Earl of Huntingdon
Earl and Countess
of Airlie
Duchess of
Grafton
Lady Rupert Nevill
Lord Hussey and
Lady Susan Hussey

Brides for Prince William?
Princess Theodora
of Greece
Princess Madeleine
of Sweden
Charlotte Casiraghi
Lady Edwina
Grosvenor
Archduchess Marie
Christine of
Habsburg
Athina Roussel
Lana Palumbo
Holly Branson
Leonora Knatchbull
Lady Eloise Anson
Princess Florentina
Massimo
Ivanka Trump
Anouska Beckwith
Fifi Trixibelle
Geldof

Lady Alexandra
Gordon-Lennox
Lady Mary
Wellesley
Elizabeth Scarlett
Jagger
Lady Philippa
Howard
Charlotte Goldsmith
Poppy or Chloe
Delevingne
Lydia Forte
Augusta Ogilvy
Clover Kelly
Dandelion Richards
Lady Isabella
Somerset
Saoirse Herbert
Arabella Llewellyn
Birgitte Sumner
Jade Farmiloe

The Chazza/Camilla Set
Simon and
Annabel Elliot
Lord and
Lady Romsey
Earl and Countess
of Halifax
Kirsty Smallwood
Duchess of
Devonshire
Duke and Duchess
of Westminster
Baroness Lulu
de Waldner
Shan and William
Legge-Bourke
Earl and Countess
of Shelburne
Earl and Countess
of Shaftesbury

Charles and Patti
Palmer-Tomkinson
Lady Charles
Spencer-Churchill
Hugh and Emilie
van Cutsem
Nic and Sukie
Paravacini
Nicholas and
Serena Soames
Lord and Lady
Hindlip
Carolyn Benson
Ian and Pammy
Farqhuar

Princess Margaret's 'Carers'
Lord and Lady
Glenconner
Ned Ryan
Janey Stevens
Earl and Countess
Alexander of Tunis
Ben Holland-Martin
Sir Jocelyn Stevens
Roddy and
Tania Llewellyn
Sir Mark Weinberg
and Anouska
Hempel
Lord Napier
Earl and Countess
de la Warr
Charles and
Pandora
Delevingne
Norman Lonsdale
Earl of Lichfield

Plutocrat Peers
Duke of
  Westminster
Duke of Buccleuch
Earl of Iveagh
Lord Howard
  de Walden
Earl Cadogan
Lord Sainsbury
Viscount Portman
Marquess of
  Tavistock
Earl of Stockton
Lord Daresbury
Marquess of Bute
Marquess of
  Northampton
Marquess of
  Salisbury
Marquess of
  Cholmondeley

**Coroneted Fun-
Lovers**
Duke of Roxburghe
Earl of Suffolk
  and Berkshire
Lord Cobbold
Duke of St Albans
Lord Rathcavan
Earl of
  Mount Charles
Viscount Norwich
Earl of Gowrie
Earl of Erroll
Earl Spencer
Earl of Verulam
Viscount Petersham
Marquess of
  Milford Haven
Earl Alexander
  of Tunis
Marquess of Bute
Earl of Drogheda

Eligible Nobles
Earl of Ulster
Lord Nicholas
  Windsor
Lord Freddie
  Windsor
Marquess of Lorne
Lord Edward
  Spencer-Churchill
Viscount Weymouth
Lord Bingham
William Stanhope
Ralph Montagu
Earl of Hardwicke
Henry Channon
Lord Howland
Viscount
  Castlereagh
Viscount Anson
Lord Seymour
Earl of Mornington
Viscount Crichton
Viscount Newport
Lord Herbert
Viscount Somerton
Marquess of
  Douglas
Jasset Ormsby-Gore
Earl Compton
Jenico Preston

Buzzy Baronets
Sir Benjamin Slade
Sir Tatton Sykes
Sir Stephen
  Waley-Cohen
Sir Charles Elton
Sir Nigel Seely
Sir Denis Thatcher
Sir Ranulph
  Fiennes
Sir Humphrey
  Wakefield
Sir John Leon

Sir Tobias Clarke
Sir Bruce Tuck
Sir Nicholas Nuttall
Sir Nicholas Bonsor
Sir Harry Llewellyn
Sir Peter Osborne
Sir Euan
  Anstruther-Gough-
  Calthorpe

**Blue-blooded
Eccentrics**
Marquess of
  Northampton
Earl of Longford
Marquess of Bath
Earl of Haddington
Earl of Clancarty
Viscount
  Gormanston
Sir Mark Palmer
Earl of St Germans
Earl of Yarborough
Earl of Seafield
Lord Bicester
Lord Sudeley
Lord Neidpath
Earl of Cardigan
Earl of Mulgrave
Viscount Reidhaven
Lord Kilbracken

**Noble
Pomposities**
Duke of Edinburgh
The Aga Khan
Duke of
  Marlborough
Lord Tryon
Earl of Caithness
Lord Armstrong
Lord Kingsdown
Lord Hussey

Aristoprats
Duke of Manchester
Marquess of Bristol
Marquess of
Blandford
Lord Brocket
Peter Curzon

D. Phils in Society
Peter Gwynn-Jones
Sir Malcolm Innes
of Edingight
Peter Townend
Richard
Fitzwilliams
John Brooke-Little
Charles Kidd
David Williamson
Robert Smith
Lady Celestria Noel
Ewa Lewis
Robert Noel

**Titled Beauty
Queens**
The Princess
of Hanover
Archduchess
Francesca
of Habsburg
Lady Porchester
Countess of Arundel
Marchioness of
Milford Haven
Lady Carolyn
Warren
Lady Romsey
Countess of Woolton
Countess Leopold
von Bismarck
Lady (Alaia) Forte
Duchess of
Roxburghe

Marchioness of
Huntly
Lady Brocket
Lady Marcia
Bulmer
Countess of
Normanton
Marchioness of
Douro

**Stately Home
Eligibles**
Countess of
Lichfield
Lady Serena
Andrew
Rosie Marchioness
of Northampton
Marchioness of
Bristol
Lady Henrietta
Spencer-Churchill
Lady Jane Wellesley
Lady Alexandra
Carnegie
Lady Annunziata
Asquith
Yvonne
Marchioness
of Bristol

Nubile Aristos
Lady Rose Windsor
Jessica de
Rothschild
Lady Davina
Windsor
Lady Ella Windsor
Lady Frances
Armstrong-Jones
Lady Lenka Thynn
Isabella Anstruther-
Gough-Calthorpe

Lady Louise FitzRoy
Camilla Astor
Lady Lucinda Savile
Zoe Tryon
Lady Rose Anson

**Royal To
Themselves**
Vicomte
Guy de Montfort
Princess
Alia Ali Khan
Princess Helena
Moutafian
Princess Nina
Mamasakhlisi
Prince Stash
Klossowski de Rola
Lord Lambton
Baron Claus von
Bulow
Maureen
Marchioness of
Dufferin and Ava
Baron Enrico di
Portanova
Prince Frederick
Anhalt
Sir James Swann
Baron Marc Burca
Lord MacDillen
Count Carlo
Colombotti
Lady Rosemary
Aberdour
Prince Alexius
Bassey
Count Andre de
Moller

3 Café Society

Legendary Beauties

Princess Salimah
 Aga Khan
Baroness Fiona
 Thyssen
Lady Annunziata
 Asquith
Lady Charlotte
 Dinan
Lady Mary-Gaye
 Shaw
Marchioness of
 Tavistock
Bronwen Lady Astor
Princess George
 Galitzine
Eva Rueber-Staier

Gracious Battleaxes

Jennifer Patterson
Christina Foyle
Helen Lady Delves-
 Broughton
Julia Morley
Frances Shand
 Kydd
Duchess of
 St Albans
Lady Falkender
Janey Stevens
Joan Wyndham
Lady Teresa Waugh
Lady Sarah
 Spencer-Churchill
Lady Wynne-Jones
Jacqueline
 Lady Killearn

Swingin' Middle-agers

Princess Firyal
 of Jordan
Soraya Khashoggi
Lady de la Rue
Diane Moran
Gloria Hunniford
Susan Barrantes
Davina Phillips
Lady Carolyn
 Townshend
Molly Parkin
Rosie Marchioness
 of Northampton
June Thirlby
Elizabeth Rogerson
Sara Leighton
Lady Jacqueline
 Thomson
Lesley Burton
Ricci Lewis
Tracy Reed
Sonia Sinclair
Nicole Bulgari
Aldine Honey
Gabrielle Crawford

Knightsbridge Tina Turners

Yvonne
 Marchioness
 of Bristol
Una-Mary Parker
Jill Melford
Kate Lady Vestey
Lady (Virginia)
 White
Elizabeth Harris
Marlen Bovell
Viviane Ventura
Tina Lubner
Jenny Viscountess
 Chelsea

Lesley Lake
Georgiana
 Bronfman
Countess Michele
 Griaznof
Nancy Beck
Deborah Wingate
Dorit Moussaieff

Eligible Dames (of a Certain Age)

Greta Scacchi
Isobel Goldsmith
Emma Soames
Jacqueline Bisset
Sabrina Guinness
Carol Thatcher
Marella Oppenheim
Liz Brewer
Amanda Donohoe
Paula Hamilton
Sally Burton
Lindka Cierach
Annabel Heseltine

Haute Hostesses

Donatella Flick
Lady McAlpine
Lady Lloyd-
 Webber
Lady Powell
Sue Sangster
Anne-Marie Graff
Anouska Hempel
Olga Polizzi
Lady Bell
Vivien Duffield
Lady Annabel
 Goldsmith
Gail Ronson
Helen Moran
Lady Renwick
Lady Palumbo

Lady Stephens
Madeleine Curtiss
Lady Young
  of Graffham

**Magical
Personalities**
Pippa Irwin
Diana Lloyd
Ellie Hedley
Countess Kristina
  von Merveldt
Wendy Baines
Sandi Mason
Celeste Mitchell
Vanessa Rhode
Shelagh Routh
Nola Fontaine
Jill Thornton
Lucienne Camille
Carolyn Cavele
Tui Esser
Marilyn Warnick
Althea Lloyd
Anne-Louise Fisher
Angela Beddall
Fran Morrison
Beth Coventry
Susannah de Fere
Jackie Modlinger
Bonnie Morris
Princess Atalanta
  Massimo
Steffi Callan

Class Acts
Camilla Parker
  Bowles
Yasmin Le Bon
Tessa Dahl
Laraine Ashton
Julia Verdin
Catherine Bailey

Rosie Cheetham
Anne Heseltine
Lady Rawlinson
Helen Pennant-Rea
Shakira Caine
Lady Camilla
  Dempster
Lucy Ferry
Juanita Kerman
Lady Tana Focke
Pat Nimmo
Meredeth
  Etherington-Smith
Sue MacGregor
Victoria Watson
Candida Lycett-
  Green
Bryony Brind

Patient Wives
Cheryl Barrymore
Susan Ferguson
Lady Glenconner
Jane Clark
Lady Archer
Louise Fennell
Diane Hoare
Lady Hattersley
Joan Branson
Diane Thatcher
Diane Yeo
Lady Teresa Waugh

**Feisty
Pulchritude**
Glenda Jackson
Rabbi Julia
  Neuberger
Barbara Taylor
  Bradford
Chiquita Dumont
Anna Raeburn
Glenys Kinnock

Rosie Boycott
Marsha Hunt
Pamela
  Lady Harlech
Fay Maschler
Elaine Paige
Lucretia Stewart
Erika Bergman
Caroline Michel
Carol Smith
Carmen Callil
Patricia Hewitt

Female Dynamoes
Cherie Booth
Olga Polizzi
Lynne Franks
Baroness
  Oppenheim
Anna Wintour
Josephine Hart
Tina Brown
Mo Mowlam
Baroness Dean
Liz Calder
Yoko Ono
Fiona Shackleton
Baroness O'Cathain
Julie Cecil
Baroness Mallalieu
Marcelle
  d'Argy-Smith
Lady Victoria
  Leatham
Alexandra Shulman
Mary Kenny
Maureen Smith
Susan Douglas
Beryl Vertue
Jenny Pitman
Eva Jiricna
Doris Saatchi
Baroness
  Ewart-Biggs

Frances Blois
Julia Peyton-
Jones

Funny Ladies
Linda Agran
Jennifer Patterson
Sue Lloyd
Princess Margaret
Annegret Easterman
Jill Melford
Kate Morris

Embarrastocrats
Paula Yates
Ruby Wax
Shirley Bassey
Vivienne Westwood
Teresa Gorman
Zandra Rhodes
Anita Pallenberg
Clare Short
Baroness
de Stempel
Soraya Khashoggi
Dannii Minogue
Dorothy Squires
Gillian Taylforth
Jeanette Charles
Sarah Keays
Cynthia Payne
Lady Georgie
Campbell

Fantasy Figures
Elizabeth Hurley
Selina Scott
Mariella Frostrup
Ulrika Jonsson
Catherine Zeta-
Jones
Anna Ford

Flawed Meissen
Marina Mowatt
Koo Stark
Paula Hamilton
Marilyn Galsworthy
Ghislaine Maxwell
Marie-Louise
Johnson
Suzanna Leigh
Mary Parkinson
Anna Pasternak
Jo-Jo Laine
Sally Thompsett
Mirabel Edgedale
Jo Fairley
Lizzie Humphries
Cass McClancey
Belinda Harley
Lady Waldegrave
Carole Caplin

**Ladies With
Attitude**
Vanessa Redgrave
Jo Brand
Barbara Amiel
Clarissa
Dickson-Wright
Celestia Fox
Susie Arthur
Harriet Crawley
Annette Howard
Nigella Lawson

**Sharons of
Belgravia**
Lesley Player
Bienvenida Sokolow
Sally Ann Lasson
Marilyn Cole
Nicola Formby
Claire Gordon
Antonia de Sancha

Kim Lady
Kenilworth
Solweiga Wallach
Stacey Young
Gae Exton
Jilly Johnson
Sally Faber
Gaynor Goodman
Carol Edge

Yum Yums
Normandie Keith
Tamara Beckwith
Tara Palmer-
Tomkinson
Amanda de Cadenet
Caprice Bourret
Letitia Cash
Lady Victoria
Hervey
Beverley Bloom
Arabella Zamoyska
Lisa B
Katharin
Zuberbuehler
Annabel Elwes
Rachel Tatton-
Browne
Samantha Phillips
Jennifer Halpern
Cristina Odone
Tamara Yeardye
Plum Sykes
Emily Bearne
Daisy Donovan
Laura Patten

**Heiresses Worth
Cultivating**
Holly Branson
Elizabeth Scarlett
Jagger
Natasha Caine

Stella McCartney
Mary McCartney
Eva Rice
Alison Grade
Seraphima Watts
Imogen Lloyd
 Webber
Kate Sangster
Lee Starkey
Laura Lubner
Jessica Rothschild
Tara Bernerd
Tamara Vestey
Victoria Tompkins
Emily Oppenheimer

**Drawing-Room
Temptresses**
Marie Helvin
Valerie Campbell
Jerry Hall
Elizabeth Hurley
Miranda Pothecary
April Tod
Sally Farmiloe
Sally Burton
Ingrid Seward
Rosemary Segal
Jackie Roffe
Chantal d'Orthez
Glenda Pearson
Camilla Shihwarg
Patricia Madden
Gloria Morningstar
Annie Foster-Firth
Fran Findlater
Lady Boothby

**Society
Bedazzlers**
Christina Estrada
Polly Havers
Anka Dineley

Georgia Coleridge
Susannah
 Constantine
Lucy Sangster
Fiona Sangster
Julie-Anne Rhodes
Catherine
 Fairweather
Lucy Portman
Pandora Delevingne
Katie Braine
Clare Wentworth-
 Stanley
Anne Dunhill
Gilly Mackwood
Petronella Wyatt
Emma Sergeant
Lady Lisa Campbell
Santa Palmer-
 Tomkinson
Emily Todhunter
Sarah Giles
Tattie Bourdillon
Anastasia Cooke

**Gold Ankle-
Chainies**
Mandy Smith
Sam Fox
Fiona Wright
Sheryl Gascoigne
Kara Noble
Linda Lusardi
Gillian Taylforth
Christine Salata
Basia Briggs
Kathy Lloyd
Sinitta
Cheryl Baker
Rose Marie
Nike Clarke
Jackie St Clair
Barbara Windsor
Jasmine Duggan

Sassy Ladies
Jemima Khan
Julia Carling
Nabila Khashoggi
Kate Slater
Princess Katya
 Galitzine
Darcey Bussell
Alison Doody
Marianne Faithfull
Greta Morrison
Catrina Skepper
Christa d'Souza
Tania Kindersley
Sarah Forbes
Alix Billen
Lady Louisa Stuart
Helen Stewart
Lady Bell
Susan Ferguson
Jane MacQuitty
Carolyn Waters
Trinny Woodall
Jane Bonham-
 Carter
Caroline Kellett

**Paladins of
Charm**
Cardinal Basil
 Home
Lord Rawlinson
Nicholas Coleridge
Lord Charles
 Spencer-Churchill
Lord Carrington
Paddy Leigh-
 Fermor
Sir Stephen Tumim
Willy Bauer
Sir George Martin
Patrick Grayson
Charles Benson
Willie Landels

Roger Phillips
John Tovey
Viscount Norwich
Julian Payne
Digby Willoughby
Bruce Fogle
Terence Feely
Henry Sanford
Neil Durden-Smith
Derek Grainger

Sherpa Tensings of Social Affairs

David Tang
Claus von Bulow
Martin Miller
Mark Thatcher
Harold Brooks-
  Baker
James Sherwood
Anthony Andrews
Neil Balfour
Jools Holland
Roberto Devorik
Francis Kyle
Jonathan Shalitt
David Shilling
Derek Nimmo
Bryan Ferry

Loveable Eccentrics

Patrick Moore
John McCririck
David Bellamy
Richard Booth
Patrick Procktor
Screaming
  Lord Sutch
Spike Milligan
Brian Keenan
Nicholas Treadwell
Terry Major-Ball

Duggie Fields
Dudley
  Winterbottom
Eddie Edwards
David Icke

Glittering Hosts

J Paul Getty
Lord McAlpine
  of West Green
Martin Summers
Wafic Said
Lord Archer
Sir David Frost
Michael White
Ken Follett

Byronic Figures

Jon Barrowman
James Hewitt
Mogens Tholstrup
Tim Jefferies
Charlie Brooks
Michael Naylor-
  Leyland

Crumpled Adonises

Duke of Beaufort
Theo Fennell
Michael Heseltine
Charlie Carter
David Essex
Darius Guppy
John Goedhuis
Michael Wood
Mark Burns
Prince Stefano
  Massimo
Christopher Wilson
James Fox
Hugh Millais

Cheever Hardwick
Julian Allason
Jess Conrad

Professional Bachelors

Sir Edward Heath
Sir Cliff Richard
Sam Mendes
Frank Johnson
Mike Reid
Ben Holland-Martin
Wayne Sleep
Jimmy Young
Danny La Rue
Neil Tennant
Bruce Oldfield
Simon Sainsbury
Alan Whicker
Sir Jimmy Savile
Jonathan King
Alan Bennett
Gordon Honeycombe
Ian Greer

Geriatric Eligibles

Terence Stamp
Viscount Lewisham
John Bowes-Lyon
Ned Ryan
Jason Donovan
Peter Mandelson
Michael Winner
Paddy McNally
Christopher Cole
Brian Stone
Bernard Levin
Peter Sheridan
Aziz Radwan
Bevis Hillier
Raymond Salisbury-
  Jones

George Bruce
Christopher Balfour

**Fashionable
Heirlings**
Zack Goldsmith
Jamie Palumbo
Robert Hanson
Prince Valerio
  Massimo
Lucas White
James McCartney
Tarka Cordell
Christian Moore
Robin Birley
Sean Lennon
Bassa Aspinall
Nicholas Lloyd-
  Webber
Dhani Harrison
Mohammed
  Khashoggi
William van
  Straubenzee
Peter Phillips
Tom Parker-Bowles
Jamie Packer
Lachlan Murdoch
James Archer

**Tweenybopper
Eligibles**
Earl Grosvenor
Benjy Fry
William Vestey
Sebastian Flick
Alexander
  Gladstone
Michael Thatcher
James Jagger
Miles Frost
Stavros Niarchos
Joshua Andrews

Ned Sangster
Taylor Stringfellow
  Roberts
Joe Sumner

**Seasoned
Revellers**
Paul Callan
Hurricane Higgins
Simon Becker
George Best
Gray Jolliffe
Peter Boizot
Geoffrey Van-Hay
Shura Shihvarg
Tony Le-Ray Cook
Jack Milroy
Michael Parkin
Richard Berens
Michael White
Jeremy Lloyd
George Melly
Geoffrey
  Wheatcroft
Alain de Cadenet
Paul Kiernan

Reformed Rakes
Sean Shelley
Bill Wiggins
John Walsh
Michael Proudlock
Josh Astor
Michael Corry-Reid
Carlo Colombotti
Nicky Kerman
Torquil Macleod
David Olivestone
Anthony Haden-
  Guest
Michael Heath
Rodney Kinsman
Willie Robertson

Michael Dupree
Daniel Topolski
Mark Shand
Anton Kristensen
Baron Steven
  Bentinck
Robert Windsor
Andrew Maconie
Leszek Nowicki

Big Dame Hunters
Peter Stringfellow
Taki
  Theodoracopulos
Tim Jefferies
Didier Milinaire
Count
  Paolo della Torre
James Hewitt
Andrew Neil
Mark Macauley
Charles Glass
Dai Llewellyn
Brod Munro-Wilson
Marc Burca
Roger Howe
James Watson
Prince Adam
  Czartoryski
Nick Monson
Luis Sosa
  Basualdo
Comte Jean-Francois
  de Chambrun

Celebrity Wooers
Christopher Biggins
Nicholas Haslam
Roddy Llewellyn
Robin Hurlstone
Michael Szell
Ned Ryan
Robin Anderson

John St Clair
James Kelly
David Shilling
Antony Underwood
Bruce Oldfield
Charles Castle
Anwer Bhatti

**Retired
Hellraisers**
Oliver Reed
Viscount Cowdray
Tony Booth
Earl of Suffolk
 and Berkshire
Earl of Kimberley
Keith Floyd
Trevor Baines
Earl of Stockton
Peter O'Toole
Barry Humphries
Richard Harris
Jeffrey Bernard
John Knight
Pete Townshend
Tony Nathan
Toby Bonham
Alan Crompton-Batt
Willie Donaldson
Tony Brainsby

**Knightsbridge
Scallywags**
Rupert Deen
Sebastian Taylor
Prince Conky
 Galitzine
Anthony Freeland
Anthony Mackay
Richard Connolly
Marcus Scriven
Alexander Atkinson
Jeremy Taylor

Rupert Heseltine
Oliver Gilmour
Andrew Brewis
Costi Countouris
Giles Gordon

**Husbands in the
Shadows**
Prince Michael
 of Kent
Peter Bottomley
Sir Denis Thatcher
Bobby Willis
Desmond Wilcox
Sir Nicholas Lloyd
Raymond Currie
Michael Williams

Flamboyants
Elton John
Eddie Izzard
Lord St John of
 Fawsley
Quentin Crisp
John Reid
Boy George
Ned Sherrin
Simon Callow
Michael Barrymore
Victor Spinetti
Gary Glitter
Ricci Burns
Lionel Bart
Richard O'Brien
Jack Woolf
Dale Winton
Robert Carrier
Allan Warren
Stewart Grimshaw
Jason Pollock
Simon Napier-Bell
Julius Just

Bons Oeufs
Richard Shepherd
Barry Lategan
Hugh Poole-
 Warren
Billy Keating
Simon Worrall
Robin Hanbury-
 Tenison
Roger Wren
Sir George
 Christie
Philip Hoare
John Downing
Quentin King
William Drummond

Sultans of Smarm
Paul Raymond
Des O'Connor
Bruno Brooks
Eric Morley
Sir Ralph Halpern
David Crewe-Reid
'Dandy Kim'
 Waterfield
Tim Gwynne-Jones
Gary Davies
Frank Warren
Ivor Spencer
Marquess of Bristol
Ronnie Knight

Blustercrats
John Prescott
Rev Ian Paisley
Maxwell
 Hutchinson
Sir Jerry Wiggin
James Pickles
Timothy Clifford
Sir Rhodes Boyson
Edward Pearce

Bernard Matthews
Sir Teddy Taylor

Dandies
Duke of Beaufort
Henry Cecil
Bill Cash
Sir Peregrine
  Worsthorne
Lord Charles
  Spencer-Churchill
Mark Birley
Marquess of
  Hartington
Nicholas Coleridge
Barry Humphries
Michael Cole
Charles Anson
Archie Stirling
Gay Kindersley
Charles Delevingne

Raconteurs
Sir Peter Ustinov
Henry Kelly
Dave Allen
Anthony Clare
Ned Sherrin
Frank Muir
Matthew Parris
Denis Norden
Peter Tory
Lord Moyne
Jonathan Routh
Johnny Bevan
Frank Delaney
Billy Connolly

Poseur Princes
Michael Flatley
AA Gill
Chris Eubank

Robert Kilroy-Silk
Dr Hilary Jones
Jeremy Irons
Simon Sebag-
  Montefiore
David Flint Wood
Ross Benson

**Nature's
Gentlemen**
John Frieda
Bernard Coral
Ken Clarke
Allan Hall
Percy Savage
Bob Holness
Patrick Gwynn-
  Jones
Barry Wieland
Jim Dunn
Laurence Tarlo
Ken Williams
Mike Molloy
Fenton Bresler
Barry Grigg
David Wigg
John Davy

4 Show Business

Hollywood Emperors
Sean Connery
Michael Caine
Sir Anthony
  Hopkins
Pierce Brosnan
Ralph Fiennes
Roger Moore
Liam Neeson
Daniel Day-Lewis
Albert Finney
Hugh Grant
John Hurt
Bob Hoskins
Jeremy Irons
Timothy Dalton
Ben Kingsley
Alan Rickman
Jonathan Pryce
Sean Bean
Charles Dance
Richard E Grant

Deposed Hollywood Royalty
Sir Peter Ustinov
Dudley Moore
Peter O'Toole
Richard Harris
Oliver Reed
Malcolm McDowell
Michael York
Sir Dirk Bogarde
Alan Bates
Terence Stamp

Big-Time Mummers
Sir John Gielgud
Sir Alec Guinness
Sir Alec McCowen
Sir Ian McKellen
Sir Roy Dotrice
Paul Scofield
Sir Donald Sinden
Christopher Lee
Leo McKern
Timothy West
Patrick McGoohan
Robert Hardy
Herbert Lom
Sir John Mills

Budding Oliviers
Kenneth Branagh
Sir Derek Jacobi
Ian Holm
Anthony Sher
Dennis Quilley
Michael Gambon
Simon Callow
Nigel Hawthorne
Alan Howard
Roger Rees
Peter Firth
David Warner
John Wood

A-Class Heartthrobs
Colin Firth
Gary Oldman
John Hannah
Adrian Dunbar
Julian Sands
Paul McGann
James Wilby
Tim Roth
Patrick Bergin

Steven Waddington
Gabriel Byrne
Cary Elwes
Gary Kemp
Nathaniel Parker
Anthony Calfe

Small-Screen Stallions
Greg Wise
Rufus Sewell
Sam West
Jeremy Northam
Rupert Graves
Toby Stephens
Ben Chaplin
Edward Atherton
Joseph Fiennes
Owen Teale
Craig McLachlan
Linus Roache
Jason Flemyng

Telly Princes
Richard Wilson
David Jason
Jimmy Nail
Robert Lindsay
Nick Berry
Robert Carlyle
Ian Richardson
George Cole
John Thaw
David Suchet
Peter Bowles
Edward Woodward
Jack Shephard
Paul Shane
George Baker
Bernard Hill

Loaded Lads
Frank Skinner
David Baddiel
Harry Hill
Steve Coogan
Eddie Izzard
Sean Hughes
Dennis Pennis
Jack Dee

Star Turns
Neil Pearson
Nicholas Lyndhurst
Trevor Eve
Tim Healy
Bill Nighy
Michael Elphick
Frazer Hines
Peter Davison
Warren Clarke
Timothy Spall
Neil Morrissey
Brian Murphy
Martin Clunes
Roy Marsden
Jonathan Morris
Peter Howitt
Patrick Malahide
Ben Cross

Ageing Beefcake
Nigel Havers
Christopher Cazenove
Robert Powell
Ian McShane
Max Caulfield
Tom Conti
Anthony Andrews
Christopher Timothy
Ian Ogilvy
Simon Williams

Patrick Ryecart
Leigh Lawson
Peter Egan
Martin Shaw
John Nettles
Dennis Waterman

Scene Thieves
Brian Cox
Joss Ackland
Steven Berkoff
Ian Bannen
Tom Wilkinson
Pete Postlethwaite
Peter Capaldi
Tim Pigott-Smith
Terence Alexander
Peter Barkworth
Nikolas Grace
Peter Vaughan
Richard Gibson
Nigel Davenport
Dudley Sutton
Roger Lloyd-Pack
Ciaran Hinds
Glynn Edwards
William Franklyn
Donald Gee

Stardom Mislaid
Nicol Williamson
Richard Johnson
Tom Courtenay
Tom Bell
David Hemmings
Gerald Harper
Simon
    McCorkindale
Jack Hedley
Oliver Tobias
Patrick Mower
Francis Matthews
Tony Britton

Lewis Collins
Simon Ward
Robin Askwith
Tom Adams
Gareth Hunt
David McCallum
Robin Nedwell
Richard O'Sullivan
Patrick Macnee

Stage Chanteurs
Michael Crawford
Tommy Steele
Jon Barrowman
Paul Nicholas
Philip Schofield
Michael Ball
Keith Michel
Jason Donovan
Tim Flavin
Lon Satton
Clarke Peters
Jim Dale
David Essex
Paul Jones
Richard O'Brien
Michael Praed
Dave Willetts

**Cardinals of
Comedy**
Barry Humphries
John Cleese
Michael Palin
Rowan Atkinson
Stephen Fry
Hugh Laurie
Griff Rhys Jones
Mel Smith
Ken Dodd
John Wells
Frank Muir
Eric Idle

Jasper Carrott
Terry Gilliam
Alexei Sayle
Terry Jones
Derek Nimmo
Ronnie Corbett
Dennis Norden
Barry Took

**Comic
Exhilerators**
Lenny Henry
Rory Bremner
Tony Slattery
Paul Merton
Rik Mayall
Angus Deayton
Ben Elton
Chris Morris
Clive Anderson
Vic Reeves
Harry Enfield
Jimmy Mulville
Nick Hancock
Bob Mortimer
Paul Whitehouse
Julian Clary
Nigel Planer
John Sessions
Mike McShane
Patrick Kielty

**Light
Entertainment
Heavies**
Freddie Starr
Dale Winton
Des O'Connor
Rolf Harris
Michael Barrymore
Jimmy Tarbuck
Sir Jimmy Savile
Val Doonican

Lionel Blair
Mike Yarwood
Russell Grant
Yuri Geller
Paul Daniels
Jim Davidson
Shane Richie
Bobby Davro
Paul Ross
Ross King
Nicky Campbell
Mark Lamarr

Cilla Black
Lily Savage
Caroline Aherne
Sandi Toksvig
Jennie Eclair
Katie Puckrik

**Hollywood
Dowagers**
Elizabeth Taylor
Julie Andrews
Claire Bloom
Angela Lansbury
Glenda Jackson
  (retd)
Vanessa Redgrave
Jacqueline Bisset
Susannah York
Joan Collins
Charlotte Rampling
Rita Tushingham

**Hollywood
Princesses**
Kristin Scott
  Thomas
Emma Thompson
Joely Richardson
Greta Scacchi
Elizabeth Hurley

Helena Bonham-
  Carter
Julia Ormond
Natasha Richardson
Catherine Zeta-
  Jones
Amanda Pays
Sadie Frost
Jane March
Maryam d'Abo
Emily Lloyd

**Bankable Movie
Babes**
Therese Russell
Amanda Donohoe
Joanne Whalley
Miranda Richardson
Jane Seymour
Kate Neligan
Rachel Ward
Lesley-Ann Down
Stephanie Beacham
Emma Samms
Fiona Fullerton
Lysette Anthony
Jenny Agutter
Hayley Mills
Twiggy

Brill Queens
Helen Mirren
Imogen Stubbs
Imelda Staunton
Janet McTeer
Lia Williams
Jane Horrocks
Frances Barber
Penelope Wilton
Niamh Cusack
Jemma Redgrave
Geraldine James
Juliet Stevenson

Lisa Harrow
Brenda Blethyn
Jane Asher
Jenny Quayle
Saskia Reeves
Caroline Goodall
Phyllis Logan

**Demi Moore
Wannabes**
Kate Winslet
Minnie Driver
Dervla Kirwan
Anna Friel
Jennifer Ehle
Louise Lombard
Patsy Kensit
Emily Watson
Katrine Boorman
Beatie Edney
Gina Bellman
Alex Kingston
Amanda Burton
Julia Sawalha
Serena Scott
  Thomas
Thandie Newton
Susannah Doyle
Siobhan Redmond
Joanna Kanska
Cathryn Harrison
Samantha
  Beckinsale
Suzannah Harker
Victoria Smurfit

Drama Queens
Dame Maggie Smith
Dame Judi Dench
Geraldine McEwan
Dame Diana Rigg
Joan Plowright
Angela Lansbury

Sian Phillips
Dorothy Tutin
Jean Boht
Wendy Craig
Nanette Newman
Joanna David
Lynn Redgrave
Anna Massey
Susan Hampshire
Patricia Hodge
Hannah Gordon
Kate O'Mara
Dulcie Gray

Scene Stealers
Pam Ferris
Mollie Sugden
Patricia Routledge
Miriam Margolyes
Sylvia Sims
Carmen Silvera
Una Stubbs
Dora Bryan
June Whitfield
Dilys Watling
Sheila Hancock
Prunella Scales
Nerys Hughes
Polly James

Opportunity Knocked
Julie Christie
Sarah Miles
Britt Ekland
Shirley Anne Field
Virginia McKenna
Jane Birkin
Ingrid Pitt
Suzy Kendall
Nyree Dawn Porter
Samantha Eggar
Alexandra Bastedo

Catherine Schell
Gayle Hunnicutt
Prunella Gee
Mary Tamm
Gabrielle Drake
Suzanne Danielle
Catherine Oxenberg
Lucy Gutteridge

Stage Nightingales
Elaine Paige
Sarah Brightman
Ruthie Henshall
Petula Clark
Gemma Craven
Maria Freedman
Toyah Willcox
Frances Ruffelle
Liz Robertson
Barbara Dickson
Stephanie Lawrence
Diane Langton
Sarah Payne
Bonnie Langford
Lena Zavaroni
Sarah Hobson

Mirth Makers
Ruby Wax
Felicity Kendal
Linda Robson
Victoria Wood
Maureen Lipman
Jennifer Saunders
Dawn French
Caroline Quentin
Pauline Quirke
Julie Walters
Tracey Ullman
Jo Brand
Faith Brown
Stephanie Cole

Lesley Joseph
Julie McKenzie
Su Pollard
Lynda Bellingham
Josie Lawrence

Showbiz Unions
Anthea Turner
 and Peter Powell
Sting and
 Trudie Styler
Trevor Nunn
 and Imogen Stubbs
Timothy West and
 Prunella Scales
Dame Judi Dench
 and Michael
 Williams
John Thaw and
 Sheila Hancock
John Alderton and
 Pauline Collins
George Cole
 and Penny Morrell
Caron Keating
 and Russ Lindsay
Trevor Eve and
 Sharon Maughan
Anton Rodgers
 and Liz Garvie
Mike Smith
 and Sarah Greene

Movie Magicians
James Ivory
Alan Parker
Ridley Scott
Mike Figgis
Neil Jordan
Anthony Minghella
Tony Scott
Mike Leigh
Stephen Frears

Mike Newell
Lord Attenborough
Michael Caton-
  Jones
Adrian Lyne
Nick Park
Stanley Kubrick
John Boorman
John Schlesinger
Bill Forsyth
Michael Apted
Ken Russell
Hugh Hudson
Danny Boyle

**Spielberg
Wannabes**
Tim Bevan
Eric Fellner
Lord Puttnam
Jeremy Thomas
Steve Woolley
Ishmail Merchant
John Daly
Nik Powell

**Stage
Panjandrums**
Sir Cameron
  Mackintosh
Janet Holmes à
  Court
Lord Lloyd-Webber
Bill Kenwright
Michael White
Duncan Weldon
Michael Codron
Robert Fox
Nick Allott
Ed Mirvish
Thelma Holt

West End Bards
Lord Lloyd-Webber
Sir Alan Ayckbourn
Sir Tim Rice
Harold Pinter
Sir Tom Stoppard
Alan Bennett
Simon Gray
Michael Frayn
Peter Nichols
David Hare
Willy Russell
Julian Mitchell
Patrick Marber
David Storey
Anthony Shaffer
Christopher
  Hampton
Pam Gems
Stephen Poliakoff
Hanif Kureishi
Keith Waterhouse
Heathcote Williams
Peter Shaffer
Mark Ravenhill
Barrie Keeffe

**Footlights'
Svengalis**
Sir Peter Hall
Nicholas Hytner
Sam Mendes
Trevor Nunn
Stephen Daldry
Sir Richard Eyre
Patrick Garland
Adrian Noble
Michael Bogdanov
Jonathan Kent
Deborah Warner
Ned Sherrin
Dr Jonathan Miller
Michael Rudman
Peter Brook

Vocal Dinosaurs
Sir Paul McCartney
Mick Jagger
Sir Cliff Richard
Eric Clapton
George Harrison
Gary Glitter
Tom Jones
Ringo Starr
Engelbert
  Humperdinck
Joe Cocker
David Essex
Eric Burdon
Ray Davies
Gary Booker
Ginger Baker
Frankie Vaughan

Antique Melodies
Phil Collins
Elton John
Rod Stewart
David Bowie
Mark Knopfler
Bryan Ferry
Ronnie Wood
Francis Rossi
Noddy Holder
Robert Palmer
Robin and Maurice
  Gibb
Ozzy Osbourne
Justin Hayward
Rick Parfitt

**Teenybopper
Idols**
Liam Gallagher
Noel Gallagher
Damon Albarn
Jason Kay
Jarvis Cocker

Gary Barlow
Robbie Williams
Mark Owen
Jason Orange
Brian Harvey
Crispian Mills
Mark E Smith

Mellow Yellers
Shirley Bassey
Dusty Springfield
Marianne Faithfull
Sheena Easton
Elkie Brooks
Chrissie Hynde
Lynsey de Paul
Alison Moyet
Anita Harris
Lulu
Madeleine Bell
Helen Shapiro

Wannabe Madonnas
Sinead O'Connor
Geri Halliwell
Enya
Emma Bunton
Neneh Cherry
Katrina Leskanich
Annie Lennox
Kyle Minogue
Lisa Stansfield
Bonnie Tyler
Kim Wilde
Dolores O'Riordan
Lisa B
Mica Paris
Alanis Morisette
Dina Carroll
Yazz
Kate Bush

Divas
Dame Kiri Te Kanawa
Lesley Garrett
Rosemary Joshua
Anne Evans
Josephine Barstow
Jane Eaglen
Sally Burgess
Dame Joan Sutherland
Marie McLaughlin
Rosalind Plowright
Elizabeth Connell
Amanda Roocroft
Della Jones
Felicity Lott
Ann Murray
Dame Gwynneth Jones
Marilyn Horne
Catrin Wyn-Davies

Ballet Thoroughbreds
Darcey Bussell
Viviana Durante
Deborah Bull
Sylvie Guillem
Miyako Yoshida

Bachs With Bite
Richard Rodney Bennett
John Tavener
Philip Glass
Sir Malcolm Arnold
Michael Nyman
Sir Harrison Birtwistle
Malcolm Williamson
Michael Berkeley

5
Media

Box Legends
Sir David Attenborough
Alan Whicker
Sir Robin Day
Sir Ludovic Kennedy
Michael Aspel
Bob Monkhouse
Tom Mangold
Terry Wogan
Magnus Magnusson
Charles Wheeler
Shaw Taylor
Sandy Gall

Angela Rippon
Esther Rantzen
Joan Bakewell
Judith Chalmers
Barbara Kelly
Katie Boyle
Mavis Nicholson
Valerie Singleton

Telly's Heavy Mob
Jeremy Paxman
David Dimbleby
Jonathan Dimbleby
Sir David Frost
Melvyn Bragg
Trevor McDonald
Judy Finnigan
Peter Sissons
Michael Buerk
Jon Snow

Sue Lawley
Selina Scott

Anna Ford
Julia Somerville
Carol Barnes
Sue Barker
Anne Robinson
Kirsty Wark
Sue Cook
Gloria Hunniford
Judith Hann
Moira Stuart
Anne Diamond

Cathode-Tube Warriors
Clive Anderson
Nick Ross
Eamonn Holmes
Richard Madeley
Jonathan Ross
Desmond Lynam
Nicholas Witchell
Robert Kilroy-Silk
John Simpson
John Stapleton
Martin Lewis
James Bellini
Alan Titchmarsh
Alistair Stewart
John Suchet
Martin Bashir

Small-Screen Originals
Loyd Grossman
Keith Floyd
Sir John Harvey-Jones
Lady Lucinda Lambton
Patrick Moore
Jennifer Patterson
Jimmy Hill
Dr Desmond Morris

Hugh Fearnley-Whittingstall
Ian McCaskill
Jimmy Greaves
Andrew Graham-Dixon
Clarissa Dickson-Wright

Britannic Oprahs
Jill Dando
Fiona Phillips
Lorraine Kelly
Fiona Armstrong
Penny Smith
Sally Magnusson
Jo Sheldon
Emma Forbes

Would-be Selinas
Anneka Rice
Caron Keating
Paula Yates
Sarah Greene
Jilly Goolden
Muriel Gray
Jayne Irving

Small-Screen Shakespeares
Alan Bleasdale
Andrew Davies
Lynda La Plante
Lucy Gannon
Jimmy McGovern
Richard Curtis
Colin Dexter
Paula Milne
Roy Clarke
Maurice Gran
Laurence Marks
John Sullivan

John MacUre
Andy Hamilton
Hanif Kureishi
Jack Rosenthal
Sir Antony Jay
Ian La Frenais
Dick Clement

Killer Scribes
Lynda Lee-Potter
Chrissie Iley
Lynne Barber
Ann Leslie
Deborah Ross
Julie Burchill

Fleet Street Chaucers
Bernard Levin
Keith Waterhouse
Ian Wooldridge
Lord Deedes
Peter Tory
Paul Callan
Godfrey Smith

Papsqueaks
Richard Young
Dave Benett
Alan Davidson
Jason Fraser
Julian Parker
Jim Bennett
Alan Grisbrook

Snap Magicians
David Bailey
Earl of Lichfield
Terry O'Neill
Clive Arrowsmith
Earl of Snowdon

Don McCullin
Barry Lategan
Tony McGee
Bob Carlos-Clarke
John Downing
John Swannell
Fergus Greer

**Merchants of
Venom**
Peter McKay
Brian Sewell
Nigel Dempster
Val Hennessy
Auberon Waugh
AA Gill
Sir Julian Critchley
AN Wilson
Tim Satchell
Jonathan Meades

**Influence
Peddlers**
Sir Tim Bell
Lord Chadlington
Philip Gould
Charles Saatchi
Lord Saatchi
Howell James
Sir Gordon Reece
Sir Bernard Ingham

PR Richelicus
Alistair Campbell
Michael Cole
Mark Bolland
Brian Basham
Dave Hill
Alan Parker
Peter Thompson
Mark Borkowski
Will Whitehorn

Keith Samuel
Chris Griffin-Beale
Brian McLaurin
Bernard Docherty
Chris Wright
Nigel Massey
Michael Shea
Christopher Morgan
David Burnside
Max Clifford
Quentin Bell
Matthew Freud

**Piranhas of
Persuasion**
Liz Brewer
Diana Colbert
Ailsa Macalister
Barbara Charone
Liz Sich
Caroline Neville
Jane Atkinson
Judy Tarlo
Connie Fillipello
Elizabeth
  Crompton-Batt
Janie Ironside-Wood
Julie Hobsbawm
Sarah Macaulay
Ba Ba Hobart
Roxy Meade
Myrto Cutler
Deborah Bennett
Carolyn Cavele
Jill Thornton
Sarah Keene
Lynne Kirwan
Dotti Irving
Georgie Gibbs
Sue Hyman
Jenny Halpern
Jenny Halsall
Judith Dagworthy

6
Books

Literary Colossi
Anthony Powell
Richard Adams
Sir VS Naipaul
Arthur Hailey
John Fowles
JG Ballard
Simon Raven

Booker Brilliants
Ben Okri
William Boyd
Martin Amis
Julian Barnes
Ian McEwen
Piers Paul Read
David Lodge
Timothy Mo
Sebastian Faulks
Michael Ondaatje
Barry Unsworth
Salman Rushdie
Paul Bailey
Kazuo Ishiguro
Graham Swift
Peter Carey
William Trevor
Robert McCrum
Will Self

**Jane Austen
Wannabes**
Dame Iris Murdoch
Margaret Drabble
Muriel Spark
Beryl Bainbridge

Fay Weldon
Jeanette Winterson
Nina Bawden
Anita Brookner
Edna O'Brien
Bernice Rubens
Margaret Atwood
Alice Thomas Ellis
Angela Carter
Penelope Lively
AS Byatt
Margaret Forster
Rose Tremain
Candia McWilliam
Penelope Fitzgerald
Lisa St Aubin de
   Teran
Emma Tennant

**Paperback
Goliaths**
Lord Archer
Frederick Forsyth
John Le Carre
Len Deighton
Jack Higgins
Michael Dobbs
Douglas Adams
Terry Pratchett
Dick Francis
Ken Follett
James Herbert
Andy McNab
Arthur C Clarke
Colin Dexter
Leslie Thomas
Tom Sharpe
Robert Harris
Gerald Seymour
Malcolm Bradbury
John Mortimer
Bernard Cornwell
Brian Freemantle

**Bonkbuster
Princesses**
Jilly Cooper
Jackie Collins
Una-Mary Parker
Shirley Conran
Joan Collins
Trudi Pacter
Celia Brayfield
Pat Booth
Penny Vincenzi
Sally Beauman
Deborah Moggach
Lynne Pemberton
Pamela Townley
Eve Pollard

Paperback Divas
Barbara Taylor
   Bradford
Dame Catherine
   Cookson
Rosamund Pilcher
MM Kaye
PD James
Mary Wesley
Joanna Trollope
Ruth Rendell
Maeve Binchy
Susan Howatch
Sue Townsend
Jung Chang
Lynne Reid Banks
Mary Stewart

**Golden Letters
Men**
Paddy Leigh-
   Fermor
Michael Holroyd
Philip Ziegler
Robert Lacey

Peter Ackroyd
Stephen Hawking
Desmond Morris
Jonathan Raban
AN Wilson
Martin Gilbert
Colin Thubron
Will Hutton
Hunter Davies
Philip Norman
Eric Newby
Brian Masters
Anthony Sampson
Norman Stone

**Golden Letters
Women**
Countess of
   Longford
Delia Smith
Jan Morris
Marina Warner
Claire Tomalin
Lady Antonia
   Fraser
Elizabeth Jane
   Howard

7
Trade

Models of Distinction
Kate Moss
Naomi Campbell
Sophie Anderton
Lisa Hogan
Karen Ferrari
Kirsty Hume
India Hicks
Cecilia Chancellor
Karen Elsen
Lisa Butcher
Jerry Hall
Yasmin Le Bon
Marie Helvin
Rachel Hunter
Laura Bailey
Christina Estrada
Gail Elliott

Scissor Stars
Vidal Sassoon
John Frieda
Daniel Galvin
Nicky Clarke
Michael Rasser
Stephen Way
Sam McKnight
John Isaacs
Andrew Collinge
Denise McAdam
Charles
   Worthington
Heinz Schumi
Antony Yacomine
Jo Hansford
Stephen August
Anthony Mascolo
Trevor Sorbie

The Fashionista
Vivienne Westwood
Alexander McQueen
Catherine Walker
Anouska Hempel
John Galliano
Tomasz Starzewski
Stella McCartney
Amanda Wakeley
Betty Jackson
Ronit Zilkha
Ben de Lisi
Paul Smith
Nicole Farhi
John Rocha
Rifat Ozbek
Zandra Rhodes
Paul Costelloe
Katharine Hamnett
Jasper Conran
Bruce Oldfield
Caroline Charles
Isabell Kristensen
Lindka Cierach
Lady Tryon
Nadia LaValle
Antony Price

Tyrants of Taste
Suzy Menkes
Alexandra Shulman
Hilary Alexander
Fiona Macpherson
Sally O'Sullivan
Jane Procter
Glenda Bailey
Anna Wintour
Liz Tilberis
Tina Brown
Kate Reardon
Annette Worsley-
   Taylor
Mimi Spencer
Sophie Laybourne

Creative Power-Houses
Viscount Linley
Emma Hope
Anya Hindmarsh
Philip Somerville
Johnny Moke
Patrick Cox
Sara Pothecary
Ken Turner
Tom Gilbey
Selina Blow
Doug Hayward
Manolo Blahnik
Kaffe Fassett
Philip Treacy
Nick Ashley
Stephen Jones
Ozwald Boateng
Domenico Dolce
Stefano Gabbana
Lulu Guinness
Mandy Barber
Jane Packer
Laura Jamieson
Jimmy Choo
Emma Bridgewater

Retail Wonders
Sir Peter Osborne
Roberto Devorik
Anthony Little
Joseph Ettedgui
Stephen Marks
Rosa Monckton
Peter Bertelsen
Roger Saul
Patsy Seddon
Jeremy Hackett
Ashley Lloyd-
   Jennings
Christopher Wray
Marilyn Anselm
George Cazenove

Joan Burstein
Carolyn Hadden-
 Paton
Neil Zarach
John Lobb
John Saumarez-
 Smith
Ken Williams

**John Fowler
Wannabes**
John Stefanides
David Mlinaric
Nicky Haslam
Christophe Gollut

Sultanas of Style
Nina Campbell
Tricia Guild
Jane Churchill
Emily Todhunter
Nathalie Hambro
Melissa Wyndham
Jocasta Innes
Lady Victoria
 Waymouth
Tessa Kennedy
Jenny Armit
Mary Fox-Linton
Lady Henrietta
 Spencer-Churchill
Sarah Woodhouse
Maddy O'Power
Countess of Caledon

**Panthers of the
Palette**
David Hockney
Lucian Freud
Ron Kitaj
Peter Blake

Sir Howard
 Hodgkin
Allen Jones
Leon Kossoff
Sir Eduardo
 Paolozzi
Bridget Riley
Patrick Caulfield
Damien Hirst
Rachel Whiteread
Craigie Aitchison

**Social
Brushstrokers**
Andre Durand
Tom Merrifield
Patrick Procktor
Paul Gaisford
Adrian George
Emma Sergeant
Andrew Logan
George Bruce
Julian Barrow
India-Jane Birley
David Shepherd
Richard Foster
Graham Rust
Lady Rose Cecil
Lincoln Seligman
Patrick Hughes
Pandora Mond
Gilbert and George
Matthew Carr
Duggie Fields
John Dewe
 Matthews

**Would-Be
Duveens**
Richard Green
Roy Miles
David Mason
Raymond O'Shea

Christopher Wood
Anthony d'Offay
Philip Mould
Martin Summers
Leslie Waddington
Anthony Speelman
Francis Kyle
Julia Peyton-Jones
Bernard Jacobson
John Kasmin
Julian Agnew
Michael Parkin
Angela Flowers
Rafael Valls
Johnny van Haeften
Philip Harari
Alan Cristea
Rebecca Hossack
Ivor Braka

**Nightlife
Napoleons**
John Gold
Mark Birley
Peter Stringfellow
Jamie Palumbo
Piers Adam
David Phelps
Joel Cadbury
Gavin Rankin
Roger Howe
Eddie Davenport

Food Dudes
Marco Pierre White
Nico Ladenis
Anton Mosimann
Albert Roux
Michel Roux
Raymond Blanc
Gary Rhodes
Antony Worrall
 Thompson

Rick Stein
Jean-Christophe
  Novelli
Bruno Loubet
Anton Edelman
Christian Delteil
Pierre Koffman
Brian Turner
Alistair Little
Rowley Leigh
Stephen Bull
Gordon Ramsay
Garry Hollihead
Richard Corrigan
Shaun Hill
Simon Hopkinson

**Bels Monstres de
Cuisine**
Roy Ackerman
Richard Shepherd
Lorenzo Berni
Jeremy King
Christopher Gilmour
Laurence Isaacson
Neville Abraham
Dan Whitehead
Michael Proudlock
Patrick Gwynn-
  Jones
Andrew Leeman
Roger Wren
Oliver Payton
Simon Slater
Michael Chow
John Brinkley
Nick Smallwood
Michael Gottlieb
Richard Polo
Eddie Lim
Claudio Pulze
Enzo Cecconi
Rex Leyland

**5 Star Suite-
Talkers**
Michael Gray
John Tovey
Peter Herbert
Martin Skan
Ramon Pajares
Tim Hart
Rudi Yagersbacher
Greta Hobbs
Francis Coulson
Brian Sack
David Levin
Jeremy Casse
Anouska Hempel
David
  Naylor-Leyland
Sally Bullock
Diana Wallace
Nigel Corbett
John Tham
Derek Picot

8 City & Politics

Squillionaires Who Revel In It
Duke of
  Westminster
Lord Rothschild
Sir Chips Keswick
Lord Palumbo
Lord Hanson
Robert Sangster
Lord McAlpine
  of West Green
Michael Smurfit
Viscount
  Rothermere
Jack Dellal
Sir Donald Gosling
Sir Bernard Ashley
Ken Bates
Sir Jack Hayward

Anglophile Plutocrats
J Paul Getty
Baron Heini
  Thyssen
Wafic Said
John Latsis
John Kluge
Mick and Muck
  Flick
Gunter Sachs
Alfred Taubman
George Soros
Prince Al-Waleed
Prince Rupert
  Loewenstein
Edgar Bronfman
Ann Getty

Prince Jefri
  of Brunei
Adnan Khashoggi
Mark McCormack
Baron Enrico
  di Portanova

**Grand-Daddies of
High Finance**
Lord King
Tiny Rowland
Lord MacLaurin
Sir Trevor Chinn
Lord Weinstock
Lord Sainsbury
Lord Forte
Lord Harris

**Entrepreneurial
Enigmas**
Elliott Bernerd
Robert Gibbons
Bernie Ecclestone
David and
  Frederick Barclay
Sir Evelyn de
  Rothschild
Lord Hollick
Sir John Ritblat
Stephan Wingate
Joe Lewis
David Kirch
Harry Hyams
Baron Bruno
  Schroder
Sir Anthony
  Bamford
Richard Szpiro
Rolf Schild
Geoffrey Robinson
Sir David Alliance
Lord Wolfson

**Panacheful
Tycoons**
Conrad Black
Alan Sugar
Sir William Purves
Sir Michael Bishop
Sir Mark Weinberg
Lord Sterling
David Davies
Richard Gabriel
Paul Hamlyn
Christopher
  Sporborg
Henry Keswick
Christopher Heath
Michael Grade
Brian Souter
John and
  Peter Beckwith
Douglas Bunn
Algy Cluff
Jarvis Astaire
Christopher Moran
Sir John Hall
Tim Holley
Peter Middleton
David Goldstone
Bob Ayling
Howard Hodgson
Chris Collins

Merchant Princes
Mohammed
  Al-Fayed
Dr Tony O'Reilly
Sir Terence Conran
Lord Vestey
Garry and
  Galen Weston
Sir Stanley Kalms
Bernard Matthews
Sir Geoffey Mulcahy
Peter Davis

Sir Richard
  Greenbury
Greg Hutchins
George Davies
Roy Bishco

**Wounded
Gladiators**
Sir Ralph Halpern
Gerald Ronson
Sir Clive Sinclair
Paul Reichmann
Sir Freddie Laker
Gerald Ratner
Asil Nadir
Ian and
  Kevin Maxwell
Roger Levitt
Jim Slater
Philip Green
Owen Oyston
John Bentley
Tim Hue-Williams
Chris Curry
Trevor Deaves
Ernest Saunders
George Walker
Alan Bond
Eddie Shah

Happening Dudes
Peter de Savary
Tim Waterstone
Dickson Poon
Michael Green
Harry Handelsman
Richard Northcott
David Lloyd
Gerry Robinson
Brian Kingham
Robert Peel
Chris Blackwell
Frank Williams

Charles Fry
Christopher
  Sharples
Wensley Hayden-
  Baillie
Julian Metcalfe
Phil Edmonds
Giles Sheppard
Stuart Lipton
John Beverton

High Rollers
Jeffrey Curtiss
Mel Morris
Michael Buckley
Charles Delevingne
Gavin Hooper
Alan Morris
Christopher Foyle
Michael Rhode
Andrew Maconie
Andrew Page
Bill Collins
Dickie Thirlby
Ian Watson
Kim Gottlieb
Julian Seddon
Nick Freeman
Bryan Morrison
Alan Judd
Manolo Olympitis

Ambitious Heirs
Sir Rocco Forte
Lachlan Murdoch
Robert Hanson
Damian Aspinall
Jonathan
  Harmsworth
Lucas White
Jamie Packer
Gavin O'Reilly

**Boardroom
Boadiceas**
Ann Gloag
Janet Holmes à
  Court
Anita Roddick
Petra Doring
Lady Wilcox
Carol Galley
Margaret Barbour
Jennifer Laing
June de Moller

Tycoon Tigresses
Mary Quant
Denise O'Donoghue
Sarah Doukas
Kimberley Fortier
Patsy Bloom
Debbie Moore
Jacqueline Gold
Jennifer d'Abo
Linda Agran
Prue Leith
José Fonseca
Lois Jacobs
Gail Rebuck
Romaine Hart
Patsy Seddon
Karren Brady
Debbie Hodges
Christine Smith
Janet Reger
Simone Mirman
Tricia Guild
Verity Lambert
Jane Godber
Liz Calder

Elder Statesmen
Lady Thatcher (Hon)
Lord Healey

Lord Hailsham
Sir Edward Heath
Lord Tebbit
Enoch Powell
Lord Callaghan
Viscount Whitelaw
Lord Jenkins
Michael Foot
Lord Lawson
Lord Owen
Lord Howe
Lord Walker
Lord Wakeham
Lord Carrington

Frisky Politicoes
Paddy Ashdown
Robin Cook
Peter Mandelson
Norman Lamont
David Mellor
Jonathan Aitken
Tim Yeo
Lord Hattersley
Winston Churchill
Alan Clark
Gerry Malone
Jerry Hayes

**Reluctant
(Labour) Toffs**
Harriet Harman
Tony Benn
John Home
  Robertson
Lord Gifford
Sir Tam Dalyell
Mark Fisher
Paul Foot
Giles Radice
Nick Raynsford

Parliamentary Troublemakers

Ken Livingstone
Tony Banks
Teresa Gorman
Jeremy Corbyn
Dennis Skinner
Diane Abbott
Bill Cash
Dennis Canavan
Richard Shepherd
Austin Mitchell

Powerbrokers

Jonathan Powell
Alastair Campbell
David Milliband
Tim Allan
Hilary Coffman
Anji Hunter
Alan Duncan
Charlie Whelan
Ed Balls
Anna Coote
Ed Milliband
Sue Nye

9 Miscellaneous

Glen Monarchs

Sean Connery
Gordon Browne
Alan McGee
Andrew Neil
Ranald Macdonald
Earl of Airlie
Robin Cook
Robbie Coltrane
Sir Jeremy Isaacs
Donald Dewar
Sandy Lyle
James Naughtie
Gregor Fisher
Jon Barrowman
Peter McKay
Gerry Malone
Sir Ludovic
  Kennedy
Jackie Stewart
Malcolm Rifkind
Sir Angus Ogilvy
John Reid
Gavin Laird
Lord Steel
Michael White
Charles Kennedy
Magnus Magnusson
Dave Stewart
Sir Alistair Burnet
Ronnie Corbett
Alex Salmond
Jimmy Knapp

Ann Gloag
Annie Lennox
Muriel Gray
Lorraine Kelly
Lady Olga
  Maitland

Carol Smyllie
Lena Zavaroni
Sheena McDonald
Barbara Dickson
Moira Shearer
Lulu
Kirsty Wark
Hannah Gordon
Nike Clarke

The Murphia

Pierce Brosnan
Henry Kelly
Philip Treacy
Dr Tony O'Reilly
Frank Delaney
Terry Wogan
The Knight
  of Glin
Dave Allen
Michael Smurfit
Dermot Smurfit
Ned Ryan
Val Doonican
Patrick Bergin
Charles Haughey
Desmond
  Guinness
Tony Ryan
Garech Browne
Philip Lawless
Lord Moyne
John McEntee
Earl of Iveagh
Ronan O'Rahilly
The McGillycuddy of
  the Reeks

Maeve Binchy
Dolores O'Riordan
Dervla Kirwan
Josephine Hart
Alison Doody
Enya

Mary Kenny
Olivia O'Leary
Linda Nolan
Sinead Cusack
Sorcha Cusack
Niamh Cusack
Lisa Hogan
Sinead O'Connor
Victoria Smurfit
Brione Atkinson

The Taffia
Lord Callaghan
Sir Harry Secombe
Ron Davies
Lord Tonypandy
Sir Harry Llewellyn
Andrew Davies
Michael Foot
Tom Jones
Ian Rush
Michael Howard
Barry John
Howell James
Sir Anthony
  Hopkins
Aled Jones
Shakin' Stevens
Patrick Gwynn-
  Jones
Howell Williams
Vince Power
Bryn Terfel
Simon Weston
Ian Woosnam
Victor Spinetti
Dai Llewellyn
Daffyd Jones
Steve Strange

Dame Gwynneth
  Jones
Glenys Kinnock
Mavis Nicholson

Molly Parkin
Sian Phillips
Ruth Madoc
Carol Vorderman
Alice Thomas Ellis
Shirley Bassey
Catherine Zeta-
  Jones
Sian Lloyd
Bonnie Tyler
Della Jones
Angharad Rees
Lalla Ward
Mary Hopkin
Iris Williams
Ffion Jenkins

Ulster Tornadoes
Kenneth Branagh
Sir Brian
  Mawhinney
Eamonn Holmes
Liam Neeson
Van Morrison
Patrick Kielty
James Galway
Lord Rathcavan
David Trimble
George Best
David Montgomery
David Burnside
Adrian Dunbar
Ronnie Flanagan
Alexander Walker
John Cole
Stephen Rea
Brian Keenan
Rev Ian Paisley
Beechey Colclough
Sir Hugh Annesley
Cieran Hinds
William MacQuitty
Alex Higgins
Barry McGuigan

Gloria Hunniford
Amanda Burton
Frances Tomelty
Rose Marie
Mary Peters
Bernadette
  McAliskey
Caron Keating
Clodagh Rogers
Jennifer Johnson
Philippa Kennedy

Top of the Tykes
William Hague
Geoff Boycott
David Hockney
Tom Courtenay
Alan Bennett
Tom Bell
Michael Parkinson
Alan Bates
Michael Palin
Sir Bernard Ingham
Jack Higgins
Kevin Keegan
Lord Hanson
Marco Pierre White
Peter Stringfellow
Peter Townend
Sir Fred Trueman
Lord Hattersley
Sean Bean
Vic Reeves
Malcolm Bradbury
Alan Plater
Harvey Smith
Arthur Scargill
Keith Waterhouse
James Pickles
Charlie Williams
Frazer Hines

Selina Scott
Dame Diana Rigg

*Barbara Taylor
  Bradford
Lesley Garrett
Dame
  Catherine Cookson
Jenni Murray
Lynda Lee-Potter
Shelagh Routh*

Scouse Superstars
John Birt
Sir Paul McCartney
George Harrison
Ringo Starr
Paul O'Grady
Alan Bleasdale
Bill Kenwright
Roy Miles
Michael Williams
Jimmy McGovern
Craig Charles
Steven Norris
Peter Sissons
John Peel
Jimmy Tarbuck
Gerry Marsden
Derek Hatton
Willy Russell
Keith Chegwin
Ken Dodd
Phil Redmond
Roger McGough
Alexei Sayle
Paul Raymond
Tom Baker

**Mancunian
Meteorites**
Liam Gallagher
Noel Gallagher
Gerald Kaufman
Mick Hucknall
Caroline Aherne

Gary Barlow
Ryan Giggs
Ian McShane
Morrissey
Karen Elsen
Mark Owen
Jason Orange
Nigel Martin-Smith
Kevin Godley
Liz Dawn
Bernard Manning
Terry Christian
Peter Noone
Peter Hook
Paula Wilcox

Geordie Genii
Paul Gascoigne
Terry Farrell
Rowan Atkinson
Michael Pemberton
Sting
Eric Burdon
Robson Green
Chris Ryan
Jimmy Nail
Jack Cunningham
Paddy McAloon
Wendy Richard
Bobby Robson
Sir John Hall
Alan Price
Alan Shearer
Mark Knopfler
Viscount Ridley
Carol Malone

**Brummie
Brilliants**
Dame Barbara
  Cartland
Trevor Eve

Sir Anthony
  Beaumont-Dark
Sir Euan
  Anstruther-Gough-
  Calthorpe
Julie Walters
Michael Buerk
Toyah Willcox
Trudie Styler
Simon Le Bon
Clare Short

**Proud
Lancastrians**
Victoria Wood
Sir Ian McKellen
Anna Friel
Eric Sykes
Jane Horrocks
Dame Thora Hird
Warren Clarke
Colin Welland
Georgie Fame
Julie Goodyear
Mike Atherton
Anthony Holden
Joan Bakewell
Mike Read
Lord Waddington

Manx Maestros
Robert Sangster
Trevor Baines
Marquess
  Conyngham
Cynthia Lennon
Norman Wisdom
Kevin Woodford
Fred Parkes
Graham Ferguson-
  Lacey
Eunice Salmond
Rick Wakeman

Brill
Brightelmstonians
Natascha McElhone
Dora Bryan
Carol Barnes
Michael Heath
Derek Grainger
Annie Nightingale
Roy Greenslade
Noreen Taylor
Desmond Lynam

Black
Conquistadores
Lord Taylor
Trevor McDonald
Lenny Henry
Bruce Oldfield
Michael Roberts
Frank Bruno
Oliver Skeete
Clarke Peters
Daley Thompson
Chris Eubank
Paul Boateng
Craig Charles
Benjamin
  Zephaniah
Bernie Grant
Ozwald Boateng
Linford Christie
Baz Bamigboye
Kenny Lynch
John Barnes
Bill Morris
John Fashanu
Ben Okri

Dame Cleo Laine
Fatima Whitbread
Baroness Scotland
Naomi Campbell
Shirley Bassey
Diane Abbott

Caroline Lee
  Johnson
Moira Stuart
Hazel Collins
Tessa Sanderson
Cathy Tyson
Sade
Nola Fontaine
Lucienne Camille
Rusty Lee

Asian Aces
Lord Desai
Salman Rushdie
Hanif Kureishi
Lord Paul
Ben Kingsley
Waheed Ali
Naveen Andrews
Keith Vaz
Ravi Shankar
James Ivory
Eddie Shah
Amin Ali
Gulu Lalvani
Art Malik
Martin Bashir
Ravi Tikkoo
Gopi Hinduja
Sri Hinduja
Anwer Bhatti
Robin Dutt

Madhur Jaffrey
Meera Syal
Viscountess de Vesci
Lisa Aziz
Anak
Lady Tanlaw
Namita Panjabi
Sunetra Atkinson
Vimla Lalvani
Sunita Russell
Pamella Bordes

Oriental Noblesse
Timothy Mo
Michael Chow
David Tang
Kazuo Ishiguro
Bert Kwouk
Ken Hom
Dickson Poon

Vanessa-Mae
  Nicholson
Lady Rothermere
Lin Cook
Nancy Lam
Monica Chong
Countess of Cromer
Christina Ong
Linda Wong
Jung Chang
Lady Albery
Jenny Lo
Linda Davies

24-Carat Oz
Mel Gibson
Rupert Murdoch
Barry Humphries
Jon Bannenberg
Barry Tuckwell
Robert Hughes
Earl of Stradbroke
Clive James
David Helfgott
Richie Benaud
Bruce Gyngell
Peter Carey
Leo McKern
Kerry Packer
Peter Weir
John Pilger
Bruce Beresford
Barrington
  Pheloung
Rolf Harris

Tom Merrifield
Rod Laver
Paul Hogan
Frank Ifield
Bryan Hayes
Geoffrey Robertson
Alan Freeman

Janet Holmes à
Court
Jillian Duchess of
Hamilton
Dr Germaine Greer
Carmen Callil
Lady Tryon
Pamela Stephenson
Rebecca Hossack
Anouska Hempel
Olivia Newton-John
Kylie Minogue
Lady Bell
Arkie Whiteley
Helen Montagu
Susan O'Reilly
Dame Joan
Sutherland
Dee Nolan
Carolyn Parker
Bowles
Patricia Hewitt
Kathy Lette
Lady Mancham
Lady (Susan)
Renouf
Pat Tudor
Scarth Flett
Lady (Michele)
Renouf

Kiwi Fruits
Sir Edmund Hillary
Dame Kiri Te
Kanawa
Keri Hulme

Sam Chisholm
Sir Frank Renouf
Bryan Gould
Jane Campion
Roger Cook
Sir Richard Hadlee
Rachel Hunter
Glynn Christian
Des Wilson
Nicholas Garland
Michael Forster
Sam Neill
Sir Ron Brierley

Randlads
(and Ladies)
Anthony Sher
Sir Mark
Weinberg
Sol Kerzner
Robin Anderson
Prue Leith
Janet Suzman
Aldine Honey
Lesley Lake
Dani Behr
Charles Castle
Moira Lister
Professor Christiaan
Barnard
Glynis Barber
Wilbur Smith
Garth Gibbs
Gavin Robinson
Hildegarde Neil
David Benson
Peter Hain
Alice Krige
Tina Lubner
Herbert Kretzmer
Kim Lady
Kenilworth
Connie Dredzen

Canadian
Doyen(ne)s
Conrad Black
Celine Dion
Lois Maxwell
Milton Shulman
Garry Weston
Galen Weston
Paul Reichmann
Linda Evangelista
Edgar Bronfman
Andre Durand
David Furnish
Kid Jensen
Maya Even
Ian Watson
Linda Thorson
Barbara Kelly

Yank Sensations
J Paul Getty
Alfred Taubman
Robert Carrier
Steve Wyatt
Michael Gottlieb
Richard Polo
Billy Keating
Andrew Wylie
Bob Worcester
Loyd Grossman
Ed Victor
Larry Adler
Paul Fuller
Alexander Atkinson
Michael Rudman
Peter Morton
James Ferman
Andrew Roth

Stars and
Stripettes
Lady Rawlinson
Ivana Trump

Caroline Benn
Jerry Hall
Marianne Wiggins
Marguerite Littman
Mary Spillane
Ruby Wax
Caprice Bourret
Gayle Hunnicutt
Countess of
  Westmoreland
Koo Stark
Katie Puckrik
Sandra Dickinson
Ruthie Rogers
Shelley
  von Strunckel
Celeste Mitchell
Susie Arthur
Pamela
  Lady Harlech
Nicole Petschek
Geraldine Sharpe-
  Newton
Fleur Cowles
Debbie Owen
Diane Thatcher
Barbara Amiel
Gwen Humble
Bonnie Morris

Italian Delicacies
Lord Forte
Enzo Cecconi
Lady Powell
Luisa Moore
Milena Canonero
Alvaro Maccioni
Mario d'Urso
Willie Landels
Prince Stefano
  Massimo
Elena Salvoni
Piero de Monzi
Nadia LaValle

Riccardo
  Mazzucchelli
Mara and Lorenzo
  Berni
Count Paulo filo
  della Torre
Walter Mariti
Katie Boyle
Marisa Masters
Lady Dashwood
Countess of
  St Andrews

French Rarities
Suzanne Duchess
  of St Albans
Catherine Walker
Raymond Blanc
Duchess of Bedford
Michael Roux
Albert Roux
Joseph Ettedgui
Eric Cantona
Claudine Charlton
Lady Ampthill
Elizabeth Maxwell
Jacqueline Green
Didier Milinaire
Nathalie Hambro
Marchioness of
  Hertford
Marchioness of Bath
Anne-Marie Graff
Antoine de Caunes

**The Teutonic
Tendency**
The Prince of
  Hanover
Rudi Jagersbacher
Count Leopold
  von Bismarck
Willy Bauer

Heinz Schumi
Renate Blauel
Erika Bergman
Marietta Parfitt
Kristiane Backer
Eva Ruber-Staier
Dieter Klostermann
Mickie Becker

Dutch Delights
Emilie van Cutsem
Baron
  Steven Bentinck
Johnny van Haeften
Rutger Hauer
Baroness Issy
  van Randwyck
Henriette Countess
  of Northampton

Platinum Arabs
King Hussein
Prince Khalid
  Abdullah
Sheik Maktoum
  al-Maktoum
Adnan
  Khashoggi
Aziz Radwan
Omar Sharif
Mona Bauwens
Prince Al-Waleed
Sheik Mohammed
Julia Sawalha
Wafic Said
Mohammed
  Al-Fayed
Charles Riachi
Sheik Hamdan
Zeinab Badawi
Nabila Khashoggi
Sheik Yamani
Naim Attallah

Iranian Locomotives

Lady Renwick
Kokoly Fallah
Olfat Esfandiari
Hamoosh Bolwer
Mebri Esfandiari

Grade 1 Expats

Anthony Haden-
  Guest
Duke of Bedford
Tina Brown
Antony Lambton
Lady Sarah
  Spencer-Churchill
Liz Tilberis
Paddy Leigh-
  Fermor
Harold Evans
Earl of Warwick
Jacqueline Bisset
Moura Lympany
Frederic Raphael
Angela Lansbury
Kelly Le Brock
Serge Beddington-
  Berens
Matthew Spender
Michael Roberts
Quentin Crisp
Anthea Disney
William Cash

Dynamic Diminutives

Nicholas Witchell
Martin Amis
Lord Forte
Keith Floyd
Lord Steel
David Sullivan
Dick Francis

Lionel Bart
Lord Stephens
Ronnie Corbett
Dennis Selinger
Anthony Blond
Lester Piggott
Earl of Snowdon
Lord Wyatt
Donald Trelford
Joseph Ettedgui
Wayne Sleep
Lord Palumbo
Matthew Evans
Freddie Starr
Albert Roux
Dudley Moore
John Reid
David Hamilton
George Davies
Lord Moynihan
Eric Morley
Larry Adler
Noel Edmonds
Adam Faith

Thomasina Thumbs

Princess Margaret
Lynsey de Paul
Laura Blond
Koo Stark
Mara Berni
Elizabeth Emanuel
Barbara Windsor
Susan Penhaligon
Catherine Oxenberg
Felicity Kendal
Anouska Hempel
Elaine Paige
Lulu
Sheena Easton
Suzi Quatro
Pamela Armstrong
Toyah Willcox

Beanstalkers

Lord Alexander
Robert Peel
Lord Dilhorne
Douglas Adams
Johnny Kidd
Chris Collins
Jeremy King
Sir Alan Ayckbourn
Ian Mackeson-
  Sandbach
Bertie Way
John Cleese
Aldy Maynard-
  Taylor
Lord Charles
  Spencer-Churchill
Gillon Aitken
Duke of
  Marlborough
Ed Victor
Terry Waite
Max Hastings
Patrick Procktor
Peter Snow
Algy Cluff
Gordon Honeycombe
Michael Barrymore

Red Setters

Robin Cook
Jane Asher
Mick Hucknall
Chris Evans
Prince Harry
Neil Kinnock
Paul Johnson
Charles Kennedy
Charles Dance
Alan McGee
Patsy Palmer
Bonnie Langford
Simon Heffer
Anne Robinson

Cilla Black
Miranda Richardson
Baroness Castle
Sally O'Sullivan
Nicholas Witchell
Rula Lenska
Emma Nicholson
Patricia Hodge
Cheryl Barrymore
Millicent Martin

Giantesses

Princess Michael
  of Kent
Jodie Kidd
Duchess of
  St Albans
Una-Mary Parker
Tessa Dahl
Lady Brown
Lady Sarah
  Spencer-Churchill
Hilly Boyd
Arianna
  Stassinopoulos
Victoria Burgoyne
Lady Earle
Cass McClancey
Rachel Tatton-
  Browne
Valerie Wade

Dorian Gray Denied

Jimmy Nail
Donald Dewar
Lord Caithness
Alexei Sayle
Ian Hislop
Gerald Kaufman
Rowan Atkinson
Bruce Grobbelaar
John Sergeant

Frances de la Tour
Kerry Packer
Roger Levitt
Jimmy Knapp
Clive James
Mark Lamarr
Jack Higgins
Mel Smith
Adnan Khashoggi
Sir George Gardiner

Face-Ruggies

Robin Cook
Prince Michael
  of Kent
Sir Ranulph
  Fiennes
Chris Bonington
Frank Dobson
Terry Waite
Noel Edmonds
Alan Sugar
David Aukin
Marquess of Bath
Lord Hollick
Sir Peter Ustinov
Roy Ackerman
Dennis Marks
Eric Clapton
Lord Attenborough
Salman Rushdie
Sir Peter Hall
Ken Bates
Brian Blessed
Rolf Harris
David Bellamy
Sir Rhodes Boyson
Gerry Adams
Jeremy King
Trevor Nunn
Earl of Stockton
Bernie Grant

'Tachmen

Sultan of
  Brunei
Alan Whicker
Peter Tory
Ian Botham
Leslie Thomas
Viscount Thurso
Sir John Harvey-
  Jones
Dickie Davies
John Cleese
Desmond Lynam
Mike Morris
Mike Molloy
Lorenzo Berni

Wonder-Baldies

Lord Montagu of
  Beaulieu
Peter de Savary
Nicholas Coleridge
John Bryan
Bob Hoskins
Auberon Waugh
Phil Collins
Alexei Sayle
Warren Mitchell
Steven Berkoff
Duncan Goodhew
Bryan Morrison
Richard O'Brien
David Swift

Grating Saws

Janet Street-Porter
Antoine de Caunes
Loyd Grossman
Danny Baker
John Cole
Lorraine Chase
Rev Ian Paisley